mindfulness skills
for trauma and ptsd

mindfulness skills
for trauma and ptsd

PRACTICES FOR RECOVERY AND RESILIENCE

Rachel Goldsmith Turow

W.W. NORTON & COMPANY

Independent Publishers Since 1923

New York • London

Important Note: *Mindfulness Skills for Trauma and PTSD* is intended to provide general information on the subject of health and well-being; it is not a substitute for medical or psychological treatment and may not be relied upon for purposes of diagnosing or treating any illness. Please seek out the care of a professional healthcare provider if you are pregnant, nursing, or experiencing symptoms of any potentially serious condition.

For information about permission to reproduce selections from this book, write to Permissions, W. W. Norton & Company, Inc., 500 Fifth Avenue, New York, NY 10110

For information about special discounts for bulk purchases, please contact W. W. Norton Special Sales at specialsales@wwnorton.com or 800-233-4830

Manufacturing by Edwards Brothers Malloy
Book design by Vicki Fischman
Production manager: Christine Critelli

Library of Congress Cataloging-in-Publication Data

Names: Turow, Rachel Goldsmith, author.
Title: Mindfulness skills for trauma and PTSD : practices for
recovery and resilience / Rachel Goldsmith Turow.
Description: First edition. | New York : W. W Norton & Company, [2017] |
Includes bibliographical references and index.
Identifiers: LCCN 2016029070 | ISBN 9780393711264 (pbk.)
Subjects: | MESH: Trauma and Stressor Related Disorders—therapy | Mindfulness—methods
Classification: LCC RC552.T7 | NLM WM 172.5 | DDC 616.85/21—dc23 LC
record available at https://lccn.loc.gov/2016029070

W. W. Norton & Company, Inc., 500 Fifth Avenue, New York, N.Y. 10110
www.wwnorton.com

W. W. Norton & Company Ltd., 15 Carlisle Street, London W1D, 3BS

1 2 3 4 5 6 7 8 9 0

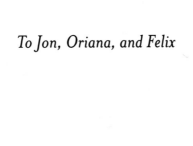

To Jon, Oriana, and Felix

contents

acknowledgments

I am grateful to Jon Turow and to Oriana Turow for giving me the kindness, space and time necessary for this work to emerge, and to the many others who provided encouragement, feedback, and logistical support, as well as training, collaboration, and wisdom regarding traumatic stress, recovery, mindfulness, and self-compassion: Melanie Langlois, Kristin Kane, Alyson Bingham, Alicia Boccellari, Martha Shumway, Jennifer Freyd and the University of Oregon Dynamics Lab, Pamela Birrell, M. Rose Barlow, Lisa DeMarni Cromer, Anne DePrince, Rudrani Farbman Brown, Susie Kessler and the Makom Center for Meditation and Mindfulness at JCC Manhattan, Joy Levitt, Michael Strassfeld, Jonathan Slater, Jon Aaron, Rachel Cowan, Sheila Lewis, Bernice Todres, Shalom Gorewitz, Adrienne Schure, Aimee Beyda, Chaya Weinstein, Elissa Bloom, Eli Shapiro, Amelia Romanowsky, L Barbour, Marie Leznicki, Julie Schnur, Anna Rusiewicz Neff, Matthew Porter, Guy Montgomery, Marlene Reiss, Sarah Weintraub, Gina Ortola, Amy Wagner, Lynn van Male, Stevan Hobfoll, Brighid Kleinman, Samantha Chesney, Megan Hood, John Burns, James Gerhart, Eric Russ, Joyce Corsica, Sharon Jedel, the Department of Behavioral Sciences Incubator Grant Committee at Rush University Medical Center, Wendy Millstine, Amy Cherry, Rebecca Ryder Neipris, Eva Berlin, Lisa Stewart, Anne Mannering, Amy Bornemeier, Rachel Nussbaum, Kristina

Visscher, Rebecca Hendrickson, Jessica Kessler Marshall, Amy Eva, Bethany Kreitl, David Green, Joy Drovdahl, Aimée Coonerty-Femiano, Hillary Locke, Ajahn Amaro, Yaffa Maritz, David Kearney, Brad Rappaport, Yelena Neuman, Steven Neuman, Rachel Wilhelm Esguerra, Adrian Wilhelm Esguerra, Danielle Abbott, Andrea McDowell, Jen Tilghman-Havens, Claire Escobosa, Erin Gilbert, Monica Lloyd, Shelley Katsh, Donald Goldsmith, Rose Black, Judith Turow, Joseph Turow, and Jane Goldsmith. Special thanks to my editor, Deborah Malmud, and to her colleagues at Norton Professional Books. Many thanks as well to the anonymous contributors who offered their own stories of trauma and recovery and provided permission for them to be included in this book. I am also grateful to my past patients and students who shared their experiences, thoughts, and growth with me during the course of our work together. Thanks to all.

introduction

SEVERAL YEARS AGO, I helped facilitate a mindfulness class for Veterans that took place in a room surrounded by busy corridors on all sides. We practiced a variety of mindfulness exercises, including paying attention to our breathing and using the "body scan" approach to observe sensations from head to toe. Many of the participants described frustration or anger at the sounds that people made as they passed by, especially directed toward a particular unseen person wearing shoes that produced a sharp click-clack-click against the floor. The sounds seemed to interfere with what participants were "supposed" to be concentrating on—the practice of mindfulness. Our practice emphasized noticing our thoughts and reactions, without judging our experience, while returning our attention over and over again to our chosen point of focus.

After a few weeks, the participants discovered that their reactions to the sounds of people passing had shifted. The same people who had expressed anger at the sound of loud shoes noticed that they were no longer bothered by them. Something had changed. The sounds of people passing by remained consistent, so the change must have occurred within the perceiver. The Veterans described surprise, awe, and gratitude at this change, which came about through their paying attention in a nonjudgmental way to their own experiences when hearing the loud shoes, over and over, rather than pushing away or ignoring their reactions. Their process reminded me of my own evolving responses—distraction, changing to annoyance, then acceptance, and finally intense fondness—to the *ding!* of the elevator outside the room in the community center where I first practiced meditation. What had seemed like a problem or obstacle turned out to be a vehicle for managing feelings using mindfulness practice; a marker of internal movement; and a sign of hope that other thoughts and emotions could transform in the same way.

Trauma impacts our lives on multiple levels—our thoughts, emotions, physical health, relationships, and our overall ability to function. People can and do recover from trauma to lead healthy, fulfilling lives, and there are many ways to heal. With practice, we can acknowledge the truth of our trauma while also developing new life skills and perspectives. Mindfulness and self-compassion can help us tolerate and reduce distress, decrease self-criticism, build kindness towards ourselves and others, clarify feelings, direct attention, make wise choices, and promote bodily relaxation—all of which can reduce trauma symptoms and improve our overall well-being.

Practicing the small stuff can help with the big stuff. We can begin by attending with care and interest to present-moment sensations of walking or breathing, experiences that are usually not as highly charged as our trauma. Whereas trauma often leaves us feeling helpless, our mindfulness practice can empower us. We get to choose the exercises that feel best, and determine how to handle our experiences moment by moment. We can also *titrate* our exposure to painful material—that is, continuously adjust how much we address deliberately at any given time. By practicing new skills over and over, we create changes in our thinking, emotions, and brain systems that can assist us in handling past trauma, as well as current and future challenges.

The conventions of life—as well as many traumatic environments themselves—can push us to hide our trauma and our related thoughts and feelings. Most of us do not want to sob on the bus or during a business meeting, and we certainly do not have to share every aspect of our experience with others in order to be authentic. However, we can become caught in the other extreme—feeling pressure to pretend that things are fine when they are not. In his story "The Lady with the Little Dog," the writer Anton Chekhov (2000) describes a character who is leading

> two lives, an apparent one, seen and known by all who needed it, filled with conventional truth and conventional deceit, which perfectly resembled the lives of his acquaintances and friends, and another that went on in secret. And by some strange coincidence, perhaps an accidental one, everything that he found important, interesting, necessary, in which he was sincere and did not deceive himself, which constituted the core of his life, occurred in secret from others. (p. 374)

In addition to concealing our feelings from others, as Chekhov illustrates, we often keep parts of our emotional lives hidden even from ourselves.

To make positive changes, we usually need to pay attention to what is truly happening, rather than to how we are "supposed" to feel or act. This attention can occur when we are on our own, or in the company of supportive friends, family, or health professionals. In a world that often does not acknowledge trauma and its effects, I have found the spaces that emphasize the reality of our experiences—such as meditation rooms, therapy offices, and many books and relationships—to be extremely comforting. Even though each context can contain imperfections, I appreciate the focus on what is really happening, rather than on image or pretense. I wish for everyone who wants it the space, time, and compassion to provide kind attention to their actual experiences.

This book approaches trauma and recovery as universal themes not confined to a specific problem and population, even as it recognizes the meaningful differences among trauma types and trauma responses. It treats the challenge of how to manage our minds effectively as a central task of being human, rather than as an individual problem or a necessity only for those of us with mental health difficulties. As a research scientist, educator, and psychotherapist, I aim to provide information that is grounded in scientific evidence. I have incorporated research studies throughout the book that can illuminate processes of trauma adaptations, trauma recovery, and resilience. The book also notes a range of frameworks and strategies offered by mindfulness teachers. Many of the skills and perspectives that they describe have generated robust scientific evidence demonstrating their accuracy and effectiveness. I have also included "In Their Own Words" sections—first-person accounts of experiences with trauma, mindfulness, and self-compassion. These stories were submitted by friends and colleagues, rather than by my own patients or students, and all of the contributors provided permission for their experiences to be included anonymously.

I have written this book so that it might be helpful for a broad range of circumstances: for trauma survivors to learn specific skills to handle one or more challenges; as an overview of different mindfulness practices for trauma; as a guide for health practitioners to provide their patients with new tools; and as a reference for students, researchers, and interested others. In fact, I view the divide between these groups as somewhat artificial, given that we have all experienced stress, trauma, difficult thoughts, and disturbing feelings. The research evidence indicates that mindfulness and self-compassion skills can improve a vast array of circumstances, including the task of providing effective care and understanding to others.

If you are currently in the midst of trauma or trauma recovery, I recommend reading this book in small portions rather than all at once, and paying careful attention to when you are feeling overwhelmed to determine how much reading or practice to do. You can also decide what sorts of modifications to make to the practice to increase your comfort (for instance, keeping your eyes open, or infusing your efforts with self-encouragement). You might keep in mind the idea of a "therapeutic window"[1] for trauma recovery—approaching difficult thoughts and feelings a little bit at a time, so that it does not feel like too much or exceed your current ability to cope, but enough that you can challenge avoidance or other difficult patterns and create positive changes. Many people find it helpful to concentrate on building general coping skills—such as tolerating minor discomforts or practicing bodily relaxation—before addressing trauma-related material. Practicing coping skills across a range of situations makes them more accessible when facing more challenging experiences.

Trauma and its effects are extremely diverse, and what is most helpful for one of us may not resonate for another. After introductory chapters on core mindfulness perspectives and skills, trauma, and self-compassion, the book is organized according to common challenges related to trauma—such as intrusive thoughts and memories, depression, avoidance, dissociation, and relationship difficulties. Each chapter contains background information, summaries of scientific research, personal experiences, and guidelines for specific mindfulness practices. You do not need to learn or practice all of the dozens of skills offered here, or even read the chapters in order. Finding and cultivating one, two, or three skills that work well for you can produce meaningful changes. Or, if simply learning more about trauma and its effects helps you to feel more validated and less alone in your experiences, reading the book from that perspective may also be valuable.

It can be somewhat odd to read a book that describes doing something else—especially activities incompatible with reading—because the experience of reading is so different from putting the book down and actually doing it. However, mindfulness and self-compassion *practice* strongly predicts positive changes. If you do want to practice the skills instead of just reading about them, you might plan out how much time you want to spend reading, and set aside additional time devoted to the practices themselves. Our intentions are important and powerful (for example, "I should be nicer to myself/practice mindfulness/take some time for myself"). However, the experience of *doing* is usually essential to actually making changes in our lives. Like learning a language or a new set of physical exercises, consistent *practice* is what makes the skills second nature. We are most likely to practice our skills if we determine a specific time and place for the endeavor, identify a particular practice to pursue, and actually do it repeatedly. I do not mean to oversimplify the learning process, as certainly there can be moments of mystery, epiphany, and spontaneous growth; however, the evidence points to practice as the most effective way to develop new skills.

The term *practice* provides a helpful reminder that it is unrealistic to expect that a skill should work right away or that we should immediately be "good" at our chosen activities. When I first started practicing mindfulness, it was very hard not to interrupt my sessions. I would sit down to practice mindful breathing, and almost immediately I would notice a bunch of thoughts in my head saying things like, "you need to get up right now, and do this, and do that, and also this other thing." I did not want those thoughts. It seemed to me that they were interrupting my practice or signifying that I was doing it wrong. However, working with them *was* my practice. For several months, I made an effort to notice my impulse to get up, my thoughts about the practice or about myself, and then redirect my attention back to the sensation of breathing. Over time I became used to this particular effort. Gradually, it became easier to observe thoughts about getting up and accomplishing tasks without judging them or wishing they were not there. Next, I noticed that they were still there, but that they did not bother me as much. Eventually they disappeared. My practice shifted to address other issues that were still challenging, but with the benefit of my lived experience of managing my attention, impulses, and self-judgment.

After trauma, the way that we hold our pain can make a subtle but substantial difference. Our experience changes depending upon whether we approach pain with self-criticism, avoidance, and despair, or whether we surround it with kindness, encouragement, and hope. Learning healthy ways of managing pain is more complex than a simple choice, but mindfulness and self-compassion practice provide a way forward. The psychiatrist and mindfulness writer Mark Epstein (2013, p. 97) describes how mindfulness can help us to approach pain in a different way: "The balance of mindfulness between relaxation and investigation allows us to enter into emotional experience in a full way while simultaneously offering us distance from it . . . to 'hold' it in meditative embrace."

As we recover from trauma and build resilience, we may find that we are different than we were before the trauma occurred, and that we can respect those differences. The cover of this book reflects the Japanese ceramic tradition of *kintsukuroi* ("golden mend"). When pottery is broken, instead of discarding it, ceramic artists repair it with silver or gold. The mended cracks in the pottery are not viewed as faults, but as symbols of enrichment, resilience, and meaning. The object does not resume its previous shape, but honors both its past history and its new form.

We rarely determine the cracks and breaks in our lives, but we do have choices in the ways that we handle them afterwards. We too can bring our ingenuity and care to ennoble our experiences. Just like *kintsukuroi* bowls, we cannot go back in time or be fully restored to the way that we were. We can, however, honor our brokenness and transform it into strength through our attention, creativity, and compassion.

mindfulness skills
for trauma and ptsd

MINDFULNESS

LIFE IS CHALLENGING. Most of us face a complex tangle of external stressors and internal struggles. Surviving life's hardest moments is a victory, but we are often left feeling anxious, depressed, lonely, and self-critical. Remnants of past trauma can stick around for years, and can frustrate us immensely.

Transforming trauma into growth and resilience is a process, and it involves balancing our attention and building our inner resources. After trauma, it is often wise to approach difficult thoughts and feelings in small portions, and to practice focusing on nontraumatic experiences as well. Cultivating kindness towards ourselves also provides strength, encouragement to keep going, and a boundless way to hold the full range of our experiences.

A mindful perspective helps us to understand the reasons for our thoughts and emotions after trauma, and opens new avenues for healing. Thoughts and feelings after trauma may confuse us, especially when they clash with our current circumstances. After a trauma, we might think, "I'm safe now, so why am I still on edge?" We may find ourselves struggling to concentrate, to meet new people, or to enjoy life's small pleasures. Our suffering intensifies when we blame ourselves for our feelings, censor them, or attack them as unreasonable. Engaging mindfulness towards our experiences reveals that our responses to stress and trauma are normal, understandable, workable, and worthy of compassion.

Mindfulness refers to paying attention to our experiences in this moment in a caring and curious way. It takes practice. When we practice mindfulness, we intentionally focus our attention on what is happening in the present moment. Mindfulness emphasizes this moment, right now—not because the past and future are unimportant, but because the present moment offers us the richest source of material and the most flexibility for making changes. When other thoughts arise (as they frequently do) during mindfulness practice, the goal is to observe them and to then redirect our attention to awareness of present-moment experiences. The word *meditation* is often used to describe the specific time and techniques that we use to practice new ways of relating to our thoughts and feelings, whereas *mindfulness* commonly refers to a broader way of being with ourselves and in the world.

Mindfulness cultivates balance. Rather than feeling all of our overwhelming emotions at once, we can carefully titrate our approach to them. After trauma, we can easily become flooded or retraumatized; however, suppressing thoughts and emotions can block healing. A balanced path means modulating our contact with difficult material, so that we touch it a little bit at a time. We can also balance our attention towards our own thoughts and feelings with the practice of new skills that can provide strategies and confidence for handling difficulties. As we practice mindfulness, we also work to cultivate a gentle, kind, and loving approach to noticing our experiences.

Mindfulness involves taking a stance that is open and curious about our experiences in the moment, rather than judging them. Whether we notice ourselves feeling distracted, calm, frustrated, or insightful in the moment, we can build awareness for what we notice without judging the experience or ourselves as good, bad, appropriate, or unacceptable. When judgments arise during mindfulness practices, we try to treat them like any other thought—after observing the judgment, we redirect our attention back to our present-moment experiences.

Mindful recovery from trauma emphasizes the actual felt experience of directing attention and care to our sensations in this moment, and encourages balanced attention between trauma-related feelings and a broader array of thoughts, emotions, and sensations. However, there is no one right way to heal after a trauma, and no one right way to practice mindfulness. There are many different types of traumas, and people have diverse emotional reactions to trauma and to recovery processes. The task is to identify which approaches to healing (including mindfulness practices) are most helpful for you.

The words *healing* and *recovery* do not indicate that the trauma has completely disappeared; rather, they reflect the process of change that occurs when trauma and trauma-related feelings transition from feeling like a central, overwhelming aspect of life to a more manageable circumstance—a circumstance that is but one part of a much fuller life. For some of us, practicing mindfulness is the "main street" of healing; for others, mindfulness enhances other roads to recovery.

We can benefit from practicing mindfulness once, practicing consistently, or from making mindfulness a way of life. It may also be helpful to learn more about common responses to trauma and the ways that specific mindfulness practices can help us recover. Scientific studies offer important evidence regarding the usefulness of mindfulness and self-compassion skills for decreasing anxiety, depression, and posttraumatic stress disorder (PTSD), and for increasing relaxation, interpersonal connections, and well-being.

Mindfulness Practices Can Help After Trauma

After trauma, mindfulness practice can help us heal in several ways:

- *By increasing our emotional tolerance and flexibility.* Mindfulness is linked with the capacity to tolerate difficult experiences, and with the ability to shift our emotions. We might experience feelings like fear, anger, sadness, and self-blame, but we gain confidence that they will not last forever and that we can navigate through them.

- *By promoting relaxation.* Mindfulness practice influences the way that both our bodies and minds respond to our own thoughts and to the environment. We learn to relate to our feelings with less tension and with a greater sense of ease. Cultivating relaxation can soothe the physical feelings of being overly alert, agitated, and keyed up after trauma.

- *By reducing automatic reactions.* With practice, we have fewer "default" responses to our own experiences. We develop more perspectives and increase our options in choosing how we respond to things.

- *By increasing our attentional control.* As we learn to notice where our minds go and practice shifting our attention, we can change patterns of attention that keep our thoughts on past traumas and future worries.

- *By cultivating self-compassion.* Mindfulness practice provides opportunities to observe and change how we treat ourselves. We can learn to relate to ourselves and to our challenges with kindness, interest, patience, encouragement, and compassion.

- *By reducing avoidance.* Pushing away painful thoughts and feelings can worsen them or leave us feeling numb, tense, and constricted. When we allow challenging feelings to be present, they lose some of their power. We gain a calmer and more expansive approach to difficult feelings.

- *By reducing self-judgment.* Mindfulness practice promotes nonjudgment of our thoughts and emotions. Reducing judgment helps lessen depression and PTSD, along with the shame and self-blame that can maintain them. Mindfulness skills can help shift common "add-ons" after trauma—the ways that we interpret the trauma to mean something negative about ourselves or the world.

- *By making this moment bigger.* Even though this moment might have pain, there may be some other neutral or pleasant aspects about it that we are missing. If we can broaden our experience of this moment a bit in a positive way, it can feel easier to handle our past suffering and worries about the future.

- *By cultivating a balanced perspective.* As we mindfully notice our thoughts and feelings, we build up the part of ourselves that does the noticing, so that we feel less personally identified with the pain and less submerged in it. We may still hurt, but we are less likely to feel as though we ourselves *are* the pain. Conversely, mindfulness also helps us reconnect to our emotions and physical sensations if we have coped with trauma by numbing or distancing ourselves from our experiences.

- *By reperceiving ourselves and the world.* Mindfulness practice develops our ability to see the same situation in a different way—to find new possibilities when things feel like the "same old same old." We learn ways to adjust our mindset when we encounter problems.

RESEARCH STUDIES SHOW that mindfulness practice is linked with improvements in PTSD symptoms, depression, self-care, self-acceptance, sleep, physical health problems, physical health behaviors, anger, attention, self-efficacy, self-empowerment, and peace.[2] Studies of mindfulness programs for trauma survivors also report decreases in self-blame and shame, along with fewer bodily manifestations of stress.[3] Across health conditions and sample populations, mindfulness practice is generally associated with reductions in anxiety, stress, and physical pain, and with improvements in coping, health, and well-being.

In one research study, King and colleagues[4] evaluated whether 8 weeks of mindfulness-based cognitive therapy (MBCT) could improve chronic PTSD in Veterans who reported enduring combat trauma. The researchers compared 20 Veterans who received MBCT with 17 people who received other types of group therapy (including one group that provided PTSD education and skills and another group that addressed nightmares). Veterans in the MBCT group (but not the other groups) experienced meaningful reductions in the severity of PTSD, especially in their tendencies to use avoidance and numbing to handle distress. Veterans in the MBCT group also reported having less self-blame than they had before starting the MBCT group.

In another study, Vujanovic, Youngwirth, Johnson, and Zvolensky (2009) reported that among 239 adults who reported a range of traumatic events, participants' self-reported abilities to accept their thoughts and feelings without judging them corresponded to their reporting fewer PTSD symptoms, even after controlling for the extent of participants' trauma exposure and negative emotions. Other research studies have confirmed that accepting thoughts and emotions without judging them is associated with fewer PTSD symptoms[5] and positively linked with trauma recovery.[6]

Core Concepts of Mindfulness

Core concepts of mindfulness include attention, present-moment awareness, beginner's mind, nonjudgment, nonstriving, patience, letting be, overidentification, and mindful reactions and actions (rather than automatic ones). When we practice mindfulness, these elements seem to work together and build on each other. We also have the opportunity to notice and change how we relate to ourselves. Compassion, self-compassion, and loving-kindness practices are closely related to mindfulness skills, and can complement other aspects of mindfulness by building capacities of friendship and kindness towards ourselves.

Attention

We have a *lot* on our minds. We are typically thinking many things at once, with various degrees of conscious awareness. We can also direct our attention to some degree. For instance, you can focus your attention on the sensations in your shoulders (such as observing their position, or any feelings of tension), and then you can transfer your attention down to the feelings in your toes and feet. Just the fact that we can do that—that we can shift our attention from our shoulders to feet—can give us hope and empower us with the knowledge that we have some choice and control over where our minds go.

We can also notice where our attention is in a given moment. Our attention often wanders all over the place. With practice we can get more skilled at observing when it roams, where it goes, and at redirecting it. The faster we notice where the mind has gone, the more choices we have in how to handle it. With mindfulness practice, the mind still wanders, but we become less caught up in it. We can begin to observe our thoughts and feelings with a greater sense of perspective.

Present-Moment Awareness

Our daily lives usually involve an intricate mixture of thoughts and feelings about the past, our experience of this very moment, and our hopes, plans, and concerns about the future. With mindfulness practice, we learn to prioritize this moment, right now. This emphasis is not meant to invalidate the importance of what has happened or what is to come. Rather, the present moment contains the most workable material for shifting our thoughts and feelings, and for improving our experience of life in general.

For instance, it is easier to investigate a painful feeling in this moment than one that we recall having felt last week, because in this moment we have much more immediate access to the specific thoughts, images, and memories that accompany the feeling, as well as its "felt sense"—the sensations in our bodies that seem related to the emotion. Plus, if we try out a new approach to a painful feeling in this moment, we will gain immediate experiential (rather than hypothetical) feedback about how the new practice might shift our experience.

When we enlarge and deepen the present moment through mindfulness practice, we often find that we are less distressed by the pain that we have been through in the past or by our worries about what will happen in the future. Present-moment awareness shapes our challenges into bite-sized pieces. The past and future are literally unmanageable, but the idea of getting through *just this one moment* is usually tolerable. In mindfulness practice, we only need to handle one moment at a time.

Beginner's Mind

A common mindfulness practice involves encountering a raisin as if it were a completely new object. We can use our five senses to investigate the raisin in a curious and open way. We might notice the color of the raisin, the geography of its folds and crevices, the ways that the light of the room touches the raisin, its texture and smooshiness, the sound or vibrations that result from touching the raisin or from dropping it on the table, and finally its smell and taste. When other thoughts arise (e.g., "I hate raisins," "I'm so glad I got a big, plump raisin instead of one of those hard little ones," or "I feel quite skeptical that this silly exercise could help me"), we redirect our attention to the present-moment, specific experience of that particular raisin as if it were our first. Another exercise to cultivate beginner's mind involves finding five new things about the room or area that you are in right now that you have never noticed before.

The beginner's mind perspective is an expansive way of encountering the world, and can allow us to open up to new dimensions of situations that seem hopeless or closed. We are so frequently jaded about life, and quick to label, categorize, and dismiss our experiences. The beginner's mind attitude builds hope. It cultivates the sense that every object and moment actually contains more than we think—that the possibilities of how we experience life are greater than we may have imagined.

Nonjudgment

We evaluate, label, and judge things in order to make sense of the world. This impulse to categorize can be quite helpful. For instance, we need to differentiate between safe and dangerous animals, and to determine whether it is cold or warm so that we can dress appropriately. When we encounter a feeling, object, or a person, we commonly project ideas resulting from our past experiences and thoughts. This process is usually rapid and automatic, and reflects basic learning processes. Over time, it can become our normal way of interacting with the world.

However, there are a few problems with automatic judgments. When we judge something quickly, we miss out on experiencing its other dimensions. If we categorize rainy days as unpleasant, it is harder to notice the smell of the leaves, the feeling of warm socks, or the look of raindrops on the grass. Judging can also become a self-fulfilling prophecy: If I wake up and judge that it is a bad day, I will be less likely to notice things that are pleasant, funny, or interesting. Judging can create additional pain. When we judge or criticize ourselves for our emotional responses after trauma, we experience an extra layer of pain on top of the trauma itself. When we judge other people, we are less likely to interact with them respectfully, or to feel calm after the interaction.

The alternative is to practice *not judging*; rather, to try approaching experiences with an open curiosity. Each mindfulness exercise in this book contains the opportunity to just observe thoughts, feelings, and sensations—without labeling them as good, bad, or anything else. When practicing mindfulness, judgments commonly arise. For instance, we often have thoughts such as, "I'm not breathing right!" or "I'm bad at this mindfulness stuff," or "I have so many problems that nothing is ever going to help me." When such thoughts arise, our goal is to treat them like any other thoughts: to notice their presence, but then to return attention back to the chosen object of mindfulness practice without getting caught up in the judgment.

Sometimes when practicing nonjudgment we observe that we are judging our judgments. We might think, "Judgment is bad, and here I am judging when I'm not supposed to do that! There I go again." The idea is to try not to judge experiences during mindfulness practice, and when judgments come, to try not to judge the judgment. The capacity to have experiences without immediately judging them gradually becomes easier with practice. Refraining from judging creates more room to have other experiences, and can help soothe pain.

Nonstriving

Most of us would like life, and ourselves, to be at least a little bit different, and probably a lot different. We can be so wrapped up in our need to change things that we deny ourselves permission to feel exactly how we are feeling right now, in this moment. Mindfulness creates a space to open to what is actually happening. Even though many of us practice mindfulness to advance a specific goal, such as improving our health and well-being, the practice of mindfulness itself involves inhabiting the moment without striving for it to change. It can be strange, agonizing, or refreshing to practice not trying to change anything, but instead to sit with our experiences and let them be. It may also seem counterintuitive that recovery from painful experiences could involve allowing the actual feelings to be present for a time.

During mindfulness practice, thoughts about goals for the practice itself might emerge, such as "I want this practice to calm me down," or "I want my mind to work differently than it does right now." The practice of mindfulness involves opening to the different ways that any one practice session might develop, and trying to stay present with the actual experiences in the moment. It is common to have one session of mindfulness practice that feels meaningful and refreshing, followed by another that feels like a dud. Hopefully, we can accept these fluctuations, and continue to practice. Our goal is not to have one amazing mindfulness session, or to have 100% of our mindfulness practices be uplifting, but to cultivate new ways of relating to ourselves and to our experiences.

Patience

Some changes are fast, but most emotional changes unfold gradually. There is a reason that the term *practice* is commonly heard in discussions of mindfulness. Developing new ways of thinking and feeling takes time and repetition. That may seem obvious, but many of us believe that we should be able to change the ways that we think (for example, to "think positive") just by deciding to do so. The reason that this rarely works is that so many of our thoughts are automatic, and they reflect specific patterns and structures in the brain. Our old habits are powerful because we have repeated them so many times; to make a new habit, we need to practice it over and over, so that our brains can build new patterns and structures. The best way to change them involves paying careful attention to the ways that we encounter our feelings and the world, and by deliberately practicing new ways of handling thoughts and feelings—over and over and over.

Through mindfulness practice, we are literally rewiring our brains, and we need to strengthen the new patterns until they stick. Research demonstrates that many people report benefits from mindfulness interventions that are 4, 6, or 8 weeks long, and also shows that longstanding mindfulness practices are positively associated with well-being. Consistent practice appears more important than the length of practice;[7] that is, it is more helpful for people to practice mindfulness skills for 10 minutes a day than to practice for 60 minutes straight once a week.

It may be hard to wait for changes, and to keep on practicing new skills until they become more habitual. A mindful way to handle impatience or frustration is to approach those feelings themselves with attention and care. The impatience then becomes another set of thoughts and feelings, with sensations that we can observe and feel in the moment that they arise. We can practice treating them in the most caring way possible.

Letting Be

The idea of "letting go" is a common one. It illustrates that we have a relationship to the thoughts and feelings that we encounter—a relationship that is adjustable. Many people find relief in the idea of letting go. However, for others, it is confusing or even infuriating. People often ask how they can let something go. Even when we want to let something go, it is difficult in practice. Where does it "go"? Does that mean that the thought or feeling is banished, never to return again? Letting go also conveys an all-or-nothing perspective. Many of us desperately want to let things go, especially after trauma, but find that in practice doing so is extremely difficult.

"Letting be" is an alternative to letting go that retains the idea of changing our relationship to a source of difficulty and reducing our sense of struggle. However, letting be is different from letting go because it does not put any pressure on a person to censor aspects of experience. Letting be conveys the idea that we can make space for all of our thoughts and feelings, even the ones that are difficult. When we allow them and let them be, we relinquish a sense of control or pressure, sensations that often add pain to the original trauma.

Letting be is not all-or-nothing; rather, it is a process. The meditation teacher Alison Laichter uses the metaphor of a snow globe to describe this process. In our usual experience, our thoughts and feelings are agitated, confused, and all shaken up together. Through mindfulness practice, the snow settles as we let our thoughts and feelings be. They are still there—they have not gone anywhere—but they are there in a more calm and peaceful way.

Letting be relates to the idea of *acceptance*. Acceptance in this instance does not mean that an emotion or sensation is good or acceptable. Rather, it is an acknowledgement that something exists. Because we commonly avoid our feelings or edit them when we are around other people, we need to practice recognizing what we actually feel. An accepting, "letting be" approach to feelings is strongly related to well-being and to recovery from trauma.

Overidentification

Overidentification with feelings is common, and refers to the sense that you *are* a feeling, rather than a person experiencing it. Suffering is often so intense that it blurs our sense of self with the painful emotions themselves. Loss, depression, and anxiety can seem to take over to the extent that they feel like defining personal characteristics, rather than a set of thoughts and feelings that could change. We might start to think of ourselves as "an anxious person" or "an angry person" rather than a person who experiences a range of emotions. We also get caught up in our thoughts. Thoughts often present themselves as truths, but offer a biased view of ourselves and our experiences.[8] Joseph Goldstein (2015) observed that although thoughts can be considered "the dictators of our mind: *Go here, go there, do this, do that,*" becoming aware of them can liberate us.

Mindfulness practice disentangles us from our thoughts and feelings. By cultivating the part of ourselves that is the observer or witness of our feelings, we become less identified with the feelings themselves. This process is sometimes called "*decentering*" or "*reperceiving.*"[9] Attention, nonjudgment, and letting be are each practices that can help us reduce overidentification.

When we notice ourselves caught up in a thought or feeling, we can direct our attention to observing it without judging it—just allowing it to exist. We can notice any subtleties about the experience, rather than getting so swept up in the feeling itself. This is often easier to do with a passing physical sensation, like breathing, than with a complex set of emotions. Noticing subtle changes in our experiences can help reduce overidentification and can lessen the sense that our suffering is permanent and unchanging. For instance, even if we are suffering for a long time, there may be slight variations in the sensations of suffering throughout the day. Observing variability can spark hope, because experiences appear less fixed and more workable.

As we practice mindfulness, new spaces open up between ourselves and our feelings. It is as if we are the sky, and our thoughts and feelings are the weather. The sky is more expansive and stable than the different shades of weather that it contains. Another common metaphor is "leaves on a river," in which we, as the river, can notice the different thoughts that flow down our stream of consciousness, and let them float by without agitating us.

Mindful Reactions and Actions

Mindfulness practice provides opportunities to notice our reactions—our immediate and automatic thinking, emotional responses, and impulses in response to everything we encounter. Reactions are usually fast and unintentional. At the grocery store, if the person ringing up my groceries glowers and barely looks at me, I may automatically assume that he is not friendly, and feel offended. In reality, he may be tired, or in pain, or deep in thought. It can take a moment to notice my reaction and to consider other possibilities. However, doing so can improve my experience, and make our interaction better. The more mindful we can be about our reactions and consider alternatives, the more choices we have about how to manage our feelings and conversations.

Our reactions portray a mix of our own past experiences and vulnerabilities. They also usually make sense given the context of what we have been through—they correspond to the blueprint of our past. However, they can be inappropriate and even destructive. For example, someone who was assaulted may be wary of strangers. This is an entirely natural inclination, and reflects the way that our brains learn through experiences. The problem is that such automatic reactions can limit our lives—in this case, the possibility of forming new connections to other people.

Bringing mindfulness to our reactions and impulses gives us more choices about how to handle them. A much-cited anonymous quote—often misattributed to Victor Frankl—states, "Between stimulus and response there is a space. In that space is our power to choose our response. In our response lies our growth and our freedom." Mindfulness practice increases our awareness of subtle sensations, so that we can notice when our feelings are starting to simmer and address them before they boil over. The earlier that a driver can spot anger arising and the urge to yell at a jaywalking pedestrian, the better chance he or she has to thoughtfully consider whether to act upon the impulse or to handle the feelings in a different way. The same is true for struggles with addictions. The sooner a craving is identified after it begins, the more opportunities a person has to mobilize support, pursue a contrasting activity, or engage other resources to resist the urge. Finally, building mindfulness for our impulses and reactions helps our actions themselves to be more mindful—that is, more deliberately chosen and more in line with our values. A mindful action is one that occurs with conscious awareness and that is intentional rather than automatic.

Compassion, Self-Compassion, and Loving-Kindness

As we build our capacity to observe our thoughts and feelings, we have the opportunity to treat them—and ourselves—with respect, compassion, care, love, and kindness. These attitudes towards our own pain and suffering have an enormous influence on healing and recovery. Like other mental shifts, developing compassion towards oneself takes time and practice. Practicing self-compassion means learning to be a kind friend to ourselves in any circumstance.

The idea of being kind to ourselves can seem very strange, especially if we have experienced trauma. Trauma often leaves us with deep feelings of shame and self-blame, which can prolong depression and other types of posttraumatic stress. Such feelings make it harder to access care and kindness towards ourselves. However, cultivating self-compassion after trauma becomes easier with intentional practice. Compassion, love, and kindness can soothe all types of pain. Even though these are big concepts, and often involve a lifelong process, we can meaningfully increase our self-kindness and self-compassion with just a few weeks of practice (see Chapter 4).

Compassion

The word *compassion* literally means to "suffer with." Compassion is also regarded as the movement in the heart when we encounter suffering.[10] In mindfulness practice, compassion has several facets. One facet of compassion is the genuine recognition of pain, in which we do not shy away from pain, but bravely acknowledge its presence. It involves an openness to the reality of suffering, and the understanding that pain is part of the human experience. Another facet of compassion involves the commitment to help decrease pain in others and ourselves. This commitment necessitates practicing compassion, and acting with compassion. Compassion involves feeling connected to the pain that we or others experience—staying present instead of running away. It includes a sense of companionship, an idea that people should not feel alone in their distress. However, compassion also incorporates a spacious perspective—a space that allows us to draw upon our own strength to help reduce suffering, so that we do not become lost or submerged in suffering.

Compassion is not the same as empathy, although both conditions reflect sensitivity to the pain of others. However, empathy rests upon the sense of having the same feelings as someone else, whereas compassion involves much more than that: listening; deep understanding; care and concern for someone else; a sense of perspective that allows us to be present with the pain while recognizing that it is one part of a larger picture; and both motivation and action to improve that person's situation. Compassion does not involve allowing people to hurt you or take advantage of you; rather, it involves taking very good care of yourself and others to prevent further suffering. Compassion can be viewed as combining care, kindness, soothing, empathy, generosity, nonjudgment, acceptance, courage, tolerance, and patience.[11]

In his book *The Compassionate Life*, the Dalai Lama defined compassion and love as "positive thoughts and feelings that give rise to such essential things in life as hope, courage, determination, and inner strength" (2003, p. 17). He clarified that "compassion is the wish for another being to be free from suffering; love is wanting them to have happiness."

Self-Compassion

Self-compassion turns all facets of compassion towards ourselves. The practice of self-compassion cultivates the quality of being an encouraging friend to oneself in any circumstance or situation, and of taking action to help our situation. Many people refrain from being kind to themselves unless things are going well or unless they have succeeded in some way. However, self-compassion can soothe suffering, and it is valuable across a full range of feelings and situations.

Self-compassion is not wimpy, self-indulgent, thinking positive, fake, going easy on yourself, or censoring attention to problems. Rather, it involves acknowledging suffering bravely, kindly, and with an open presence. It is a way of relating to ourselves that is open and caring towards *all* of our experiences, without pushing away or censoring them. Self-compassion involves taking a wide, mindful perspective on all of our feelings and needs, and serving our best interests in both the short- and long-term.

Many people who have experienced trauma feel the impulse to isolate themselves at home. People who are feeling this urge and practicing self-compassion might say to themselves something like, "It's normal and understandable that you would feel this way after what you went through. Your feelings are real and important, and I'm here for you. It's also important for your own well-being that you mail your rent check today, and I think that once you are outside, a walk could actually feel good. And certainly it's OK to balance some exertion with some relaxation." Other thoughts might take the form of offering kindness and care towards the parts of ourselves that are experiencing pain: "I'm sorry you are feeling this way, and I care about you and want to help make things better, both today and in general."

In her book *Self-Compassion*, Kristin Neff (2011) clarified the difference between self-compassion and self-esteem. Self-esteem, the way we evaluate ourselves as being competent or worthy, appears to be unstable and contingent on external circumstances. For instance, if I view myself as smart but then fail to understand an article or do not pass an exam, my self-esteem plummets. Self-esteem also relies on comparisons with other people in order to maintain a view of ourselves as superior—and of others as inferior. This is problematic because self-esteem rises or falls depending on the other people that we encounter. Finally, self-esteem involves constant judgment of both others and of oneself. Judgments often create pain, as is the case when we judge ourselves or someone else as unacceptable in some way. They also narrow our field of vision to the one quality that we are appraising, so that we fail to notice other important characteristics. Self-esteem processes can also prevent compassion, because our recognition or care is conditional, or dependent on the results of our own judgment and evaluation.

A common impediment to self-compassion is the habit of self-criticism. Many cultures seem to encourage negative self-evaluations. Self-criticism can be further reinforced through unrealistic media images or the marketing of products to help us overcome supposed flaws. People are also more likely to criticize themselves when they have experienced trauma, criticism from others, emotional abuse, or neglect. Other people think that they need to criticize themselves to stay sharp or to meet their own high standards. However, research shows that self-criticism sabotages us. Self-criticism is strongly linked to depression and anxiety, whereas self-compassion is positively associated with well-being, motivation, and accomplishments, and negatively related to distress.[12]

The practice of self-compassion changes our brains and bodies. For instance, when we encounter stress, our bodies respond, but self-compassion practice appears to decrease bodily activation to stress.[13] Although how we relate to ourselves may feel nebulous, unimportant, or "woo woo," the ways that we treat ourselves seem to have observable biological consequences. Self-criticism and self-encouragement appear to activate distinct brain regions.[14] Even though self-compassion practice might seem abstract, it can help to remember that it works on a physical level.

Loving-Kindness

Loving-kindness is a word that reflects qualities of friendliness, unconditional love, benevolence, kind intentions, and goodwill. It is a translation of the Pali word *metta* and is close to the Pali word *mitta*, which means friend. The concept of metta includes a recognition that all beings wish to be happy, and reflects strong, genuine wishes for well-being and happiness for oneself and for others. The meditation teacher and psychologist Sylvia Boorstein described *metta* as "complete and unrestrained friendliness" (1997, p. 128) and as "friendly, congenial well-wishing." *Metta* involves sensitivity and empathy, because it highlights openness, understanding, and care for one's own feelings and for those of others. In her book *Lovingkindness*, Sharon Salzberg defined *metta* as "the ability to embrace all parts of ourselves, as well as parts of the world" (1995, p. 22). The teacher Acharya Buddharakkhita wrote that *metta* "evokes within a warm-hearted feeling of fellowship, sympathy and love, which grows boundless with practice and overcomes all social, religious, racial, political and economic barriers" (1995, Introduction section, para. 1).

Many of us find it easier to feel love and kindness towards others than towards ourselves. This is an exceedingly common challenge. The good news is that love and friendliness are already within us all, even if we need to work on redirecting those qualities to include ourselves. It is very similar to exercising a new muscle, or using it in a different way.

Conversely, many of us find it hard to feel friendly feelings towards others, especially if other people have hurt us. In that case, it may help to know that traditional practices of loving-kindness begin by developing care for ourselves. Once this becomes more comfortable and habitual, the next steps involve slowly practicing loving-kindness towards others—beginning with people who are respected or beloved, then moving to people who seem more neutral, and only progressing to those who provoke painful feelings when loving-kindness towards others feels more established.

When trauma occurs, loving-kindness can feel very far away. It can be extremely hard to believe that anything will help. Practicing self-compassion and loving-kindness can be difficult or strange at first, like an extra, odd ingredient in a dish to which one is accustomed. Compassion, self-compassion, and loving-kindness each get easier with practice. They begin to feel normal and helpful. As the Dalai Lama (1998) pointed out, "love and compassion are necessities, not luxuries. Without them humanity cannot survive."

Resolving Misconceptions and Stumbling Blocks

The idea of mindfulness and its practices have grown more widespread over the past several decades. This growth is exciting, as it has brought the benefits of mindfulness to so many people, as well as a general understanding that it is possible to cultivate new mental patterns. However, misconceptions about mindfulness are pervasive, and can prevent us either from trying out mindfulness practices in the first place, or from continuing to practice them if we encounter obstacles. Common misconceptions include the idea that the point of mindfulness is to clear your mind; the view that some people are just not good at it or that it does not work for them; the idea that mindfulness practice can solve all problems; the assumption that mindfulness requires a specific religious affiliation; that practicing mindfulness is boring or self-indulgent; and that people who have experienced trauma should be wary of mindfulness or compassion practices.

The Point of Mindfulness Is Not to Clear Your Mind.

Minds have tons of thoughts, and they wander all over the place. With practice, we can observe our thoughts, feelings, and patterns more clearly. However, the goal of any specific mindfulness practice session or the work of mindfulness in general is usually *not* to empty the mind of thoughts. This misconception often leads us to think that we are failing at mindfulness if we notice ourselves being distracted while practicing mindfulness, or having lots of thoughts. This is not the case. Mindfulness works to build awareness and to train attention in the following way: When a thought, feeling, or image arises, we notice it, try not to judge it or the fact that it has arisen, and then gently return our attention to our chosen object of focus, such as the breath or the sensation of walking.

If the mind were always still or empty of thoughts during mindfulness practice, there would be few opportunities to develop the skills of mindfulness. We actual *need* the material that arises so that we can use it to practice new mental habits. In fact, the moment of noticing that our minds have wandered away is so important that the meditation teacher Sharon Salzberg (2011) called it "the magic moment": "The moment that we realize our attention has wandered is the magic moment of the practice, because that's the moment we have the chance to be really different. Instead of judging ourselves, and berating ourselves, and condemning ourselves, we can be gentle with ourselves." Observing and gently changing our attention is the true work of mindfulness—it is the essential step that builds our mindfulness "muscles."

Mindfulness Involves Balance, Rather Than Feeling All of Our Feelings All of the Time

The idea that mindfulness involves attending to this moment does not mean that we need to be fully present with all of our feelings all of the time. Mindfulness is not a contest or an endurance test to evaluate levels of mental presence.

In fact, sometimes the wisest thing to do is to turn our attention elsewhere. We may need to take an exam, drive a car, listen to another person, or take shelter in a storm—situations in which it would be inappropriate to focus on all of our feelings.

Healing from trauma often requires a delicate approach: touching emotional material a little bit at a time, and then backing away. We titrate or modulate our approach to trauma so that it does not overwhelm us, and so that we can also focus on developing new skills and self-compassion. After trauma, it is often wise to first establish safety, stability, and self-compassion, so that we can approach trauma from the perspective of "being with, but not being overwhelmed" by it.[15]

We might consider trauma to be a large body of water. We do not need to be fully submerged in it in order to be present with it. Instead, we may be present by touching, smelling, or seeing the water; by observing its effects on the rocks and sand; by standing in the water; or by building a raft or learning to swim to get across the water. We can consciously choose how to approach difficult thoughts and feelings as we become more comfortable with them.

Overcoming the Idea That "I'm Just Not Good at It"

It can be frustrating when mindfulness practice does not produce immediate results. Often, the thought arises that "I'm just not good at this." Although this thought can feel true, it is not. Mindfulness skills take time and effort, and the practice of mindfulness contains challenges by its very nature. When those challenges arise, they are rich opportunities with which to work, and not an indication that the practitioner is personally flawed or incapable. Most of us enjoy doing things that we feel "good" at, and avoid things that are harder for us.

The idea that "I'm not good at it," often reflects confusion about what mindfulness is. If you think that mindfulness means maintaining unwavering attention and concentration, it is easy to interpret moments of distraction as failure. If you recall that it is OK and even normal for your mind to wander a million times, you may be less likely to think that there is a problem with your practice. The way that we *relate* to the ups and downs of our practice is, in fact, the cornerstone of mindfulness practice.

The real, deep mental work of life is often hard. If we stick only to doing what feels easy, we are unlikely to change difficult patterns and to develop new skills. The feeling that "I'm just not good at it" may also reflect a general tendency to blame ourselves when something is hard. If that is the case, that tendency becomes another pattern that we can observe mindfully, and then gently shift our attention back to our chosen focus of mindfulness practice. The point of mindfulness practice is not to become "good" at the skills themselves; rather, the techniques exist as vehicles to help us develop new ways of living our lives.

Mindfulness Practice Cannot Solve All Problems

The buzz about the benefits of mindfulness can be so intense that it is easy to believe that mindfulness is a panacea. A range of scientific studies do demonstrate that the majority of people who practice mindfulness in a sustained way, over the course of several weeks, report benefits to their well-being. These reported benefits, however, do not mean that mindfulness makes all problems disappear. Personal mindfulness practice alone cannot erase all of the pain and suffering in the world, but it may reduce problems, make them easier to handle, or help guide effective actions to prevent or lessen suffering.

Mindfulness needs to be combined with other positive actions. Sometimes it is necessary to visit a doctor, to change a living situation, to take prescribed medications, or to provide tangible care to another person. In fact, mindfulness practices have been shown to be highly effective when combined with conventional treatments for psychological or physical health problems.[16]

Mindfulness is not the best approach for every problem. It can be ineffective and even dangerous to view all problems as located within individual people. Problems such as a discriminatory workplace or a harmful chemical in the environment are not challenges to be solved with individual mindfulness, but with structural changes.

Although most people report benefits from mindfulness practice, some people describe negative experiences, or a mix of positive and negative consequences.[17] Briere (2015) noted that for individuals with overwhelming intrusive memories or emotional pain, it can be problematic to reduce avoidance (as commonly occurs during mindfulness practice) in the absence of other effective coping strategies for tolerating and regulating emotions. Briere recommends that in those cases it may be helpful to begin with loving-kindness meditation (see Chapter 4), or other practices that open awareness for thoughts and feelings less directly. Some challenges with mindfulness are to be expected, which present opportunities for growth; however, if you find that your feelings worsen with mindfulness practice, and that the setback persists, it is important to seek help.

The idea that we are in complete control of our experience is misguided, and it can create internal pressure. Rather, our experience is a combination of the circumstances we face and our own internal dynamics. We need to do the best we can to develop skills and actions to promote our well-being. For some, this process may include cultivating mindfulness, but different people benefit from a range of approaches to handling distress. Recognizing that mindfulness is not a cure-all may help us put aside unrealistic expectations, and remind us to consider various kinds of helpful actions towards ourselves and the world.

Mindfulness Practice Can Be Secular, Spiritual, or Religious
Mindfulness teachings abound in diverse cultural and religious traditions, and span thousands of years. Mindfulness is not the province of any one religion.

It is a common misconception that mindfulness is solely aligned with Buddhist traditions. Certainly, Buddhism contains a strong emphasis on mindfulness training, as well as teachings about mindfulness that many people (not only Buddhists) find valuable. However, mindfulness traditions also exist within Christianity, Hinduism, Judaism, Jainism, Sikhism, Taoism, Sufism, and among Native American and other traditions. In addition, many people who do not identify with any religious tradition find benefits from mindfulness practice—practicing mindfulness does not mean that a person is taking part in a religious observance. Many people do have important spiritual or religious dimensions to their meditation; however, many others experience benefits from secular mindfulness practice.

Regardless of their religious affiliations, people often find that mindfulness shifts how they view themselves and the world. Each person can decide whether or not to link mindfulness practice with other religious or spiritual traditions. However, even when practiced "secularly"—that is, without any specific religious connection—mindfulness practices are not neutral. They are linked with a strong set of values: of awareness, nonjudgment, compassion, loving-kindness, and actions to enhance the well-being and happiness of ourselves and others.

Fear of Mindfulness and Self-Compassion

Even when habitual thoughts and emotions are painful, there can be some comfort in them because we are used to them. The idea of trying out or feeling new things can be scary. In addition, the concept of being calmer or kinder with ourselves may feel especially threatening, as though we are "letting down our guard." In a way, this is true. Mindfulness practice and self-compassion facilitate a balanced awareness of the world around us—an awareness that balances attention to potential threats with openness to other experiences. It may help to recognize that no sudden changes are necessary, and to give ourselves permission to make changes as slowly as we need and as they feel comfortable.

Overcoming the Idea That Mindfulness Practice Is Boring

We might also be wary of mindfulness or self-compassion practice because it sounds boring, or because we feel worried that it will make us boring, selfish, or self-absorbed. It might help to consider that we are used to high levels of stimulation, and that we may pay attention only to things that are intensely pleasant or unpleasant, rather than anything in between. We often crave immediate reinforcement for our actions, and practicing mindfulness might not always provide that.

Often, when we turn our full attention to something, it becomes more interesting than we anticipated (who knew that there was a tiny little Lincoln statue within the Lincoln memorial on the back of a penny?). We can also expand our emotional experiences beyond negative ones by paying attention to a broader range of thoughts and feelings. It is true that mindfulness practice is not always immediately uplifting; however, it does appear to help the majority of people over time, and each moment of practice provides something that we can work with. As for the concern that it will make us boring or self-centered, we might take comfort in the research evidence that people who practice mindfulness, self-compassion, and loving-kindness are relatively more helpful and less prejudiced towards others.[18]

Challenges as Mindfulness Opportunities

"Wherever you are, that is the entry point" (2002, p. 35). This advice from the 15th century poet Kabir is useful when encountering obstacles to mindfulness. Everyone has challenges in mindfulness practice. However, what begins as a challenge can become a catalyst to practice observing a problem in the present moment without focusing on fixing it. The obstacles to practicing mindfulness can include physical discomfort, falling asleep, self-judgments, restlessness, or disturbances in the environment. Our tendencies to become distracted, to blame ourselves, or to want a "quick fix" can also challenge our practice.

Each mindfulness challenge provides an opportunity to engage and strengthen our mindfulness skills with respect to the challenge itself. For instance, every time you sit down to practice, you might notice discomfort in your hips that settles down after a few minutes. Instead of viewing the discomfort as an obstacle to practice, you might try being curious about it and observing how it changes; noting the discomfort but then redirecting your attention, over and over; or offering yourself compassion for the discomfort. Over time, you can observe shifts in your relationship to sources of discomfort and distraction. These challenges can also serve as touchstones or markers that help us observe changes.

Practicing Mindfulness

Practice is a key word in mindfulness, because cultivating mindfulness takes intentional effort and unfolds over time. To get started, it can help to identify a setting, a time, and a specific practice. We are generally more likely to practice if we make a plan or have a routine. You can use any of the suggestions below, or you may choose to incorporate mindfulness groups, books, apps, or audio recordings into your practice.

Setting

The setting should be a place where you feel relatively comfortable, without too many distractions, and one that is easy to access. Many people practice at home. If this is your preference, you might identify a specific spot within your home that you want to link to your practice. Over time, it is important to practice mindfulness out in the world as well, but having a mindfulness "home" can assist in developing mindfulness skills.

Having a specific spot helps cue our mental processes—that is, the space can become associated with mindfulness efforts and reinforce them, so that they become easier to access over time. The spot can be anywhere (some people even convert a closet to be their mindfulness space), except for your bed. People often find that when they practice mindfulness in bed, they fall asleep. There's nothing inherently wrong with falling asleep; many people even find that mindful relaxation helps to relieve sleep problems. However, in order to develop skills for managing the mind during wakeful states, we need to be in a wakeful state when we practice. You can practice in a chair, or on a cushion on the floor. Try to find a posture that is both relaxed and composed, and that balances some degree of energy and calmness, or to sit in a way that reflects how you want to feel. You may find it helpful to decorate your mindfulness space in such a way that marks it as special in developing your mindfulness skills.

Many people like to practice as part of a group, either as their primary way to practice mindfulness, or as a complement to their individual practice. Group mindfulness meetings often provide opportunities to share experiences and to ask questions.

Time

Figuring out a time to practice mindfulness is often a challenge for people. It seems to be most effective to plan for mindfulness practice in advance, rather than hoping that it can fit into the week somehow as the idea arises. The morning is a popular time for mindfulness practice—either first thing or after breakfast. People often find that a morning practice can set a positive tone for the rest of the day. However, other times are fine as well, with the exception of right before bed, because you may fall asleep and miss out on some of the benefits of practicing during wakefulness. To make mindfulness a routine, it is most helpful to practice at the same time every day (or on the days that you practice).

People often ask how much time is necessary for mindfulness practice. The teacher Sharon Salzberg (2015) often recommends at least 20 minutes, because minds often take this long to settle down, but advises that 5 minutes can be enough when we are starting out. However, there is no specific set time that is necessary, so you can experiment to see what amount of time seems most helpful for you. It seems as though consistency of mindfulness practice is more important than the number of minutes you practice per day.

Soler and colleagues (2014) investigated mindfulness practices and self-reported mindfulness skills in 670 individuals. They found that the frequency of mindfulness practice and the extent of people's lifetime experience practicing mindfulness were linked to their mindfulness skills of observing, nonreacting, and decentering; however, the length and type of their mindfulness practice sessions were not. The researchers suggest that practicing 20 minutes daily offers more benefits than longer weekly practices.

Posture

We can benefit from mindfulness practice without any specific posture. However, our emotions respond to physical cues from our bodies. Our posture can help us to feel more confident, empowered, and positive. You might try sitting or walking as if you were royal, with an open chest and shoulders, but in a way that is also flexible rather than tense. You can also sit in the posture of how you want to feel. You might try for a balanced posture, in which you feel both dignified and relaxed.

Our posture can benefit our mindfulness practice, but it can also provoke discomfort. When our posture feels tense or uncomfortable, we can use it as a vehicle to curiously investigate our thoughts and experiences. Learning to handle small amounts of physical discomfort can help us build our capacity to handle emotional pain. If you find yourself judging your posture, you might use it as an opportunity to notice judgment and to practice nonjudgment. It is common to begin with an upright posture and then to slump. If this happens, or if you are uncomfortable, you can reset your posture. You can experiment with short phrases to remind you of the posture that you are aiming for (such as "straight back" or "soft belly"). On the whole, posture should be an asset to mindfulness practice, rather than a source of stress.

Special Considerations for Practicing Mindfulness After Trauma

After trauma, it is especially important to approach mindfulness practice in a way that feels safe, caring, and gentle. Remember that your intention is to heal, rather than to cause more stress. You can choose to go at your own pace, and to pay careful attention to your physical and emotional comfort. If you observe any tendencies to criticize yourself about your mindfulness practice (e.g., "I'm not doing a good job"), try to observe them gently as thoughts rather than facts.

There are some practical considerations that can help you to feel safe practicing mindfulness after trauma. The first is your physical location. Try to choose a spot where you feel relatively safe and calm. The second is the position of your body. During mindfulness practice, it is helpful to sit in such a way that you feel comfortable. You can choose to practice with your eyes open, or with your eyes closed. If you decide to practice with your eyes open, find a spot about a foot or two in front of you where your gaze can rest gently. The third consideration is to give yourself permission to change or stop your practice session if you feel overwhelmed. For instance, you might decide to focus on self-compassion or mindful breathing, rather than attending to traumatic material. If you do attend to painful emotions, you can set a time limit or an intention to help soothe yourself afterwards. You might even decide to shift your practice emphasis to cultivating self-compassion or mindful breathing. Once you have developed some mindfulness skills through your practice, you may choose to stay present with difficult feelings for longer periods. However, you can give yourself the option to stop ahead of time if you need to help yourself feel more safe and secure.

If you need to stop your practice session because you are feeling very upset, it can be helpful to have ideas for how to help yourself that you have thought out in advance. For instance, the list could go something like, "1. Make and drink tea; 2. Call a friend; 3. Read or watch television." Do not include activities that cause harm (such as using drugs or alcohol; engaging in self-harm) on the list. These are not long-term solutions, but tools to tolerate especially strong emotions if they arise. Although mindfulness practice can help people with a range of distressing feelings, it is easiest to try out new ways to handle challenges when they are at a moderate level.

If you consider rating your distress on a level of 0 (no distress) to 10 (extreme distress to the point of danger of harming oneself or feeling physically out of control), beginning mindfulness practice often works best in the 1–7 range. With no distress, there are no opportunities to practice new approaches to challenges; with extreme distress, it is essential to seek emergency care by calling 911, phoning a suicide hotline, or going to a hospital emergency room.

A variety of sensations, feelings, and memories can emerge during mindfulness practice after trauma. After trauma, it is common to experience *dissociation*—interruptions in the normally integrated processes of attention, concentration, and memory. You may also experience *depersonalization*, the feeling that you are not yourself or that you are not in your body. Some people experience *flashbacks*—the sensation of being either partly or completely back in the midst of a memory. Others experience bodily memories or sensations, such as a physical feeling linked to the trauma, or sensations in a specific part of the body where the trauma seems to reside. When these arise, you might use your five senses to ground yourself in the present moment and to build your sense of safety. You might open your eyes if they are closed, focus on this very breath in this moment, or feel the texture of a chair or rug in order to anchor yourself. If the sensations are mild and tolerable, you can use mindfulness to observe them in a caring way.

It is always wise to notice the way mindfulness practice affects you personally, and to establish conditions that will enhance your feeling of safety and comfort. Every person is different. If you notice trauma-related difficulties becoming worse, rather than better, after mindfulness practice, it is important to try a different approach or to consult a healthcare professional.

As we recover from trauma, it can help to feel a sense of empowerment and choice. We can choose the specific practices to try, and we can decide if they seem to be helping. In this book, I try to use language in the mindfulness exercises to convey invitations and suggestions, rather than implying that there is anything you have to do. My hope is that the mindfulness practices will feel empowering as you develop more options for handling challenging thoughts and feelings.

Choosing a Specific Practice

When we pay attention during mindfulness practice, we purposefully focus on something, such as the breath or the experience of walking. When the mind wanders away, we notice that it has wandered, and we may observe where it has gone (sometimes people call this "noting"). We then return our attention to the facet of experience chosen for that practice, such as breathing or walking, while we try to refrain from judging that the mind wandered or where it went. That process is likely to happen over and over. Even if it happens 100 times in 20 minutes, remember that noticing distraction highlights the "magic moment," when we can practice a new way to handle thoughts and feelings when they arise.

The following pages describe many specific mindfulness practices, and explain the ways that different mindfulness skills can address common difficulties after trauma. To get started, you might choose one of the following practices: mindful breathing, body scan, or mindful walking. Chapter 3 describes each of these practices in more detail, along with other ways to begin and deepen mindfulness skills. For each of these mindfulness practices, your only job is to pay attention to the sensations that you have chosen, without judgment, and to return your focus when it moves away, over and over.

Mindful Breathing

The breath is a convenient entry point into mindfulness because it is always there, and because the present breath is the only one that we can observe. The breath anchors us to the present moment. You can take a moment to just be—to just notice your breath without trying to change anything. Each breath has a lot to observe, including the air going into the nostrils, the sensations in the chest, and the transitions between inhaling and exhaling. You can consider resting your attention wherever you feel the breath most strongly. You can also try being present for your breathing while counting 10 breaths in a row. When your attention drifts or you lose count, you can start over again at 1. If breathing is stressful or difficult for you, you might start your mindfulness practice with the body scan or mindful walking.

Body Scan

In the body scan exercise, we practice focusing our attention to scan the physical sensations throughout our bodies. We practice shifting our attention slowly from the top of the head down our bodies to our feet. If you prefer, you can start with the feet and then work your way up to your head. We might notice sensations in our head; next in our shoulders, chest, arms, and back;

then our stomach, pelvis, and seat; and then in our legs and feet. We might notice many bodily sensations about which we had been unaware, or we may feel not much at all. However, we build our mindfulness skills by noticing our sensations without judgment, and by redirecting our attention to our feelings in this moment.

Mindful Walking

Like breathing, walking is an activity that we rarely think about consciously, especially if we do not have any physical problems that impede it. We can bring mindfulness to our walking by observing our movements and sensations as we walk. It might seem at first as though there's not much to notice. Once we practice tuning in to walking, we can notice more complexity: the way that we land and balance on our feet; our posture; the process of shifting our weight; and the movement of our arms. This practice of mindful walking can be a good place to start when we feel too restless to sit still.

Encouragement to Keep Going

Trauma hurts. Because our pain can be quite deep and complex, healing from trauma often requires careful attention. By practicing new ways of handling our thoughts and feelings, we can transform our suffering into strength. Choosing how we recover from trauma can feel empowering, and practicing new skills can help provide a framework for recovery. Because the journey of healing after trauma takes time and energy, we can benefit from our own self-encouragement to keep going. It can be helpful to acknowledge and reinforce *all* of our efforts—even one moment of mindfulness practice. In every moment and in every breath after trauma, we are engaged in the hard work of healing our pain and building peace.

TRAUMA AND PTSD

T RAUMA TOUCHES EVERY life. Both the moments of trauma and its aftermath can bring deep pain. It can help to learn that our feelings make sense, and that we are not alone in our suffering. It may feel validating to learn about common reactions to trauma, and to understand how constellations of trauma symptoms fit together. We often judge ourselves for our feelings after trauma—especially in the context of a culture that prioritizes "getting over" trauma or insinuates that feeling traumatized is a choice related to our strength or character. Surveying the science of trauma and PTSD can soothe those judgments, and demonstrates that trauma strongly impacts a range of mental and emotional processes.

It can feel empowering to know that there are many routes to trauma recovery, and to remember that each of us gets to decide what route to follow. For instance, some treatment approaches emphasize building mindfulness, self-compassion, and skills to regulate emotions; other treatments focus on paying attention to the trauma itself and related feelings; and some programs combine these approaches. Each of these kinds of treatments has been effective in reducing PTSD and depression symptoms. This indicates that there is no "one size fits all" way to heal from trauma.

You may choose to read the information below to obtain more knowledge about trauma and its effects, or you might want to skip over it and go on to the next chapter. It might feel upsetting to reflect about the ways that trauma can impact our lives, but it can also feel interesting to learn more, or even comforting to learn that a trauma response is common. At times, there may be a fine line between feeling validated about the seriousness of trauma and its effects, and feeling discouraged. It might help to know that the evidence shows that we can recover from trauma, and illuminates several successful ways to do so. If you decide that you do want to read about trauma, but that it provokes some pain or discomfort, you might try out some of the self-compassion exercises (see Chapter 4) to care for your distress. Either way is fine, and a matter of personal choice about how much you feel that this information can help in your trauma recovery.

What Is Trauma?

When people hear the word *trauma*, they often think of something that is immediate and intensely horrific, such as a sudden car accident or a violent assault. Trauma does indeed include some of the most terrifying parts of human experience, such as war, disaster, illness or disease, sexual or physical violence, and accidents. However, there is now strong scientific evidence that other types of situations—such as emotional abuse, bullying, grief, losing jobs, and ending relationships—can lead to traumatic reactions that are just as strong, or even stronger, than trauma that involves actual or threatened bodily harm.

A common definition of trauma is an overwhelming event or situation that we experience as potentially harmful, that exceeds our coping capacities at the time, and that has lasting negative effects.[19] It is common to experience many different traumas throughout life. It is our cumulative trauma exposure, rather than our experience of one specific trauma, that has the most impact on our mental and physical health.[20]

Effects of Trauma

A full range of experiences can arise after trauma, including depression, anxiety, shock, grief, anger, numbness, hopelessness, shame, sleep problems, betrayal, alienation, and guilt. Trauma can impact how we think by disrupting our attention and concentration, by shading our thoughts with negative judgments and expectations, and by creating patterns of self-blame and self-criticism. It can also lead us to avoid things that trigger anxiety or painful memories, and it can influence how we interact with other people.

We can recover from trauma. To start, it often helps to observe our trauma-related thoughts and feelings with a curious and caring intention. Understanding common emotional responses to trauma can help us from ove-ridentifying with our own feelings, or thinking that there is something wrong with us. Trauma-related mental experiences then become just mental experiences, rather than reflections of our character. Gaining more knowledge about normal responses to trauma may not make trauma-related suffering less painful, but it can make the pain feel less alienating and personal, so that it loses some of its sting.

RESEARCH HIGHLIGHT Which Events Are Traumatic?

IT MAY BE SURPRISING to learn that traumas such as relationship conflicts, relationships ending, losing a job, financial worries, and emotional abuse can lead to mental health problems that are just as severe, or more severe, as the effects of life-threatening danger or sexual trauma.

Anders, Frazier, and Frankfurt (2011) analyzed connections between the types of traumatic events that 884 women reported and their mental health symptoms.

The researchers determined that experiences like losing a job or a relationship were just as strongly linked to PTSD and depression as were life-threatening or sexual traumas. Similarly, Gibb, Chelminski, and Zimmerman (2007) asked 857 adult psychiatric outpatients about their experiences of sexual abuse, physical abuse, and emotional abuse in childhood. Childhood emotional abuse, rather than sexual or physical abuse, contributed most strongly to depression and social phobia in adulthood.

The social aspects of trauma have a substantial impact on survivors' responses. Interpersonal traumas usually cause us more anxiety, depression, and PTSD than do noninterpersonal traumas such as accidents or disasters, with the worst suffering linked to trauma perpetrated by someone with whom we were close.[21] Our social environments after trauma also influence mental health. For instance, survivors of sexual abuse who are believed and supported fare better than those who are not.[22] Veterans' and firefighters' levels of social support are closely linked to the severity of their posttraumatic stress, despite the amount of trauma they endured.[23]

Types of Traumatic Events and Situations

- Emotional, physical, and sexual abuse
- Child emotional neglect and child physical neglect
- Abuse in educational, religious, incarceration, or work settings
- Intimate partner violence
- Physical assault
- Rape
- Harassment
- Stalking
- Loss of a job

- Major financial hardships and poverty
- Legal difficulties
- Accidents and disasters
- Combat trauma
- Military sexual trauma
- Grief and loss
- Illness and disease
- War, genocide, and refugee trauma
- Discrimination
- Terrorism
- Kidnapping, being held hostage, and torture
- Community violence, police violence, robberies, and muggings
- Racism
- Sexism
- Bullying
- Homophobia
- Microaggressions (subtle, automatic insults or biased behavior) involving racism, sexism, bullying, and homophobia
- Political repression and discrimination
- Institutional betrayal—traumas perpetrated by an institution on individuals who depend on that institution, including the failure to prevent or respond supportively to traumas[24]
- Systemic trauma—the ways that institutions, cultures, and communities exacerbate or mitigate trauma and people's responses

Trauma and Social Contexts

Our social world strongly impacts the type of traumas that we experience, as well as our recovery processes. We seem to absorb cultural messages about how we "should" feel and whether or not we should express our feelings. Our environments may ignore or condone trauma, or blame trauma survivors. However, our environments can also help prevent trauma and provide resources for healing.

Whereas unsupportive environments make trauma worse, social support can help us heal from trauma. When trauma occurs within a relationship, it leaves deep emotional scars and we are likely to feel shame, betrayal, anger, and alienation, and to blame ourselves. These types of feelings can then fuel posttraumatic stress and depression. Conversely, healing from trauma often involves having positive experiences within the context of relationships—feeling believed, understood, cared for, or supported.

We often hear phrases about trauma and its effects, many of which are not true and are even harmful. "What doesn't kill you makes you stronger" and "Sticks and stones may break my bones, but words will never hurt me" express myths that have been refuted by clear research evidence. In fact, both our total amount of trauma exposure and our experiences of verbal abuse are *strongly* linked to mental and physical health problems throughout our lives. Untrue ideas about trauma are pervasive, and they can make us judge ourselves or others unfairly.

Many cultures seem to convey the idea that mental health is created entirely by our own internal attitude and determination, rather than by a complex interplay of circumstances and behaviors. We often regard normal emotional responses to trauma as failures of character, rather than as part of being human. We commonly *pathologize* normal responses to trauma as being odd or disordered; that is, we treat the person or the problem as abnormal or unhealthy. My graduate professor and supervisor Dr. Pamela Birrell compared trauma exposure to toxic gas pouring into a room packed with people. If some people felt slightly queasy, but others fainted or became ill, would we blame anyone for their body's natural response to the toxic gas?

We may keep our suffering hidden because of shame or self-blame, or the idea of not wanting to burden others. However, overcoming the hurdle of seeking help or talking about trauma with someone supportive can help us heal. In fact, supportive relationships themselves can be a vehicle for healing—especially if our trauma occurred within the context of relationships.

Emotion Socialization and Posttraumatic Stress

Learning to manage challenging emotions is a bit like learning how to swim. Most of us need careful guidance at first, and then it becomes easier and easier until we can do it without trying very hard. Our capacity to manage challenging thoughts and feelings evolves in a similar way. We typically need a lot of assistance and care as we build our skills; however, that guidance is more readily available in some environments than others.

Ideally, parents or other caregivers teach us how to cope with difficult feelings and situations—how to soothe ourselves, think about the situation as a learning experience, tolerate distress, and improve our circumstances. However, many environments do not provide this instruction. We may be discouraged—either explicitly or implicitly—from noticing or talking about our feelings. Other environments pay minimal attention to emotions in general. Although culture and gender appear to contribute somewhat to the way that we identify and discuss emotions, the way our parents "socialized" our emotions has the strongest impact on how we approach our own feelings.[25]

Emotional neglect, or inadequate attention and care for emotional experiences, is a common phenomenon. It can occur on its own, or alongside emotional, physical, or sexual abuse—all situations that ignore or degrade a child's emotional needs. *Invalidating environments* [26] in which children's emotional experiences are ignored, minimized, criticized, punished, or ridiculed, are traumas themselves and contribute to mental health problems in adulthood. Childhood environments that include abuse or neglect also impact brain development, because they overactivate brain circuits involved in responding to threat, and underactivate brain systems that regulate anxiety and other challenging emotions. If we learn new coping skills and build resilience after trauma, however, we can modify the way that the brain works both in this moment and in the long term.

Common Challenges After Trauma

We typically experience a constellation of difficulties after trauma. Sometimes the sheer number of problems can make them feel insurmountable. However, each challenge is understandable and workable. Every problem reflects an understandable adaptation to the exact circumstances that we endured. For instance, if we were to be assaulted by an acquaintance, we might feel wary of interactions with new people, overly alert to potential dangers, jaded and disillusioned about life, afraid of going outside to walk or exercise, and unable to calm down without alcohol or other drugs. Rather than seeing these difficulties as a long list of separate issues or "disorders," we can view them as a set of expectable, interconnected, and learned responses. In fact, being ultra-alert, not leaving home, being disillusioned with the goodness of the world and with life itself, and not calming down can each be viewed as potentially effective strategies to reduce the likelihood of being assaulted again.

Our symptoms after trauma make sense, and they fit together. Many people feel some relief from observing the ways that their symptoms reflect normal adaptations to trauma, rather than indications that there is something wrong with them. Because these trauma responses are learned behaviors, they can be changed over time. We can learn new responses that disrupt the old patterns. Although not everyone will respond in the same way to the same trauma, the trauma responses below are extremely common. In fact, the degree of trauma exposure we experience predicts the likelihood that we will experience each of the difficulties below.

It is a difficult paradox that the same behaviors that help us adapt to trauma can also diminish our overall well-being. After trauma, it can feel tremendously uncomfortable to learn to relax, to go outside, or to talk with strangers or acquaintances. We can feel conflicted when the same behaviors (such as being on guard at all times, or not caring about anything) that were once adaptive come to be a source of long-term suffering. We can benefit from acknowledging this tension, and by compassionately understanding our patterns as normal responses even as we work to change them.

Depression

Depression is an exceedingly common response to trauma. Depression can include feeling sad or down more often than not; feeling less interest or enjoyment in activities; feeling worthless, hopeless, or helpless; feeling irritable; criticizing or blaming ourselves for real or perceived faults; having trouble concentrating or making decisions; crying; not liking ourselves; feeling like a failure; sleeping or eating either too much or too little; wanting to die; and experiencing reduced interest in sex. Several factors appear to contribute to depression and other mental health problems, including trauma exposure, coping skills, genetics, and early home environments. Depression is treatable, and can be substantially reduced through several approaches, including psychotherapy, increased activities, medication, mindfulness practice, and exercise.

Depression that is related to traumatic experiences seems to be different from other types of depression.[27] When depression is related to trauma, we may benefit from acknowledging the role of trauma, rather than by approaching the depression as if it were unrelated. Because depression often involves negative judgments about ourselves and our feelings, developing an understanding of those tendencies as common responses to trauma can shift the self-criticism that maintains depressed mood.

Anxiety

Anxiety is a normal response to trauma that can persist long after the immediate danger has passed. When a trauma triggers an involuntary "fight, flight, or freeze" signal in the nervous system, our brains and bodies quickly engage an emergency reaction. Anxiety symptoms include being overly alert to potential threats; feeling tense or wound up; feeling as though the world or other people are dangerous; feeling worried all of the time; feeling jumpy or easily startled; never being able to relax; having difficulty sleeping; having panic attacks; blaming oneself for feeling anxious; feeling exhausted from expending so much energy worrying, and feeling tense or keyed up. Repeated stress results in overlearning how to respond effectively to danger, and underlearning how to calm down. Therapy, medications, and exercise have each shown utility in reducing anxiety. Mindfulness practices also show benefits in reducing overall levels of anxiety, as well as anxiety related to trauma.

Emotion Regulation Difficulties

Trauma disrupts the ways that we relate to our own emotions. During times of extreme stress, it may be adaptive to decrease awareness for feelings in general, or to prioritize attention to extreme feelings rather than more subtle emotions. Patterns of *emotion regulation*—the ways in which we observe and manage our emotions—play a key role in mental health following trauma. We often imitate the models of emotion regulation that we observe around us. When we see others model effective ways of noticing, communicating, and handling their emotions, we are more likely to develop these capacities ourselves. Fortunately, we can improve our emotion regulation skills by using mindfulness techniques and other forms of conscious practice.

Emotion regulation difficulties often arise from our past trauma experiences. Whereas strategies of avoiding, suppressing, or internalizing distress are related to PTSD, anxiety, and depression, strategies of accepting emotional experiences and reappraising the trauma and its meaning are associated with fewer psychological problems. Both psychotherapy and mindfulness techniques can result in improved emotion regulation skills.

Negative Trauma Appraisals

After trauma, we often develop *negative appraisals*—negative beliefs or feelings about our experience of trauma and what it means. Negative trauma appraisals can include guilt, shame and self-blame. For instance, we may have thoughts along the lines of "I'm an awful person for not wanting to see my parents more often, even though they hurt me," or "I'm pathetic for not having more energy since my relationship ended." Negative appraisals are so powerful that they influence levels of depression and posttraumatic stress to a degree beyond the contributions of the trauma itself.[28] However, we can change our appraisals through therapy, mindfulness, and self-compassion.

Posttraumatic Stress Disorder (PTSD)

The term posttraumatic stress disorder (PTSD) describes problems that are common following trauma. Although this label might give the impression that reactions to trauma are consistent, they actually vary widely across individuals in terms of which symptoms occur and how severe they are. The precise combination of problems included under the PTSD classification continues to shift as health professionals gradually incorporate research advances. The PTSD category reflects some of the ways that trauma impacts the nervous system, as well as how we think and feel about ourselves, the trauma, our own emotions, and the world.

Posttraumatic Stress Disorder (PTSD) Symptoms

- Having intrusive thoughts, images and memories about the trauma (*intrusions*)
- Avoiding people, places, and other cues related to the trauma (*avoidance*)
- Feeling alert, on guard, or watchful; feeling jumpy or easily startled (*hypervigilance*)
- Having nightmares or difficulty sleeping
- Feeling depressed
- Having problems managing emotional experiences in general
- Feeling fear, helplessness, shame, and guilt
- Having negative beliefs about oneself, others, and the world

---

The symptoms of PTSD reflect the ways in which trauma can be such a huge disruption in a person's life. During trauma and afterwards, our energy and resources become redirected toward coping. Our bodies respond to extreme stress by going on high alert, feeling jumpy, being on guard to potential signals of danger in the environment, and having difficulty relaxing—feelings known as *hypervigilance* and *hyperarousal*. These responses happen involuntarily. Our minds respond to trauma by trying to remember it, to process the trauma to handle the feelings that spring up after the trauma, and to make it somehow fit in with the way things were before. We typically experience *intrusions*—thoughts, memories, and sensations about the trauma that seem to pop up out of the blue, along with urges and behaviors to avoid thoughts, feelings, people, actions, or places related to the trauma.

Our minds seem to chew on the trauma with an intrusion-avoidance-intrusion-avoidance motion. The *cognitive processing* view of PTSD explains how intrusive symptoms such as trauma-related thoughts, memories, and nightmares cycle back and forth with avoidance symptoms after trauma. When intrusions arise, it's as though a voice emerges that says, "Argh! This is way too upsetting and painful. I need to push it away." However, when we avoid trauma-related material, the intrusions rebound, essentially saying, "Hey, this really happened. I need you to pay attention to it so that the memory can be integrated into the general flow of life experiences, so that my feelings can get cared for, and so that I can stay safe in the future." In this way, intrusions and avoidance tug on each other, and keep us stuck.[29]

The world itself changes after trauma. It may feel impossible to fit the trauma into the frame of life that existed before the trauma occurred. The *shattered assumptions* perspective on PTSD emphasizes the disconnection between life before and after the trauma. Trauma can challenge common core assumptions: fundamental beliefs that the world is a safe or manageable place, that people can be trusted, and that there is goodness and meaning in the world.[30] We struggle to reconstruct the ways that we understand ourselves, others, and the world. This struggle can emerge as PTSD, depression, or other difficulties.

Identifying the specific problems that are most troubling can help us heal. For instance, some people may find the most benefit from techniques that promote relaxation, whereas others benefit from attending carefully to negative beliefs. Many people consider it helpful to simultaneously address multiple aspects of PTSD, while cultivating a sense of kindness and understanding towards the experiences themselves. Several different approaches can result in recovery from PTSD, including therapy, mindfulness, self-compassion, and exercise.

Complex Posttraumatic Stress Disorder

Complex posttraumatic stress disorder is used to refer to the symptoms that develop following prolonged or chronic interpersonal trauma (some people also use the term *disorders of extreme stress not otherwise specified*, or DESNOS). The PTSD diagnosis initially reflected the experiences of adults who experienced trauma within a relatively limited place and time (such as serving in the Vietnam war or being raped by a stranger), and emphasized fear-related responses. Complex trauma describes situations in which we have to depend on the same people who hurt us. Childhood abuse fits into this category, as does domestic violence, trafficking, torture or hostage situations; and many types of violence that occur in religious, work, educational, or correctional settings. After complex trauma, we may experience one or more of the difficulties listed below:

Complex Posttraumatic Stress Disorder Symptoms

- Depression
- Difficulty understanding and managing emotions
- Problems trusting others or having healthy relationships
- Pessimism about the world and one's place in it

- Feeling unlovable, defective, or not good enough
- Disturbances in awareness, attention, and memory
- Shame and guilt
- Physical symptoms that do not necessarily have a clear medical cause

After complex trauma, we often learn to be highly attuned to the moods and triggers of those hurting us, and we might learn to ignore our own feelings and emotional needs. We commonly develop negative beliefs about ourselves, other people and the world. For instance, we might internalize that we are bad people who should expect bad things to happen, other people to be untrustworthy, and the world to be unfair. Complex trauma is especially detrimental when it occurs during childhood, because it interacts with our developing sense of who we are as people and of the social world. Even if we are aware to some extent that the treatment that we are receiving is inappropriate, the negative messages usually seep in.

Complex PTSD is different from "regular" PTSD because it shapes our sense of ourselves. It is inherently personal; that is, it *feels* deeply personal, even though the behavior typically arises from the perpetrator's own problems and would have been directed towards any other person in the same position. Because of the deeply personal nature of the injury, recovery from complex PTSD requires a deep level of care. Care—from both ourselves and from others—helps heal the feeling of being unlovable that complex trauma typically instills. Mindfulness, self-compassion, and therapy each can contribute to healing as well. These strategies help us identify and manage our thoughts, feelings, and beliefs after complex trauma.

THE WHOLE BODY reacts to trauma. A traumatic event or situation triggers an automatic sequence of reactions throughout the brain, nervous system, and viscera (guts). Our brains and bodies react not only to external stressors, but to the ways that we process stress on an internal, physical level. Trauma often results in meaningful long-term biological changes in both brain structure and function. In this way, trauma is a whole-body, physical experience.

"Everyone's brain learns from the environment how safe, on average, things are likely to be," explains Dr. Rebecca Hendrickson, a neuroscientist and psychiatrist at the University of Washington and the Veterans Affairs Medical Center, Puget Sound (personal communication, May 21, 2016). When our brains learn that the world is mostly dangerous, we are more likely to interpret ambiguous situations as dangerous. Conversely, if we learn from our environments that the world is a safe place and that people can be trusted, we are more likely to interpret stimuli as reflecting that learning. Neither pattern of learning or resulting belief system is right or wrong; rather, the brain is doing an excellent job of learning from the environment, with the aim of keeping us alive and optimally functional in a given situation. In a dangerous environment, being exceptionally aware of all possible threats can help keep us from getting hurt, and our brains adapt to that circumstance. PTSD is thought to reflect long-term alterations in brain systems—changes in brain circuitry that sensitize responses to potential threats.[31] For instance, abused children have heightened reactions to cues of emotional faces (even to those presented subliminally), and respond faster to fearful faces than nonmaltreated children.[32] Trauma can also steer our brains towards interpreting ambiguous information as threatening.[33] Childhood abuse and neglect can have a strong influence on brain development. In abusive environments, individuals' brains learn to be closely attuned to potential threats. Brain circuits involved in responding to threat become highly activated, whereas brain systems that regulate anxiety and other challenging emotions become less activated. These long-term changes can then contribute to the development of PTSD and other mental health difficulties in response to trauma in adulthood.[34]

After trauma, the brain's patterns of responding to the environment often persist. Brain pathways that process information about fear and emotional memories become more highly developed and responsive after trauma, whereas the brain expends fewer resources toward processing information that is ambiguous or nonthreatening, so that we develop an *attentional bias* towards potentially threatening stimuli.[35]

By consciously recognizing how we are processing the information that arises in our environments, we can practice and establish new patterns. We can ask ourselves whether an interpretation of an event in our current lives is accurate or healthy, or if it reflects our brain's learning in the context of past trauma. Then, we can consciously practice new interpretations—including viewing current experiences as safe or neutral—to alter mental biases that may not serve us well.

As we heal from trauma, we can benefit from mindfulness skills in changing the brain's networks of attention[36] and emotional responses to stimuli.[37] Our practice of observing without judging shifts brain patterns of *evaluative processing* that can keep us stuck in negative emotions.[38] That is, mindfulness practice can change how our brains organize and respond to thoughts, emotions, and events, so that we can recover from trauma and build effective ways of coping with stress.

Dissociation

When we find ourselves in stressful situations that we cannot escape, we may dissociate, or distance ourselves mentally from our present reality. *Dissociation* is often defined as a disruption in the normally integrated stream of attention and memory. Dissociation can be an adaptive way to get through traumatic circumstances. It can also help us handle thoughts or experiences that are incompatible. For instance, victims of abuse are commonly forced to depend on their abusers, and even to act in ways that will ensure continued caregiving. People who are sexually assaulted in the military often describe being pressured to keep it secret and to continue to function as they had before. The two parts—the experience of mistreatment and the expectation to function and to fit in with the other parts of life—just do not fit together. Coping with this sort of situation can create separate mental tracks in which we compartmentalize our thoughts and experiences. Many trauma victims are warned or threatened with further harm if they disclose what happened. In such situations, there is an additional incentive to dissociate.

Dissociative experiences can have diverse presentations. Some trauma survivors may feel relatively "spacey" and have trouble remembering things, including trauma experiences. Others may create distance between themselves and emotions in general—essentially dissociating from feelings themselves. We may feel numb, distant, or cut off from emotions. After trauma, we are more likely to experience *alexithymia*, or a lack of words for feelings. Many trauma survivors experience difficulties with attention, and may be misdiagnosed with attention deficit disorder. *Dissociative identity disorder* (formerly called multiple personality disorder) reflects the dissociative splitting of experiences into separate identities, and is usually a response to severe abuse. Dissociative adaptations to trauma each reflect a separation between pockets of attention, feelings, and memories. With care and attention, we can reduce dissociation, and build awareness and integration for our experiences.

Self-Criticism

Self-criticism is common. It often takes the shape of an ongoing negative commentary about ourselves. After verbal and emotional abuse, we often absorb the negative statements that we hear ("You're bad" or "you're an idiot"), and continue to tell ourselves such things. In fact, research demonstrates that self-criticism fully accounts for the link between experiencing verbal abuse as a child and feeling anxiety or depression as an adult.[39] Even when mistreatment does not contain explicit negative statements about us, we might internalize its presence in our lives as evidence that we are bad or deserving of the abuse. We may also criticize ourselves as a way of preserving a sense of control and trying to reduce the likelihood that we will be revictimized ("It's your fault; you should have gotten out of there before it happened.").

Self-criticism can also reflect the hypervigilance aspect of PTSD. Self-criticism can emerge as an internal hypervigilance—a way of continually examining ourselves for anything that could contribute to further trauma. Although self-criticism may seem to provide a sense of safety or control, self-criticism is strongly linked to depression, anxiety, and PTSD. Furthermore, we often criticize ourselves for *having* PTSD, depression, and other trauma-related problems. Unfortunately, the self-criticism adds another layer to the suffering.

People often think that self-criticism is motivating, or that it keeps them accountable to high standards. However, research studies show that self-criticism decreases motivation and accomplishments, whereas self-compassion increases motivation and achievement. Our tendencies to criticize ourselves are not fixed, and can change with practice. Techniques for working with self-criticism are discussed further in Chapter 4 and Chapter 8.

Alcohol and Other Drugs

After trauma, we are at increased risk for problems with alcohol and other drugs. We might use alcohol or other drugs to decrease negative emotions and to quell intrusive thoughts and memories of trauma. Research indicates that when we use alcohol to cope with emotional problems, we become more likely to develop alcohol-related disorders. Being intoxicated also makes us more vulnerable to both experiencing and perpetrating trauma.

Using alcohol or other drugs to cope with trauma and PTSD can produce a cognitive, emotional, and physiological pattern that maintains both substance use problems and PTSD. Excessive use of alcohol or other drugs can maintain PTSD and other trauma-related symptoms by preventing cognitive and emotional processing. In this way, using alcohol or drugs constitutes avoidance, which then worsens intrusive symptoms. Long-term use of alcohol may also worsen PTSD through biological pathways that include sleep disturbances and nerve damage. Healing involves managing both difficult emotional material and cravings for drugs and alcohol, while paying careful attention to the interplay between emotional symptoms and addictive behaviors.

Eating

There are many ways that trauma can lead to unhealthy eating: through feeling depressed, through feeling unworthy of taking care of ourselves, through trying to regulate difficult feelings, through feeling numb or cut off from our own bodies, through paying inadequate attention to other ways of caring for ourselves, and through living in neglectful environments that do not teach other ways to handle difficult emotions. Feeling as though we can control our eating may promote some sense of security. On the other hand, eating excessively may help to distract or numb ourselves from trauma-related pain, by "stuffing feelings" with food. Difficulty managing emotions is a central problem in disordered eating—a problem that links past trauma to disordered eating behavior.[40] After trauma, we are at increased risk for eating disorders, as well as for being overweight or obese.[41] Forming effective ways to notice, accept, and manage emotions helps us improve eating behavior.

Physical Health Problems

Although people may have the idea that trauma, PTSD, and related problems are "all in the head," they are very much in the body as well. Trauma is strongly linked to a range of physical health problems, including heart disease, cancer, asthma, diabetes, sleep problems, and irritable bowel syndrome.[42]

Trauma can relate to physical health directly. For example, we might become physically injured during a disaster or assault, develop a sexually transmitted disease after being raped, or experience the trauma of physical illness. We may also develop health problems in our attempts to cope with trauma. For instance, we might use alcohol excessively, smoke cigarettes, or overeat in response to emotional suffering—behaviors that then worsen health. Trauma and PTSD also make it less likely that we will obtain preventive health care such as pap smears, mammograms, or prostate cancer screening. Finally, trauma can alter our inflammatory and immune processes.

It is often helpful to address PTSD, depression, and physical health difficulties simultaneously. Physical exercise and mindfulness meditation can improve both emotional and physical health. We can benefit from a mindful "whole person" approach to our bodies and behaviors.

Relationship Problems

Trauma can often result in feelings of alienation and loneliness. Perhaps no one was there to witness the trauma or to help, or no one can quite understand the experience. The rest of the world seems to go on and on, and it can seem as though we and our trauma do not fit in anywhere. When we isolate from others because of our discomfort, we can wind up perpetuating our loneliness.

After trauma, we might feel uncomfortable trusting others or expressing our needs. We may also find ourselves caring too much about other people's opinions—especially if we have survived situations where others' opinions were potentially dangerous. PTSD and depression can also get in the way of connecting effectively with our partners, friends, or communities.

Traumas that occur within relationships alter our *relational schemas*, or our sense of what we expect from a relationship. Depending on the nature of our past relationships, we are likely to have widely differing expectations of future relationships, ranging from being cherished and respected, for example, to being neglected, or even abused. We also develop a style of *attachment*, or our own personal style in relating to other people. Attachment styles can be *secure* (where the connection we experience is trustworthy and consistent) or *insecure* (where the connection is characterized by anxiety, inconsistency, avoidance, rejection, uncertainty, or detachment). People often approach important adult relationships with the same schemas and attachment styles that emerged in relationships with their first caregivers. However, these styles can change with attention and care, and through healing from trauma-related depression or PTSD.

Healing From Trauma and PTSD

After trauma, we each develop a specific assortment of challenges. The process of identifying and observing our symptoms is a helpful first step in trauma recovery, especially because many symptoms are rather sneaky. It may not be initially obvious that our trauma has influenced problems with depression, attention, or relationships. Similarly, avoidance tendencies may become so ingrained that they may not even seem like avoidance, but just a part of the everyday fabric of our lives. It takes energy, openness, and courage to spot the ways that trauma has influenced us.

This book introduces mindfulness practices that may help reduce trauma-related distress in people who are now adolescents and adults. It is organized according to the challenges themselves, so that trauma survivors and health practitioners can readily find practices to address depression, anxiety, intrusions, avoidance, self-criticism, or other problems. These practices can be helpful on their own, and they can also complement other treatments to trauma. In addition, the skills described in this book can be used to handle challenges and to improve well-being in general, rather than only to deal with situations that involve trauma.

Many people find psychotherapy to be an integral part of trauma recovery. Therapy provides opportunities to verbalize and share experiences, to connect with another person on a deep level, and to practice directing attention, care, and new skills towards painful feelings. If you are looking for a therapist to help heal from trauma, it is important to find someone with specific expertise in trauma recovery. People's experiences of psychotherapy vary widely. They are influenced by the "fit" and quality of the relationship between the therapist and patient; the level of training, experience, and skill of the therapist; the specific kind of treatment provided; and the therapist's level of empathy, warmth, and collaboration with the patient.

Care from a therapist can feel healing, especially if part of the trauma involved receiving insufficient care from other people. Working through different aspects of the patient-therapist relationship, including building trust and comfort, and feeling respected or understood, can generalize to other relationships and propel us towards trauma recovery. However, it can also be hard for trauma survivors to advocate for their own needs. I encourage my patients to tell me if I make a mistake, or if they would prefer another approach, because both their specific input and the process of communicating it can advance our work together. Negative experiences with a therapist that do not change after efforts to communicate about them may be a sign that the situation is not the best fit. I encourage people to try multiple therapists if necessary in order to find a fit that feels right, and to ask for the specific kinds of care that they would like.

Many therapists do not have training or experience in handling trauma. Some therapeutic approaches emphasize the current moment, and may even dissuade people from talking about the past. For trauma survivors, this can feel hurtful or invalidating. I have had several patients (still suffering from trauma and its effects) tell me that their last therapist told them not to think about the trauma or talk about it, or advised them to "focus on the present" or "move on." When making an inquiry or an appointment, or during an initial session, you can ask about the therapist's specific training in trauma and PTSD, and find out which approaches the therapist uses.

Therapy is not the only way to heal from trauma. We can also benefit from help from other kinds of health providers, including psychiatrists and primary care physicians; from support groups or mindfulness groups; from having positive relationships and experiences; from spiritual or religious perspectives, or from our own efforts and care.

Providing Effective Support After Trauma

When I talk with someone who tells me about a trauma, I want to listen as well as I can, and to provide my support. I try to make lots of room for each person's full range of memories and emotions. I work on being mindfully present with the person and with their experiences. I notice within myself the sense of care that I have for the person, and I try to convey that care. I also find it helpful to communicate that I am sorry that the person had to experience the trauma.

I emphasize that a person's emotional responses and behaviors are normal given the situation, and that it is in fact understandable and smart that the person adapted to the trauma in whatever way that he or she did (for example, avoiding trauma-related thoughts or behaviors, becoming hypervigilant, or dissociating). I want to impart that "there is hope for you, I'm here to help, and I absolutely believe that you can feel better than you feel now." I assert that, "You deserve care and support—from me, from other people, and from yourself."

If you are someone providing support to trauma survivors, keep in mind that your genuine care and presence are just as important as the specific skills that you might help facilitate. Depending on the trauma, the person might be wary of sharing personal material or might be nervous around other people. People are often worried about the effect that their story and feelings have on others. For this reason, those helping trauma survivors need to genuinely provide reassurance that it is OK for them to share their experiences.

Beginning therapists may be so worried about doing a good job or about implementing specific skills that they have trouble relaxing. They may temporarily forget about being present and caring when they focus on the problems instead of the person in front of them. In addition, health professionals and others can pathologize trauma survivors and patients in general—that is, they might treat a person as a group of symptoms or disorders to be fixed, rather than as a whole, unique, and complex individual deserving of respect as an equal.

The way that a therapist responds when hearing about trauma is important, because it can influence a person's mental health outcomes. The psychologists Melissa Foynes and Jennifer Freyd (2011) created a helpful set of guidelines for responding to trauma disclosures. These include using attentive body language (upright or leaning forward), not making facial expressions that are incongruent with the trauma survivor's emotions (like smiling when someone is talking about something upsetting), and showing engagement through eye contact (look directly at the person for brief periods of 3–6 seconds, then look away for a moment, then reconnect). It is helpful to encourage the speaker to keep talking, and to refrain from changing the topic. Even though it can be hard, it is important to allow silences. You might periodically make short responses like "hmmm" and "uh-uh," reflect back the feelings that the person describes, and ask questions that require responses longer than one word, such as "What was that like for you?"

It is important not to minimize the person's experience (by saying, for example, "That happened a long time ago; it's more important to focus on the here and now") or to judge their decisions. You might refrain from giving advice unless the person asks for it. Trauma survivors benefit from hearing their emotions validated in a genuine way ("Given what you went through, it makes sense that you feel this way" or "Anyone would be overwhelmed if that happened to them"). When providing support to someone after trauma, remember to focus on that person's experience, rather than on yours as you listen. Finally, it can help to point out the person's many strengths ("You've worked hard to keep your life going despite everything that happened," or "I'm deeply impressed by your courage, and by the ways that you've managed to cope with this.")[43]

When we provide support to trauma survivors as health professionals, friends, and family members, or engage in seeking support, keep in mind the idea of a "therapeutic window." The term describes a psychological position between the two extremes of avoidance and exposure. Ideally, we will experience just the right amount of exposure, so that feelings of trauma can shift and change. If we undershoot the window, we can maintain patterns of avoidance, and fail to challenge and address trauma symptoms effectively. If we overshoot the window, we risk exceeding a person's available self-regulation capacities, and can contribute to their feeling overwhelmed and unable to handle it.[44] Ideally, we want to aim in the middle, so that we address the trauma to an extent that is effective but does not surpass a person's ability to tolerate the distress it might provoke. This can involve taking stock of what coping capacities exist, and building more skills if needed.

The idea of a workable "window" can also apply to a session of therapy, talking with another person, or addressing trauma on our own. We can consider "opening" and "closing" the window gently. For instance, we might frame discussions of trauma with conversations about topics that are less intense, or plan a fun or distracting activity to help us calm down after addressing trauma.

To restore a sense of empowerment, it can help to offer specific choices, and to be up front about our limitations. When a patient begins to disclose trauma, I emphasize that it is the person's choice whether, when, and how much to share with me. At other times, I might consider saying something like, "I have 20 more minutes right now, and I'd be happy to listen. Or, if that doesn't feel like enough time, should we plan a different time to talk about this?" I also check in about whether a person might prefer to first work on building more coping skills, or on becoming more comfortable working together, before we address trauma.

Posttraumatic Growth and Resilience

We often change following trauma, and not all of the changes are negative. The term *posttraumatic growth* refers to the positive changes that can occur, and reflects that surviving trauma can open up new capacities and connections. For instance, in some cases, having endured trauma may enhance our ability to cope with other difficult life events.[45]

Richard Tedeschi and Lawrence Calhoun (2004) described five different dimensions of posttraumatic growth: (1) new possibilities or opportunities that did not exist before the trauma; (2) an increased sense of closeness or connection to others, including others who are suffering; (3) an enhanced appreciation for one's own strength in being able to survive hardships; (4) more appreciation for life in general; and (5) changes or deepening in one's religious, spiritual, or belief systems. After trauma, many people report more favorable attitudes toward other people who are suffering, along with more actions to benefit others, like helping, sharing, donating, or volunteering.

The experience of posttraumatic growth does not run counter to pain or distress; rather, it is very common for people to report PTSD along with posttraumatic growth. Tedeschi and Calhoun note that not everyone reports posttraumatic growth, and that the concept of posttraumatic growth should not imply that trauma is good. Rather, the term is helpful in recognizing and explaining the types of positive changes that some people experience after trauma.

As we work to heal from trauma, we also build new skills for handling stressful circumstances. That way, when new hardships emerge, we feel more confident that we can handle them, even when they shake us. The same skills that can help us recover from trauma can buoy our overall mental health and our resilience to future stress. Despite our very real suffering, the process of healing from trauma and PTSD can be empowering, and we can gain new skills or perspectives along the way.

chapter 3

ANCHOR IN THE PRESENT TO HANDLE PAIN FROM THE PAST: BASIC MINDFULNESS SKILLS FOR TRAUMA AND PTSD

TRAUMA BENDS TIME. It intertwines whatever we encounter today with strands of suffering that originated in the past, so that we are here and not here all at the same time. Noticing and shifting how we experience time—including our past memories and worries about the future—can empower us and help us heal.

We have numerous complex mental "threads" that engage our minds with the past and the future. For instance, we might replay an argument over and over again in our minds, or we may feel anxious about everything that we need to do tomorrow. Our minds can feel so crowded. Thinking about *just this one moment* can provide some relief. Spending time in this moment so that it becomes bigger, fuller, and richer can make the past and future seem less overwhelming.

After trauma, the suggestion to "focus on the here and now" can feel invalidating or dismissive, and can come across as blame or judgment. It can insinuate that we are *choosing* to be caught up in the trauma rather than trying very hard to live our lives amidst our suffering. Sometimes the advice to concentrate on the present moment comes from friends, family members, or professionals who do not understand, or who are themselves scared or unprepared to venture near the realm of trauma. I encourage working with the present moment not to invalidate the past or its relevance, but to provide stability and empowerment during trauma recovery.

The present moment is an anchor that can help keep us grounded as we heal from trauma. It can balance us. We do not have to abandon or push away the reality of the trauma to benefit from the gifts of this moment—that is, attending to the present moment does not mean ignoring the thoughts and feelings about the trauma that might actually be part of our present-moment experience. However, we can begin to notice and deepen our connection to other aspects of this moment besides our traumatized feelings, and those connections can help us along. Deepening our experience of this moment as an anchor can help us feel safe enough to reflect about the trauma and how it has affected us, because we know that we will not drift away entirely. It can also help us feel grounded enough to try out a new skill to handle our distress.

This very moment can be our home, and it can feel better and better the more we visit. Our minds can still spend some time journeying to the past and to the future, and then we can return home. The present moment may contain some trauma-related pain, but it can also offer us new perspectives and possibilities. There does not need to be tension or judgment about where our minds go. Instead of blaming ourselves for having thoughts about the past, we can see the present moment as offering us some balance when we feel rocky.

During trauma and in its aftermath, we often avoid the present moment. Mentally separating ourselves from the moment may seem to give us more control. If we keep ourselves away from reality, it can feel as though we are protecting ourselves. In fact, some internal manipulations of time, such as dividing or moving our attention away from the present moment, splitting the past, present, and future apart, or suppressing the past may be adaptive during trauma.[46] However, if these become our only approaches for coping with challenges, we can miss out on some of the possibilities that this moment offers.

The present moment is where we have the most opportunity and power. It is the place where we can work most directly and flexibly with our bodily sensations, thoughts, and emotions. We can observe more in this moment than we can notice in the past or the future. It is also the place where we have the most choices about how we respond. For instance, if I read a news article that triggers a cascade of past trauma memories, I might become upset even without recognizing why. I might even stay upset for most of the day. However, if I consciously try to observe my feelings in the moment, I have more choices about how to handle them. For instance, I could practice self-compassion by offering myself care and kindness for the feelings as I feel them, engage in some physical activity, or connect with other people in order to improve my mood and shift my thinking.

The present moment is a key ingredient in trauma recovery. We remain traumatized and depressed through strong mental patterns—normal patterns that make sense, but that also reflect habits of mind. These mental patterns literally change our brains, both momentarily and over time. We recover from trauma through noticing our thoughts and feelings in this moment, and by repeatedly practicing new habits with the exact material that presents itself right now. To do this, though, we need to attend to our mental activity *in the moment*—for instance, by consciously experiencing neutral, pleasant, and changing sensations instead of paying attention only to negative ones; or by relating to our feelings with kindness—in order to make real changes. Each of the skills described in this book uses this very moment as the springboard to meaningfully change our habits. Just as the old habits correspond to actual brain structure and function, new habits change our brains as well, and can create lasting recovery and emotional resilience.[47]

As we work with our feelings in the present moment, we can benefit from mindful awareness of how our minds usually encounter the past, present, and future. We can then practice new skills to strengthen our connection to this moment and its opportunities for healing and well-being.

Time and Trauma Recovery

Trauma triggers in our everyday lives are like wormholes that whisk us away into a trauma universe. When this happens, we can use some aspect of our present-moment experience to help bring our minds back, and incorporate practices such as There's More in This Moment (in Chapter 3, below), Mindful Breathing (in Chapter 1), or Grounding (in Chapters 5 and 11) to do so. Devoting our attention to this moment can keep us tethered when we feel adrift in painful memories, and can provide a foundation for building new ways of relating to ourselves and to the world around us.

Trauma can change our perception of time, because we often experience unwanted thoughts and memories of past events, hopelessness about the future, and *dissociation*—that is, disruptions in the normal flow of attention, concentration, and memory. Trauma impedes our ability to live in the present moment.[48] Trauma can also create a feeling of being split off from reality. Healing from trauma may include building understanding and control of how we experience time.

Whether time is linear—proceeding consistently in one direction through the past, present, and future—remains an open scientific question. However, it is clear that "psychological time" is often experienced in a nonlinear way.[49] It is relatively easy to manipulate the ways that we perceive the duration of time and the temporal order of events.[50] As the writer Julian Barnes observed, "It takes only the smallest pleasure or pain to teach us time's malleability" (2011, p. 3).

Indeed, time often seems drawn out or endless during traumatic moments,[51] perhaps because we are absorbing such a large amount of information, and because trauma is so emotionally overwhelming.

We can use the malleability of time to our advantage as we heal from trauma. If we can give ourselves permission to approach this moment with curiosity and compassion, we can increase our comfort in this moment, even if this moment includes suffering. Although we do not have a choice about whether or not we have experienced trauma in the past, we have choices in this moment about how to handle our feelings. Tuning into our breathing or our bodily sensations in this moment can also help us feel more synchronized with the flow of time—a connection that can feel helpful when we feel stuck in the past or cut off from the future. By enhancing our engagement with this moment, we can change its scope, its length, and its tone.

As we build our connection to the present moment, we can also cultivate appreciation for the complex ways that we experience time. The poet David St. John (2014) described "the braiding of time" as a literary technique in which poets weave together many temporal threads to enrich a poem and make it more intricate and resilient. For instance, the Philip Levine (2000) poem "Call It Music" intertwines the speaker's present-moment breathing and listening to Charlie Parker on the radio with imagined scenes of Parker's struggles with addiction 50 years ago, with recollections of past conversations about Parker, high school memories, and with reflections about working on the loading docks years ago while singing songs that his grandfather had taught him even more years before. The poem richly portrays the many elements of the past that we experience as folded into this moment.

Our jumbled-up experience of time can present interesting opportunities for healing from trauma. For instance, you might bring a mindful perspective to the experience of feeling triggered by a present-moment reminder of trauma by noticing where your mind has gone, observing your emotional responses to the trigger in this moment and to the past memories it evokes, and witnessing how you return to this moment. Or, you may prefer the idea of mentally sending yourself some care, comfort, and understanding back through time. For instance, you can imagine yourself around the time of the trauma, and say something to yourself such as, "I see you, my friend, back in that moment. I offer you my support and care, and I send it to you back through time" (see the exercise Remember With Self-Compassion, in Chapter 5).

Time Orientation

To function well, we need to pay attention to the past, present, and future. We have to remember things like paying the rent next week, or instructions about how to take medications. Consider the enterprise of farming. A farmer needs to have learned from experience what techniques have worked in the past; to pay attention to planting and harvesting as they are happening; and to think ahead to determine the type and quantity of crops to cultivate.

Time orientation, or *time perspective*, refers to an overall orientation towards the past, present, and future, and to how our approach to time shapes our behavior.[52] We can also consider *time relatedness*, or the ways that we experience the past, present, and future to be connected or disconnected, as well as *time dominance*, or the importance that we ascribe to the past, present, or future.[53] Our perception of time is highly complex; interestingly, we do not appear to have a specific part of our brain that processes time[54].

There is nothing inherently wrong with having our minds in the past or in the future. In fact, a future time orientation is related to several positive behaviors, such as less smoking, more academic engagement, and enhanced decision-making strategies.[55] A future time orientation can also provide a sense of hope during trauma.[56] When things seem very bleak, we can take comfort that they may improve in the future.

Problems arise when our minds get stuck in past pain or future worries. Sadness often cues thoughts about the past, whereas anxiety can spin our thoughts towards the future.[57] We are also impacted by the *way* in which we think of the past. It is specifically negative thinking about the past that seems to diminish life satisfaction.[58] However, sometimes even positive thinking about the past, such as nostalgia, can worsen our mental health.[59] Ideally, we can develop a balance between thinking about the past, present, and future, as well as some choice about where our minds go. A balanced time perspective is positively related to well-being.[60]

Mindfulness practice seems to shift the information that we gather and remember about the past. For instance, individuals who participated in 12 weeks of mindfulness training had significantly greater increases in memory for positive words (but not for negative words or for the total amount of words) on a word-recall test compared with individuals in a control group without mindfulness training.[61] The groups did not have meaningful differences at the beginning of the 12 weeks, with the exception that the control group actually remembered more positive words during the word recall task. At the end of the 12 weeks, the mindfulness participants' improvements in positive word recall were linked to their significant reductions in depression and anxiety, and to their increases in well-being. The study suggests that mindfulness training can change how we process and remember past information—changes that can then improve mental health in the present.

Often, our minds are several places at once—here in the present moment and elsewhere simultaneously. Sometimes this capacity is helpful. For instance, when we drive a car, we need to pay attention to this part of the road, anticipate the turns up ahead, and recall our destination. However, in other circumstances, dividing our attention can cause problems. It can impede learning and memory,[62] and bias our attention towards negative information and away from pleasant or neutral information.[63]

We can bring a curious and caring intention with us as we explore where our minds go in time. If we notice ourselves being critical about where our minds go, we can observe that criticism as another thought, and then redirect our attention back to our chosen focus. We do not develop new mental habits by just deciding to develop them or by criticizing ourselves, but through the consistent practice of new skills.

Mindfulness Practices to Anchor in the Present Moment

The practices below focus on expanding our experience of the present moment, but they do not address trauma specifically. Some people find it more helpful to combine present-focused practices with those that address trauma and PTSD symptoms directly (see Chapters 5, 6, 7, 8, 9, 10, and 11). Many individuals and trauma treatment programs do this sequentially, in stage-based protocols. That is, they first build up mindfulness practices to connect with the present moment, increase abilities to tolerate distress, and cultivate capacities to regulate emotions; and only *then* do they address traumatic material itself.[64] Other people and research studies find that mindfulness and self-compassion practices alone, without specific attention to traumatic material, can also lead to meaningful healing.[65]

Mindfulness is not merely about being present, but about the *way* in which we are present. For instance, it is common to *ruminate*, or to passively mull over distress and its causes again and again[66] without taking active steps to make positive changes.[67] Rumination is strongly related to depression and anxiety,[68] and appears to link stressful life events to those conditions.[69] We might be present with ourselves in the moment as we ruminate, but our presence alone does not improve our feelings. We are better off paying attention to our experiences themselves than developing analyses and interpretations about them, or mulling over the plot or story of what happened.[70]

We can remind ourselves that "Mindfulness means paying attention in a particular way: On purpose, in the present moment, and nonjudgmentally" (Kabat-Zinn, 1994, p. 4). When we practice mindfulness, we choose where we want to focus our minds, and aim to stay present with our experiences without evaluating them.

Encountering obstacles to being in this moment is a normal part of mindfulness practice. It is common for practice sessions to vary widely—to have one relatively easy session followed by another that seems challenging or pointless. You can keep practicing throughout these ups and downs. You might find yourself thinking, "That session was so disappointing! I sat for 15 minutes and I was only present in the moment for about three breaths, and then my foot fell asleep." You can then remind yourself that, "Being present for three breaths is a start. In one instance, I was able to notice that my mind wandered to a conversation I had yesterday, and to bring my attention back to this moment. Plus, I noticed the sensations in my foot. Now I can be present in the moment with my feeling of disappointment, even though it is unpleasant." Over time, handling those ups and downs in a curious and patient way can branch out into other areas of our lives.

One common challenge is that a part of our minds is engaged in paying attention to the present moment, and other parts are off doing other things. This is tricky, because we are in fact engaged in a mindfulness exercise to some degree. For instance, we can pay some degree of attention to breathing while also thinking other thoughts. Over time, we can observe and increase our degree of engagement with a chosen mindfulness exercise.

For instance, if I choose to observe my breathing for 10 breaths at a time, I might notice that I am quite present for breaths 1 and 2, beginning to drift off somewhere else for breaths 3 and 4, and basically absent for breaths 5, 6, and 7. After I consciously notice that my mind has drifted away—what Sharon Salzberg (2011) and others call "the magic moment"—I like to return my attention to the breath in an enthusiastic and affirmative way ("Yay! I'm fully here for breath number 8! Hello, breath 8!"). I find that generating a boost of positivity during my mental return helps me to reengage with the practice. Because it is often hard to keep going in mindfulness practice, we can use all of the self-encouragement that we can summon.

Some of the mindfulness practices below involve tuning in to bodily sensations, and some do not. Bodily sensations can be conducive to mindfulness practice because they often help us to anchor in this moment. For instance, if I tune in to the feeling of breathing, I am most likely to observe this very breath right now, rather than a breath in the past or one in the future. However, after trauma, it can feel strange or scary to pay attention to bodily sensations, or uncomfortable to receive suggestions or directions about your body (see "Special Considerations for Practicing Mindfulness After Trauma," in Chapter 1). You can decide to implement another practice, or you can stop if you feel that the practice is not the right one for you at this time. By observing your own inclinations and responses to mindfulness practice, you can become more and more empowered to proceed in the way that is best for you.

Practice #1: There's More in This Moment—What Else Is Here?

Most of us can handle just this one moment, right now. We get into trouble when we consider how hard the whole day might be, or how hard our lives might be. We tend to project our present feelings into the future—for instance, thinking that "it's never going to get better," or "how am I going to survive this upcoming month?" This practice can help us focus on this moment without worrying about its broader implications ("this just shows how incapable I am at handling things"). We may feel pain in this moment, and there are also other aspects of this moment besides our pain that may be hidden until we look. This practice is designed to make this moment bigger and more nuanced.

You can use "There's More in this Moment" in relatively short bursts (3–5 minutes), or for longer periods. It works best with your eyes open. I encourage you to pause for a moment, and check in with your mind and body. After noticing your state of mind and bodily sensations, you might ask yourself, "What else is here?" You can then engage your five senses to observe other facets of this moment. For instance, if you explore the feeling of touch, you might notice the sensation of your fingers touching your other fingers and hand, the texture of your clothing, a couch or chair, and the book or electronic reader that you are holding. You may also investigate what you hear. At first, it might seem like "nothing." But if you spend a few moments with whatever sounds arise, you can observe the hum of a radiator or a whoosh of plumbing. You might also look around and find a few things about your surroundings that you had not noticed before, such as the variations in the fabric on a lamp or intricacies in how the books are stacked on a table.

You can also ask "What else is here?" about your thoughts and feelings. It may seem as though one particular worry or feeling is so dominant that it crowds out everything else. I encourage you to stay open for a moment, and observe both what feels obvious and what feels obscure. By bringing patience, curiosity, and persistence to the question "What else is here?" we can broaden our view of our own experience. Even if you are worried about an outing tomorrow, you might observe other thoughts and feelings alongside this worry. By asking "What else is here?" you might notice gladness that a heat wave has passed, anticipation of a yummy lunch, or a feeling of physical comfort in your posture.

Practice #2: Boats on a River

There is a delicate balance in thinking about challenges in our lives. A certain amount of investigation can provide helpful insights, but sometimes we might think about the same things over and over in such a way that we become lost in the thoughts without any benefit. Mindfulness differs from *rumination*, which involves unintentional, repetitive thinking about specific content other than our present-moment experiences. When we practice mindfulness, we observe our thoughts as a witness; whereas when we ruminate, we become absorbed in them. With practice, we can begin to discern when we are engaged in useful reflection and when we would be better served by disengaging from a thought process. Boats on a River is an exercise that empowers us to decide how much to engage with thoughts or feelings.

I invite you to set aside about 10 minutes to imagine a river that has many different cargo boats floating down it. If imagining boats does not feel right, you can imagine something similar, like a conveyor belt of suitcases. In this visualization, you can consider that there are only a few types of boats or suitcases, filled with basically the same items, and that they repeat. These boats or suitcases represent specific topics in our lives, and they are packed with our thoughts and feelings about those themes. Sometimes it can be helpful or informative to board the boat (or take the suitcase off of the conveyor belt), open the compartments, and unpack the cargo to see what is there. However, it is not necessary to do this for every boat that goes by. We can recognize some "boats" by their basic color or shape, and we can allow them to keep moving through the river without climbing onto them, or we can disembark without surveying the cargo. Because we basically know what is inside, we can watch the boat go by. We get to decide how to manage each one, and we can change our approach. You might try boarding one boat, and letting the next one go by, and notice if you experience any differences between those two approaches.

This practice promotes the ability to observe thoughts and feelings without overidentifying with them. The practice can also extend to the metaphor of "trains of thought." We rarely notice it when we board a train; but once we notice, we have the opportunity to step off and change trains, as many times as we want.

Practice #3: This Breath, This Moment

There are many ways to use the breath to cultivate mindfulness. The "Mindful Breathing" section in Chapter 1 introduced the basic practice of paying attention to the breath wherever the sensation of breathing is felt most strongly, along with the variation of counting 10 breaths in a row to help maintain a mental connection to the breath.

We can also practice mindful breathing with an emphasis on exploration and curiosity. Every breath is different. Each breath holds multitudes: the sensations of the breath entering the body, the temperature of the air, where the breath goes next, the length of in-breaths and out-breaths, the quality of transitions between our breaths, spots of tension in our bodies as we breathe, and the ways in which different body parts engage in the breathing process.

Each breath contains a new opportunity, distinct from all past breaths and the experiences that went with them. We might feel a bit jaded ("Oh, yeah, breathing. I know what that feels like. Just how many new sensations could there possibly be?"). Approaching a new breath in a curious way, however, can remind us that there are *unlimited* new possibilities in this moment.

Many people practice mindful breathing in a sitting position. There are different views on sitting postures that are conducive to paying attention to the breath; some people prefer to sit cross-legged, whereas others sit with legs together and their feet on the floor. Our posture can affect our breathing. If we slouch too much, it can make it harder to breathe. You might try a posture that feels both relaxed and dignified—or more broadly, a posture that reflects the way you want to feel.

As you sit, you might notice parts of your body along with the breath, or feelings related to the breath. Does this breath have a sense of calmness? Choppiness? Squeezing? Discomfort? Ease? When you notice these types of "flavors" to breathing, you can use them to investigate the related physical sensations ("Hmmm, I have a sense of tension and constriction. What's going on there? Let's see where I feel that the most strongly. Huh, it seems to be in the top part of my chest. There's something there that seems to shut down the breath a bit . . . right . . . there. That part of my body seems to generate an urge to stop inhaling and start exhaling even though I've only taken in a small amount of breath. Let's stay right there and notice that for a bit.").

It is extremely common to experience judgments as we practice mindful breathing. These are usually negative interpretations about the meaning of the experience: "I'm so bad at this," "I can't believe I keep getting so distracted; what is wrong with me?" "This tightness in my gut has been there since the trauma, and I don't think it will ever go away," or "I have this heaviness in my chest because I'm a terrible person." When these sorts of judgments arise, we can observe them with curiosity (in the same manner in which we observe our breathing), and then return our focus to the actual sensation of breathing in this moment. Such judgments can seem like truth, but they are rarely true. However, it does not even matter whether or not they are true for the purpose of our practice: to observe them without engaging with them. Treating them in this way helps us escape their pull.

Paying attention to our breathing can be uncomfortable, and we might feel restless. I encourage you to *keep going* even when discomfort or restlessness arises. If it is too difficult, you can certainly stop and resume another time. If it is moderately difficult, you might choose to keep going. If we stick it out, we gain confidence that we can endure discomfort. We can also observe that discomfort does not last forever.

You can gradually build the amount of time that you spend practicing mindful breathing, and work up to at least 20 minutes. For many people, it takes at least 20 minutes to get into the zone of noticing breathing and disentangling from other thoughts.

RESEARCH HIGHLIGHT What Benefits Have Been Identified for Mindful Breathing (also called Sitting Meditation)?

RESEARCHERS HAVE DEMONSTRATED that sitting meditation reduces anxiety, anger, depression, stress, and impulsivity.[71] Beng and colleagues (2015) conducted a single 5-minute mindful breathing session with terminally ill patients and their caregivers. They found that mindful breathing significantly reduced distress, and that mindful breathing was more effective than a listening intervention. However, they also noted that after participants completed the mindful breathing session, their distress levels rose again, a result that might mean that more sustained or consistent practice would be beneficial.

Other studies confirm that regular practice produces positive results. For instance, a research study of 174 participants in an 8-week mindfulness program demonstrated that their time spent engaging in sitting meditation was positively related to their overall well-being, and to greater mindfulness.[72] Specifically, participants who reported more time practicing sitting meditation reported gains in acting with awareness (rather than acting impulsively or on "autopilot"), and increases in nonreactivity to inner experiences (the ability to notice thoughts and feelings without reacting to them or getting lost in them).

Mindful breathing also seems to improve attention. In an experiment that involved 40 participants without prior mindfulness experience, researchers observed that participants who engaged in 16 weeks of regular mindful breathing demonstrated significant changes in brain activity related to attentional control.[73]

Practice #4: Mindful Walking

Like breathing, walking is an activity that many of us can do without conscious thought, but that can also provide opportunities for cultivating mindful attention. Walking involves a complex series of coordinated movements. So many body parts are involved—hips, legs, feet, arms—even the posture of our back and shoulders. As we walk, our whole body moves through space.

If you have physical limitations that prevent you from walking, you can still benefit from some form of moving meditation. If you cannot walk, you can focus instead on moving any part of your body in a way that feels comfortable, and on observing all of the sensations that you can.

You can aim for at least 20 minutes of mindful movement. Our task is to stay present with the sensations of walking or other movement in a curious way. When we notice that we have slipped away from conscious awareness of our movements and have resumed moving on "autopilot," we can return our focus to our bodily sensations.

You can practice mindful walking at your regular pace, or you can experiment with changing the speed of your walking. Many people practice walking meditation by walking in extreme slow motion. This allows us to observe the minuscule movements involved in raising our feet, placing our feet on the ground, and shifting our weight from one side of the body to another. You can also observe your breath as you walk.

If you are able to walk, you can walk anywhere. You can walk indoors or outdoors; you can walk in a straight line or you can zigzag; you can even stay standing and notice the sensations of shifting your weight from side to side. Interestingly, walking in nature helps people decrease stress and rumination, and also produces measureable positive changes in the brain.[74]

Although most mindful walking practices focus on bodily sensations, you can also practice what my friend Melanie calls a "magic walk." A magic walk uses our sense of vision to notice the features in the world around us. You might notice the pattern in the bark of a tree, clouds, a ladybug, someone else's outfit, or variations in the sidewalk. The idea of going outside and noticing the world around you can seem like a cliché. However, it is common to notice our surroundings for a mere moment or two before getting swept back up into our own thoughts. We may need to refocus over and over again on the external world. You might do this by repeating "magic walk" to yourself when you find that your mind has wandered. The "magic" in the magic walk stems from our intention: we set out with (and may need to reestablish) a mindset that is open to magic. It is our "magic" attitude that helps us observe the world around us as if it were new and unlimited.

Practice #5: Body Scan

In Douglas Coupland's novel *Microserfs*, the narrator Dan reflects that, "my relationship with my body has gone all weird . . . I feel like my body is a station wagon in which I drive my brain around" (1995, p. 4). If we are physically well, it is common to pay our bodies little or no attention. If we are in pain, we may notice only the body parts that hurt, and ignore the rest. Over time, we get in the habit of ignoring our bodies, or at least ignoring the majority of our body parts.

In the body scan meditation, we direct attention to our different body parts in turn. You can start at the top of your head, or with your feet and toes. For each part of the body, you can notice its position, its temperature, spots of tension, or other sensations. You can also observe the body part's contact with clothing or furniture, and feelings of weight or gravity. You might find that a part of your body is numb or that you cannot feel anything. If that happens, try to remain open and curious about not feeling anything.

It is often helpful to hear someone's voice talking us through the body scan. Hearing directions can help us remember to notice parts of the body that we might otherwise forget, and to return our focus to our bodies when our minds wander. There are many good audio and video instructions of the body scan freely available on the internet, and you can experiment with finding the one that most suits your preferences. You can choose one guided by a voice that you find soothing and pleasant, and with a length that seems right to you. Many people find that the body scan takes them 15–30 minutes.

At the beginning of the body scan, we often take a few minutes to try to mentally arrive in our bodies. We can tune in to the feeling of breathing or of reclining, and we can set our intention to be in this present moment with our bodily sensations. You might prioritize depth over speed; that is, rather than mentally zipping down your body, you can give yourself permission to rest your attention on any body part to the extent that keeping your focus there feels right to you. Sometimes it takes several moments for our attention to arrive at a body part, or for us to notice how it feels.

If you are beginning at the top of your body, you might start scanning your body by noticing the sensations on the very top of your head. You can then gradually shift your attention down your body. You can notice your feelings along the way as you focus on your:

1. Scalp, forehead, eyes and eyelids, nose, cheeks, eyes, lips, tongue, jaw
2. Neck, collarbone, shoulders, chest, and ribs
3. Upper back and lower back

4. Left upper arm, elbow, lower arm, wrist, hand and fingers; right upper arm, elbow, lower arm, wrist, hands, and fingers

5. Stomach and gut

6. Pelvis, genitals, and bottom

7. Left hip, thigh, knee, calf, ankle, foot and toes; Right hip, thigh, knee, calf, ankle, foot and toes

You can end the body scan the same way that you started—by allowing your attention to reside in your body for a few minutes as you consider more general feelings throughout your body. You might do this by noticing your breathing again, or by feeling some of the sensations that you noticed during the body scan.

Sometimes noticing our body parts produces discomfort. Until I tune in to bodily sensations, I might be unaware that my eye is itchy or that my toes are scrunched up. Although the body scan is often relaxing, you might notice difficult feelings as well. Or you may experience an increase in pleasant sensations, or a sense that physical pain becomes more nuanced or bearable. Ussher and colleagues (2014) reported that people with chronic pain experienced immediate reductions in distress related to physical pain using the body scan. Consistent practice of the body scan can promote well-being and the ability to notice thoughts and feelings without reacting to them or getting swept up in them, and can reduce anxiety.[75]

You may find yourself falling asleep during the body scan. In fact, many people use the body scan to help them fall asleep. It can help us fall asleep by providing an alternative to the rumination that prevents sleep, and by helping us observe and relax bodily tension. If you fall asleep, you might remember that it is normal and to try to refrain from judging yourself. It is fine to use the body scan to promote sleep. However, to get the most benefit from mindfulness practice, it is important to implement some form of mindfulness practice in a wakeful state, because it is through wakeful practice that we learn more effective ways to handle life's challenges.

If you want to avoid falling asleep, you might try practicing the body scan in a seated position, rather than lying down. Finally, you can practice the body scan at times of day when you are less likely to fall asleep.

Practice #6: Find the Emotion in Your Body

The Buddhist monk and teacher Ajahn Amaro described a simple but powerful practice in his 2010 lecture "Don't Push: Just Use the Weight of Your Own Body." He shared that he tended to worry and fret consistently, and that he began to respond to those worries by turning his attention to where he felt the worry in his body. He focused on exploring the bodily sensation of the worry in a curious way, and then on relaxing the part of the body where he felt it. As he practiced this technique for over a year, his relationship to the worry shifted.

To practice this technique, I invite you to consider an emotion of medium intensity that you feel in this moment, rather than one that troubles you generally or one that is closely linked with past trauma. For instance, you might try it when you feel irritated at yourself for making a small mistake, or disappointed about something that happened today. You can sit in a comfortable position, and take a few breaths as you check in with how you are feeling emotionally. You can then invite yourself to explore and notice all that you can about the feeling of the emotion in your body. If the emotion seems elusive and hard to locate physically, you can practice some patience for the feeling of openness and exploration without a quick answer, or self-compassion about any frustrations that arise. If you do notice a body region or sensation that seems to correspond to the emotion, I encourage you to stay with it for several moments. You can investigate its subtleties. After staying with the feeling for a bit, you can then bring an intention of relaxation to the physical sensation.

If you find yourself swept back up in the details of the events that provoked the feeling (or otherwise distracted), you can practice returning your focus to the bodily sensation itself. If you notice that focusing on a physical sensation has triggered difficult memories of past trauma, you might implement grounding techniques to return your focus to the present moment (Chapter 11, Practice #1) or self-compassion for painful memories (Chapter 5, Practice #3).

Bringing a curious perspective to the bodily sensations of an emotion can reduce its power, because we observe its physical feeling in this moment, rather than becoming overwhelmed by our thoughts and by all of the external factors that impact us. We also notice the feeling's variations and the way that it changes, so that difficult emotions seem less fixed and permanent, and more workable.

Practice #7: Where Is My Mind in Time?

When you consider where your mind has been today, it might help to consider a visual representation. If you make a pie chart, you can slice it up according to the proportion of time that your thinking today has been in the past, present, or future. As another variation, you can consider whether the proportion of mental time in each category is related to positive events and perspectives, or to negative ones. You can also ask yourself which part of the "time pie" feels the strongest or most dominant, or reflect about how clear the boundaries feel to you. Are all of the time periods mixed together in your mind? Or, does the past or future feel closed off by a big wall?

Figure 3.1 shows some possibilities for the ways our attention may feel distributed in time:

Figure 3.1: Proportions of Mental Time Spent in the Past, Present, or Future

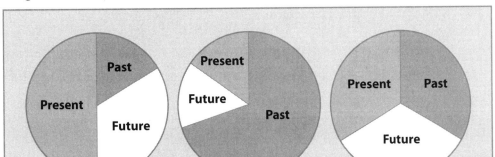

Of course, any "pie chart" representation of how we experience time will be an oversimplification, especially as our mind may seem to be many places (including past, present, and future) at once. However, it can be a starting point for enhancing awareness about where our minds reside.

In Their Own Words

I was initially drawn to mindfulness and meditation after hearing that it was an effective way to increase energy and focus. I was going through an emotionally draining period and have a job as a teacher that requires me to be fully present. I dabbled on my own for about 9 months before taking part in a mindfulness training program. I practiced for 10 minutes a day and attended 2-hour group sessions twice a month. Over the course of 10 months, the change I experienced was profound. Without a doubt, my mindfulness practice is the single best thing I have ever done to enhance the quality of my life. It has dramatically decreased my stress levels and improved my focus, energy, and relationships.

The practice of learning to be mindful provided me with a roller coaster of emotions for a long time because I had to retrain my thinking. Sitting

with myself without the busyness that I was used to creating as a life strategy was uncomfortable. Looking back, what changed for me was that I started to notice the power of returning to my breath when faced with the challenge of a misbehaving student, a wave of emotion, or a tough decision to be made. Returning to my breath slows things down, calms my systems, and allows me to respond appropriately with kindness and compassion towards not only myself, but to others.

As we build our ability to connect with the present moment, we notice more and more that things change. Trauma can make us feel stuck in time, and our pain often seems permanent. Observing even small changes—a stiff muscle that relaxes, a breath that differs from the last one—can build hope that our suffering will not last forever in its present form. It will change shape over time and become more bearable.

In addition to noticing your experience of time, you may observe how mindfulness practice impacts your sense of space. As we practice aligning our attention with a broader range of present-moment experiences, rather than with wherever our minds gravitate by default, we often experience shifts in perspective. This can feel like a sense of opening or spaciousness, whereas our rumination often feels tense and constricted because it is confined to a much smaller portion of our experiences. A spacious perspective can shift suffering. As Jack Kornfield wrote, "A spoon of salt in a glass of water makes the water undrinkable. A spoon of salt in a lake is almost unnoticed" (1994, p. 21).

Our minds are full of so many thoughts, experiences, and memories, all woven together. That fullness can feel deeply overwhelming, and even more so after we are shaken by trauma. However, we can absolutely develop more awareness and control of how we navigate the mental landscape. In the Kusala

Sutta the Buddha says, "One can cultivate the skillful. If it were not possible, I would not ask you to do it" (as cited in Salzberg, 1995, p. 4). This encouragement is supported by the scientific literature demonstrating that people can and do develop new mindfulness skills that enhance their well-being. Your own wisdom and experience can help you determine which practices are most helpful for you as you deepen your connection to this moment and all of the opportunities it can provide.

SELF-COMPASSION:
THE KIND WITNESS WITHIN

SELF-COMPASSION IS a powerful practice. It leads us sturdily towards trauma recovery and emotional health. It is strong medicine for suffering, and a resilient way of relating to ourselves and to our experiences. However, developing self-compassion is a path that many of us do not anticipate taking.

Self-compassion may sound remote or foreign—a niche behavior like parasailing or playing the bassoon. It might seem theoretically appealing, but as more of an aspiration than a true possibility. The word self-compassion can give the impression that it is weak, lenient, or soft, rather than a resource of great power. The idea of self-compassion may even sound disagreeable or dangerous. Whatever our assumptions about self-compassion might be, every person can build self-compassion and benefit from it.

You already have a relationship with yourself. What kind of relationship is it? Do you criticize yourself for your faults or your feelings? Are you kind to yourself when things are hard? Do you treat yourself as well as you treat other important people in your life? Is your care for yourself contingent on how you are feeling or what happens?

Your relationship with yourself matters. It might seem surprising that the way we treat ourselves could do much to change our feelings. After all, trauma and pain are still there, whether we are self-critical or self-encouraging. But the way that we treat ourselves does, in fact, have a huge impact: It *strongly* predicts our levels of stress, anxiety, depression, and PTSD.

You can change your relationship with yourself, and it is not as hard as it might seem. Even if you are your own worst critic, you do not have to take that position forever. The relationship that you have with yourself is not static. Instead of just assuming we will always be mean to ourselves, we can pay attention to the ways that we relate to ourselves, and we can build kinder and more effective ways of relating.

A few weeks of self-compassion practice can make a substantial difference in shifting old patterns, and can bring about meaningful improvements in mental health and well-being. When we practice new habits of relating to ourselves, they elicit real physical changes in our brains and bodies.

After trauma, we have a range of vulnerabilities—including fear, shame, upsetting memories, numbing, a lack of control, worry, and self-blame—that can be soothed with self-compassion. Although self-compassion may feel unfamiliar or scary for trauma survivors, its practice can generate meaningful shifts in suffering. Developing a sense of the "kind witness within" can reduce the self-criticism that keeps us caught in PTSD, anxiety, and depression. Self-compassion can also provide us with the care that may have been missing during the trauma itself. The practice of self-compassion reaches across time, because it helps us recover from past trauma, handle our feelings in this moment, and build resilience for coping with future challenges.

What Is Self-Compassion?

You can think of self-compassion as the practice of being a kind, helpful, and encouraging friend to yourself in any circumstance. Self-compassion is generous and unconditional. Self-compassion calls forth our most noble and caring qualities: courage, acceptance, patience, understanding, nonjudgment, sympathy, soothing, and generosity.[76] Self-compassion reflects an ability to acknowledge and remain present with whatever is happening inside us, even if the feelings are very painful. It adds the dimension of *kindness* to mindfulness skills, as we practice relating to ourselves in a caring way no matter what happens.

Self-compassion also reflects truly listening to everything that is occurring within us, as well as the genuine wish that the suffering be reduced. The historical roots of compassion practice, as reflected in the names of the Buddhist deities *Avalokitasvara* (Sanskrit) and *Kuan-yin* (Chinese), convey deep listening—literally, "sound perceiver"—(Yü, 2001). The Buddhist teacher Thích Nhất Hạnh defined *karuna* (often translated as compassion) as "the intention and capacity to relieve and transform suffering and lighten sorrows" (1998, p. 172), and he explained that it is most effectively engaged with deep concern, listening, and understanding.

Metta, or loving-kindness, is a quality closely linked to compassion. It reflects the quality of friendliness and the practice of wishing that things go well for ourselves and for others. Salzberg described *metta* as the capacity to "embrace all parts of ourselves" (1995, p. 27), and observed that it "illuminates our inner integrity because it relieves us of the need to deny different aspects of ourselves." As for the relationship between compassion and *metta* (loving-kindness), compassion is what happens when *metta* encounters pain and suffering.[77]

You can think of self-compassion as wildly expansive. There is no thought or feeling that self-compassion cannot encompass. The Buddha advised that we "develop a mind so filled with love that it resembles space" (Salzberg, 2010). When we cultivate self-compassion, we make room for all of our thoughts and feelings—no matter how difficult—and we allow them to exist. This "roominess" can make pain more bearable, and can shift the feeling that we are overwhelmed or about to burst with our suffering.

After trauma, it can be challenging to develop a balanced perspective towards our thoughts and feelings—a stance where we remain connected to our feelings as well as to a broader sense of understanding, care, and wisdom. We may cope with trauma by numbing ourselves or distancing ourselves from our feelings; however, an "observer" standpoint towards trauma and other memories is linked to higher levels of PTSD and depression.[78] It can also be problematic to feel *overly* identified with our feelings, to the extent that we feel overwhelmed by them or lose a sense of ourselves beyond our suffering.

Self-compassion practice provides the opportunity to benefit from integrating a sense of feeling our emotions from the inside and observing them from a perspective that places them within a larger context, as a "witness." As we observe and practice noticing our experiences from both perspectives, we can infuse each of them with caring. The "witness" aspect of self-compassion differs from *dissociation* (experiences of disconnection, "spacing out," or disruptions in time and consciousness that often occur following trauma). When we practice self-compassion, we remain present and connected to our feelings, even though we are not submerged in them. Self-compassion also differs from rumination or the idea of "wallowing" in feelings because it reflects a wise, expansive perspective, in which we are aware that our feelings change over time and that they reflect only one part of a more complex picture. Self-compassion practice involves approaching our feelings *themselves* with care and understanding, instead of getting lost in trains of thought connected to a specific situation.

The quality of kindness in self-compassion reflects a meeting between care and perspective. That is, the idea of being kind to myself amidst my suffering depicts that there is an "I" or an awareness beyond my feelings in this moment—a greater self from which I can offer care and understanding for the parts that are suffering. This strong kindness also reflects a resonance that suffering and pain are real, and that they hurt—along with the true wish that the suffering be alleviated.

The aspects of perspective and kindness in self-compassion are complemented by wisdom. We build wisdom over time through our experiences and other learning, and we can use it to navigate our next set of feelings more effectively. We remember things like, "the last time I got angry at myself I punched a wall and broke my hand; that didn't work out so well," or "My stomach hurt the last time I ate the whole box of cookies." Or, we learn something new—for example, that exercise often reduces PTSD and depression[79] that helps guide our actions. It is that broader, longer-term mindful approach to our life experiences, mingled with kindness, that can help us be as effective as possible as we handle our suffering and recover from trauma.

Self-compassion is brave, because it involves staying with our pain rather than running from it. Instead of pushing difficulties away, we can acknowledge what we are feeling, and keep ourselves company in the presence of those feelings. Self-compassion reflects a deep wish for suffering to be alleviated, coupled with the understanding that it may take time. Feldman and Kuyken wrote that compassion is "the capacity to open to the reality of suffering and to aspire to its healing" while acknowledging that "not all pain can be 'fixed' or 'solved'" (2011, p. 144).

Imagine for a moment that on a day where you felt awful, you had a very caring and encouraging friend who came to spend the day with you. This friend is not pushy, and does not impose any expectations about how you should feel or function. Rather, this friend just stays with you, and never balks at any of your feelings. This friend keeps you company as you wake up, as you experience the day's ups and downs, and as you engage in your daily tasks to the extent that you are able. This friend listens deeply, and conveys love for you. This friend lets you feel all of your feelings, without suggesting that you should feel differently. And if you felt so bad that you declined to eat or drink, this friend would gently encourage you to eat or drink just a little bit. If you felt drawn to harm yourself, this friend would gently prevent you from harming yourself. If you sat all day, this friend would advocate that you take a very small walk if you were able, and would help you get up to do it—not in a judging way, but in a manner that is considerate of your long-term best interests. This friend represents the qualities of self-compassion: presence, caring, allowing feelings without judging them, and encouraging wise actions.

It is common to be able to feel compassion for others but to have a hard time generating it for ourselves. When this is the case, it can help to notice feelings of compassion for others, and to recognize that compassion is already present. We can then work on redirecting those qualities to include ourselves. It is very similar to exercising a new muscle, or using it in a different way. Or, your challenge may be trying to find any caring feelings at all—for anything. You may need to engage imagination to consider what self-compassion might feel like, and to start small when locating and cultivating the seeds of compassion. You can even start by giving yourself attention, listening, and companionship for the struggle to feel care.

For some reason, self-compassion seems hardest to muster when we need it the most. This may stem from a combination of factors. We commonly blame ourselves for feeling bad, or think that we do not deserve kindness. After trauma, self-criticism, self-blaming, and prioritizing others' needs over our own can develop as "safety behaviors"[80] that then become habitual. Attending to our own needs can feel scary and uncomfortable, although it becomes much easier with practice. Also, when we are in pain, our resources can feel depleted. It is hard to engage the muscle of self-compassion if we feel barely strong enough to make it through the day, and especially if using that muscle is unfamiliar. That is why consistent practice of self-compassion is so crucial—so that it can be our default, rather than requiring an extra effort, when things are hard.

What Self-Compassion Is Not

Self-compassion is meant to be truthful, not deceptive. It is not an attempt to evade real problems that need to be fixed. It differs from "thinking positive" or "looking on the bright side" because it is deeply authentic, bravely making room and providing care for a full range of feelings. Self-compassion is not self-pity, sulking, or feeling sorry for ourselves. Self-compassion is not "going easy on yourself" or giving yourself a pass to avoid things that are hard. Rather, self-compassion involves understanding and addressing feelings as kindly and effectively as possible. Self-compassion involves taking responsibility rather than shirking it.

Self-compassion is not about boosting self-esteem. Neff (2011) clarified that self-esteem involves comparing ourselves to other people, and that it relies on external factors such as praise or achievement. As such, self-esteem is highly unstable. As soon as something goes awry—we receive negative feedback, or a new medication makes us gain weight—it crumbles. Seeking self-esteem also leads us to a constant state of judgment, both of others and of ourselves—a state which itself can elicit feelings of anxiety and depression as either we or others come up short. Self-compassion provides a stable alternative to self-esteem, because it offers kindness that does not depend on external events or comparing ourselves to others.

Self-compassion is not the same as self-indulgence. It is easy to get confused, particularly in the midst of advertisements that seem to conflate self-compassion with self-centered pleasure. Certainly, it is OK to treat ourselves with delicious food or a relaxing shower, and mindfully engaging with sensory experiences can feel kind and healing. However, the representations of self-indulgence in the media can convey the sense that self-compassion is a luxurious, extra ingredient in life—a garnish to our meal rather than the bowl itself that holds it. The Dalai Lama (n. d.) advised that, "Compassion is not religious business, it is human business, it is not luxury, it is essential for our own peace and mental stability, it is essential for human survival."

Self-compassion is not being selfish, self-involved, or self-centered. The word "self-compassion" is tricky that way, because it begins with that word, "self." We might worry that we will overdo it—that if we pay attention to our feelings and take good care of them, we will become overly immersed in them. It turns out that mindful care of our feelings enables us to manage them better, so that we are more present, available, and helpful to others. For instance, therapists' own mindfulness and self-compassion practice can improve the quality of care that they provide to patients.[81] If you have ever taken care of a screaming toddler, it can be helpful to take a moment to acknowledge something like, "this child is suffering, and in this moment, it is hard on me as well. I care about both of our experiences." Such a reflection can provide sustenance and endurance to ultimately offer more effective care than blocking out your own experience and focusing solely on the child. Noticing and tending to our feelings when they feel somewhat manageable can prevent them from overwhelming us as they develop, and can decrease our likelihood of becoming angry, resentful, apathetic, or burned out.

For some reason, self-compassion can sound fluffy, wimpy, or even girly. In many cultures, ideas of kindness and care are presented as feminine qualities.[82] However, strong and masculine representations of compassion also exist, such as the Buddhist deity Avalokitasvara, the embodiment of compassion, who is represented as a man in some traditions and a woman in others (including Guanyin in China). Exploring assumptions about self-compassion and dissolving them can feel radically liberating. We can then give ourselves permission to experiment with new ways of relating to ourselves.

RESEARCH HIGHLIGHT How Does Self-Compassion Impact our Well-Being?

SELF-CRITICISM IS STRONGLY linked with depression and anxiety,[83] whereas self-compassion is a robust indicator of well-being, motivation, and the ability to manage stress.[84] Our tendencies to be either self-critical or self-compassionate seem to have a greater influence on whether we become depressed than other mental habits such as rumination, perfectionism, and our overall abilities to regulate emotions.[85] Self-criticism and self-reassurance are also physiologically distinct, and stimulate activity in different areas of the brain.[86]

Our physical health, health attitudes, and health behaviors are also linked to self-compassion. Higher levels of self-compassion are associated with fewer physiological responses to stress,[87] and with healthier behaviors.[88] Self-compassion is also linked to healthier attitudes about body image and eating,[89] and it seems to diminish the relationship between traumatic memories and the severity of eating problems.[90] Self-compassion also appears to help people cope with illnesses such as cancer and HIV.[91]

In one study, Sirois, Kitner, and Hirsch (2015) analyzed data from 15 independent samples (totaling 3,252 students and community members) to investigate associations between self-compassion and health-promoting behaviors such as exercise, sleep, eating, and stress management. They found that self-compassion was positively linked with health-promoting behaviors across all 15 samples. Researchers Terry, Leary, Mehta, and Henderson (2013) also demonstrated a connection between self-compassion and healthy behaviors, and observed that the reasons for this connection included practicing self-compassionate thoughts, proactively approaching health issues, and having an inclination toward self-kindness.

Although experiencing trauma is linked with lower levels of self-compassion,[92] self-compassion can provide a key ingredient in trauma recovery.[93] For instance, self-compassion is associated with fewer PTSD symptoms following divorce,[94] natural disasters,[95] and military combat trauma.[96] In general, kindness towards ourselves helps us to tolerate distress[97] and handle life's stresses.[98]

A few weeks of practicing self-compassion skills confer observable benefits, including reductions in rumination and self-criticism,[99] decreased levels of bodily and psychological stress,[100] and increased optimism, resilience, and self-efficacy.[101] Neff and Germer (2013) found that an 8-week self-compassion training program increased mindfulness, well-being, and self-compassion, and that the benefits remained observable at both 6 months and 1 year after the program's completion.

Self-compassion practice can reduce PTSD, depression, and trauma-related guilt.[102] Self-compassion appears to work in part by decreasing rumination about symptoms, and by diffusing avoidance of thoughts and behaviors.[103] Self-compassion and loving-kindness meditation may also activate brain areas involved in emotional processing.[104]

Self-Criticism

Whereas self-compassion may sound odd, self-criticism often resonates as familiar. It is extremely common for people to relate to themselves through constant criticism. The habit of self-criticism can even feel comfortable because of its deep familiarity. It can masquerade as a friend, but it is not. Self-criticism sparks and perpetuates emotional pain. It gets in our way.

Why are we critical of ourselves? Many of us have the mistaken belief that self-criticism is motivating, or a normal part of having high standards. However, the evidence is clear that self-compassion, rather than self-criticism, is associated with higher levels of motivation.[105] We also absorb others' criticism and standards, and maintain them within ourselves. We may be self-critical because feeling OK or good about ourselves seems scary, like letting down our guard. Self-criticism might feel like a shield—we may believe that if we criticize ourselves constantly, others' criticism or our own failures will not hurt as much. We may have learned to criticize ourselves as a mechanism for coping with trauma ("You don't deserve anything—and if you ask for what you need, you'll get punished." or "if you were better in some way, this trauma wouldn't have happened"). We may have absorbed self-critical tendencies from our peers or parents, or have taken the value of modesty to its unhealthy extreme. Self-criticism also becomes an unconscious habit that gets stronger and more dominant with repetition.

When we look inside our self-criticism, we often find that it is more complex and nuanced than it initially seemed. The fabric of self-criticism may have threads of fear, self-doubt, past trauma, disappointment, frustration, envy, isolation, perfectionism, self-protection, conditional love, and internalized cultural messages about the "right" way to look, act, or feel. Our self-criticism may even reflect positive elements, such as our aspirations and ideals for ourselves, and arise when our experiences do not match our hopes.

Sometimes self-criticism does contain helpful information, even though we experience its presentation in a destructive way. For instance, you might be critical of yourself for not taking better care of your health, or not returning phone calls from friends. In those instances, it is possible to separate the motivation or value from the self-critical tone. That is, you can distill information from self-criticism about important values and actions without succumbing to its insinuation that you are not good enough.

Self-compassion is a highly effective way of handling self-criticism. Self-compassion can be initially hard to generate and feel a little awkward, but it gets easier and less strange with practice. Building up the "muscle" of self-compassion is the most effective way to handle self-criticism. In addition to increasing self-compassion, you can also practice directing compassion towards self-criticism itself, by meeting self-criticism in a caring, kind way, rather than with censorship (see Practice 4 below, Self-Compassion Toward Self-Critical Voices).

An internet search regarding self-criticism reveals a common exhortation to "Silence your inner critic!" Despite the prevalence of this approach, however, banishing, silencing, repressing, or shaming of self-criticism does not work. Self-criticism just returns more forcefully, because you are essentially engaging in more self-criticism, but this time it is *about the self-criticism.* This can create an escalating cycle of self-criticism if we are not careful. Instead, you can try gentle, mindful observation of self-criticism, complemented with consistent cultivation of self-compassion—or even compassionate listening and care towards the "inner critics" themselves. Any time that you notice self-criticism can signal a reminder to practice self-compassion.

Self-Compassion After Trauma

Self-compassion can feel at odds with our feelings after trauma. We might feel squeezed, as though all of our resources are taken up by just trying to cope with what happened. Because trauma is uncontrollable, we may try to control things (including ourselves) as much as we can—a style that often leads to self-criticism. Our hearts may feel hard or closed. After trauma, we often react with *hypervigilance*, or being superalert, watchful, or on guard. We may even develop the message that relaxing or caring for our own needs can be danger-ous. If we feel shame, guilt, or self-blame about the trauma—or if the trauma included hearing from others that we are defective—we might believe that we are unworthy of compassion from anyone, including ourselves.

Fear of self-compassion is a common experience. Receiving kindness from ourselves and others can elicit grief about having experienced an absence of care in the past.[106] We may find ourselves feeling afraid of positive emotions in general; feeling wary of kindness from others because it evokes memories of people in our lives who did not provide consistent support or care; feeling reluctant to be kind because we equate it with being submissive or letting others take advantage of us; and feeling reluctant to try something new that seems strange and hopeless.[107]

The good news is that all of these obstacles to self-compassion illuminate practice opportunities. We can cultivate self-compassion for the full range of our experiences: for our impulse to control things, for our limited energy, for engaging in coping mechanisms that turn out to be self-destructive, for our grief over not having had sufficient care in the past, for the feeling of being criticized by ourselves or others, for feeling as though our hearts are closed or hard, and for our fear of relaxing. To practice, we can just begin to notice any of these experiences with kindness and interest, and direct our care and good wishes towards those feelings. You do not have to change everything at once, but you can practice one small step at a time as you build your comfort with self-compassion.

What is it like to develop self-compassion after trauma? Lawrence and Lee (2014) conducted in-depth interviews with seven people who participated in compassion-focused therapy for PTSD. Several common themes emerged from their experiences. First, participants described their struggles to disengage with self-criticism, because self-criticism formed a central part of their identities and a key way that they coped with emotions. Second, they described a negative reaction to the idea of developing self-compassion, because it seemed so unfamiliar, undeserved, and even a hopeless endeavor. The third theme that emerged involved feelings about the therapy itself. Participants described feelings of acceptance, nonjudgment, and being valued and understood by their therapists as other human beings who cared about them; feeling less alone in their struggles; and experiencing "the difference between *thinking* that they were not to blame and *feeling* that they were not to blame" (Lawrence & Lee, 2014, p. 502) for their past trauma. Fourth, the participants described surprise about experiencing self-compassion in a positive way, especially after their initial reservations. Finally, participants reported an increase in positive feelings—a sense of "enjoying life rather than just living it" (p. 502)—and feeling more hopeful about the future.

We all have the seeds for self-compassion. It can feel strange and scary to try something new, and we can be kind and understanding towards that feeling. I encourage you to consider trying out one of the exercises below as an experiment, and to consider relating to yourself and to your feelings in a different way.

Practice #1: Inhale My Friend, Exhale My Friend

This exercise combines kind words with mindful breathing, so that we can generate a bodily sense of self-compassion. I invite you to pick something to call yourself. "My friend," "my love," "my dear," and "my darling" are all phrases that convey care and affection, but it could be anything kind, even "my sweet potato." If it feels a bit corny or strange, you might experiment with continuing despite that awkwardness, or with choosing another phrase that seems more authentic to you (but that is not an insult). Next, you can practice pairing that phrase, as repeated silently in your mind, with the gentle encouragement to inhale and to exhale ("inhale, my friend; exhale my friend") so that you synchronize each phrase with the physical sensations of breathing in and out.

You might try this practice for several minutes. You can return your focus to your breathing and the phrase when you become distracted. As you breathe, you might try generating a sense of keeping yourself company with kindness. You might call to mind the kind of joy that you feel when you finally get to see one of your dearest friends after months or years—a kind of delighted recognition, and the sense of relaxing into a comfortable connection that was there all along. Just as you joyfully meet your friend in the flesh after a long time, you can practice meeting yourself with this same delight and companionship. Or, you can focus on the feeling of company itself ("I'm here with you for this inhale, and now I'm here for you with this exhale, and I care about you, exactly as you are feeling right now").

Practice #2: Loving-Kindness

In the Buddhist tradition, there are specific practices for cultivating the quality of *metta* (loving-kindness). Loving-kindness meditation involves the silent repetition of specific good wishes towards yourself and others. Traditionally, practitioners begin with cultivating *metta* towards themselves, and then, once this is established, cultivating *metta* for others. The practice for ourselves is introduced below; the extended practice that includes others is described in Chapter 12 (Practice #6, Loving-Kindness Comes Full Circle).

To practice loving-kindness, find a comfortable position as you practice the silent repetition of phrases wishing yourself well. If you like, you can match the phrases to a full breath (inhale and exhale) for each phrase.

The following phrases are commonly used,[108] although there are many variations.

- May I be safe
- May I be happy
- May I be healthy
- May I live with ease

These phrases may feel just right to you, or there may be others that resonate more deeply. Variations include "May I be calm," "May I be content," "May I be joyful," "May I be free from physical danger," "May I be free from mental danger," "May my actions be skillful and kind," and "May my life unfold with ease." The sense of "ease" conveys our wish for less struggle and suffering.

You can silently repeat the phrases over several minutes as you breathe. If you notice spots of emotional or physical tension, you can try "breathing into" those sensations (that is, mentally directing your breathing towards those feelings), and even sending your kind wishes to that specific experience in the moment.

If it feels very hard to locate self-compassion within yourself and to practice it, you can try an "outside-in" approach. First, you might try to think these phrases about someone you know who has helped you, and for whom you have gratitude or affection. Next, you can practice sending those wishes towards someone whom you have seen but barely know (e.g., someone who works in a coffee shop that you frequent). Once you locate and experience compassion, it may feel easier to direct it towards yourself. After you awaken the quality of kindness and caring for others, you can practice using this same "muscle" in a different way as you practice the phrases for yourself.

In Their Own Words

Last year, my mother who has lived with MS for 50 years abruptly went into the hospital for a heart attack and life-threatening pneumonia. Our family was used to my mom having health concerns, but it was shocking to have an emergency of this magnitude. It was uncertain during all of her 10-day stay whether she would survive, and we almost lost her on two distinct occasions. I found myself at a total loss on how to cope with my fears of her dying, or how to deal with the weight of the unknown from hour to hour.

I had been meditating at a Buddhist temple off and on for about a year, and had just started going regularly before my mom entered the hospital. I reached out to a friend from the temple, desperate for advice on how meditation practice could support me. I knew it would help to watch my breathing, sit in quiet—but I just couldn't calm enough on my own. My friend sent resources on loving-kindness practices that served as an anchor and simple way to be present with the reality of what was happening, as well as be kind to myself in the process. The phrase I came back to over and over was "May I find the inner resources to be present for suffering." Having this phrase was transformative for me. It helped me feel like I could be capable to care for myself and my mother, even if in a moment I felt overwhelmed.

Practice #3: Reframe Symptoms as Normal and Adaptive

The very symptoms that cause us distress after trauma reflect a coping strategy that was once adaptive. For instance, if we are anxious and jumpy, it is often because we had a real reason to be that way during the trauma—because there was real danger in the vicinity. If we feel wary of connecting with people, it is likely because we were hurt in prior relationships.

Rather than blaming ourselves for our posttraumatic symptoms, we can instead observe the ways that the symptoms make sense given the context of our past experiences. In unsafe circumstances, it is wise to set our antennae to "high alert," to refrain from relaxing, to dissociate in order to escape the present moment, or to blame ourselves to maximize a sense of control.

Even if these tendencies cause distress now, they represent adaptations that were smart, normal, and necessary at the time. This practice can seem counterintuitive as it offers "symptoms" some degree of respect, honor, and gratitude. However, it may mitigate the self-criticism and "feeling crazy" that can worsen PTSD and other symptoms.

Step 1: You can observe and acknowledge the presence of a trauma-related symptom or difficulty, such as being on guard all the time, numbing or dissociating from feelings, or blaming yourself.

Step 2: You might offer the issue some understanding for the way that it developed as a relatively normal response to external circumstances. For instance, if you sought comfort in food, alcohol, or other drugs, you could provide yourself with the understanding that trying to escape negative feelings is an impulse that makes sense, and it may have been the best mechanism that you had available at that particular time. You can try out saying to yourself something along the lines of, "Thank you, anxiety. You developed to help keep me safe during that dangerous situation, and I needed you to handle those circumstances, even if this same anxiety remains and presents a difficult habit for me today." You might also accentuate the very normality of your experience—the fact that so many people struggle to cope with trauma, and typically handle it in one of a few similar ways.

Step 3: You can provide yourself with kindness and care about the whole shebang: the trauma that you endured, the painful feelings that arose, and any additional difficulties that occurred in trying to handle your suffering. You can use your self-compassionate stance to give space and love to the whole range of experiences and feelings.

Step 4: You can offer yourself some encouragement and hope, because you are deeply engaged in the process of healing—of trying out new ways of handling hardships. You can recognize that you are in the very midst of the difficult work of life, where we really get in there and try to change our ingrained patterns. You are working hard, and you deserve care and cheering.

Practice #4: Cultivate the "Kind Witness" Within

The mindfulness teacher Sharon Salzberg (2012) encourages practitioners to watch their emotions as a wise and compassionate elderly person might watch small children at play. From that perspective, you can be sympathetic when a child cries because of a broken shovel, rather than minimizing, invalidating or shaming the child ("stop crying, kid; it's just a shovel"). However, you also have the wisdom and experience to stay balanced yourself in the midst of the child's distress. You do not go to pieces or lie down bawling on the pavement—instead, you can stay grounded while also conveying genuine care and understanding.

This is the perspective of the "kind witness," an observer that sees the whole scene from a perspective of wisdom and deep care. We can practice this stance at any time. A good place to start is often with something rather small—our own equivalent of a broken shovel. Most of us have many opportunities on any given day: waking up at 3:00 AM and not being able to get to sleep, getting stuck in traffic, burning the toast, or becoming aggravated with another person in our lives.

Step 1: You can begin by bringing your awareness to the whole range of feelings that are present, without censoring anything. If you find yourself getting caught up in the specific details of the event ("I can't believe they sent a bill charging me for the cable service after I canceled it!"), you can try to return your focus to your physical sensations in this moment (such as a racing heart, pressure in your throat and chest, and a feeling of tension in your forehead) and your feelings (perhaps disappointment, agony, frustration, or betrayal). There is no wrong sensation or feeling; all are allowable, even if they are unpleasant.

Step 2: Next, you can call to mind the idea of a kind witness within yourself. This kind witness truly understands the complete scope of what you are experiencing, and even the context of the situation, but also brings a deep sense of wisdom and balance. The kind witness does not ask you to push aside your feelings or change them in any way. Rather, there is a sense of spaciousness, of viewing the immediate situation as one part of a vast landscape. You might also tune in to the process of changing your perspective. What is it like for you to move from being *inside* the difficult feeling to the place of observing the feeling with compassion?

It can help to verbalize the response you might receive from the kindest perspective possible, and to practice directing it towards the feeling. You might use phrases such as, "I see you in pain, and I am so sorry you are experiencing this. I offer you my support and care. I have confidence that you can get through this, and I am here for you, no matter what."

Cultivating the kind witness within ourselves builds our abilities to care for ourselves effectively when in the midst of traumatic memories, depression, and other difficulties. It helps us develop stability and perseverance, and abiding self-compassion.

Practice #5: Self-Compassion Towards Self-Critical Voices

A compassionate perspective towards our thoughts and feelings encircles everything, leaving out nothing. It even holds self-criticism. This can seem counterintuitive, because self-criticism appears to be the opposite of self-compassion, or a threat to self-compassion. However, self-compassion can contain and soothe our full range of self-critical experiences. The expansive quality of self-compassion is helpful when we consider that self-criticism rarely operates on its own, but is commonly linked with past trauma, fear, anxiety, and depression.

What is it like to be self-compassionate towards self-criticism? Often, it involves acknowledging that the self-criticism developed for a reason: as a way of coping with trauma, trying to stay safe, or from internalizing criticism or negative treatment from others. It also involves investigating whether the self-criticism is arising from a place of need. I might think to myself, "My place is such a mess! I am a real slob." If I try gently asking that self-criticism what it needs, I might discover an answer like, "I really need to be able to find clean pants, and it stresses me out when I can't find them." Then I can provide myself with some validation that yes, it is reasonable and even self-caring to want to locate clean clothing without a struggle. Often, self-critical voices calm down when they are treated with caring, respectful listening. When ignored, they often scream more loudly.

When we approach self-criticism mindfully, we can view it in the same way that we would regard any other thought or feeling—that is, we can observe it without becoming swept up in it. Then, when we add self-compassion to our mindful approach, we can notice our self-criticism from a place of care and kindness.

> **Step 1:** I invite you to notice moments of self-criticism gently, rather than "doubling up" by criticizing the criticism. How do you feel during this moment of self-criticism? Can you locate any bodily sensations that correspond to the self-criticism? Does the self-criticism elicit other emotions? Do you notice a part of yourself that is generating the self-criticism, and another part that feels criticized or wounded from the criticism? How do the different parts feel?

Step 2: After noticing the self-criticism, you can try responding to the underlying goal of the self-criticism in a validating and compassionate way (e.g., "I hear you and care about you. It sounds like you're really trying to look out for me, and that you want me to make progress in terms of _____"). If there is no underlying goal (for instance, if you find yourself thinking "I'm so stupid" because someone else told you this), you can provide yourself with compassion and understanding for how the self-criticism emerged and how it feels.

Step 3: You can provide yourself with compassion about feeling criticized. Self-criticism hurts. It can feel hopeless, or like being stuck, and it adds another level of pain, because whatever we were criticizing ourselves about was probably already painful. You might comfort yourself a bit about the feeling of criticizing yourself, and say something to yourself along the lines of, "Ugh, this self-criticism is a really painful experience. You have my care and support as you feel this self-criticism, and as you try to build new patterns of relating to yourself."

Alternatively, you might think of having a brief, respectful, and open chat (perhaps over tea or coffee) with the critical part of yourself, the part of yourself that seems to be the target of the criticism, and with your wisest, most centered, self-compassionate self. You can ask each part about how it is feeling, and inquire about its goals and deeper needs. You can also offer understanding and validation if appropriate. You might reassure each part that you want to help advance well-being, and offer each part kindness and compassion. It might seem corny or wacky to encourage dialogue among the different voices within us. However, the alternative, in which all of these parts operate outside of our conscious awareness, can cause problems. After trauma, different parts of ourselves can split off from each other, and integrating them with compassion and understanding can promote healing.

At times, it is hard to determine whether a self-critical voice stems from a genuine desire to improve things for ourselves, from a self-sabotaging impulse, or from an echo of others' criticism. It might help to investigate the tone of the criticism. Is it encouraging? Gentle? Harsh? Blaming? Punishing? Self-criticism can be pervasive and sneaky, and may have an air of objectivity, of rightness, or even self-awareness. Ultimately, it may not matter how the self-criticism arises, except as an opportunity for understanding. Regardless of its source, it can be soothed by self-compassion.

Observing self-criticisms gently and directing care towards them can reduce their intensity, our overidentification with the self-criticisms, and their contributions to anxiety, depression, or other symptoms.

Practice #6: Spot the Success

Every day, we do many things to take good care of ourselves without noticing them. As humans, our attention is biased towards things that are not going well, and this bias is often stronger after trauma. In order to shift our focus away from our flaws, we need to consciously practice spotting our successes. Taking a moment to recognize our successes is also reinforcing—it increases our motivation and confidence for additional success.

Step 1: To practice Spot the Success, you can identify (either in your mind or on paper) several things that have gone well today, and to which you contributed. You might aim for at least 10 actions. For instance, your list might look something like:

1. Got out of bed
2. Showered
3. Got dressed
4. E-mailed a friend
5. Prepared and ate breakfast
6. Went for a walk
7. Talked to my new neighbor for 5 minutes
8. Paid bills
9. Did laundry
10. Took vitamins

There is *no item too small* for Spot the Success. Even breathing is a success, and it is completely fine to include it on your list. The items on your list may all seem like nothings or no-brainers—the basic and habitual steps of life that we take for granted. We typically gloss over our efforts and accomplishments without even noticing them. However, it is especially important to notice them when life is rough, because things like showering or calling a friend often take great effort. We need all of the support that we can get, including support from ourselves. When things are very hard, getting through the moments and the day is a victory.

Step 2: You can try giving yourself support and encouragement for your positive actions (for example, leaving the house; showering; calling a friend; attending a medical appointment; practicing mindfulness). You might experiment with staying with the feelings of gratitude towards yourself for both your efforts and your accomplishments.

What does it feel like to actually take a moment and give yourself credit for your efforts, even for these small things? Many people have the urge to dismiss these actions when calling them to mind, and you might notice that impulse as well. However, when we look at our successes, we can observe that they are indeed important, and that they each reflect meaningful care. Practicing Spot the Success provides an opportunity for us to acknowledge and reinforce self-compassionate actions that are already occurring.

In Their Own Words

After a triggering conversation with my supervisor at work, I had a massive panic attack. Fortunately, as a result of my mindfulness practice, I actually felt curious about the trauma response and even looked forward to investigating. I went back to my office and meditated. When I did that, I observed the tension in my body, labeled it as fear, and noticed the thought, "I am not supposed to talk about this." I breathed into the sensation lovingly, cried for the part of me that was suffering, and felt a deep knowing that everything was going to be okay.

Self-Compassion for Trauma Recovery and Resilience

Although we often think of personal qualities as characteristics that we either have or do not have, compassion and kindness can be cultivated and can grow with practice. Salzberg reflected that the nature of *metta* is "to reteach a thing its loveliness" (1995, p. 22). That reteaching is vital after trauma.

We often feel unlovable and unloving after trauma, and those feelings often seem intractable. Even with self-compassion practice, change takes time, and you may not notice benefits immediately. It might feel comforting to ease off any pressure to change your feelings at all. You can keep the exact same thoughts and feelings that you have. If you like, you might also imagine a big pitcher full of self-kindness, which then you can pour all over everything. You can also start very small. Remember that compassion is unconditional and unlimited, and that you can have compassion even for feelings of hopelessness and frustration.

The mindfulness teacher and psychologist Tara Brach described asking people the question, "When you are caught in fear, what is it that you most want to feel" (2015)? She observed that people initially responded that they want the fear to go away. After considering the question further, they commented that they wanted to feel safe, loved, peaceful, trusting, valued, and worthwhile. Self-compassion practice generates those feelings, and is a powerful antidote to fear, shame, self-blame, and self-criticism.

As a complement to any of the exercises above, you might try placing your hands on your heart, using another gentle form of touch, or imagining being held by a loved one.[109] Brach (2015) explained that visualizing or experiencing a comforting touch can awaken feelings of safety, connectedness, and well-being. It may also elicit a "felt sense" of care and love.

When changes in self-compassion occur, they may emerge in ways we do not expect. We might first just become more aware of self-criticism—an awareness that is not particularly enjoyable. It may help to remember that noticing self-criticism can be an important step in cultivating self-compassion, because it provides an opportunity to practice a new way of relating to ourselves. We might practice self-compassion for several weeks, and then have very small but meaningful changes in our self-criticism ("I can't believe I forgot that appointment. I'm such a scatterbrain! But, it's OK. I'll reschedule and make it work, and it's not the end of the world. It's hard to remember everything, especially when I'm feeling stressed."). Over time, the habit of self-compassion becomes stronger, and we become more resilient when facing difficulties.

As you practice new mindfulness skills for handling trauma and PTSD, you can bring kindness and self-compassion to each step of the journey. In every effort to heal, you can approach the moment with friendliness towards yourself, even as you acknowledge its challenges. If something feels hard, you can encourage yourself along the lines of, "I'm so sorry this feels incredibly hard right now. I care about you and I am here with you. I am going to help you get through this." The hope is that our self-compassion practice generalizes to an overall self-compassionate way of being, so that when we make a mistake or encounter a hard moment, our self-compassion is right there, ready to engage.

chapter 5

RESPECT AND REFRAME: MINDFULNESS PRACTICES FOR INTRUSIVE THOUGHTS, TRAUMATIC MEMORIES, AND NIGHTMARES

AFTER TRAUMA, unwanted memories, thoughts, and feelings about it keep arising in our minds. Often the memories are vivid and deeply disturbing. They can interrupt our concentration and make us feel far removed from the world around us. We may wish for the thoughts to just stop, and we can become aggravated and frustrated whenever they revisit us. Far from being a respite, sleep can shake us with nightmares that leave us feeling worse.

Unwanted thoughts and memories related to trauma are called *intrusions.* They seem to come to us unbidden. At times they present themselves at random; at other times, they are "triggered" by an event or image in our environment. Intrusions can feel clearly defined, or they may blend together. They might emerge as a physical feeling, an image, a strong emotion, or as a *flashback*—the sensation of being partially or fully back in the memory, as if it is happening all over again. Intrusions can also take the form of reenactments or compulsive reexperiencing, in which we repeat the behaviors of the trauma or expose ourselves to information or situations that recall the trauma. We might experience intrusions throughout the day or week, or we might feel stuck in a sea of intrusions, where thoughts and feelings about the trauma become our primary mental experience. Although they can be highly disturbing, involuntary intrusions are a normal and common response to trauma.

The psychologist Anke Ehlers (2010) explained that there are at least four ways that intrusions differ from other types of memories. Intrusions seem to have more of a sense of "nowness" than do other memories; that is, even if we are aware that the images, sensations, or memories represent our past experiences, we feel them strongly in this moment. Although this is especially true for flashbacks, other intrusions also reflect this nowness. Intrusions also seem more fragmented and disjointed than other memories, which typically are accompanied by more contextual features. An intrusion commonly arises as a single image paired with a strong emotion. Intrusions also differ from other memories because they are triggered by a broad range of cues, including cues outside our conscious awareness. Finally, intrusions provoke more distress than do other memories.

Why do we have intrusions? After trauma, our minds work hard to protect us from future harm, and to regain a sense of safety and control. Replaying our memories may help us process them. The cycle of intrusions and avoidance may reflect a natural adaptation to trauma, even though that same cycle can also keep us stuck. Intrusive memories seem to match the moments during the trauma when our psychological or physical selves felt most threatened, and to provide rich sensory information that could help us avoid future trauma.

Intrusions are demanding. They hijack our attention and make it hard to concentrate on anything else. When we experience PTSD, intrusions bias our perception, so that we are highly responsive to information related to the trauma, and less aware of other sensations.[110] This bias means that we miss out on sensations that are pleasant or neutral. This pattern can endure over time, so that we become focused on stimuli linked to our trauma, and experience fewer and fewer feelings of ease or pleasure. We can engage mindfulness skills to help us recover by expanding our attention to aspects of ourselves or our environments that are not related to the trauma.

Integrating our experiences before and after the trauma takes time and effort. Intrusions typically diminish over time, and they become less frequent and less distressing. Intrusions can arise when our minds are engaged in the hard work of integration. At times, we can get stuck. The sticking place might be the material of the intrusion itself—we may experience the same painful memories for months or years. Alternatively, we can get stuck because we avoid every intrusion, and never allow ourselves the opportunity to work through them (see Chapter 7 for strategies to handle avoidance). We can also get stuck in our own interpretation of the trauma, such as the belief that we cannot trust anyone or that we are horribly flawed (see Chapter 8 for working with these layers of meaning). At their best, intrusions can push us to build a new, coherent perspective that reflects everything we have been through—a view that can hold the trauma itself, insights from the recovery process, and some degree of current safety and ease.

Factors that prevent intrusions from resolving include mental processes that become habitual, our appraisals and interpretations about the intrusions (add-ons), and the thoughts and behaviors with which we respond to intrusions.[111] When we judge ourselves harshly for having intrusions, we may take steps to manage them that are ultimately counterproductive, such as suppressing our thoughts and memories, ruminating, or overengaging in behaviors thought to promote safety (such as checking multiple times that doors are locked). However, we can learn more effective ways to manage intrusions, including acknowledging triggers when they occur, remembering that intrusions and related feelings are normal responses to trauma, reducing repetitive behaviors thought to promote a sense of safety, and understanding how our interpretations of intrusions might maintain or exacerbate them.

> *Upon undergoing a prophylactic bilateral mastectomy at 25, I learned anew about grief. I learned that losing a body part is unique from losing a loved one because no one else shares that loss. I learned that moving on does not mean the grief disappears. To the contrary, it evolves to become less potent, but susceptible to seemingly innocuous triggers. For me, moving on meant honoring the inevitable return of those feelings, potentially at unexpected times and in unexpected ways. It meant sitting with those feelings, weathering the waves of grief while knowing the storm would eventually pass. It meant learning that self-denigration would capsize the boat, whereas self-compassion helped batten down the hatches. Self-compassion was not selfish; it was strength.*

Intrusions, Appraisals, and Reappraisals

When we experience an intrusion, we usually have a fast reaction to the intrusion. As soon as the distressing image, emotion, or thought arises, we often have strong feelings or urges. We may feel frustration about having the same intrusion again and again; an impulse to push it out of our minds; an urge to use alcohol or other drugs to try to escape the intrusion; or a judgment towards ourselves for having intrusions. Our negative reactions to our own intrusions may actually function to maintain them, by increasing the likelihood that we will suppress our feelings or avoid trauma-related material.[112] Our negative responses to intrusions seem to be linked to behavioral avoidance and to the tendency to suppress thoughts.[113] One research study[114] examined the responses 297 motor vehicle accident survivors attributed to their intrusions. Thought suppression, distraction, and suppression during intrusions were associated with higher levels of PTSD symptoms.

Often, our negative reactions to intrusions take the form of *appraisals*, or the meaning we assign to the trauma and to ourselves. I might think, "There's clearly something wrong with me," "This just shows that I am bad at relationships," or "I can't believe this memory is still popping up all the time—I should be over this already!" The psychologists Martina Reynolds and Adrian Wells (1999) measured several different ways that people respond to their own intrusive thoughts. These included *punishment* (for instance, telling myself that I am stupid for having the intrusion, or becoming angry or shouting at myself for having it), *worry* (for example, worrying about more minor things instead), and social control (such as keeping the thought to ourselves). As people recovered from PTSD, Reynolds and Wells observed that they used punishment and worry strategies less often.

Reappraisal of intrusions is connected to recovery from trauma. Reappraisal involves attempts to open to new ways of looking at intrusions, trauma, and ourselves. We might try out thoughts such as, "It wasn't your fault that it happened to you," "It's normal that you would feel this way," or "I have confidence that you can get through this." We can become brave enough to challenge the old ways that we perceived things, and to try out different perspectives and meanings.

By observing both our intrusions and our responses to the intrusions with mindfulness and compassion, we can reduce the frequency of intrusions and the distress that they provoke. Whereas focusing on the intrusions themselves can feel scary, focusing on our *reactions* to intrusions might provide us with a workable entry point for shifting mental patterns after trauma.

Nightmares

Nightmares are considered to be closely related to intrusions. Nightmares are often linked with insomnia, because they can disrupt our sleep or cause us to resist or delay sleep. Although many trauma survivors avoid sleep because of nightmares, this behavior can result in a "REM rebound" in which nightmares become more frequent and intense. Nightmares and other sleep problems after trauma are debilitating; they are linked with PTSD severity, depression, irritability, anxiety, and impaired mental functioning during the day. After trauma, nightmares often depict the scary features of the trauma, or reflect the terrifying feelings of the trauma paired with new images.

Nightmares may reflect our efforts to process the trauma. They may help us connect emotions about the trauma to other aspects of our lives[115] or remodel negative memories.[116] However, nightmares may also become mental habits that take on a life of their own, and that maintain PTSD. On the bright side, working to change nightmares and other sleep problems can reduce their frequency and severity, and even decrease daytime PTSD symptoms (see Practices 5 and 6 below).

RESEARCH HIGHLIGHT How Does Trauma Relate to Sleep Problems and Nightmares?

TRAUMA DISRUPTS SLEEP, and disrupted sleep can worsen PTSD. This two-way process can take a toll on both mental and physical health. Trauma survivors often report nightmares along with other sleep difficulties. For instance, Chu, Dill, and Murphy (2000) observed that individuals with a history of childhood abuse were more likely to be afraid of falling asleep and more anxious when they awoke mid-sleep. Nightmares and insomnia are both strongly linked with depression and PTSD. It appears that nightmares and insomnia can worsen anxiety, irritability, and depression, while decreasing our ability to process and cope with such emotions.

It makes sense that trauma survivors would try to avoid sleep in order to escape nightmares. However, this behavior can backfire. When we deprive ourselves of sleep, our bodies respond with "REM rebound," meaning that our subsequent sleep sessions have a greater proportion of time spent dreaming, and contain more intense dreams.

Imagery rehearsal therapy (IRT), in which people imagine and rehearse a more positive resolution to their nightmares, is associated with improvements in nightmares, insomnia, and PTSD (IRT practice is described later in this chapter). For instance, imagery rehearsal therapy has been shown to decrease insomnia, the intensity and frequency of nightmares, and daytime PTSD symptoms in combat Veterans and in sexual assault survivors.[117] The benefits of imagery rehearsal therapy appear to last, and yield significant reductions in nightmares even one year after treatment[118].

Mindful Approaches to Intrusions

We can begin our mindfulness towards intrusions by noticing how we handle them now. Do we try to think about something else? Criticize ourselves for having the intrusion? Worry that they will never stop? Do we ever allow ourselves space to have the intrusions, and to notice all of the ways that we feel about them? After we notice how we handle intrusions, we can experiment with actually letting the intrusions come and go, along with the thoughts and feelings that go with them. Allowing ourselves space to actually experience intrusions, rather than pushing them away, can help us change the intrusion-avoidance dynamic that maintains PTSD.

We can shift intrusions by trying out new strategies. When intrusions arise, we can try one of several techniques depending on the severity of the intrusions, the situation at hand, and how strong we feel in the moment. First, we can give ourselves permission to actually experience them, even when they are painful. The radical approach of allowing intrusions to be present instead of pushing them away actually results in fewer intrusions over time. Second, we can sharpen our attunement to the present moment in order to ground ourselves when intrusions whirl. Third, we can implement distraction mindfully and selectively (for example, choosing to focus on sensations in our feet when our breathing feels unsteady), rather than as our default mode, for moments when we must focus or relax. Fourth, we can use imagery techniques to decrease the amount and severity of nightmares. Fifth, we can infuse self-compassion into the way that we handle our intrusions.

We can also plan ahead when we know we will encounter triggers that are likely to spark intrusions. For instance, after a traumatic break-up, it might feel awful to attend a close friend's wedding, no matter how pleased we are for that friend. We can practice mindfulness and self-care for the feelings of dread or annoyance that we have in this moment as we consider attending the event. We might also imagine sitting at the wedding and trying out one of the mindfulness strategies described below. It could help to tell a friend or fellow guest about the situation ahead of time, and ask if we might call upon this person for support. We can also give ourselves permission in advance to get up and "use the restroom" at any point to take a break.

In another example, U.S. military Veterans often say that July 4th, Independence Day, is their least favorite day of the year, because the sound of firecrackers triggers painful memories of danger or combat, and elicits physical feelings of fear associated with war. This is a situation where an avoidance strategy might be appropriate, such as going to a place where there are no audible fireworks, wearing earplugs, listening to loud music, or going to the movies. The reason that avoidance might be appropriate in this situation is that for most people, fireworks happen only once a year, and foregoing them altogether would not impede everyday levels of functioning or hinder important relationships.

Self-compassion about intrusions can help us when we are shaken and frustrated. We can picture an all-encompassing circle of self-compassion that contains everything: the intrusions themselves, our frustration, our self-judgment, our impatience, and our worries that they will not end. We can direct our own kindness, care, and encouragement to every aspect of this challenge. We can also draw on our self-compassion to help us choose and practice new strategies for handling intrusions, and to cultivate our confidence that we can learn to manage intrusions more effectively.

The mindfulness practices below offer diverse strategies for managing intrusions. The first two strategies, *Grounding* and *Change the Channel*,[119] are especially helpful for reducing the distress of intrusions in the short term. The next two strategies, *Remember With Self-Compassion* and *Waves of Intrusion*, address intrusions in the longer term; that is, they may help more for handling overall intrusions than for coping with a particular intrusion in this moment. The last two strategies, *Mindful Imagery Rehearsal for Nightmares* and *Self-Compassion Before Sleep and Waking*, are meant to help relieve nightmares.

Practice #1: Grounding (Short-Term)

This practice is particularly helpful when experiencing intrusive images, flashbacks, or dissociation. Unlike other mindfulness practices that can be practiced with eyes open or with eyes closed, grounding is best practiced with open eyes to maintain focus on your experiences in this moment. Grounding techniques engage the five senses to strengthen the feeling of connection to the present moment—our sense that "I am here in *this moment, right now.*"

Grounding With Touch

I invite you to touch an object such as a pebble or a pencil. Any object can work, as long as it is one that feels emotionally neutral or positive. You can notice its texture, its weight in your hand, and how it feels to touch or press it. Some people find that it helps them to carry the same object with them to "ground" themselves, such as a stone that fits comfortably in a pocket. You can also try touching the fabric of your clothing, or the material of a chair or sofa.

Grounding With Your Feet

We often do not direct conscious attention towards our feet, but they have a complex distribution of 26 bones, 33 joints, and over 100 tendons, ligaments, and muscles. Drawing our attention down to our feet can feel grounding, because we often experience distress in the head, chest, or stomach. When we practice mindfulness of the sensations in our feet, we might notice the feeling of our feet inside socks or shoes; the position of our feet and toes; or the way that our weight is distributed throughout our foot. We can also feel the literal ground or floor with our feet, and observe the sensation of our feet on the ground. If you have pain in your feet, you can either observe that pain as part of your mindfulness practice, or choose to focus on another body part where you do not experience pain.

Grounding With Objects in the Room or Outside

To enhance our attunement with this moment, we can try to observe 10 new things in the room around us. These can be small things that we have never noticed before (such as the way that the molding bevels into the ceiling, or the shadow of a picture frame). We can also name the shapes and colors of the objects around us. This quick exercise can help unstick our minds a bit when they become mired in distressing thoughts and feelings.

Practice #2: Change the Channel (Short-Term)

Change the Channel is a distraction technique. The first step involves developing a detailed scene from a favorite (nontraumatic) movie, television show, or personal experience. It is important to have as much detailed material in the alternate scene as possible, including specific dialogue, clothing items, and facial expressions. In the second step, we practice or rehearse the scene in our minds so that it is ready to go when we need it. While in a relatively calm state with few intrusive thoughts, we can imagine the alternate scene at least three times from beginning to end (it might help to actually watch the scene, so that it is fresh in your mind, and then to imagine it). In the third step, we use the Change the Channel technique during an intrusion. Some people like to imagine holding a television remote control, and pretending to press the button to "change the channel" away from the intrusive memory and into the imagined scene.

Practice #3: Remember With Self-Compassion (Long-Term)

Intrusive symptoms do not usually go away by avoiding or trying not to think about them. Instead, making a specific time and space to actually allow the experience and related feelings to arise, rather than suppressing them, can help them resolve. The practice involves setting aside 10 minutes to experience difficult memories and associated feelings, but in a compassionate way.

When we remember with self-compassion, we can "bookend" the experience with self-compassion before, during, and after we pay attention to our memories. That is, we can offer ourselves care as we consider letting ourselves experience the memories; compassion during the experience itself; and thoughtfulness about how we can best take care of ourselves if we experience distress. At any point before, during, and after this "scheduled feeling time," you can insert self-caring statements that feel genuine and are directed at both your past and current selves. Examples of self-caring statements are:

- I am so sorry you had to go through that.
- That was terrible, and you got through it, and I am glad you made it. I am here for you now.
- I see you, my friend, living through that experience. I offer you all of my care and respect, and send it to you back through time.
- I am sorry that you not only had to endure the trauma, but that you also have to handle all of the distress and painful memories that remain. I care about your feelings in this moment.
- These thoughts and feelings are a painful but normal response to what you have been through. They don't mean that there is anything wrong with you.
- After you sit with the feelings and memories for several moments, let's plan to do something fun and enjoyable.

Any self-caring statement can work, as long as it feels authentic and in your own voice. In addition to directing specific statements towards ourselves, we can work to cultivate a self-compassionate attitude towards traumatic memories and our responses.

Practice #4: Waves of Intrusion (Long-Term).

This practice builds on a saying from the mindfulness teacher Jon Kabat-Zinn: "You can't stop the waves, but you can learn to surf" (1994, p. 30). Many people find that imagining distress as a wave helps to manage it (however, it is not recommended for traumas that involve water). In the first step of this practice, I invite you to imagine a wave—it arrives, builds, crests, and falls away. It can help to engage your senses as you imagine the sights, sounds, and smells of the wave gathering strength and receding. In the second step of the practice, you can try pairing the wave image with a minimally distressing experience (e.g., an itch; or feeling minor irritation at having to wait in line), and observing the ebb and flow of the feeling. Finally, in the third step of this practice, you can bring the "wave" perspective to intrusive symptoms: first to less intense ones, and then to more intense intrusions. When we consider our intrusions as waves, it helps reassure us that they have an arc to them, and that they will not last forever. It can also help us from overidentifying with intrusions, and to build the "observer" stance and self-confidence that we can get through the wave.

Practice #5: Mindful Imagery Rehearsal for Nightmares

After a nightmare, we often want to forget about it as quickly as possible, so that we can escape the fear or anxiety that it evoked. However, paying attention to the content and feeling of the nightmare and reimagining the dream can help us reduce nightmares as well as daytime PTSD symptoms. In imagery rehearsal therapy (IRT), we choose a nightmare and change some aspect of it, so that it no longer ends in a scary way. We then replay or "rehearse" the new dream with the more positive ending several times a day for at least a few days.

To practice IRT, we first need to pick a recent nightmare. It is most helpful if it is not a nightmare that reflects an exact reenactment of the trauma, but one about something else. Next, you can change the nightmare in any way you like. Then, rehearse the new version of the dream in your mind for a few minutes a few times a day. Continue to rehearse the new dream (but not the old nightmare) daily. Then, try this process with a new dream every 5–7 days. Some people find it helpful to write out the revised version of the dream, but others find benefit without writing it down.

You can creatively change the dream in any way that feels right. It can help to insert a positive, peaceful, or silly resolution (e.g., a wise or supportive figure appears; the scene shifts to a safe or comforting space; you slide up a rainbow onto a comfortable cloud; a would-be attacker slips on a banana peel and falls unconscious). You can also change small details of the nightmare (e.g., put a window with a beautiful view into a room that did not have one before; change the color of a car from red to blue).

Mindfulness skills can enhance our IRT practice. We can check in with ourselves about the content of our dreams and how we feel upon awakening. We can also observe changes in fear and anxiety over the weeks that we reimagine our nightmares. Mindfulness practice can also help us cultivate the sense that we can work with our thoughts and nightmares to change them. A common barrier to IRT is the tendency to have a "nightmare sufferer identity" (Krakow, 2004); that is, a set of beliefs that we are powerless against nightmares, that they cannot be changed, or that having nightmares is part of our identity. We may also feel fearful about practicing imagery in general if we are troubled by intrusions and nightmares. Mindful awareness about our beliefs about nightmares and imagery practice can help us address them, and may help us become more open to trying something new.

Practice #6: Self-Compassion Before Sleep and Waking

This practice incorporates self-compassion to reduce fear of nightmares or being vulnerable before sleep, as well as distress after nightmares. In both instances, you can direct self-compassion towards those difficult experiences, saying things that feel authentic along the lines of, "I'm sorry this is so hard. It's very difficult to fear sleep or have a painful dream. I offer you my support and care during this experience."

Before sleep, you might take a few minutes to notice how you are feeling.

It is common to feel frightened about sleep after trauma. You may fear having nightmares, or it may be scary to sleep because we generally lose a sense of control. You might also feel tense or keyed up. As you observe your feelings, you can practice responding to them with kindness. You might reassure yourself that you are going to do your best to take good care of yourself in this moment, in your dreams, and when you wake up. If you notice the urge to avoid sleep, you can respond to that urge with compassion. You can balance your understanding of your desire to avoid sleep with your knowledge that avoiding sleep can make nightmares more severe, and could lead to other problems. You can remind yourself that no matter what happens during sleep, you will plan to provide yourself with comfort and care when you wake.

As you awaken, you can observe the transition between sleep and wakefulness. For some people this is immediate; others experience "twilight sleep" in which they are neither fully asleep nor fully awake. If you have had a dream, you might notice the content of the dream. When suffering from PTSD, depression, or other difficult daytime conditions, we might notice some dread and pessimism about the day ahead (such as waking up to think, "Ugh, this again"). We can observe all of these experiences with great kindness towards ourselves. We may even decide to begin the day with self-compassionate thoughts ("I'm here for you, and I will help you today").

In Their Own Words

My father sexually molested me for 8 years. I pretended for a long time that it had no impact on me and, when I finally told my family, I couldn't stop the cascade of memories and emotions that flooded every moment. Mindfulness helped me find a place of acceptance between those two extremes. I started with being aware of my breathing while remaining inside my body. Five seconds of being mindful was all I could manage at first. Once I figured out that mindfulness wasn't an emptying of my brain, but a filling up of the present, it became easier to focus my attention for longer periods. Now I am mindful that those memories are part of who I am, no more or less than all of my other experiences.

Respecting and Reframing Intrusions

What do you call a treated traumatic memory? The psychologist John Briere posed this question during a conference I attended. There was a pause, and the audience was quiet as they awaited the answer. "A memory," Briere said. Once a trauma memory is processed in our minds, it becomes more like a regular memory, and less like an intrusion. It is less distressing, and seems more contextualized or connected to a broader landscape of experiences. It no longer seems to appear out of the blue, over and over. We gain more control over whether and how much we think about it, and it does not distress us as much when it arises.

When we approach intrusions, we might consider our task as "Respect and Reframe." It can be tempting to disrespect ourselves and our experiences when intrusions frustrate us. Instead, we can treat our intrusions with great respect by acknowledging them as normal and worthy of our attention and care. We can open to reappraisal by considering new perspectives about the intrusions, about the trauma, and about ourselves. We can also reframe intrusions by seeing them as opportunities to practice mindfulness, tremendous patience, and self-compassion.

DEFUSE ANXIETY: MINDFULNESS PRACTICES FOR FEAR, HYPERVIGILANCE, AND HYPERAROUSAL

FEAR FEELS REAL. That is, it presents itself as the sharp, definite truth. Our bodily sensations of fear are indeed real, but that is often where the reality begins and ends. Fear can impart valuable information to us about danger in the environment, or about our own feelings. However, fear can also be deceptive. It portrays itself as a straightforward reflection of the circumstances around us, even when it is not. Working with fear and with other forms of anxiety involves investigating the degree to which our feelings reflect our present situation, past trauma, and mental habits. We defuse anxiety by treating it with kindness and understanding, by training our bodies to relax, and by consciously attending to neutral, safe, and pleasant experiences.

It is brave to acknowledge fear. During moments of trauma, we may have needed to suppress fear or to push it aside. As we work to recover from trauma, we can build our capacity to remain present with fear, instead of dissociating, numbing, or using other ways to escape. The teacher Chögyam Trungpa noted that "acknowledging fear is not a cause for depression or discouragement," and explained that, "true fearlessness is not the reduction of fear, but going beyond fear" (1984, p. 33).

When we approach fear with mindful curiosity, we see that it is not as monolithic as it appears. Common descriptions of anxiety—feelings of worry, fear, terror, nervousness, unease, panic, apprehension, or nervousness—indicate that it is complex and nuanced. Unpacking our anxiety can help us handle its contents. It might contain discomfort with uncertainty, or mental projections of a feared outcome that seems certain. We may be overwhelmed, stressed, or uncomfortable as we face unreasonable goals and expectations. We might worry about the future as a habit, as a way to generate a sense of control, or as a strategy to avoid whatever we are feeling right now. Anxiety can also reflect impatience about reaching a future outcome. Anxiety might arise as a physical sensation—a constriction in the chest, or an ache in the gut. It might emerge as a subtle current just beneath our conscious awareness, or it might announce its presence loudly. If we look beneath the anxiety, we might find sadness, anger, or hurt.

Anxiety can take the form of constant worry; the pervasive sense that the world or other people are dangerous; never feeling able to relax; an exaggerated "startle" response; or the sense that life will just not work out. We might have episodes of panic, in which we experience symptoms such as shortness of breath, a racing heart, sweating, feeling dizzy or lightheaded, and the fear of passing out or dying. Anxiety may also show up in the form of "safety behaviors," actions that seem to increase our safety but that can actually worsen anxiety, such as sitting by the door, not getting too close to other people, or carrying a weapon. Anxiety may lead to avoidance, dissociation, and numbing—strategies that can help us in the short term, but that often increase anxiety and PTSD in the long term. Anxiety can consume a large proportion of our attention and energy, and lead to our feeling depleted, withdrawn, or helpless.

After trauma, our bodies often learn to stay in an anxious state that reflects *hypervigilance* (being overly watchful, attuned, alert, or on guard for potential signals of danger). We also tend to experience *hyperarousal*, the feeling that we are always activated rather than relaxed. Hyperarousal symptoms include feeling irritable or angry, having difficulty concentrating, and problems falling or staying asleep.

Anxious feelings can arise forcefully, as wormholes that whisk us back to past traumas and swirl emotional memories together with whatever we encounter today. We feel fear when our bodies respond to trauma triggers in the environment, even when there is no present danger. Military Veterans who learned to be on guard for mines or improvised explosive devices may remain anxious about walking on grass or dirt. Similarly, survivors of sexual abuse often feel fearful about attending health care visits that involve being undressed, touched, or physically objectified. Exposure to any type of interpersonal trauma can make us wary of interacting with other people. Trauma can also lead to a pervasive sense of being nervous, worried, or scared—a charged anticipation that something will go wrong, and will then create more suffering.

As soon as we feel anxiety, we often feel a "zing" of self-blame, catastrophizing, or judgment. We might say to ourselves, "What's wrong with me? Why do I feel this way? It's a terrible problem that I feel this way! How can I get this feeling to stop right now?" Our anxiety *about* anxiety tends to make it much harder to bear. When we practice approaching our anxiety with deep understanding and kindness, it loses some of its power. We can remind ourselves that our anxiety is logical given our past experiences, and encourage ourselves as we try out new ways to handle it.

Many of my patients say, "I've just always been a very anxious person." When I hear someone say this, I note that the person seems to regard anxiety as a stable component and defining aspect of character. I also hear self-judgments about anxiety, including perceptions of being "stupid," "silly," or unable to "snap out of it." Many of the patients who make such statements also describe having endured highly stressful circumstances—circumstances that research demonstrates are strongly linked with feeling anxious—but are unaware of the connection between their trauma histories and anxiety. Often, learning about the normal ways that anxiety arises and endures following extreme stress helps us reduce our overidentification with anxiety and our self-judgments about it.

Anxiety is a normal response to threatening situations and their aftermath. In the midst of a trauma, our bodies undergo a cascade of physical reactions to promote survival. Following severe or prolonged trauma, this cascade often continues, with the result that anxiety persists. Anxiety becomes the default setting. Our brains and nervous systems adapt to the trauma and retain the physical processes that were set in motion. Some brain regions and systems become overactive, whereas others become underused. Our brains are highly responsive. Brain circuitry established during extreme stress can filter emotions, physical sensations, and the world through an anxious lens.

On the bright side, our brain's responsiveness can work in our favor in healing anxiety. Healing involves redirecting mental energy—which physically manifests as blood flow, the activation of specific brain regions, and the architecture of brain structures—away from brain systems that perpetuate anxiety and towards brain systems that help regulate and decrease anxiety. We can do this by proactively practicing relaxation, or through connecting to people or activities that help us feel more safe and supported. We can also reverse our brain's bias towards threatening information by consciously noticing and savoring experiences that feel neutral, safe, or pleasant.

Reappraising Anxiety

Anxiety can perpetuate itself in a cycle: An internal or external event triggers anxious feelings, and then we become anxious or judgmental about the feelings themselves, which then leads to more anxiety. *Cognitive reappraisal* interrupts the middle part of this cycle. When the anxiety arises, we reappraise or reframe it as a normal consequence of having endured stress, rather than as a problem or a negative character trait. In addition to being normal coping mechanisms, feelings of fear, hypervigilance, and hyperarousal are usually necessary and smart in the context of stressful situations. In dangerous situations, being very alert and attuned to potential threat can help us protect ourselves or others. Reappraising posttraumatic anxiety as understandable, normal, and smart can help us refrain from interpreting the anxiety in ways that generate additional anxiety.

After trauma, a cycle of ongoing anxiety can get stuck as our default setting, and for good reason. During circumstances of extreme stress, it is most adaptive to interpret anxiety as a sign that there is something very wrong. These interpretations usually occur outside of conscious awareness during the time of the trauma and beyond. In addition, the tendency to appraise the anxiety itself as a cause for alarm often remains after the traumatic circumstances have passed. Because these appraisals may not be conscious, it can be a bit challenging to access them. However, both accessing our appraisals and changing them can become easier with practice.

We often feel caught in the patterns of anxiety that we developed during stressful situations. For instance, some military Veterans feel that they need to conduct a perimeter check of their homes every night—anxiously observing every boundary for signs of danger. This behavior is necessary and appropriate within some contexts of military danger, but can contribute to ongoing anxiety that extends far beyond military service or any present risk. Even as adults, survivors of childhood abuse can feel anxious in interpersonal situations, because their bodies and brains at one time adapted normally to contexts that included dangerous uncertainty. Reappraising these adaptations as normal reactions to stress may not heal them completely, but can reduce some of the self-judgment and self-criticism that worsen anxiety. Reappraisal can help neutralize "double anxiety"—being anxious about our anxiety symptoms.

In Their Own Words

Fear is something that I have struggled with in my life. In the past, whenever fear would arise, it would often take charge of the moment, steering me away from myself and the things I wanted to move towards. Over the years as my practice of mindfulness has developed, my capacity to experience fear and respond in a healthier, more skillful way has grown . . . beyond even what I thought I was capable of. I sit daily for 20–30 minutes, practice periodically during the day, and have incorporated loving-kindness into my daily practice as well. When fear arises now in my experience, I can often recognize the fear, label it, ask it what it wants from me, and then watch it as it fades away. Practicing mindfulness has helped me develop this capacity of observation; this capacity to witness what arises in me and not be so reactive to it.

Contributions of Childhood Environments to Anxiety

Our experiences with anxiety are shaped by a combination of factors, including the traumas we endure, standard biological responses to stress, individual tendencies related to our unique biology and disposition, and by the environmental messages we receive about how to handle anxiety. In considering the last factor, it is helpful to consider our childhood environments.

As our brains develop during childhood, we hear messages from our caregivers and the world around us about how we should handle anxiety. Unfortunately, many of these messages communicate that we are wrong in the

136 • mindfulness skills for trauma and PTSD

assessment of our own experiences, that it is not brave or strong to feel fear, or that we should not cry or express distress. Hearing these messages as a child can result in struggles to manage stress and anxiety in adulthood.

We also learn how to manage anxiety from the models that we observe in our caregivers or others. For instance, we might have had a parent who yelled when anxious, or one who "bottled up" emotions rather than expressing them. With these sorts of models of how to manage anxiety, it is not surprising that many of us enter adulthood without effective skills for handling fear or worry. Fortunately, we can learn more effective ways to manage anxiety as adults— essentially reparenting ourselves in this domain to become stronger and more skilled.

RESEARCH HIGHLIGHT What Happens in the Brain During Posttraumatic Anxiety and Recovery?

UNDERSTANDING HOW the brain becomes stuck in anxious patterns after trauma may help us know that anxious symptoms are in fact common adaptations to trauma, rather than any sort of character deficit. It may also help to reflect that these responses are deeply biological—not made-up ideas that one can simply turn off or let go. Research demonstrates that mindfulness practices can retrain our brains to respond differently to situations that spark anxiety.

Fear is a biological process that is usually automatic and outside of our conscious awareness, and may reflect brain circuitry that evolved over time to keep us safe in dangerous environments.[120] After trauma, we experience changes in the brain. Our brains develop an attentional bias, in which we experience a reduced capacity to process information that is ambiguous or nonthreatening.[121] This attentional bias makes it more likely that we will interpret neutral stimuli as threatening.[122] When fear systems are overactivated, other brain regions are less able to control them,[123] or to engage cognitive, emotional, and behavioral responses to manage anxiety. In sum, research demonstrates that trauma often produces overactivity in regions that monitor potential threats, along with underactivity in brain regions that regulate perceptions of threat and emotional responses. This pattern may manifest as anxiety.

The good news is that both mindfulness and psychotherapy can reduce anxiety by changing our brain activity and systems. Both mindfulness practices and psychotherapy can modify brain circuits related to anxiety, and diminish brain abnormalities linked with anxiety—in essence, rewiring the brain.[124] For instance, following cognitive-behavior therapy, people suffering from spider phobia had less activity in the amygdala—a change linked with their own perceptions of fewer anxiety symptoms.[125]

Different healing approaches correspond to changes in activity and blood flow in distinct brain areas.[126] Psychotherapy increases the involvement and activity in the brain's frontal regions, including the anterior cingulate cortex, which can help us manage anxiety,[127] and can also produce changes in the amygdala and hippocampus.[128] After a person takes medications for anxiety, brain regions involved in assessing environmental threats become less overactive. These two approaches to reducing anxiety are sometimes referred to as "top-down" and "bottom-up."[129] Changing patterns of thinking may enable the brain to develop efficient connections among brain regions that assess and manage responses to potential threats,[130] transformations that can result in less anxiety.

Mindfulness practices can also reduce anxiety by altering brain activity. Following mindfulness practices, participants often report feeling less anxious, and these reductions in subjective levels of anxiety correspond to changes in the brain. For instance, one mindfulness study[131] involved four 20-minute sessions that emphasized paying attention to the feeling of breathing and bodily sensations.

After each session, participants indicated that they felt less anxious. The reductions in anxiety were associated with activation in the ventromedial prefrontal cortex and the anterior cingulate cortex—brain regions related to "executive control" over worrying, thoughts, and emotions.

Mindfulness Practices for Anxiety

Mindfulness practices are powerful tools for reducing anxiety. When we cultivate mindfulness for the ways that anxiety emerges and passes, we begin to see anxiety as a temporary condition rather than as a reflection of character. Mindfully and compassionately noticing the anxiety itself, along with the judgments and interpretations that maintain it, can advance our healing. In addition, practicing different mindfulness skills for anxiety builds confidence, as we learn that there are in fact concrete strategies that we can implement to feel better and to heal.

There are several different ways to practice mindfulness for anxiety. It is very effective to practice mindful relaxation exercises consistently in a preventive way. For instance, a daily practice of mindful breathing or the body scan (Chapter 1) seems to lower our baseline levels of anxiety, so that we become more calm and resilient when stress arises.

During times when we feel a small amount of anxiety (that is, we feel anxious, but not overwhelmed by the anxiety), it is often helpful to try to locate and relax the bodily sensations that are linked to the anxiety (see Chapter 3), or to pay attention to the anxiety in a curious and kind way. During moments where we do feel overwhelmed by anxiety or panic, grounding (Chapter 5) is an especially helpful technique. Because panic is often accompanied by disturbing physical sensations, such as difficulty breathing, we may benefit most from distracting ourselves or by choosing a practice that decreases attention to the body parts that are activated (for instance, attending to objects in the room, or to body parts that feel comfortable or neutral, such as your feet). However, progressive muscle relaxation (Practice #2 below, Tense and Release) may also help us calm down when we are panicking.

Although it may not be possible to control whether and when anxiety arises, we can develop the capacity to respond to it more effectively. Mindfulness practices show benefits in reducing overall levels of anxiety, as well as anxious responses to specific stressful situations. The amount and consistency of mindfulness practice corresponds to reported reductions in anxiety.[132] In other words, the more we practice mindfulness, the more we are able to handle anxiety effectively.

Practice #1: Circle Breathing

Circle breathing[133] facilitates smooth and gentle breathing to promote relaxation. When we feel anxious, our breathing can speed up or become shallow. We might notice that we are holding our breath, or not exhaling fully before taking the next breath. Sometimes breathing feels choppy or as if it gets stuck. Our breathing can reflect a sense of being tense or on guard. The good news is that changing our breathing can shift our emotional states.

Think for a moment about breathing in and out. Those two parts might seem distinct and opposite, or as if they proceed in different directions. Circle breathing connects these two parts and minimizes the transitions. Both parts of the breathing process form a single entity as the inhale flows seamlessly into the exhale, and then back to the inhale.

To prepare for the circle breathing exercise, find a comfortable spot where you are unlikely to be disturbed. Set aside approximately 10 minutes, and consider turning off any electronic devices that might distract you. You can close your eyes, or keep them open. As with any mindfulness exercise, it is normal to have distracting thoughts emerge. Try to observe distracting thoughts in a simple, gentle manner (rather than investigating them further) before returning your attention to your breathing. Distracting thoughts can be frustrating when you are trying to concentrate. If frustration or other emotions arise, notice them before returning your focus to your breath. If self-criticism occurs, gently observe that as well before returning your focus to the breath. Remember that returning your attention to your chosen intention is itself an important event—sometimes called the "magic moment"[134]—and is working the muscle of mindfulness. Try to encourage yourself to have an open and curious attitude towards the exercise and your experience while practicing it.

Step 1: Imagine your breath in the shape of a circle. On your next inhale, imagine that you are moving from the very bottom of the circle, up along one side. As you become full of air, you approach the top of the circle. Then, as seamlessly as possible, transition from the inhale to the exhale as you imagine rounding over the top of the circle and coming down along the other side. Make your way down the side of the circle as you exhale. Try to exhale all the way as you come down to the bottom of the circle. As you reach the bottom, prepare to transition from exhaling to inhaling as smoothly as you can.

Try to keep a steady pace of the air flow, and refrain from holding your breath at the top of the circle or pausing without any breath at the bottom. When challenges arise, notice them mindfully and try not to judge them. You may feel bumps, tension, or discomfort, or you may find yourself holding your breath or pausing when you have run out of air. Remember that if fear, anxiety, self-criticism, or other thoughts or sensations arise, you can notice them as gently and kindly as possible before returning your focus to the breath and the circle image, as illustrated in Figure 4.1.

Figure 4.1: Circle Breathing

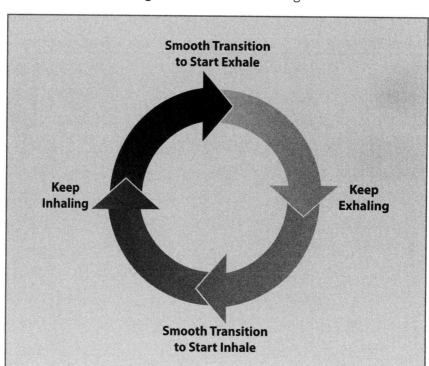

Step 2: After you have practiced circle breathing and feel fairly comfortable with the exercise, you can enhance this skill by increasing the length of both the inhale and exhale. Visualize lengthening both sides of the circle while continuing to follow the smooth arcs and transitions between in-breaths and out-breaths and back again. During an in-breath, begin to observe how many counts you can notice on both the in-breath and the out-breath. Gradually increase the counts for each breath until you reach 20 counts on the in-breath and 20 counts on the out-breath. The in-breath starts at the bottom center of the circle; proceeds smoothly up the curve of the circle; transitions as smoothly as possible to the out-breath at the top of the circle;

descends during the exhale down along the opposite curve; and shifts back into the in-breath gently at the bottom to start again.

When you are ready to end the exercise, let yourself breathe normally for a minute, without trying to change or adjust anything. Observe the feeling that you have right now in your body, and notice any emotions or thoughts that arise.

Practice #2: Tense and Release

This exercise involves tensing and releasing your muscles in a step-by-step sequence that spans the whole body. Tensing and releasing muscles promotes the body's relaxation response, and is most effective when directing mindful attention to the sensations of tension and relaxation. This practice is sometimes called "progressive muscle relaxation" or PMR.

This exercise takes approximately 15 minutes. First, you will need a comfortable spot where you feel as though you can relax without being disturbed. A seated posture in a couch or chair can work well. Many people find PMR to be so relaxing that they fall asleep. Using PMR at bedtime to promote sleep can be a useful strategy; however, to gain the practice's maximum benefit for reducing anxiety, it is important to also try it when you are unlikely to fall asleep. You can wear any type of clothing, as long as it is comfortable; however, it is important to remove your shoes so that your feet can have a full range of motion when tensing and releasing them. It is best not to practice PMR right after eating, because you will be tensing your stomach muscles. Do not practice PMR when you are intoxicated from alcohol or other drugs. Use your best judgment about how much to tense and release your muscles. You should be able to observe a strong difference between the tense and release components of the exercise, however you do not want to tense your muscles so strongly that you feel pain or injure yourself. If you have any concerns about the suitability of PMR for your own body, or how PMR might interact with any health conditions or injuries, it is best to ask a medical provider before beginning the practice.

As in any mindfulness exercise, thoughts and feelings are likely to arise. Try to notice them as they emerge, and then refocus your attention on the bodily sensations of tensing and releasing your emotions. You may also observe thoughts and feelings about the exercise. Common mental distractions while practicing PMR include concerns or self-judgments about doing it correctly, frustration when trying to activate a specific muscle, and worry about whether it will work. If you find yourself having these thoughts, you can use your mindfulness skills to observe them as events that rise and fall, and as an opportunity to refocus on your bodily sensations. If you do find yourself falling asleep, you can simply notice this and give yourself credit for having engaged this exercise and spent time practicing up until you slept.

You can keep your eyes open or closed with this exercise. If it feels comfortable, closing your eyes may help you to tune in to bodily sensations, and may reduce the possibility of being distracted by what you see. You can follow the instructions below; alternatively, there are many audio tracks of progressive muscle relaxation online that can guide you through the exercise. First, direct your attention to your breath. Count 5 long breaths. For the next 5 or 10 breaths, pay attention to how your body feels right now, in this moment, without trying to change anything. You are now ready to begin the tense-and-release sequence. Some people practice PMR from the top of the body to the bottom; others start at the bottom and work their way up. The suggestions below describe how to tense each muscle group. There are many different versions of these suggestions; these are influenced by the guidelines provided by Edmund Bourne (1995). Other instructions are readily available online.

For each of the muscle groups, you can squeeze and hold them in the "tense" position for about 5 seconds, followed by about 10 seconds of release and relaxation. You can match these processes to your breathing by squeezing as you inhale and releasing as you exhale. When tensing your muscles, engage them deliberately, but not so strongly that you risk injuring yourself. Try to notice the physical sensations when you tense the muscles and release them, as well as the differences between the two states. Some people also feel shifts in body temperature during PMR. Others find that the sensation of releasing the muscles produces an enjoyable feeling of relaxation. Even though PMR involves tensing your muscles tightly, set the intention to have a mindset towards the exercise that is gentle, caring, and curious.

1. Squint your eyes tightly shut. Feel the tension in your eyes, nose, and cheeks as you do this. Squeeze and hold for 5 seconds, then release and relax for 10 seconds.

2. Purse your lips as tightly as you can to make a point in front of your face. Imagine that you are saying the word "prune" and exaggerate it, using your whole face. Hold for 5 seconds, then release and relax for 10 seconds.

3. Open your mouth as wide as you can. Try to make a square position (rather than an "ah") so that your mouth is stretched in four different directions. Hold for 5 seconds, then release and relax for 10 seconds.

4. Raise your shoulders as high as they can go as you try to touch them to your ears. Hold for 5 seconds, then release and relax for 10 seconds.

5. Contract your chest as you bring your shoulders towards each other in front of your body. Hold for 5 seconds, then release and relax for 10 seconds.

6. Tense your back by keeping your arms by your sides as you pull the arms, shoulders, and back in towards your spine. Hold for 5 seconds, then release and relax for 10 seconds.

7. Make a bicep with your left arm as you bend the elbow. Squeeze and hold for 5 seconds, then release and relax for 10 seconds.

8. Extend your left arm, and flex your left hand as you push forward with your hand and arm. Hold for 5 seconds, then release and relax for 10 seconds.

9. Make a tight fist with your left hand. Squeeze and hold for 5 seconds, then release and relax for 10 seconds.

10. Make a bicep with your right arm as you bend the elbow. Squeeze and hold for 5 seconds, then release and relax for 10 seconds.

11. Extend your right arm, and flex your right hand as you push forward with your hand and arm. Hold for 5 seconds, then release and relax for 10 seconds.

12. Make a tight fist with your right hand. Squeeze and hold for 5 seconds, then release and relax for 10 seconds.

13. Suck in your stomach as tightly as you can. Hold for 5 seconds, then release and relax for 10 seconds.

14. Clench the muscles in your buttocks. Squeeze and hold for 5 seconds, then release and relax for 10 seconds.

15. Press your legs together as you tighten your thigh muscles. Squeeze and hold for 5 seconds, then release and relax for 10 seconds.

16. Flex your left foot as far as it will go towards your left leg. Hold for 5 seconds, then release and relax for 10 seconds.

17. Point your left toes and foot as tightly as you can. Hold for 5 seconds, then release and relax for 10 seconds.

18. Curl your left toes as tightly as you can. Scrunch them up. Hold for 5 seconds, then release and relax for 10 seconds.

19. Flex your right foot as far as it will go towards your right leg. Hold for 5 seconds, then release and relax for 10 seconds.

20. Point your right toes and foot as tightly as you can. Hold for 5 seconds, then release and relax for 10 seconds.

21. Curl your right toes as tightly as you can. Scrunch them up. Hold for 5 seconds, then release and relax for 10 seconds.

22. End by taking 10 deep breaths. Pay attention to the feelings and sensations throughout your body as you inhale and exhale. Notice the feeling of not doing anything, and allowing the chair, floor, or bed to hold you up completely. When you stand, get up slowly.

When first learning PMR, it is helpful to practice two times per day—especially because you may fall asleep during one of the practice sessions. You do not need to be feeling anxious at the time that you practice PMR. It may be easier to concentrate and to learn the skill if you first practice it when you feel relatively calm. The first few times that you practice PMR may be the most challenging, but it will get easier the more you practice. As you develop your comfort with the skill, you can build up to squeezing the muscles for a few more seconds before releasing them.

Many people report that at first they have trouble engaging specific muscles, and that they feel inclined to tense their whole bodies or larger muscle groups. This challenge seems to get easier as people practice PMR; in fact, learning how to distinguish between muscles is part of learning the PMR skill. Over time, you will learn how to use your mind to engage and relax your muscles, and you can then implement this skill during times when you are feeling anxious. By carefully attending to the sensation of muscle relaxation, you can encode it into your memory, where it will be available to you at any time.

Practice #3: Normalize and Neutralize

When learning to reappraise posttraumatic anxiety as normal and initially adaptive, it can be helpful to begin with a practice of mindful self-inquiry. As you become used to seeing anxious symptoms in a new light, you can start to notice them in the moment, and to engage your reappraisal skills after anxiety arises.

The following exercise takes about 10 or 15 minutes. It may help to keep your eyes open if you feel that thinking about the trauma might be distressing for you. Begin by checking in with yourself, and asking yourself how you feel in your mind and body in the present moment. Allow yourself to "just be" for a few moments, exactly as you are, without trying to change or fix anything. It may help to practice some mindful breathing to connect to your feelings in the present moment. Next, notice what comes up for you as you consider the following questions and ideas:

- In what way are my anxious symptoms an understandable response to what I have experienced?
- How did my anxiety symptoms initially serve me in some way? What was their adaptive function during the trauma?
- Other people have endured similar difficulties to what I experienced. What are some of the most common emotional responses to that type of trauma?
- When I think of my anxiety as a normal response, how is that different from the other ways that I have thought about it?

- How does it feel in my mind and body to view my anxiety as a normal response to what I endured?
- Does learning about the biology of trauma and anxiety (for instance, reading the information in the beginning of this chapter and in Chapter 2) help me to view my anxiety symptoms as understandable and expected consequences of the stressful circumstances that I experienced?
- Is the anxiety arising from inside myself (as a reaction to thoughts, feelings, and memories), from an external circumstance, or from a combination?
- Are there feelings underneath the anxiety, like anger, sadness, or pain? Can I allow myself to feel those feelings, view them as normal, and care for myself as I approach them?
- When anxiety arises, can I tell myself that the anxiety is understandable, residual from the trauma, and not itself a cause for alarm? How does it feel to view it this way?
- Do I notice any changes in my thoughts, feelings, or in my body after I practice mindfulness or self-compassion for anxiety?

When you are ready to end the exercise, take a few breaths to reconnect to your physical sensations and to ground yourself in this moment, as distinct from your thoughts about the past. Remind yourself that you are in the process of learning new ways to manage anxious feelings. Although research studies demonstrate that reappraisal is associated with reductions in anxiety, every person is different. It is normal to have this type of mental work trigger other thoughts and feelings related to the trauma. If this occurs, try to notice them briefly, and then return your focus to these specific questions. However, if the thoughts and feelings are very distressing, it is best to end this exercise and to focus on caring for yourself in the present moment. You can distract yourself, or implement other mindfulness skills to reduce your distress.

You can also practice reappraising anxiety about other life experiences that are less upsetting than the trauma you endured. Try engaging reappraisal when confronted with other stressful circumstances in your life, and asking yourself the question "What is another way to interpret this event or my experience in this moment—one that might generate a more positive feeling about myself, another person, or the world?"

RESEARCH HIGHLIGHT How Do Mindfulness Practices Reduce Anxiety?

THERE IS STRONG evidence demonstrating that mindfulness-based approaches are associated with decreased anxiety.[135] Mindfulness meditation appears to be especially effective.[136] Research studies indicate that practicing relaxation or mindfulness skills results in fewer anxiety symptoms, fewer and less severe panic attacks, and the maintenance of mindfulness practices among most individuals 3 years after mindfulness training.[137]

The mindfulness-based practices in this chapter each have an evidence base in the scientific literature. For instance, deep breathing reduces oxygen consumption and enhances the parasympathetic nervous system, processes that help calm the mind and promote a sense of control over the body.[138] Intentionally breathing deeply may help shift the default setting of the nervous system to have it synchronize more effectively with the brain, heart, and lungs[139]. Breathing practices can also enhance emotion regulation processes and reduce anxiety.[140]

Progressive muscle relaxation (described above) is associated with substantial reductions in anxiety and stress.[141] For example, one research study found that two sessions of progressive muscle relaxation resulted in lower heart rates and cortisol (stress hormone) levels, perceptions of less anxiety and stress, and greater levels of relaxation.[142]

Cognitive reappraisal reduces both emotional and physical feelings of anxiety, and decreases activity in the brain's fear circuit.[143] Trying out positive reappraisals for situations that provoke anxiety activates brain regions involved in regulating anxiety.[144] After practicing reappraisal, people report feeling less anxious, a shift that corresponds to the way that the brain "recruits" additional brain regions to help regulate anxiety.[145] Reappraisal may also reduce depression after stressful experiences.[146] For instance, framing symptoms of PTSD as normal can facilitate recovery from trauma.[147]

Guided imagery can also reduce anxiety and stress levels.[148] The guided imagery exercise in Chapter 1 promotes the mindfulness goal of *decentering*, because we observe our anxiety as a transitory phenomenon occurring next to us, rather than a reflection of who we are. Decentering—sometimes called *reperceiving*—reflects a shift in attitude towards thoughts and feelings. Instead of identifying strongly with thoughts and feelings and considering them to truly reflect our character or reality,[149] decentering builds the capacity to notice and label both thoughts and feelings as temporary states.[150] Research indicates that this decentering process is one of the key ways that mindfulness practice exerts its positive effects.[151]

In addition, acceptance, loving-kindness, and self-compassion practices can decrease anxiety.[152] There is compelling research evidence that this particular type of meditation reduces both perceptions of anxiety as well as physiological stress responses.[153] Repeating loving-kindness phrases has been shown to increase self-compassion,[154] and it may cultivate positive emotions that reduce the negative loop of anxiety and result in new emotional and physiological patterns.[155]

Practice #4: Walk Alongside Your Fear

In this visualization practice, you will engage mental imagery to imagine yourself walking next to your anxiety.

Find a comfortable setting where you can sit or lie down, and where you can practice this visualization without being disturbed. It may be most helpful to read the full visualization description, and then to implement it with your eyes closed if you feel comfortable. As you begin to imagine the setting for this visualization, set the intention to engage your five senses within the scene as vividly as you can. You may have thoughts or reactions in response to your own experiences or to the visualization exercise, and you can notice these with the same sort of curious approach that you bring to the anxiety itself. If distracting thoughts, emotions, or physical sensations arise, notice them gently and return your attention to the imagery practice. As you begin to imagine the setting for this visualization, set the intention to engage your five senses within the scene as vividly as you can.

Imagine that you are walking on a forest path at some short distance from a river—the river of your anxiety. To put yourself into the scene, take stock of the smells and sounds around you. In this forest, there is nothing threatening that can harm you, and you are safe as you walk along the path. It is likely that you are wearing comfortable clothing and hiking shoes. Take a moment to imagine what you have on and the bodily sensations that you might have. Perhaps the sun is shining on you, or you might feel a gentle breeze. Sounds arise intermittently—birdsongs, wind, your own footsteps, and the rushing sounds of the river. You see many colors: different shades of green trees and plants; the colors of the sky and clouds; variations of brown in tree bark and earth; and the river. The river has clear water that reflects the surrounding scene and is punctuated with white bubbles as it navigates the rocks.

You are close enough to the river that you can observe it closely, but you are also at enough of a distance that you can observe a good stretch of its length. Consider the river to be your anxiety. Notice the motion of the river. How fast is it going, and in what direction? Are there spots where the water collects or becomes stuck? Do you see any bubbles or gurgles along the surface of the water as it streams over rocks? Are there places where you can see the plants, trees, or sky reflected in the water? Notice that you are not the river, but an observer.

Next, imagine how the shades of your own anxiety might manifest in the river. If your anxiety were the river, would it move at a steady pace, or proceed in fits and starts? Are there some spots on the anxiety river that seem calm, and others that are swirling with activity? Do the twists and turns resolve predictably? What are some of its colors and shapes? If you see a pocket of agitation, take the opportunity to observe it more closely to see how it is constructed and how it unfolds. You might notice the way that the same water that is bubbly in one turn of the river flows over rocks and becomes calmer in the next section. You may also perceive a contrast between the agitation on the surface and the deeper and stiller waters underneath.

You do not need to do anything to change the flow of the river. Instead, just notice as much as you can about it, but without touching it or entering the water. Just let the river be. Rest a moment in your feeling of separateness from the river—the sense that you can observe quite a lot about it from a comfortable distance. If you have any reactions to the river, such as thinking that it is too big, unattractive, or moving faster than you would like, imagine those reactions as also being part of the river, rather than inside you. See those reactions as a secondary rivulet streaming off to the side of the river, as you continue to walk along next to it as an observer.

When you are ready to end the exercise, first stay engaged in the scene as you direct your attention away from the river. There is a whole forest out there, and much to see besides the river. Take a moment and notice the trees and plants—the leaves and branches creating numerous shapes and shadows. Tune back in to the complex sounds of the birds around you. Feel the temperature of the air, and the subtle breezes around you. You might notice how you are feeling in your body—perhaps you have a pleasant sensation in your muscles after having walked for a comfortable amount of time. See the path before you, and the topography that stretches to the horizon. Take a few breaths. Take a moment to check in with yourself, to see how you are feeling emotionally and physically in this moment. As you take the next set of breaths, let those breaths transition you back from your sense of being within the scene to your sense of being in your body right now, in this chair or room. After you open your eyes, take another few breaths, and check in with yourself again. Give yourself credit for trying something new, and for addressing your anxiety in a different way than you might have done before.

Practice #5: Loving-Kindness for Fear, Hyperarousal, and Anxiety

Anxiety symptoms are painful and distressing. It can be helpful to cultivate care for ourselves when learning new ways to manage anxiety. If we pause to imagine someone we care about as they endure distressing anxiety symptoms, it seems natural to feel care or compassion for that person. Many people find it much harder to find compassion about their own anxiety.

When we hold feelings of fear and anxiety with love, kindness, and compassion, they feel a bit different, and easier to handle. Common self-judgments about anxiety as silly or stupid can prevent us from treating ourselves kindly when we feel caught in anxiety. Sometimes it can be effective to notice the ways that self-criticism most likely originates from a caring place; on a deeper level, it arises from a wish that the anxiety and related suffering will end. However, the self-criticism can make the anxiety feel worse. Practicing self-compassion or loving-kindness can help us heal both the anxiety and our self-criticism about it. In fact, noticing self-criticism about anxiety can serve as a cue to practice the loving-kindness phrases ("May I be safe. May I be happy. May I be healthy. May I live with ease.") or another mindfulness technique.

We can learn to manage anxiety in a way that feels both caring and effective. It may help to reflect upon the ways that you might comfort someone else who is coping with anxiety—with a focus on providing a sense of care and under-standing, rather than trying to change the person's approach to their difficul-ties. The next step is to redirect that same quality of care towards ourselves.

In addition to generating feelings of care or compassion, verbally articu-lating statements that express them can enhance their impact. The statements will likely resonate best if they feel genuine; that is, true to your own man-ner of speaking and relating. We can incorporate caring self-talk that provides acknowledgement, care, and soothing for anxiety and related suffering. For instance, we might cultivate self-compassion by telling ourselves something along the lines of, "I am sorry you have to go through this. It was bad enough that you had to endure the original trauma, and now it's challenging that it takes a lot of energy to learn how to manage and calm these symptoms. What you are feeling is completely normal given what you experienced, but it is still very upsetting. I am going to help you as much as I can to get through this."

After trauma, it may feel odd to try to treat ourselves kindly. Traumatic situations may have contributed to the feeling that we can never relax or feel as though things are OK. The idea of accepting our own feelings as normal and deserving of care might feel unsafe, or just strange and new. During the trauma, it is unlikely that anyone was available and offering care and comfort. Building new, caring voices can address this level of recovery. Finding a caring voice within may reflect a level of parental care that we never experienced. However, we all have the capacity to access this level of caring towards ourselves, and to practice it. If the feeling is strange or uncomfortable, it may work to direct some caring towards that strangeness or discomfort.

The classic loving-kindness meditation, "May I be safe. May I be happy. May I be healthy. May I live with ease," has been shown to be effective in helping people to access a sense of caring for themselves. The practice of this meditation involves silently repeating these phrases over and over, for a period of several minutes. All of these wishes form powerful antidotes to the fear, discomfort, and struggle of anxiety and other trauma-related symptoms. They cultivate the part of us that genuinely wishes ourselves well—a part that can calm distress.

To practice loving-kindness for anxiety, begin by taking a moment to tune in to how you feel right now, in this moment. Observe the physical sensations and thoughts that arise. It may be helpful to trace the rise and fall of a few breaths. After a few minutes, begin to repeat the phrases to yourself. To the extent that you can, say them with a positive intention of kindness towards yourself. As in other mindfulness exercises, it is quite normal for your mind to wander. When this happens, bring as much of your attention as you can back to the repetition of the phrases, over and over. During the moment of noticing that your mind has wandered, you can try to notice the wandering and return your mind to the phrases using a kind and gentle manner.

As you consider the phrases and your positive intention, you might try being mindful of the ways that these phrases reflect positive wishes about anxiety. Each of the phrases can express a dimension of recovery from anxiety. You might focus on wishes for freedom from physical or mental danger, for example.[156] The loving-kindness statements express kind hopes for freedom from all aspects of anxiety—danger, perceptions of danger, emotional suffering, and physical suffering. The last statement, "may I live with ease," also imparts a positive wish to experience life in a manner that is calm, relaxed, and pleasant.

When you are ready to complete your practice, take a moment to check in with yourself about your feelings in this moment. You can also acknowledge that you put time and effort into the practice. Observing the feeling in your mind and body after loving-kindness practice can make it easier to return to that sensibility throughout the day and in difficult moments. Loving-kindness practice and self-compassionate statements form powerful remedies for the fear, discomfort, and struggle of anxiety and other trauma-related symptoms. They cultivate the part of us that genuinely wishes ourselves well—a part that can help calm distress.

In Their Own Words

My best friend always says, "Worry is not preparation." This has led me to wonder why we worry instead of hope, and why our giant brains that typically do so much for us, like helping us breathe when we're asleep, work against us when it comes to imagining our futures. So now I think of worry as a call to action to breathe, to be in the present. Our brains are amazing. They are our most powerful employees. They just need some guidance. So, I am working on, every time I envision a catastrophic future, either 30 seconds or 30 years from now, replacing that vision with a positive version of it. It's a long practice, but it calms me immediately.

Anxiety is hard, and usually very unpleasant. It also signals a need: the need to mobilize to keep ourselves safe; the need to care for our feelings after trauma; the need to relearn how to relax; or the need to cultivate a greater sense of well-being. If we do not pay attention, it is easy to misinterpret the signal of anxiety, and to respond as if it always indicates danger in this moment. A mindful approach to anxiety helps us uncover its different components—such as sadness, a need for control, a physical habit of being tense, or our judgment about what anxiety means—and defuse the ways that these components interact. By addressing one piece of anxiety at a time with interest, patience, and kindness, we become more confident and steady as we face anything that arises.

Chapter 7

FORGE AHEAD GENTLY: MINDFULNESS PRACTICES FOR AVOIDANCE

YOU MIGHT HAVE the urge to avoid the chapter on avoidance. To reduce our suffering after trauma, we often avoid reminders about it to the extent that we can. Because avoidance can often be effective in the short term, it can become a comfortable habit, and one to which we become attached or which we feel that we need. However, avoidance keeps us stuck within our current set of emotional experiences and behaviors, and can impede trauma recovery. Avoidance can provide some comfort and respite, but over time we will feel more free when avoidance becomes less necessary. We can gradually reduce avoidance in a gentle way, by touching only a little bit of avoided material at a time, and by supporting ourselves in the process.

A mindful approach to avoidance involves care and curiosity. We can explore how our avoidance works, experiment with small changes, and observe how those changes affect us. We may fear that shifting our avoidance patterns will open the floodgates of trauma and negative emotions. It may help to know that we do not have to relive the trauma or feel everything at once in order to heal. Instead, we can approach difficult thoughts and feelings in small doses, so that we gradually build more comfort and confidence.

Avoidance brings relief. We experience that relief as a physical sense of release, calmness and ease. Imagine for a moment that you see someone on the street who treated you poorly at your last job. Your heart rate increases, your muscles tighten, you start to sweat, your mind races, and you feel generally shaken up. Then, you duck into a coffee shop, and the person passes by without seeing you. Phew! You relax, your heartbeat slows, and you feel cooler and calmer.

There is wisdom in avoidance. It makes sense to avoid people, places, or things that will trigger trauma-related feelings, as well as potential sources of new pain. It can even be adaptive to distance ourselves from painful thoughts and feelings so that we can get through the day or survive in dangerous situations. Avoidance reflects our drive for self-preservation. However, over time, avoidance can take the shape of shutting down or narrowing our focus, and it can perpetuate PTSD and depression.

Avoidance takes many forms. We so desperately want relief from painful feelings that we will do anything to distract ourselves and keep them at bay: watching hours of TV shows or movies, reading all the time, playing video games, gambling, never being alone, trying not to sleep in order to escape from nightmares, or overworking. We might avoid people, places, or things related to past trauma. Avoidance can arise through potentially beneficial behaviors as well, such as immersing ourselves in current events, exercising, or helping others. Even worry can function as a form of avoidance if we occupy ourselves with future problems in order to shield ourselves from our current feelings.

We may also try to mentally distance ourselves from painful thoughts and feelings, or even from feeling anything. This might take the form of *dissociation*— mentally "spacing out" or detaching ourselves from reality. We may cope with trauma by denying its reality, or by suppressing information about it from conscious awareness. We might also try to numb out or escape our feelings through overeating, engaging in romantic relationships or sexual activity in which we would not otherwise take part, or by using alcohol and other drugs. To the extent that any of these behaviors function to keep ourselves from undesired thoughts and feelings, they are avoidance strategies.

Although we often think of avoidance as related to our *external* activities (such as avoiding seeing specific people or going to certain places), our avoidance of *internal* experiences may play a larger role in PTSD and in trauma recovery. The ability to accept our own emotions is related to having fewer PTSD symptoms, and plays a stronger role than the amount of trauma we experience or the extent of our negative emotions.[157] Avoiding feelings can lead to a general emotional numbness that might lessen painful feelings but also distances us from neutral or pleasant feelings as well.

The term *experiential avoidance* refers to the unwillingness to experience unpleasant emotions, thoughts, bodily sensations, and memories, and to efforts to alter those experiences.[158] Experiential avoidance may worsen mental health because it requires directing some mental energy towards the unpleasant, avoided material; because it establishes pathways in the brain that maintain fear; and because it can severely limit our activities.[159] Mindfulness-based approaches to PTSD and depression appear to work in part by reducing experiential avoidance[160] and by cultivating the ability to remain present with difficult feelings.

Avoidance is closely related to *numbing* (having trouble experiencing positive feelings; feeling distant from other people, and losing interest in important activities), and to *dissociation* (disconnection among different parts of our thoughts, emotions, and experiences). However, there is evidence that they operate separately. Whereas avoidance usually limits thoughts, feelings, and experiences to a smaller repertoire, dissociation and numbing involve a broader separation from our feelings and other experiences. Avoidance, numbing, and dissociation also each contribute independently to alcohol and other drug use.[161]

Mindfulness skills that reconnect us with a fuller range of internal and external experiences can benefit each of these symptoms; however, they each have some specific features that may respond best to different practices. For instance, avoidance appears especially helped by exposure,[162] whereas numbing may improve through reconnection to bodily sensations. Exercises for working with avoidance are included in this chapter; practices for working with numbing are included in Chapter 10; and skills for managing dissociation are discussed in Chapter 11.

It can be tempting to judge ourselves for our avoidance. As we learn about the problems associated with avoidance, we may start to think that, "Avoidance is bad, and because I engage in avoidance, I am bad too, and probably to blame for having PTSD." Instead, I encourage you to recognize avoidance as normal, human, and often the wisest choice for many stressful situations, and to develop curiosity about avoidance and how to work with it. If self-criticism arises, we can take the opportunity to observe it mindfully and to practice self-compassion. All of us have challenging mental patterns, and we have the capacity to work with them gently and effectively.

When Is Avoidance Helpful, and When Is It Harmful?

It can be useful to differentiate *problematic avoidance* from *unproblematic avoidance*. The distinction is important because we might have the impression that we must do everything that scares us, such as skydiving or bungee jumping. However, we do not have to do everything that scares us to be happy or to recover from trauma. It is clearly wise to avoid toxic waste, perpetrators of violence and abuse, and sharks and grizzly bears, as they can worsen our health without providing any lasting benefit. After painfully ending a romantic relationship, the urge to cancel a Valentine's Day cruise may be the wisest and most caring course of action.

Avoidance is unproblematic if it does not interfere with our health, our values, or our relationships. If you avoid violent movies because they give you nightmares, and doing so does not compromise your well-being, values, or connections to other people, then it is not a problem. If you are experiencing difficult feelings that interfere with sleep, you may find that distracting yourself for a while helps you relax. Distraction may also be a valuable short-term way to cope with urges to self-harm; however, some level of self-awareness is also needed to remove dangerous objects and to call a crisis hotline, 911, or visit an emergency room if needed.

During trauma, avoidance may not be exactly unproblematic, but it may be the best course of action at the time. For instance, a high school student who identifies as a sexual minority, such as gay, lesbian, bisexual, or transgender, might cope with a hostile, homophobic environment by avoiding the worst bullies and the places where they gather, and by pushing away painful thoughts and feelings in order to minimize additional traumatization and to concentrate in class. In areas impacted by war or high levels of community violence, avoiding certain places, thoughts, and feelings may promote survival. Unfortunately, avoidance that helps us in the short term (for instance, distraction in order to tolerate severe emotional distress) may generate patterns that harm us in the long term.

Because avoidance works extremely well in the short term, it is a very popular strategy. It is also rather sneaky. Even after avoidance has outgrown its initial function of getting through the trauma itself, it stays around and can appear to be helping us, rather than hurting us. The reason to decrease avoidance is that it can grow and grow until it takes over. We might avoid every person who has the same hair color or gender as someone who perpetrated violence—or even refrain from getting close to people in general. Survivors of sexual abuse or assault commonly avoid preventive health appointments, such as pap smears or mammograms.[163] Although this behavior may temporarily reduce anxiety—because it could prevent trauma "triggers" like being undressed in front of strangers[164]—missing health appointments could hurt our health in the long term.

Avoidance is problematic if it impedes our ability to recover from depression, anxiety, or PTSD, compromises our health, gets in the way of living a full life, conflicts with our values, or prevents us from connecting to other people. For instance, if after being mugged one night at 9:00 P.M. in a neighborhood that generally has low levels of violence, I decline all evening invitations and do not go outside after dark for the next 5 years, my avoidance is likely to be problematic. I might miss cultural events—music, theater, or celebrations—that are linked to my values and happiness. My relationships with friends and family members would probably suffer, and my isolation could make me feel more depressed.

Avoidance can be self-perpetuating. When we choose to avoid something, we experience a sense of relief that signals to us that on an immediate, physiological level, we made the right choice. It can be very hard to override the urge to avoid and the release of tension that it brings. After a mugging, making a decision to stay inside probably brings an immediate sense of calm, and reinforces the belief that the decision has increased safety and well-being. The problem with continuing avoidance patterns is that we refrain from generating—and learning from—alternative evidence. Having a positive or neutral experience of going out at night provides a lived experience of relearning that it can be safe and enjoyable. Without exposure to situations that might trigger trauma, the behavior pattern (and related PTSD symptoms) often remains.

Perhaps the most important drawback to avoidance is that we miss out on opportunities to heal. Avoidance keeps us stuck in the same limited assortment of thoughts, emotions, and behaviors—and it can even increase our experience of PTSD symptoms.[165] By shifting our relationship to avoidance, we can develop new skills and confidence in our ability to handle challenges.

RESEARCH HIGHLIGHT What's the Problem With Avoidance?

TRAUMA SURVIVORS COMMONLY assume that avoiding trauma-related thoughts and feelings is helpful.[166] However, the evidence shows that experiential avoidance—the reluctance to have difficult feelings, thoughts, sensations, or memories, and efforts to change them[167]—contributes to general emotional distress, PTSD, and depression.[168] In fact, suppressing thoughts seems to tighten the connection between PTSD and negative moods after trauma.[169]

Avoidance also seems to bias our interpretations of the world around us. In one study, researchers asked 108 undergraduate students to infer emotions from vignettes describing everyday events. Those with high levels of experiential avoidance demonstrated a bias towards inferring negative emotions.[170] However, this bias appears to be reversible. Another research study demonstrated that trauma survivors' attentional bias towards negative information diminished after they completed therapy to reduce their PTSD symptoms.[171]

Besides contributing to negative moods and PTSD, avoidance is related to problematic alcohol use after trauma[172] and to risky sexual behaviors.[173] Avoidance also contributes to emotional numbing, or the inability to feel much of anything.[174] When we avoid feelings, we might not really know what we feel at all. This is problematic, because the ability to distinguish different emotions is linked to lower levels of fear, worry, rumination, and depression.[175]

Avoidance preserves our mental associations between the trauma and other aspects of our experience—associations that maintain and expand our fear structures. PTSD involves resistance to extinction learning,[176] an obstacle that may even influence PTSD to a greater extent than trauma experiences themselves.[177] Our ability to experience thoughts and feelings is inversely associated with the extent of our avoidance symptoms.[178]

Reducing avoidance through exposure—that is, systematically facing trauma-related material—is very effective.[179] Exposure to a new experience enhances fear extinction in the brain,[180] so that we can become less fearful. Reducing avoidance appears to be a key mechanism through which mindfulness skills improve well-being.[181]

Avoidance may prevent us from growing and learning after trauma. One study[182] found that trauma survivors who reported high levels of distress but low levels of avoidance found the most posttraumatic growth and meaning in life, whereas those who engaged in high levels of avoidance described less growth after trauma. It seems clear that feeling our feelings, rather than avoiding them, helps us to move through trauma and to build new strength and wisdom.

Learning and Unlearning Avoidance

After trauma, we commonly develop a structure of fear in our minds—an assortment of thoughts and ideas that are associated with each other and tend to occur together. We rarely form this structure intentionally; however, it is quite intricate. It includes painful memories, uncomfortable emotional experiences, interpretations about the trauma and about ourselves, and assumptions about the world and other people. Avoidance plays a key role in maintaining our fear structure. It keeps everything in its place. However, it also prevents us from remodeling the architecture in ways that better serve us.

Our fear structures contain objective information related to the trauma.

However, they also encompass a great deal of material that is linked with the trauma in our minds only. This feature of fear arises from the nature of human learning—how we make connections and generalizations as we process the world around us. The smell of charcoal and lighter fluid on a summer day is not tantalizing by itself, but often seems delicious because we associate it with barbecue. The association is automatic, involuntary, and usually occurs outside of our conscious awareness.

This phenomenon is called *classical conditioning*—the same one that the researcher Ivan Pavlov (1927) demonstrated by training dogs to salivate when he rang a bell right before presenting them with their food. The bell and the food became linked—paired—in the dogs' minds. There was nothing special about the bell to begin with; rather, it was a neutral stimulus that became associated with the food through experience. The dogs then generalized the bell to other similar sounds, so that those sounds also made them salivate. The more similar to the original bell the signal was, the more likely that the dogs would salivate upon hearing it. Classical conditioning works across animal species, including humans.

In our minds, we match the trauma to a range of contextual features that may or may not have had anything to do with the trauma itself, and experience fear in our bodies in response to these learned cues. Vietnam Veterans may have a strong aversion to palm trees or humid weather, whereas a survivor of domestic violence may feel agitated by the cologne, music, or clothing favored by a perpetrator. A car accident survivor may come to associate red cars with danger after being hit by a red car, or a person assaulted at sunset may become fearful during sunsets. Our learned fear generalizes, and we involuntarily become scared and physiologically activated even in situations that were previously neutral.[183]

We also link our thoughts during the trauma to our general beliefs about ourselves (for instance, thoughts such as, "I should have prevented this from happening," or "I am incompetent to handle anything").[184] We develop *conditioned emotional responses*, such as panicking during moments of stress because they remind us of our trauma and our inability to escape threats. Our fear structures become rigid and resistant to changes, even as the associations with them often do not reflect reality.[185]

From a learning perspective, avoidance is a form of *operant conditioning*. Whereas classical conditioning is involuntary, operant conditioning involves taking some action to influence an outcome. When we avoid something that we anticipate will be unpleasant—like going to the Department of Motor Vehicles—we are rewarded by not having the discomfort or anxiety that goes with it. Any behaviors that decrease our anxiety reinforce our avoidance, and make it more likely that we will continue to avoid it.

Once we have learned to associate different environmental cues with danger, and to avoid them, how do we unlearn those mental associations and our avoidance? For the answer, we can return to Pavlov's dogs. They could unlearn the association between the bell and the food through a process called *extinction*. After hearing the bell ring many times without the presentation of food, the dogs stopped associating it with the food. The association between the bell and the food gradually became extinct.

You might think that our human access to logic, a conscious form of reasoning that dogs lack, would enable us to recognize the associations we have between environmental cues and danger, and simply decide to extinguish our automatic responses. However, logic alone can do little to dissolve classical conditioning. Fear and fear-related learning seem to operate at a very basic and automatic biological level. We can no more decide that, "I get it. Palm trees, red cars, sunsets, or feeling stressed are not truly dangerous, so I will no longer be afraid of them from this moment forward," than we can decide not to feel sick when confronting a food that we recently ate right before vomiting. Instead we require an embodied, felt *experience* of a stimulus as safe in order to learn to calm down in its presence.

When we avoid trauma-related thoughts, emotions, and sensations, we prevent ourselves from experiencing evidence that can disconfirm danger. Our fear structures then remain intact, including our fear-based thoughts about ourselves. When we intentionally approach stimuli that we have mentally paired with trauma (a technique known as *exposure*), we increase our mental flexibility and generate new experiences and meanings. Exposure can thus lead to extinction of problematic, mental associations with trauma.

Exposure is the key to unlearning avoidance. It unlocks our fear structures so that we can observe and change them. Whereas avoidance keeps our fear structures rigid, exposure makes them malleable. Once we open the door of avoidance by allowing ourselves to experience difficult feelings and thoughts, we may indeed face some pain, but we also gain new opportunities. We can remodel our ideas about the meaning of the trauma or about ourselves, and we can refurbish old fear structures to reflect our developing effectiveness, wisdom, and resilience.

What Helps With Avoidance?

We dissolve avoidance through letting ourselves experience some of our feared thoughts and feelings, and by approaching some of the stimuli that we have learned to fear but that are not themselves dangerous on their own. Mindfulness practice provides opportunities to be present with our thoughts and feelings, even when they are difficult. There is no rush or time limit. We can titrate carefully, so that we stretch our comfort level a bit at a time.

We can start with a mindfulness practice that feels manageable: feeling the sensations of walking or breathing, or directing kindness towards our thoughts and feelings. These practices build our muscles of allowing ourselves to experience a range of thoughts and feelings. We might then be on the lookout for opportunities to stay present with feelings related to minor challenges in our lives, such as having to wait in line or spilling a drink. Building our curiosity and tolerance for emotions like frustration or annoyance can help us feel more confident and effective as we work towards opening our experience to more thoughts and feelings.

We can then pay attention to the different ways that we avoid, and begin to experiment with small changes. The exercises below include skills for approaching rather than avoiding trauma-related thoughts, feelings, places, and behaviors. Several kinds of exposure can help reduce avoidance and other PTSD symptoms, including *imaginal exposure* (thinking or talking about the trauma) and *in vivo* exposure (experiencing situations related to the trauma). Virtual reality, or using technological exposure to a controllable, multisensory environment, is also effective in reducing avoidance and PTSD.[186] The main goal of any sort of exposure is to reduce our avoidance and its grip on our fear structures.

Many people assume that it is necessary to relive trauma in order to heal. Although it is common to feel an urge to repeat the trauma in our minds or to reenact it through our behaviors—urges that may reflect our need to process the experience—there is no one right way to heal from trauma.

Talking about the trauma can be helpful, especially for those of us with long-term PTSD,[187] but discussing trauma-related thoughts and feelings may actually contribute more strongly to recovery than retelling the story of the trauma itself.[188] Whether we decide to reduce avoidance through addressing trauma-related feelings, thinking about the trauma itself, or talking about it, we are not reliving the trauma exactly. Rather, we are approaching it from a place of increased safety, understanding, and care—ingredients that help transform structures of fear.

Reducing avoidance may cause PTSD symptoms to get worse before they get better. Because avoidance keeps us from experiencing difficult feelings to some extent, removing it is likely to result in some discomfort. You might think of this temporary increase as similar to the "pins and needles" feeling you get from walking on your foot after it has fallen asleep. Exposure to trauma-related material after avoidance can initially increase intrusive symptoms of PTSD; however, after that initial increase, the symptoms will typically fall to levels much lower than where they started.[189] Reducing avoidance is crucial for remodeling our fear structures and for building confidence in working with difficult experiences.

Many people find it helpful to work with a therapist to help reduce avoidance. Therapists with backgrounds in trauma treatment can help you determine appropriate levels of exposure, and can also provide care and encouragement for shifting patterns of avoidance. Whether you address avoidance on your own or with a therapist, you might want to keep in mind the idea of a "therapeutic window"[190]—that is, you can approach difficult emotions gently, make contact with them in a way that stretches your comfort level without overwhelming you, and then shift your attention to other thoughts and feelings as you wind down.

Exposure

Graded exposure is a method for tackling our avoidance a little bit at a time— in bite-sized pieces—as we build confidence in our ability to handle difficult material. The general practice of mindfulness may serve as an exposure all on its own, because it involves building awareness for thoughts and feelings. However, graded exposure has been shown to be a remarkably effective process for reducing PTSD and other forms of anxiety.

When we practice exposure, we deliberately approach situations that we have avoided. We choose things that *feel* dangerous because of our past trauma, rather than things that are objectively dangerous. For instance, if you and your partner had an upsetting argument and broke up in the supermarket closest to you, you may want to avoid shopping there. However, the supermarket is not itself problematic—it is only its unfortunate association with the trauma that makes it feel uncomfortable. In another example, survivors of interpersonal trauma might feel wary about talking with anyone, including a bank teller or a receptionist. However, becoming more comfortable with interpersonal interactions could make life easier in many ways. On the other hand, activities like driving over the speed limit, going to a stranger's home, or walking through a violent neighborhood alone at night are behaviors that might actually result in harm, and it is wise to avoid them.

There is a fine line between learning to tolerate difficult situations and becoming retraumatized. It is rarely necessary to return to the scene of an accident, or to watch violent movies after being attacked. Optimal opportunities for exposure consist of situations that are safe but still provoke distress. This includes allowing yourself to have thoughts and feelings related to the trauma, or facing situations that remind you of the trauma in some way but that pose minimal present danger.

Graded exposure involves either *imaginal exposure* (confronting difficult thoughts, feelings, and memories in our minds) or *in vivo exposure* (approaching avoided people, places, or situations). The "graded" part of graded exposure describes how we begin with experiences that are somewhat easier, and gradually move up the exposure hierarchy or "ladder" to material that is more difficult. Mindful awareness about our distress and our avoidance forms a key role in the exposure process.

Action is an important element of in vivo exposure. We have to actually experience feared situations in order to shift our distress. Experiencing the situation without traumatic outcomes sends a message to our brains and bodies that we are safe and that we can handle the avoided circumstances better than we may have thought.

In Their Own Words

One insight that I have carried with me is that I truly learn so much more by doing than by just thinking about doing. For instance, in practicing balancing poses in a yoga class conducted on wobbly tumbling mats, I finally "got" the idea that balancing poses aren't about holding balance; they are about practicing time and again how to right myself when I lose balance. Losing my way isn't failure; it's simply a chance to practice getting back on track.

Mindfulness Practices for Avoidance

We can change patterns of avoidance by allowing our thoughts and feelings to be present. Many of the exercises in this book are powerful tools for reducing avoidance. For instance, practicing self-compassion for our full range of feelings entails allowing them to exist, without restricting them or pushing them away. We can also practice with our physical sensations, as after trauma, we may need to learn even to tolerate having a body.[191] Practicing mindfulness for our thoughts and bodily sensations enhances our awareness for whatever arises.

We need to be careful, because it is also possible to use mindfulness techniques as an avoidance strategy. For instance, spending a lot of time inside in order to practice mindfulness might enable us to avoid the outside world.

We could even use it as an excuse to avoid engaging with people or with our other goals or interests. As we develop increased control over our attention and concentration through practicing mindfulness, we may be tempted to use it to focus our attention away from trauma-related material. We therefore need to be aware of how we are using our mindfulness skills. If we are using them effectively, mindfulness skills should help increase our ability to tolerate distress, difficult interactions with other people, and trauma-related thoughts and feelings.

Practice #1: Noting Avoidance Behaviors

Although most of our fear structures may be outside of our conscious awareness, we can cultivate mindfulness for the way that they operate. Understanding more about our fear structures and the ways that we reinforce them through avoidance gives us the opportunity to make changes, or to engage in avoidance or distraction if we decide that it is the wisest course of action for that situation (for instance, if we need to focus on an exam, helping another person, or driving a car).

Noticing avoidance empowers us to make a choice about whether and when to use it, rather than falling into avoidance unconsciously. Avoidance is tricky; it can become ingrained and relatively unconscious. When trying to notice our avoidance, it may help to set an intention to approach avoidance, rather than avoiding the avoidance.

We can cultivate a curious, nonjudgmental attitude towards our avoidance. This is hard to do, but making friends with our avoidance can reduce the tension and control in our relationship with it. We might start by noticing what we can about the avoidance, without any pressure to change it. Remember that avoidance can occur in the form of keeping ourselves away from people, places, and things that remind us of trauma, but that it can also emerge as narrowing our range of thoughts and feelings. Our aim is to notice avoidance and escape in any form—any time we use a strategy to change our feelings.

There are many ways to avoid traumatic material. You might consider whether you experience avoidance in any of the following situations:

- Interacting with other people
- Making eye contact or smiling at strangers
- Spending time in stores, restaurants, parks, or public transportation
- Dating or intimate relationships
- Participating in recreational activities like team sports, band, or choir
- Attending religious or spiritual gatherings
- Going places alone at night
- Accessing news or current events
- Seeing pictures or movies
- Attending social situations such as parties or other events
- Being in crowded places
- Having health appointments (checkups, preventive screenings, dentist visits)
- Delaying or avoiding sleep
- Using alcohol or other drugs to avoid thoughts or feelings
- Engaging in constant activity (work, reading, television or movies, video games, gambling, hobbies, volunteering, dating, or socializing, to avoid thoughts or feelings
- Worrying about the future in order to avoid challenging thoughts or feelings in the present
- Encountering reminders of the trauma, including objects, places, people, foods, and smells

After identifying the avoidance behavior itself, you can open up to learning more information about it. You might ask yourself the questions below. In order to benefit from the full range of your wisdom, including your mental, emotional, and physical senses, you might try engaging in some mindful breathing, a body scan, or grounding. You can try to feel your answers to these questions, rather than engaging your logical mind alone.

- What is the function of the avoidance?
- Do I consciously notice avoidance when it is occurring, or only afterwards?
- How does the avoidance behavior increase or decrease pain in the short and long term?
- What contributes to engaging in this type of avoidance, and what helps me use a different strategy if I decide that would be best for me?

We may decide that the avoidance is in fact serving us well in the moment, or we may choose to try a different approach such as the exercises listed below. Bringing our avoidance into conscious awareness provides insight and choices about how to handle it.

Practice #2: Self-Compassion for Avoidance

If we are tempted to feel bad about any of our avoidance, self-compassion is the antidote. Practicing self-compassion can lessen the self-blame related to avoidance. Self-blame often keeps us stuck or feeling hopeless. Self-compassion can sustain us as we notice our avoidance, consider changes, and try out new behaviors.

You can practice self-compassion for avoidance by calling to mind an avoidance behavior that you have noticed. You might reflect a bit on the following questions. Just as you may have practiced using your felt experience, rather than your intellect, to answer the questions above in Practice #1, Noticing Avoidance, you might find that you need to "feel" the response to these questions, rather than thinking them.

To practice self-compassion for avoidance, it may help to first tune in to your general feelings of self-compassion and loving-kindness (for example, using the exercises in Chapter 4). You might hold your body in a way that feels especially kind or comforting, such as hugging yourself or placing your hands on your heart, as you approach your experience from a caring perspective. You might then call to mind one form of avoidance as you consider the following questions:

- Does the avoidance come from a caring place (such as wanting to reduce pain)?
- Can I provide care for myself about the avoidance itself, and about my wish that my pain be reduced?
- Can I feel compassion for any difficulties or challenges that the avoidance causes?
- Can I feel compassion about the challenges or anxiety I might feel about changing avoidance?

Even if the answers to these questions do not emerge right away, posing them may help cultivate self-compassion for avoidance. You might also try speaking to yourself in a way that reflects deep understanding, care, and hope about the avoidance. For instance, you might tell yourself something like, "This is where you are right now. I understand that this avoidance has served an important purpose in helping you feel safe, even if it also generates problems. It makes sense that you would feel and act this way, given what you have been through. However, other possibilities will also arise for you. I care about the whole picture—the trauma-related thoughts and feelings, the avoidance, and your feelings in this moment, right now. I offer you my support and care in exactly the place you are in right now with this avoidance. You also have my encouragement ahead for the ways that some of this avoidance may diminish or transform. I believe in you."

Self-compassion for avoidance can support us when we feel pressure to change our avoidance, when changes are uncomfortable, or when we are self-critical. We can connect to the parts of ourselves that understand the logic in our avoidance—that is, the ways that we have tried to bear the trauma in our lives. We can even glimpse elements of self-care in our avoidance, or feel gratitude for the ways that it may have gotten us through hard moments.

As we cultivate self-compassion, we may find that we need avoidance less and less. It is as though self-compassion becomes a new, stronger container for our thoughts and feelings.

Practice #3: New Breath, New Opportunity

With every breath, we have a chance for a new experience. In this breath, we can think about our situation in another way or try out a new approach. We can hold our body differently, and we can hold our avoidance differently.

You might take a moment to notice all that you can about this breath, right now. As it arises, you can observe its newness—the fact that this breath has never existed before and is just at this moment coming to life. You can observe its "nowness"—its distinctness from all past breaths or future breaths. Within the parameters of the breath, there are many opportunities for choices and control. You can make the breath longer or shorter; you can change your posture; and you can change how you attend to the breath (for instance, you can focus on the temperature of the air, the length of the breath, where the breath moves in your body, or on the transitions between inhalation and exhalation). Within the scope of just this breath, we have a great degree of mental and physical power.

As we begin a new breath, we can notice its newness in the following ways:

- What does this very breath feel like, right as it starts?
- What happens next?
- How do the sensations of this breath change as it proceeds?
- What is the arc of this particular breath—its movement through our body from inhale to exhale?
- What sensations or thoughts arise with this particular breath?
- How does the breath feel as you exhale?
- What are the sensations as this breath recedes and you begin to transition to the next breath?

We can bring this same empowered sensibility to other moments and other breaths. We might observe the urge to avoid our feelings—and the moments of avoiding them or trying another approach—with the same nonjudgment and curiosity that we can bring to a breath.

Practicing awareness and control of our breath can strengthen our ability to notice an urge (in this case, avoidance) without acting on it. We can use this very breath as the vehicle to check in with ourselves, and to help determine whether avoidance or another course of action is the wisest choice. We can use the breath to remember that we have choices and power in this moment.

Practice #4: Mindfulness in Graded Exposure

To practice graded exposure, we create an exposure hierarchy. The idea is to rank-order mental or real-life situations that generate distress. The top of the hierarchy includes situations that feel the most distressing and that are most avoided, whereas the bottom contains material that is usually avoided, but antic-ipated to elicit only mild distress.

Step 1: Identify behaviors that you might avoid and that you wish to tackle through exposure. In order for exposure to work, you need to expose your-self to situations that elicit mild and moderate discomfort. They also need to be *prolonged*—that is, it is important to remain in the situation until your distress is somewhat lowered.

Step 2: Briefly notice your feelings, thoughts, and physical sensations before you complete the exposure. Try not to spend so long that you might talk yourself out of the activity, as this is a situation where the "doing" is more important than thinking about it. Consider coming up with a "guesstimate" to quantify distress so that you can observe changes. Many exposure par-adigms use a rating scale, where we rate our levels of fear and avoidance from 0 to 100 (with 0 being absolutely no fear or avoidance, and 100 being the most distress or avoidance imaginable). We can use our awareness of our thoughts, emotions, and bodies to observe our distress and to monitor any changes that occur during or after exposure to difficult material. For instance, if my heart is pounding when I am fearful, that might help me estimate my distress level to be above 70. However, numeric ratings are not meant to overshadow our awareness for our felt experience, but to comple-ment it.

Step 3: Actually complete the exposure behavior, and mindfully observe your physical sensations, thoughts and feelings *during* the exposure itself. If possible, complete it more than one time. We reduce our distress by practic-ing a difficult situation multiple times, and preferably several times a week. For situations that are very brief (such as making eye contact or asking directions), it may be most helpful to practice several times so that the anxiety has a chance to recede. Lynch and Mack advise us to "start low and go slow" (n.d., p. 21) with exposure in order to maximize success and prevent ourselves from becoming overwhelmed.

Step 4: Mindfully observe your feelings after the exposure—immediately after you complete the exposure activity. You can also give yourself another rating to quantify your level of distress.

Table 7.1 is an example of an exposure hierarchy for someone struggling with fear and anxiety in social situations.[192]

Table 7.1: Example of an Exposure Hierarchy

Situation	Fear level (0–100)	Avoidance level (0–100)	Thoughts, emotions, and sensations when anticipating the situation
Speak with a new neighbor	95	95	"It feels impossible," dread, heart racing, sweating
Attend a party or social gathering	85	90	"This will be terrible," fear, obligation, disgust, grating feeling in my throat
Enter a crowded shopping center	80	85	Thoughts and feelings of anger about other people, fear for physical safety, tingling sensation in chest
Make eye contact with people in a public place	75	70	Concern about how other people will react, ache in ribs and stomach
Ask someone for directions	70	70	"I'm sure I will stutter," urge to run away, nausea

Ask someone for the time	65	65	Projecting that the person will judge me for not having a watch or phone on me, tense shoulders
Ask a clerk how the day has been going	65	60	Fear that the person will think I am weird, wobbly knees
Wait in line at the store	55	60	Anger at how long things seem to take, impatience, powerlessness, tense back
Sit in a waiting room	45	35	Impatience, tension in chest, thought that "it will take forever."
Phone a store to ask when they are open or where they are located	40	30	Thought that the person will judge me, tightness in jaw

To practice exposure, we start with the situations we anticipate will provoke relatively less distress (start low and go slow). We can then mindfully tune in to our feelings right before we approach the avoided situation, and to our feelings afterwards. Some people find it helpful to rate their distress using a Subjective Units of Distress (SUDS) scale of 0 to 100. For instance, 0 would be no distress at all, 30 would be mildly bothered to the point where you observe it; 50 might reflect being upset and uncomfortable, but still able to manage feelings; 80 might convey being able to handle feelings but only with great difficulty; and 100 would be the most distress imaginable (unbearably bad, as if you might faint or lose control). The numeric values can help us gauge to what extent practicing exposure reduces our distress. Table 7.2 provides an example of tracking distress before and after exposure practice:

Table 7.2: Levels of Stress Before and After Exposure

Situation	Subjective units of distress (SUDS) before exposure (0–100)	Subjective units of distress (SUDS) after exposure (0–100)	Thoughts, emotions, and sensations
Speak with a new neighbor	85	65	"Not as bad as I thought," "She has a beautiful accent," concern about how it went, feel glad that I did it, relief
Attend a party or social gathering	85	60	"I didn't like everyone there," really delicious cheese dip, enjoyed talking to Todd, felt a bit awkward
Enter a crowded shopping center	80	85	"I can't stand this," thoughts of moving to a more rural area, annoyance, wanting to shop in peace, tightness in chest
Make eye contact with people in a public place	75	50	It's not as bad as I thought, because it only lasts a few seconds. I find myself judging people's outfits and feeling pretty calm.
Ask someone for directions	65	60	I didn't stutter after all, but I didn't enjoy it. It doesn't feel like my anxiety or tension changed at all.
Ask someone for the time	55	35	This was my favorite exposure item yet, because it is over so fast. I asked four different people, and each time I felt less tense and more confident.

Ask a clerk how the day has been going	60	50	I could tell that the person was struggling with the day and with the job, just like I am. My back hurts from slouching during the conversation.
Wait in line at the store	55	55	I felt impatient, and it did not seem to get easier over time. I still feel tension in my chest.
Sit in a waiting room	45	20	I got absorbed in a magazine article and lost track of the time. At the beginning, another person's loud breathing irritated me, but I relaxed once that person left.
Phone a store to ask when they are open or where they are located	30	20	It didn't bother me as much as I thought it would. I think it helped that I didn't see the person face to face. I feel relatively calm.

After trauma, we often engage in *safety behaviors*, in addition to avoiding feared situations. Safety behaviors are habits, superstitions, and rituals that we use to assuage our distress. The phrase reflects behaviors that might make us feel calmer, but do not objectively make us any safer. For instance, checking to see that a door is locked or the oven is off 10 times does not make us any safer. Other examples include always sitting with your back to the wall, checking the perimeter of your home, visually scanning the environment for threats, and carrying a weapon.[193] The temporary relief that these behaviors may provide also comes with a cost: They reinforce our anxious thinking. We can decrease our reliance on these safety behaviors by building our recognition of them and observing our thoughts and feelings as we take steps to change them. Addressing safety behaviors works similarly to exposure for avoidance: The goal is to not engage in the safety behavior, and to instead complete an alternate behavior that would correspond to a lower level of anxiety (such as sitting without your back to the wall).

As we face and withstand difficult situations, we gain a sense of mastery and empowerment. We build the sense of having more control, because we consciously choose the situation and the length of time for the exposure. We also build our mindfulness skills by noticing our thoughts, feelings, and sensations as we practice. We might ask ourselves what feelings we are trying to prevent through our avoidance and our safety behaviors, and consider how we might support ourselves through them. Finally, we can gain new levels of awareness by comparing our imagined projections of feared situations with our actual experience, and by seeing our experiences change over time.

Practice #5: Spot the Success for Exposure

Exposure is a brave step for tackling avoidance. Every small step is a victory, and a path to meaningful change. When we consciously observe and reinforce our successes, we are more likely to repeat them.

Self-encouragement can support us through every step of the exposure process. We might say to ourselves something like, "I thought I would never be able to stomach another date again, and yet I was able to arrange a date. Well done!" Or, "Even though I feel anxious about safety, I was able to leave the house after checking the door only one time. That's a step in the right direction."

We can try treating each step of the exposure process with our own kindness and support:

- As we consider tackling avoidance
- As we generate an exposure hierarchy
- As we consider thoughts, feelings, and sensations related to avoided experiences
- As we notice ambivalence or trepidation
- As we challenge ourselves gently to keep going
- As we acknowledge our own efforts when taking action
- As we observe our feelings when approaching things that we have avoided
- As we recognize having tried something that we had avoided
- As we notice the full range of our feelings after exposure (such as fear, confidence, surprise, relief)

There is no success that is too small for our appreciation and encouragement. In fact, for people who have trouble leaving the house, it can be effective to applaud success in taking one step outside, or one lungful of fresh air. Making a mental note of the success—and offering ourselves care and support in the process—helps us to reinforce our successes and to build upon them.

Avoidance offers temporary and needed relief from trauma-related thoughts and feelings. However, avoidance comes with a cost. Avoidance prevents healing and moving through trauma-related feelings and habits, and can keep us from important goals and positive life experiences.

Because avoidance cuts off access to difficult thoughts and feelings, it can obstruct opportunities to change them, or even to change our ability to tolerate them. If we hide from our own feelings, we can miss chances to make them better, and to get the support we need. We may also miss out on different sources of internal information or wisdom. Mindfulness practices may help us rebuild a connection to different parts of ourselves that we ignored because of our avoidance, and help us integrate them. Mindfulness skills provide a framework through which we can pause and attend to a "felt sense"—an implicit resonance among our thoughts, emotions, and sensations that is often beyond words or logic.[194]

Making changes to our avoidance can seem daunting. However, it can be easier to think about making changes to moments. After waking up from a nightmare, we can pause to acknowledge and care for our feelings before rushing into our day. If we find ourselves binge-watching television, we can take a few breaths between episodes to tune in with how we are feeling and to encourage ourselves. If we find ourselves reaching for our phone or surfing the internet, we can pause and explore our motivation (Boredom? Avoidance? Loneliness? Interest?). Those short moments may be all we need, or they might be springboards that bounce us towards another way to handle challenging thoughts and feelings. Making room for awareness of avoidance opens us up to other options for handling pain.

We can also observe how the urge for avoidance presents itself. Perhaps avoidance comes as a gentle tug, or as a screaming imperative. It may be obvious to us what we are doing, or our avoidance may be teeming below the surface of our consciousness. We can also notice our feelings as we engage in avoidance or try a new strategy.

We do not construct our fear structures consciously, but we do have the opportunity to use mindfulness to change them. Approaching feared material from the perspective of safety, comfort, and care helps us shift our trauma-related thoughts and feelings, because we gain the lived experience of holding the trauma differently. As we develop and shift our relationship to avoidance, we change our experience of trauma, and cultivate new senses of power, confidence, and flexibility.

LAYERS OF MEANING: MINDFULNESS PRACTICES FOR SHAME, SELF-BLAME, SELF-CRITICISM, ANGER, AND GUILT

THE PAIN OF TRAUMA is often complex. It arises from the event or events themselves, which may have caused emotional or physical wounds. On top of that pain may reside many other layers, such as emotions, thoughts, and interpretations about the trauma and its meaning, or judgments about how we are handling it. Those layers can hurt just as much or even more than the original trauma.

You can picture the layers of trauma like a layer cake. The first, or bottom level, represents the raw pain or hurt caused directly by the trauma itself. The second layer contains our mental and emotional activity *about* the trauma and the pain that it caused—including our beliefs about why it happened or what it means, as well as feelings such as shame, self-blame, anger, betrayal, alienation, and guilt. These reactions to our experiences are sometimes called "add-ons." We may even observe a third layer on top that reflects our thoughts and judgments about the second layer (for instance, the idea that we are thinking about it all wrong, or the belief that we should be recovering faster).

We often experience all of the layers of trauma at once, and they can be overwhelming. It works best to attend to the layers one at a time, little by little. We usually cannot change the bottom layer—that is, the trauma itself and its immediate impact. The top layers, however, can change. Their changeability does not mean that they are voluntary—we usually do not consciously choose to feel angry, betrayed, or ashamed—but we can work with them and gradually shift them around. Even if our thoughts and feelings about our trauma seem fixed, certain, and out of our control, our mindful attention and care can transform them.

It is normal to make *appraisals* about what the trauma and our own responses mean about ourselves, other people, and the world (represented above as the second layer of the cake). However, these appraisals often worsen suffering. For instance, someone who has been attacked might carry painful memories and feelings directly associated with that experience, another layer of shame or self-blame, and perhaps even another layer of self-judgment that judges those feelings as irrational. Those appraisals or "secondary emotions"—particularly internalized senses of shame, self-blame, feeling bad, weak, unacceptable, or unlovable, or having deserved being hurt—strongly contribute to PTSD and depression above and beyond the impact of the trauma itself. Because they can keep us stuck, loosening the grip of our trauma appraisals can be a powerful approach to healing.

Another type of layer involves the fear of emotions. We might fear the feeling of not being in control, or of our own anger. Some people claim that they would prefer to have no emotions at all, like the character Data on *Star Trek: Next Generation* (it is worth noting that Data is not human, but an android, or robot with a human appearance). Emotions can provide several benefits, such as connecting us to other people or signaling information, but even if they did not, doing away with emotions is not an option. We can try to separate ourselves from emotions, but when we do so we constrict our lives and develop other problems. Alternatively, we can acknowledge our fear of emotions, offer ourselves some understanding and compassion about that fear, and try to gradually open up to our emotions until we feel more and more comfortable. The less fearful we feel of our emotions, the fewer PTSD symptoms we are likely to experience;[195] therefore, addressing this layer of trauma may help us heal. Interestingly, building attentional control—a common benefit from mindfulness practice—seems to play a role in reducing fear of emotions and related PTSD symptoms.[196]

Some layers of trauma may be subtle, hidden, or contradictory. For instance, a part of ourselves might know that a trauma could not have been anticipated or avoided, while another part maintains a belief that people get what they deserve, or that we are somehow defective. Because our brains automatically try to promote consistency and to resolve conflicting ideas (thereby reducing "cognitive dissonance"), we might push conflicting mental experiences out of awareness ("I know I'm basically fine, so I'm going to just disregard the smaller parts of me that are still struggling"). However, even if they are outside of our conscious awareness, those layers of trauma still affect us.

Other layers of trauma are so loud or strong that they seem incontrovertible. Thoughts are very powerful, and they often feel truly real (for instance, "I'm a failure," or "It's my own fault that I'm depressed") even when they are highly subjective. Add some feeling onto these sorts of thoughts, such as shame or despair, and they can take off like a rocket. The mindfulness teacher Joseph Goldstein (2015) has called thoughts the "dictators" of our minds. Thoughts often assume power and run with it, disregarding any contradictory data or information. It is often most effective not to engage with our thoughts through arguments or by accepting their decrees as facts. Instead, we can observe them using a broader perspective that sees our thoughts as small parts of a much larger picture, and that understands that they may be untrue.

Layers of trauma exist not only within us, but as part of our social world. Others' perceptions and messages about trauma can affect us. For instance, we might develop an all-or-nothing approach to trauma and mental health—the idea that we are either perfectly healthy or else have deep problems. The phrase "getting over" something also implies that we can or should reach a state in which a trauma no longer impacts us in any way. Or, we grow up hearing Cinderella stories or watching action films, in which the protagonists experience trauma with no apparent mental health repercussions.

Our own appraisals about how we are feeling and what it means tend to swirl around in our minds with ideas that we have absorbed from other people and our own concerns about what others might think of us. We can feel so caught up in these ideas that it is hard to step back and pay attention to what we are actually feeling. When we regard our layers of meaning with curious interest, rather than following them as though they were our dictators, those layers begin to lose their hold on us. They become ordinary thoughts, passing mental experiences. We can notice them without necessarily believing them, and we can become more open to alternative interpretations.

Directing mindfulness and care towards these layers of meaning can reduce our suffering and promote healing. The changes may unfold gradually, but they can also be easier than we expect. Even the simple practice of mentally labeling a layer of trauma as a thought or a feeling can soften it, so that we recognize it as a transitory mental event rather than an objective truth.

We can also attend in a curious and caring way to how our thoughts and feelings are related. For instance, we might observe that "when I keep thinking of what I should have done to prevent the trauma, I get really down on myself," or the pattern that "I tell myself repeatedly that I should be able to just put this behind me, and I feel angry and frustrated." Just noticing the patterns can help shift them, and can provide an opportunity to try out new approaches.

When we try a new approach to the trauma and to our feelings, we can notice any changes that arise. What happens if you try a very curious approach to the trauma layers? Or a very understanding one? Or a very kind approach? You might also observe how general mindfulness practice impacts the trauma layers, because they often broaden our perspectives, shift our thinking, promote nonjudgment, and cultivate compassion.

RESEARCH HIGHLIGHT How Does Changing Appraisals Influence Trauma Recovery?

MANY RESEARCH STUDIES have demonstrated that a focus on reducing trauma appraisals leads to healing from PTSD. This body of work makes a compelling case that addressing appraisals forms a key ingredient of successful treatments for PTSD.

For example, one study of 195 Veterans with PTSD tracked trauma-related thoughts and PTSD symptoms over time as the Veterans participated in a therapy program. The researchers noticed that the improvements in trauma-related thoughts such as self-blame and negative beliefs about themselves occurred first, and that Veterans' levels of PTSD diminished *after* those changes. They also reported that Veterans' changes in negative beliefs about themselves preceded reductions in their levels of depression.[197] A study of 61 assault victims similarly demonstrated that changes in negative trauma-related cognitions led to reductions in PTSD and depression.[198]

In another study, 92 survivors of physical or sexual assault provided information about their trauma appraisals, their PTSD symptoms in the month after the assault, and their enduring PTSD symptoms.[199] The authors demonstrated that the following categories of trauma appraisals were linked with both the onset and maintenance of PTSD:

- Mental defeat ("I mentally gave up")
- Mental confusion ("I couldn't believe this was happening to me'"; "My mind went blank"), Emotions ("If I can react like that, I must be very unstable"; "I cannot accept the emotions that I had")
- Trauma-related symptoms ("My reactions since the assault mean that I must be losing my mind")
- Perceptions of others' reactions ("I feel like other people are ashamed of me now")
- Permanent change ("I will never recover")
- Avoidance and safety ("Trying to push thoughts of the assault to the back of my mind"; "Sleeping with lights or radio on")
- Global beliefs ("I cannot rely on other people"; "There is no justice in the world")

Many studies demonstrate how powerful trauma appraisals are. In fact, negative trauma appraisals predict symptoms of PTSD and depression *above and beyond* the amount and severity of trauma that people experience.[200] On the bright side, research demonstrates that people can change their trauma appraisals and related PTSD symptoms.[201]

Common Trauma Appraisals

The sections below consider some of the most common trauma appraisals:

- Shame
- Self-Blame
- Self-Criticism
- Betrayal
- Anger
- Guilt
- Alienation

Shame, Self-Blame, and Self-Criticism

Shame, self-blame, and self-criticism are all logical responses to trauma. In many traumatic situations, it is not possible to escape, and the feeling of uncontrollability is terrifying. We often respond by *internalizing* the trauma. As strange as it might sound, interpreting trauma so that we ourselves are the problem—and so that the trauma itself seems deserved or unsurprising—can actually be a useful way to adapt to traumatic circumstances in the short term.

Viewing (or rather, misperceiving) ourselves as wholly responsible for what happens to us can help us feel a bit more in control. The same is true for our approach to posttraumatic symptoms: We might blame or criticize ourselves for feeling how we feel or for taking longer to heal than we would like, thus assuming that we are completely in control of our trauma-related thoughts and feelings. Even though it might help us feel more control during trauma, internalizing trauma is linked with a range of negative outcomes.

Shame, or the sense of feeling embarrassed, foolish, humiliated, or defective, is linked to the severity of PTSD symptoms and to physical responses to trauma reminders.[202] Shame involves global evaluations of the self,[203] along with behavioral tendencies to avoid and withdraw.[204] It can take the shape of a nagging disregard towards ourselves, or even a visceral disgust that involves viewing ourselves as dirty or contaminated. We may also feel and express shame physically. For instance, we might contract our bodies, look downwards, or have a drooping posture.[205]

Although shame may announce its presence strongly, it is often subtle and elusive. We may experience it as more of a feeling than as a set of thoughts with words attached. Shame's tendency to skim below the surface may explain some of its relationship to aggression and violence. Shame also tends to grow. It might start out as a reaction to trauma, but it can expand so that we become ashamed to go out, to talk to people, or even to exist in the world. Noticing and understanding our shame can help us dissolve it, little by little. Reducing levels of shame can help diminish PTSD symptoms.[206]

Self-blame may be easier to identify than shame, because it often involves words or a story in our minds, rather than just feelings alone ("The trauma happened to me because I . . . was not driving carefully / am a bad person / upset someone else"). Whether or not there is an element of truth to the story, we often convince ourselves that we are *entirely* responsible for the trauma. One exercise that can dissolve this assumption involves broadening our perspectives to consider other factors that might have contributed to the trauma, beyond our own role (for instance, icy roads; decisions by world leaders to instigate armed conflicts; having a human body that is by its very nature vulnerable to injury and disease). Once we discover our patterns of self-blame, we have options. We can try out a new story and see if it shifts anything; practice mindfully noticing our feelings in this moment without judging ourselves; or offer ourselves compassion for the discomfort related to self-blame. Because self-blame influences our psychological adjustment after trauma,[207] addressing and shifting self-blame can help us heal.

Self-criticism is another way that we internalize trauma. We commonly absorb and maintain the negative messages that we receive from others, especially in the case of insults and other forms of verbal abuse. We may also use self-criticism as a way to cope with trauma, with uncertainty, or with feeling out of control. Self-criticism might provide a false sense of security in the form of an endless self-improvement campaign ("To avoid trauma in the future, all I have to do is be perfect in the following ways . . .") or of being our own harshest critic ("no one else could ever be meaner to me than I am to myself"). Because it is often habitual, self-criticism can seem comforting in its familiarity, and in its sense that there is nowhere lower down to go.

Even if it seems protective, self-criticism is quite destructive. Self-criticism is strongly related to the severity of PTSD symptoms after trauma[208] and to depression.[209] Self-criticism is a mental habit that keeps us stuck. For instance, it seems to link past abuse experiences to current levels of depression[210]—in essence, self-criticism keeps the abuse going internally. The good news is that we can reduce self-criticism by noticing it and by trying out new approaches like self-compassion.

In Their Own Words

"My trauma happened when I was 13. I was ashamed and never told anyone. I felt responsible for what happened to me, and I believed that I was bad and unworthy. Those feelings led to staying in unhealthy relationships in my late teens and early 20s. In my current therapy, which I started at age 52, I began to write letters to my therapist between sessions, telling him about experiences, thoughts and feelings that I had trouble expressing during therapy sessions. Usually, I would write when I was alone, without distractions, which allowed me to connect to the memories, thoughts and feelings in a safe place, and to write about them in a very spontaneous manner. The writing is a very important part of my journey and my healing. A lot of my therapy has been about changing my self-concept from one of being bad and unworthy. My therapy has helped me realize that the trauma was not my fault, and did not make me a bad, unlovable person"

Betrayal

Trauma often breaks social contracts. When we are hurt by family members, friends, colleagues, or romantic partners, our trust is shattered. In the trauma literature, betrayal is used in a couple of different ways. *Betrayal trauma* describes trauma that is perpetrated by a person's family members, caregivers, or close others—people who are supposed to be providing help and support, rather than hurting those in their care.[211] For instance, research shows that this type of interpersonal trauma is more strongly associated with PTSD symptoms than are other forms of trauma.[212] The word *betrayal* is also used to indicate our appraisals of the trauma—the extent to which we feel betrayed. For instance, we might have betrayal appraisals such as "The people that I was supposed to trust the most hurt me;" or "I feel double-crossed."[213]

We might also feel betrayed by the world, by ourselves, or by our bodies. Trauma can shake common basic beliefs—for instance, that the world is safe or that we can fully control our own well-being.[214] We may feel suddenly lost, or as if the foundation of the world as we knew it has crumbled.

The discomfort of betrayal highlights the phenomenon of *cognitive dissonance*, our mental preference for thoughts to be compatible ("The trauma happened, and the world is clearly a terrible place") rather than contrasting ("The trauma happened, and there are still a lot of good people and things about the world"). As humans, we generally try to resolve cognitive dissonance in our minds by picking an overarching belief. In the case of betrayal, the dissonance is also emotionally charged, which may make the need to resolve it (rather than holding contrasting thoughts) feel more urgent.

Mindfulness provides several ways of working with betrayal. As we widen our perspectives, we often become more comfortable with contradictory pieces of information ("That person was both wonderful and horrible to me," or "I have some control over my health, but not total control"). Mindfulness practices that redirect our attention to our sensory experiences this moment, rather than to our thoughts, also help us disengage from retelling ourselves the same type of information, over and over, in a manner that can keep us stuck. Finally, through mindfulness practices, we can also provide ourselves with understanding for the full range of our betrayal experiences: shock, grief, loss, hurt, fear, distrust, anger, and sadness. We can offer ourselves the care that the betrayal seemed to steal away.

Anger

Anger often feels clear, or even obvious in its content and urgency ("I can't believe she did that to me!" or "How dare they overcharge me?"). However, when we look at anger in a curious way—a challenging feat when in its throes—we often discover many different parts to it. For instance, anger might occur as a response to sadness, shame, guilt, alienation, or humiliation. We might feel outrage that someone else's actions provoked those feelings in us, or dismay at ourselves for having those feelings. Anger can reflect our dislike for other emotions, and our struggle to tolerate them.

Anger can signal our own unmet needs. Most humans have a strong need to feel liked, respected, cared for, and valued—on top of our basic physical needs such as food, shelter, safety, and access to medical care. When these needs go unmet, we may feel angry at a person or a system, at ourselves, or at the world. Anger often leads us to shift our focus away from the unmet need itself onto the person or system influencing the problem. We then commonly ruminate on the details of the story, perhaps to the extent that we neglect the need itself, or struggle to identify other effective ways to get the need met.

Anger can also arise from the basic challenge of living in a world full of people with conflicting needs and priorities. For instance, if a line is moving very slowly when boarding a bus, I might feel angry that this slowness could make me late for an appointment. Even if I recognize that a person in the line has a physical disability, I may feel agitated at the conflict between that person's needs and my own. Romantic feelings might go unrequited; someone else might get a job that I wanted; or I might argue with family members who prefer different music, movies, or vacations. These types of conflicts happen all the time, and can contribute to an "us versus them" or "me against the world" mentality that can compound anger.

Anger reflects a strong disconnect between what we experience and how we feel things should be. This facet of anger ("it shouldn't be this way!") can highlight unfairness, and help motivate us to address it. For instance, our anger might provide us with energy to help us advocate for a better healthcare system, measures to slow global climate change, or a living wage.

Another dimension of anger that we can explore is its physical sensations. We might notice ourselves feeling warm or tense, or observe our hearts pound or race. We may feel tremendous energy that we can redirect towards useful ends, such as cleaning the kitchen. After prolonged periods of anger, we might feel immobilized or exhausted. Anger can wear us out.

Even though anger often presents itself loudly, we might not notice that it is there at all, or try to push it aside. We may fear anger, or the actions that we might take if we were to become angry. Many of us received the message in childhood that we should not be angry. We might therefore repress anger before we can even detect its presence. However, even "undercover" anger can still affect us, and can emerge as irritation, depression, or the avoidance of potentially upsetting things.

There are many interconnections between anger, trauma, and PTSD. We commonly feel angry that the trauma occurred, angry at all of the contributing circumstances, and angry about having to navigate posttraumatic stress symptoms. In fact, levels of anger correspond with the severity of PTSD symptoms.[215] Anger may also connect PTSD to behavioral impulsivity and substance use,[216] and anger seems to increase the likelihood of ending PTSD treatment early.[217] On the bright side, therapeutic treatments for anger reduce both PTSD symptoms and anger itself.[218]

Guilt

Guilt can feel like an undertow, dragging us down into murky depths of jumbled thoughts and feelings. We might be gripped by self-blame as our default reaction to negative life events; we may feel "survivor guilt" at having survived a trauma when others did not; or we might believe that guilt is a necessary part of having a conscience or being a good person.

There is a qualitative difference between feeling responsible for something, blaming ourselves for it, and feeling guilty about it. There are certainly times we recognize that we have harmed someone or made a mistake, and a feeling of responsibility kicks in. For instance, if I accidentally run into a woman on the street and her bag of groceries tumbles to the ground, I might wish that I had not knocked over the groceries, and feel regret that I inconvenienced and upset her. Those feelings might spur me to take helpful or restorative action, such as helping her pick up the groceries and communicating an apology. However, the concepts of self-blame and guilt typically extend beyond these feelings, and convey more than *responsibility* or *regret* to include a self-judgment that we are bad—it is "my fault" that something happened, rather than "I take responsibility for it." Self-blame is a milder form of this judgment, whereas feeling guilty involves a more profound disapproval and self-rejection—the belief that our actions reflect deep flaws in our character.

Guilt often involves cognitive errors—common mistakes in thinking that somehow appear to us to be logical and true. For instance, Kubany and colleagues[219] describe four different types of cognitive errors that frequently emerge among survivors of trauma:

- **Hindsight bias** – believing that the outcome was foreseeable at the time of the trauma
- **Lack of justification** – believing there was no possible justification for an action

- Responsibility – believing that we were completely or primarily responsible for the trauma
- Wrongdoing – believing that we intentionally did something wrong or against our values

These patterns of thinking can ensnare us. However, once we recognize them as cognitive errors, we may be able to shift our thinking and related feelings. For instance, we might investigate one of our strongly held beliefs, such as, "I should have left 15 minutes earlier so that the accident would not have happened," and locate the threads of hindsight bias and responsibility that run through it. Or, we might address our assumption of responsibility by considering a broader range of factors that contributed to an outcome. Addressing these cognitive errors can contribute to healing from trauma-related guilt.

We might also investigate the *function* of guilt. Guilt can keep us from feeling other emotions, such as fear ("If continue to feel guilty, it can help me feel more in control and guard against the trauma happening again") or sadness ("perhaps I can stave off sadness by concentrating on the story of what I did wrong, and going over it again and again"). We can also use guilt to justify avoidance ("I'm so awful, no one will want to get close to me anyway, so there's no point in making an effort socially."). We might also believe that our guilt honors those who did not survive, or that it is an important part of sustaining our values. Observing the function of our guilt may help us to resolve it. For instance, we might seek another way to honor others besides feeling guilty; make a realistic plan for reparative action if we have caused pain; or intentionally plan how to lead a life that reflects our values.[220]

The concept of *moral injury* conveys another dimension of trauma-related guilt and shame. A moral injury can feel like having "a hole in the soul," or as though trauma has sliced through core values. This experience can occur through "perpetrating, failing to prevent, bearing witness to, or learning about acts that transgress deeply held moral beliefs and expectations" (Litz et al., 2009, p. 700). Recovery often involves speaking about these aspects of the trauma, and engaging in actions that provide a sense of connection and moral healing.[221]

Alienation

Trauma can leave us feeling alone, empty, and disconnected. We might feel lonely even when we are around other people, struggle to trust people, or have trouble getting close to anyone. Even when we recognize that other people have been through trauma, our own experience can feel deeply alienating, as though we are "marked" or fundamentally separate from others. Trauma can also remove us from the thinking and rhythms of daily life, which can then make it hard to connect to those around us. Both trauma and depression increase the likelihood that we will isolate ourselves and avoid interpersonal connections—behaviors that keep us feeling more and more alone.

It makes sense that we would feel alone after trauma. Isolation may have contributed to the trauma itself (for instance, getting hurt when there was no one helpful around to intercede), and we may still be in a similar environment. Many traumas leave no visible marks, so those around us may have no idea that we are suffering. That invisibility can make us feel more alienated—as though we "should" fit in, but cannot. Because people often keep their traumas private, we often feel alone in having gone through something harrowing, and do not realize that others have had similar experiences. Similarly, after trauma, we may have the sense of being the only person struggling with PTSD or other trauma-related challenges.

The alienation layer of trauma appears to have a major impact on our well-being. Feelings of alienation are associated with higher levels of PTSD symptoms, depression, and dissociation after trauma.[222] It is likely that those connections are bidirectional; that is, the worse our trauma and depression symptoms, the more alienated we feel, and vice versa.

Addressing feelings of alienation can be challenging, because they require attention both to our thinking and to our behaviors. A sense of alienation may also be intertwined with other layers of trauma, such as self-blame or shame. On the bright side, changing our thoughts and behaviors so that we relate to people more effectively can substantially improve PTSD and depression.

Mindfulness and Layers of Meaning

Many ingredients in mindfulness practice make it a balm for transforming negative trauma appraisals. Practicing nonjudgment towards thoughts and feelings, a core mindfulness skill, can reduce our tendencies towards self-criticism, self-blame, and guilt—appraisals that each contain elements of self-judgment. Cultivating self-compassion can also shift the layers of trauma that involve judging ourselves. Setting an intention to notice our thoughts and feelings in a curious way also challenges the idea that we need to push away undesirable parts of ourselves. Viewing thoughts as a constantly changing mental landscape—rather than as indications of a supposedly objective reality—can help us challenge and change our layers of trauma.

Mindfulness practice pushes us to develop patience with ourselves. Building up our ability to be patient with our mental processes can help us relate to our layers of trauma in a more gentle way. Over time, we can become more comfortable tolerating feelings such as anger or loneliness. As we reduce our resistance to difficult emotions, those emotions themselves may change. Practicing mindfulness after trauma can promote acceptance of emotional experiences, and decrease shame.[223] Finally, because mindfulness and self-compassion practice can reduce difficulties such as PTSD and depression, the way that we make sense of our trauma—the layers of meaning that we assign to it—may change as we recover.

Mindfulness Practices for Layers of Meaning

Practice #1: Noting

The practice of *noting* involves labeling mental material that arises during mindfulness practice with a simple word that reflects a broader category. For instance, when trying to focus on mindful breathing, we may find ourselves swept up in other thoughts. At the moment we recognize that this has happened, we can calmly and silently note it as "thinking," and then return our attention to the breath. Noting can prevent us from getting carried away further on a train of thought, from overidentifying with our thoughts, or from judging ourselves when we recognize that we have become distracted. It builds up the "witnessing" part of our minds, and can be a helpful pivot point for redirecting our focus.

We think and feel so many things at once that it is often overwhelming. Labeling experiences by category ("thinking," "discomfort," "smelling") can make them feel a bit more manageable, and less personally charged. For instance, I might hear a noise that I recognize as a neighbor entering the apartment next door. This recognition could easily provoke a complex array of mental activity—such as my feelings towards this neighbor, unresolved questions about the person's life, and memories of interacting with the person. Simply noting the sound of the neighbor entering as "hearing" might help me refocus on my own sensory experience in this moment, rather than going down a long path of related mental content.

Noting can be a useful strategy as we become more aware of the mental layers that reside on top of our trauma. Traumatic memories, thoughts, and feelings often intrude during mindfulness practice. The practice of noting is not meant to deny that this material is complex, but to help steer our practice so that we can more easily navigate through the layers of material. When trauma-related content arises, we might silently note it as "fear," "sadness," "pain," "self-blame," or "anger" before redirecting our attention to the object of our mindfulness practice. If trauma arises as bodily sensations, we can label what emerges (for example, "heat," "tension," or "restlessness").

Noting it may help this material feel less intensely personal. When we label a feeling, we reframe it: It is no longer a personal problem, but merely one of many types of human experience. It can also prevent us from becoming submerged in it, because our perspective involves witnessing the feeling. Another benefit of noting is that it can highlight patterns. For instance, some people find that they are especially distracted during the first 10 minutes of mindfulness practice, and that their focus settles a bit after that. When we practice noting, we may be surprised to observe these sorts of patterns, and the extent to which we become angry, distracted by smells, or have the urge to stop the practice and get up.

The practice of noting can change our brains as well as our minds. Labeling feelings seems to diminish activation in the amygdala, a brain region involved in recognizing and reacting to fear, in situations that involve exposure to negative emotional stimuli.[224] Noting may therefore keep us from getting too agitated when we encounter difficult material.

To practice noting, we first need to choose another mindfulness exercise.

Examples in Chapter 1 include mindful breathing, the body scan, or mindful walking. We can set an intention to do our best to keep our focus on the object of our meditation, but to respond by "noting" when our minds wander and by using that moment as a pivot to redirect our attention back to the exercise. We might even anticipate the exercise by planning to note thinking as "thinking," and to note emotions by category, such as fear, anger, and sadness.

Next, we begin the mindfulness exercise, and try to note calmly where the mind goes. If we find that we are judging ourselves after noting (e.g., "I shouldn't be so scared/distracted/impatient"), we can note it as "judging." It is likely that during any mindfulness practice session, we will have many opportunities to practice the skill of noting. However, even if we are able to note thinking, feelings, or sensations only once or twice, the practice can still be valuable. We can also practice this skill in everyday life as thoughts and feelings emerge.

Practice #2: Observe Layers of Meaning

Our layers of meaning often operate in subtle and sneaky ways, outside of our conscious awareness. As we notice these layers, their power diminishes. Mindfulness practice builds our capacity to observe thoughts in general as changeable, and increases our ability to watch even subtle thoughts go by without necessarily believing them or getting wrapped up in them (*overidentifying*). We can begin to choose how to interpret the trauma and its meaning, rather than letting our unintentional interpretations take charge.

This process begins with the intention to just notice. In order to get into the "noticing" mindset, it can be helpful to start with something less emotionally charged than our interpretations of trauma, such as noticing our breathing or other bodily sensations.

You can then direct this same observational perspective—*just noticing*—

towards noticing layers of meaning, or "trauma-related appraisals" about yourself, others, and the world. It may be hard to just notice, without getting whisked away on a speeding train of thought. Layers of trauma are mentally "sticky," because they are entangled with so many other memories, thoughts and emotions. Our aim is to notice all of these layers, but to maintain our "witness" perspective, where we notice what is there and then let it pass. Some layers of meaning may emerge suddenly, whereas others may take some time to discern.

When we work to observe layers of trauma, it may help to base our curiosity around specific questions, such as the following:

- What beliefs have I developed about myself in response to the trauma?
- Do I have any shame/guilt/self-blame/anger about what happened?
- Do I have any judgments about my emotional response to trauma—for instance, the idea that I should not feel the way that I feel?
- How has my view of myself changed after the trauma?
- What are my ideas and assumptions about the world—that is, my sense of whether the world is safe or dangerous, or what kinds of things are likely to happen to me in the future?
- When I meet new people, do I project assumptions on them that stem from the trauma?
- How do I feel connected to other people, communities, nature, or the world? How do I feel disconnected?

When we observe our responses to these questions, it can be natural to judge them. The answers to these questions might feel unwanted or upsetting, and contradict our ideas of how we "should" feel or think.

Another common experience when noticing layers of thoughts and feelings is that we become overwhelmed with the quantity and interconnections of all of the layers. To the extent that we can, we might benefit from trying to notice them one at a time, and by trying to observe all we can about one before moving on to the next. It is also fine to return to noticing breathing or bodily sensations at any time when becoming upset or overwhelmed. It might also be helpful to offer self-compassion for any painful layers that emerge (see Practice #5 below). Before ending the exercise, we can return our attention to the breath or other neutral object of focus in order to reengage a nonjudging, observational stance.

Practice #3: Notice the Add-Ons in Everyday Life

As we go through life, we often "add on" to our daily experience with thoughts that reflect interpretations, hypothetical situations, or projections about the future. This process usually occurs unintentionally and somewhat unconsciously. Often, this feature of mental activity works in our favor. For instance, if I read a recipe for a new side dish that sounds delicious, I might try to recall what ingredients I already have at home, plan how I will acquire the others, admire the person who imagined the dish, and anticipate making substitutions that reflect my own preferences or food allergies. I might also enjoy imagining how the new dish will taste, even though I am not tasting it right now.

In other circumstances, our add-ons can magnify our distress. If I recall that I left a message for a friend a couple weeks ago but received no response, my mind might become busy supplying add-ons: "This friend does not like me anymore, and no longer wants to be my friend," "This is all my fault, because I got depressed and isolated myself last month, and now everyone has given up on me," or, "This means that I am just bad at having friendships." However, through mindfulness practice I can try out noticing these thoughts as add-ons, unnecessary (and often inaccurate) extra ingredients that worsen my experience.

To separate the add-ons from the basics of our experience, we might ask, "what is true for me in this moment, right now?" In the example of my wait to hear back from my friend, I might answer myself with, "as far as I know, my friend has not called back, and I feel worry and self-blame." Although that scope of thought might still be unpleasant, it does not contain the added suffering of projections into the future that seem definitive, or interpretations about what the situation means about me or whether the friend still likes me.

As we notice our add-ons, we can also notice to what extent they are entwined with past trauma. When we respond to everyday events with thoughts such as, "This means that I am bad," or "Nothing will ever work out for me," we are most likely adding trauma-related material to our experiences—that is, filtering them through a trauma lens that can maintain suffering. It can help to notice the trauma-related add-ons and to label them as such.

Most of us are "adding on" to our experiences throughout the day. For instance, if a stranger cuts in front of me in line, I might think, "Everyone is so disrespectful these days. The world is changing for the worse. I'm going to be late now. This is going to make my day worse." Add-ons can arise in response to anything—an electric bill, someone's facial expression, a grade on a test, or bodily pain. One way to spot add-ons is to look for generalizations from a specific incident to a broader belief, or to ideas about the future that seem true but are in fact uncertain.

If our thoughts project into the future in a way that feels encouraging and hopeful, we do not necessarily need to change them. For instance, I might plan to consult with my household members to figure out a way to pay bills on time, or decide to reach out to a different friend every day. However, these differ from add-ons that increase suffering, because they involve a realistic plan to improve my circumstances, rather than an unpleasant projection of how I assume the future will take shape.

To notice add-ons in everyday life, we need to set the intention to do so. It may help to practice in a situation where there are other people who might elicit our judgments about them, or our judgments about ourselves when interacting with others. An errand to get a cup of coffee or tea can provide a good opportunity for noticing add-ons. We can also notice add-ons during our mindfulness practice, as thoughts and feelings arise and we respond by interpreting them or projecting our assumptions into the future. We can note this type of mental activity as an add-on and then resume our mindfulness practice.

Practice #4: Normalize Layers of Meaning

It can be very helpful to reappraise the layers of meaning that we ascribe to our trauma as normal and initially adaptive. Layers of meaning can be exceedingly challenging to work with. They often contain assumed certainty (they *seem* so true), habits (we reinforce our interpretations every time we believe them), personalization (they appear to reflect something meaningful about our own character), and pain (such as the idea that we are bad or doomed). Learning that our layers of pain are normal can decrease some of the certainty, personalization, and pain that perpetuate them, and can help us change our habits.

Negative appraisals about ourselves are not pleasant; however, there is often a very logical reason for their development. Developing a "layer of meaning" that we are bad, weak, or should have behaved differently might promote a sense of control that was necessary to cope with the trauma. This coping style presumes that we are the cause of the trauma, rather than an unpredictable and problematic external world.

Negative appraisals about ourselves and others can contribute to depression and other trauma-related symptoms. As we work to change our appraisals, we need to be careful not to attack ourselves for having negative thoughts, because that can lead to yet another layer of self-judgment ("See how screwed up I am? Since the trauma, all my thoughts are so negative, which just shows that I'll never feel better and that it's all my fault that I feel this way anyway"). We can avoid entering into another cycle of self-blame by regarding negative thinking as very normal after trauma.

In addition to its potential contribution to a sense of control, negative appraisals might be realistic if we have just had an extremely salient negative experience. Distrust or dislike for other people and the world might seem to protect us from the additional trauma that could occur if we had a more positive view of the world or fully engaged with it. Finally, negative appraisals might help us maintain a consistent mental perspective, which can be necessary to keep going after trauma. It is hard to think about ourselves (or the world) as containing both wonderful and difficult qualities. Our minds often crave a simpler view of things (for instance, "I am bad," "the world is a scary, dangerous place," or "people can never be trusted"). Normalizing negative appraisals and understanding how they may have been adaptive in context can soften their sting.

To normalize our layers of meaning, we need to set aside a few minutes for quiet reflection. To elicit an open and nonjudgmental mindset, it may help to first engage in some mindful breathing or a body scan. We can check in with ourselves about how we are feeling, physically and emotionally, right in this moment. Then, we can set an intention that we will bring the same perspective of curiosity and nonjudgment as we shift our focus to our trauma-related thoughts. It can help to try this exercise after already having identified a few specific appraisals with which to work. For instance, I might choose to work with the appraisal that "It is all my fault that I feel so bad."

After identifying an appraisal to address, we can then open to the question: "In what ways does this feeling make sense, given what I have experienced? How can I understand this feeling as a normal, human response to trauma?" We might also ask ourselves whether the appraisal contains common cognitive errors, such as hindsight bias, that are "normal" but often problematic.

Next, we might pay attention to the thoughts and feelings that arise. There might be a determined part of ourselves that argues back, "No! This appraisal is my own problem, not a normal response. I am certain that I am abnormal!" We may even feel bodily tension as we try to consider our appraisals in a new way. When we encounter mental or bodily resistance to the task of "normalizing" our posttraumatic appraisals, we can note that resistance gently, but then refocus our efforts on the question of understanding how our appraisals make sense as normal responses.

We may be surprised by the responses that arise when we ask, "In what way can I understand this appraisal as a normal response to trauma?" For the example of "It is all my fault that I feel so bad," I might recall that self-blame is a common response after trauma. I can observe that self-blame often arises out of a wish to control past or future events—essentially functioning as a protective shield. It may occur to me that the default thought of "it's all my fault" was one that I internalized from others in my life who communicated that I was always solely to blame for feeling upset. I can tell myself that such self-blame makes complete sense given those past circumstances. Or, I may realize that the idea that I could ever completely control my feelings is a normal human hope, but unrealistic.

Opening up to the possibility that our layers of trauma are normal and understandable can feel like a big leap. However, the practice of "normalizing" them can help us become unstuck from untrue assumptions about what trauma means about us and about the world. Reappraising our trauma experiences as human and normal may help reduce some of our negative feelings about them.

Practice #5: Reappraise Layers of Meaning

Even if they seem certain or fixed, our layers of meaning can change. After we go through the process of noticing our layers, we might try out some alternatives. In addition to normalizing our feelings about trauma, we might also try to see new sides of our experiences. We can benefit from intentionally trying to shift our appraisals, bit by bit. For instance, one kind of shift involves noticing any healing or positive changes that we have encountered. Even when trauma brings suffering, it can also elicit different layers of personal growth (sometimes called *posttraumatic growth*). Noticing positive changes mindfully can encourage us.

To reappraise layers of meaning, we can begin with the same method and intention identified in Practice #4 above, Normalize Layers of Meaning. When we reach the self-inquiry part of our meditation, we can ask ourselves one or more of the following questions:

- What strengths within myself do I notice following this experience?
- What new coping skills have I learned during my recovery from trauma?
- What new information have I learned about how my mind works?
- How has this experience changed how I want to relate to myself, or to other people, for the better?
- Do some of my appraisals seem to contain cognitive errors, such as hindsight bias or the assumption of total responsibility? If so, can I revise the appraisal (reappraise it) so that it is more accurate and reflects the fact that I did not know how things would turn out, or the fact that many variables contributed to what happened?
- What is a more balanced, wise, or caring way of looking at the situation?

After pondering these questions, we can observe whatever thoughts and feelings arise, and try to sit with them for a few minutes. We may need several "reappraisal sessions" as we work to shift our firmly held beliefs. It may help to remember that the ability to reappraise our experience is strongly associated with mental health.

Practice #6: Self-Compassion for Layers of Meaning

Handling our layers of meaning can be one of the most challenging aspects of trauma. Because these layers reflect our core sense of ourselves, others, and the world, layers of meaning can hurt enormously when those views are painful. As we work to address the layers, we can provide ourselves with boundless love and support. In being kind and supportive of ourselves, we strengthen our recognition of our own essential goodness. This stance presents a stark contrast to the negative view of ourselves that is often embedded in our layers of meaning.

It can seem like a huge leap to be mentally kind to ourselves, especially if trauma leaves us with the sense that we are shameful, bad, or unworthy. It can take time to see those views as residue from trauma, rather than feelings that reflect the truth. Even as we work in that direction, we can acknowledge the simple fact that feeling bad hurts.

Self-compassion can help us dissolve self-criticism and other negative ways of relating to ourselves. In this practice, we direct self-compassion specifically to negative trauma appraisals. As we notice difficult appraisals or struggle to work with them, we can practice offering ourselves kindness and support. We might try out phrases such as the following:

- I'm so sorry that you are suffering in this way. I offer you my care and support.
- I recognize how painful it is to have this belief about yourself.

- I acknowledge that the process of trying to shift layers of meaning can be very difficult.
- I want to validate you for all the energy and care you have put into your healing process.
- Anyone would feel bad when experiencing this belief about themselves.
- I hope for your healing and happiness.
- I have confidence in your ability to recover, learn, and grow.

In addition to offering ourselves compassion specifically about our trauma appraisals, we can try offering ourselves compassion more generally. Practicing any form of self-compassion can shift the way we think and the way that we relate to ourselves. Self-compassion makes it less likely that we will view ourselves with shame, criticism, or blame, and can help "unstick" us from negative trauma appraisals.

Layers of meaning (also known as "trauma appraisals") are important because they can intensify and maintain our suffering after trauma. However, they can also work in the other direction. Mindfully noticing our layers of meaning can diminish their power over us, and make room for alternate perspectives about why the trauma happened and what it means. When we consciously build new layers of meaning through normalizing our responses, reappraising them, or having self-compassion, we make powerful strides in our trauma recovery.

MINDING THE MOONLIGHT: MINDFULNESS SKILLS FOR DEPRESSION AFTER TRAUMA

DEPRESSION CAN TAKE many shapes: a heaviness in the chest, a dense fog clouding other thoughts, a powerful inertia that makes simple activities seem impossible, or a feeling that nothing matters. Depression can come sporadically, as part of "ups and downs," or as a pervasive feeling of "blah." Depression seems to swallow other parts of our identities, so that we are unable to separate the depressive thoughts and feelings from anything else. We become ensnared in the double whammy of both physical symptoms and negative thoughts that intertwine and hold us in their grasp.

Depression is also shape-shifting: It often appears to us that everything is truly and hopelessly terrible, rather than a reflection of a condition or circumstances that could improve. One of the most painful parts of depression is a mixture of pain and self-blame that can lead us to think, "I feel bad, so I *am* bad," or "there's something unacceptable about me—my core, my character, who I am as person." Navigating through depression often involves attending to its different facets simultaneously—to the physical feelings of depression, to our thinking, and to our emotions.

Depression is an exceedingly common response to trauma. Trauma can disrupt our confidence in ourselves, in others, and in the world, and leave us feeling discouraged. As an alternative to blaming ourselves for being depressed after trauma, we can think of depression as a very normal and understandable reaction, and offer ourselves oodles of compassion. Something or someone has caused us great pain; therefore, it makes sense that we want to retreat and withdraw in order to focus on healing, and to reduce the possibility of being hurt again. Depression may reflect profound grief and loss, and the sense that our whole world is diminished. Once a depressive "lens" is formed, it is difficult to remove, and it colors our vision. Depression's pervasiveness obscures that it is there at all—rather, it seems as if we ourselves, life itself, and other people are painfully, fundamentally awful. Depression often produces the sense that things will never improve. Interacting with a cranky store clerk, getting caught in a rainstorm, or forgetting your wallet at home can appear as evidence that nothing will ever work out. It is often a huge mental leap to think of the depression as a temporary condition rather than as a fundamental characteristic.

Mindfulness skills allow us to observe the different sides of our experience: the part that feels stuck in the trauma, the part that is skeptical about recovery, the part that wants to feel better, and the part that holds some hope for change. Depression can be a signal that some part of our experience needs greater attention and care.

Depression usually includes some combination of the following symptoms:

- Feeling sad or down nearly every day, for more of the day than not
- Losing interest or enjoyment in activities that used to be interesting or fun
- Feeling worthless
- Feeling hopeless
- Feeling irritable or agitated
- Criticizing or blaming oneself for real or perceived faults
- Having trouble concentrating

- Having trouble making decisions
- Ruminating (replaying negative thoughts and memories over and over)
- Feeling tired and fatigued
- Losing energy
- Crying
- Disliking oneself
- Feeling like a failure
- Sleeping either too much or too little
- Eating either too much or too little (changes in appetite)
- Sleeping either too much or too little
- Wanting to die or wishing to be dead
- Feeling helpless
- Losing interest in sex

Several factors appear to contribute to depression, including trauma exposure, coping skills, genetics, and early home environment. Interestingly, depression that is related to traumatic experiences seems to be different from other types of depression. Trauma-related depression is associated with specific changes in the brain, and it appears to respond differently to therapy and to medication than do forms of depression without traumatic antecedents.[225] Furthermore, depressions can vary with respect to the challenges that they present and the therapeutic approaches that seem to be most helpful.

Understanding Depression After Trauma

Trauma-related depression can be depicted through the model of *learned helplessness*. This model is based on the observation that when bad things happen in ways that are unpredictable and inescapable, we (both humans and animals) often respond by giving up. We feel defeated, as if there is no point in trying.

This belief may have been logical within the context of the trauma that we endured. In fact, expending effort to improve or control the situation might have wasted valuable energy necessary for survival. Even after the traumatic situation ends, however, the learned depression often remains, and we continue to feel withdrawn, defeated, and fatigued. Fortunately, we can use mindfulness skills and other tools to incorporate new situations and patterns that replace the old learning with new experiences and skills.

Another common route from trauma to depression involves *internalizing*. We commonly internalize negative experiences. Either consciously or unconsciously, we often interpret traumas as deserved—as reflections of one's own character or worthiness, rather than as events that could happen to anyone. Many survivors of interpersonal trauma are told by perpetrators that their treatment is deserved. Such statements can easily become internalized and result in depression. Abused children or victims of domestic violence may also find it easier to believe that they deserve their maltreatment than to understand that a caregiver or partner—someone on whom they must depend—is abusing them.[226] The sense that we get what we deserve might help us feel a bit more in control (even though this is a false sense of control), but it can lead to depression.

Similarly, it is common to ruminate on *counterfactual thinking* after trauma (e.g., "If I had only started the drive 5 minutes earlier, the accident wouldn't have happened . . ." or "If I had run left instead of right, I could have saved that soldier . . . "). Counterfactual thinking reflects a sense of oneself as the problem—a mindset linked to depression. Counterfactual thinking can easily segue into self-blame ("I was carrying so much cash on me because I'm an idiot . . . basically, I was asking to be mugged because I didn't have the sense to take only what I needed for the day and to leave the rest at home") and then into depression.

Learned helplessness, internalizing, and counterfactual thinking each seem maladaptive, but these tendencies may offer a temporary sense of control and stability. If we consider a trauma to have occurred because of something about ourselves or our actions, we may believe that we can control future events more successfully. The alternative perspective—that we often cannot control what happens to us, and that awful things happen to people who do not deserve them—seems to be extremely difficult for humans to accept. Even trauma survivors who know fully on one level that the trauma was not their fault may become aware of deeper levels of self-blame. Observing our tendencies toward learned helplessness, internalizing, and counterfactual thinking can help us to manage those patterns as we embark on new pathways through depression.

How Can Mindfulness Skills Help Depression?

Mindfulness practices can help people get through depression in several ways. When we notice depression in a curious way, we can become less personally identified with the depression. The depression becomes the weather, and we become the sky. Mindfully observing depression can help us to reduce judgment and self-blame. As we cultivate the part of ourselves that is witnessing the depression as distinct from the parts of ourselves that feel inside the depression, we can gain a sense of spaciousness and room for growth.

Mindfulness practices help us to notice the feelings of depression and its lifting within our bodies. During difficult times, our bodies themselves can become depressed. We often feel fatigued and have the sense that small things take enormous effort. Physical inertia can block recovery from depression. It takes energy to try out new behaviors, thoughts, and feelings—energy that is in short supply during depression. Observing small variations in the sensation of depression helps it to feel less monolithic and more workable.

Mindfulness involves experimentation—trying out new practices and observing whether they influence thoughts and feelings. When people experience long-term depression, it can feel so familiar as to become somewhat comfortable, although it is also painful. Depression contains a certain amount of certainty—the sense that things are truly awful, and that there is nowhere further down to fall. Recovery from depression requires giving up that certainty, and risking that because things are getting better, they could get worse again. When people are used to being depressed, having different (nondepressed) thoughts and feelings can feel scary or uncomfortable. Mindfulness can become a frame for trying out new approaches to depression in a way that feels safe.

Mindfulness practices can also help us cultivate self-compassion, a balm for depression. Understanding that depression is a normal response to trauma can reduce self-blame and self-criticism. We can begin to treat our depression in a caring way, acknowledging that it is painful, understandable, and not a reflection of character. This can help us to feel less depressed *about being depressed*. Whereas self-criticism and self-blame maintain depression, mindful self-compassion generates feelings of friendship and solace towards oneself.

RESEARCH HIGHLIGHT How Do Mindfulness and Self-Compassion Decrease Depression?

RESEARCH STUDIES HAVE demonstrated that mindfulness interventions can reduce symptoms of depression among both trauma survivors and others.[227] Mindfulness may help by increasing our metacognition, or our awareness of our own thoughts from a "witness" perspective. For instance, mindful attention appears to be inversely related to rumination, or feeling stuck in replaying negative thoughts and memories over and over.[228] Mindfulness also seems to reduce depression by protecting us against cognitive reactivity—an experience in which mild negative feelings activate more general patterns of negative thinking, and a tendency that is linked with depression.[229] In addition to these cognitive changes, mindfulness appears to be linked with changes in brain activity that may decrease depression.[230]

Evidence demonstrates that self-compassion can diminish the likelihood that we will develop depression or remain depressed.[231] Low levels of self-compassion seem more closely linked to depression than other mental patterns, including rumination, perfectionistic beliefs and cognitions, and overall emotion regulation skills.[232] Self-compassion seems to work in part by reducing rumination, as well as through decreasing both mental and behavioral avoidance.[233] Self-compassion seems to play an especially strong role in protecting individuals from depression after trauma experiences such as chronic illness and cancer—to an extent beyond its impact on individuals without such challenges.[234]

Interestingly, self-compassion seems to play a stronger role than mindfulness in protecting us from depression and related mental health difficulties.[235] In one sample of 504 individuals, self-compassion was 10 times more predictive than mindfulness in influencing anxiety, depression, and quality of life.[236]

Mindfulness in the Moonlight

In the midst of our moments of pain, it can seem impossible to consider that they could offer anything of value. In the chapter "Gifts of Depression" from his extraordinary book *Care of the Soul*, Thomas Moore (1992) invites us to approach depression with care, listening, interest, and respect. He explains that this stance provides an alternative to a mainstream "hygienic" view of mental health: the idea that we can or should be happy all of the time, that we have a problem if we are not, and that we need to get rid of the negative stuff as fast as possible. Moore argues that being human involves a full array of the emotional color spectrum, a palette of both bright hues and of blues, grays, and black. Rather than rejecting the darker tones, we can allow their presence and sense how they might deepen our lives.

This perspective is not meant to invalidate the pain of depression, but to honor it as real and important. The "moonlight" of depression may offer us glimpses of the world that broaden the ways we understand our experience—shades that are obscured by bright sunshine. Even saying, "I am in the moonlight now" sounds kinder and healthier than saying, "I am depressed." Moore cautions that the "gifts of depression" may be subtle and mysterious. They may emerge as shades of patience, compassion for others, humility, new beginnings after loss, maturity, or as learning how to care for ourselves or others during times of suffering. It is unclear what we might see or learn when we allow ourselves to really *be* with depression, rather than pushing it away, criticizing it, or hiding from it. In his book *Dark Nights of the Soul*, Moore provides this invitation: "I want to encourage you to enter the darkness with all your strength and intelligence, and perhaps find a new vision and a deeper sense of self." (2004, p. xvi). Moore advises that, "We are not out to solve the dark night, but to be enriched by it."

Mindfulness for Changing Behaviors That Contribute to Depression

Mindfulness can enhance *behavioral activation*, one of the most effective ways to reduce depression. Behavioral activation is a fancy term for "doing stuff in an active way." Basically, it involves exercising, going out, accomplishing tasks, and connecting with people. People who are depressed generally do not want to do any of those things. Our minds and bodies are often stuck in a reinforcing feedback loop: we feel bad, so we do not want to do anything, so we do nothing, and then feel worse. Being active sends a new message to our minds, brains, and bodies to engage, and in this way can set in motion a new feedback loop that promotes a sense of hope, energy, and accomplishment.

Behavioral activation involves putting the behavior first, rather than waiting to want to do it. For instance, if you find it difficult to leave your home, I invite you to try getting dressed and going outside, and noticing your feet and your bodily sensations as you step outside. Sometimes it helps to act as though the behaviors are initiated by your body, rather than your mind ("After my body gets dressed, now my feet are going to put on socks and shoes and go outside. I'm not going to worry about what's going on in my mind—my feet have got this.").

This level of mindfulness involves engaging in things that you would do if you were not depressed, and observing them. After the actions are completed—after you have phoned a friend or gotten groceries—you can then be mindful of any changes in depression or other emotions. It is helpful to balance behavioral activation efforts between activities that provide a sense of accomplishment and activities that feel enjoyable. Behavioral activation is a powerful antidote to a depressed mind and body, because it sends powerful signals to the brain that it is time to engage with life rather than to withdraw and conserve energy. Engaging in behavioral activity can meaningfully reduce levels of depression and PTSD.[237]

One of the most effective forms of behavioral activation is physical exercise. I generally encourage all of my patients to exercise if they do not have a physical health barrier. Any form of physical exercise, including walking, is preferable to none; and any amount of time for exercise is preferable to none. I recommend profuse self-encouragement following even one minute of exercise, in order to reinforce the effort. You can also send yourself self-encouragement for everything that you do that promotes exercise: for getting dressed, for leaving the house, for reaching an exercise destination such as a park or gym, as you engage in exercise, and when you are done.

If physical exercise is not possible, there are many other ways to engage in nonpassive activities. You might consider calling or visiting a friend, attending a lecture, going to the library or sporting event, completing a puzzle, creating art or music, or writing and mailing a letter. Mindfully choosing to participate in any of these activities, and then following through with action, can serve as a healthy substitute to more passive activities like watching television or surfing the internet, or to destructive activities such as substance abuse.

Behavioral activation might feel like distraction, or the opposite of mindfulness. Here it may be helpful to make the distinction between *mindful distraction* and *mindless distraction*. With mindful distraction, we mindfully choose to shift our focus to a specific activity and maintain our focus to the extent that we can, and we observe how the activity shifts our thoughts and feelings. Encouraging behavioral activation is not meant to invalidate that depression exists, but to provide an opportunity to observe how an attentional and behavioral shift impacts depression. In contrast, mindless distraction is unintentional: We just fall into it, without choice or reflection. Although mindless distraction may provide some temporarily relief, research demonstrates that effortful engagement in activities is associated with greater well-being. Behavioral activation might not "work" right away; however, many people do report benefits after a single instance or after trying behavioral activation for a couple of weeks.

Mindfulness Exercises for Depression

Practice #1: Mindfulness in the Moonlight

I invite you to find a spot in your home or in the world where you feel comfortable *allowing* yourself to feel sad, depressed, or in the "moonlight." Before entering into the feelings themselves, it can be helpful to decide upon a specific amount of time, such as 10–15 minutes, that you want to devote. You can also decide if you would like to have someone whom you trust be present with you, or if you want to hold something comforting as a "key" that can help you find your way back as needed. Next, you can set the intention of feeling your feelings, of being present in the sensations of pain or depression, and of refraining from criticizing yourself. You may observe physical sensations in the body, and notice if they appear to have some connection to your emotional state. You can also observe your thinking and your emotional states. I encourage you to try to stay present with your actual sensations and feelings in this very moment, and to allow them to be just as they are without trying to change them. If you can, try not to pressure yourself to have all the answers. You might recall that depression is like being in the moonlight—you might need different senses to feel your way around, and objects may present themselves in glimmers and shadows. When you are ready to end your moonlight time, you can use your "key" to come back. You can also thank yourself for your bravery in entering the darkness. This exercise has no end goal; however, it may allow us to relate to depression in a different way, and to understand it more so that we might work with it more skillfully if we choose.

Practice #2: Mindful Behavioral Activation

This exercise involves implementing the following steps to mindfully engage in behavioral activation:

Step 1: I invite you to list at least 5 activities that you might initiate. Behavioral activation works best if these are active (such as walking around a lake) rather than passive (such as watching a movie). If you can, try to balance the activities between some that are likely to provide pleasure, some that might promote a sense of accomplishment, some that contain physical exercise, and some that might encourage a sense of connection to another person (such as sending a birthday card).

Step 2: Next, I encourage you to get specific regarding when you will complete the activities, because that specificity contributes to making it happen. Even just thinking, "I'll call my friend tomorrow after lunch," is more specific than, "I'll call my friend sometime tomorrow." If you can, it is most helpful to pick a specific day and time for each activity.

Step 3: You can next make any preparations that you might need for the activity. For instance, if you are planning to send someone a card, you might need the card, a pen, and a stamp. If you plan to exercise or to attend a social function, it is often helpful to prepare in advance by assembling your clothing or getting your equipment together. This step may sound obvious; however, small preparations can make a big difference during times of depression. We are more likely to go out or accomplish a task if the ingredients that we need are already together.

Step 4: Do the activity. Try to be fully present in the activity as you engage in it, but try not to judge yourself if your mind wanders. If barriers emerge (for instance, a strong sense of lethargy), try to notice them and to still engage in the activity anyway.

Step 5: After the activity, I invite you to appreciate yourself as much as you can for your efforts and for whatever you were able to do ("You didn't even want to go out, and you still did it. Well done! You go!").

Step 6: I invite you to mindfully observe your physical sensations, thoughts, and feelings. For behavioral activation, I have intentionally included mindfulness last rather than first. That is because behavioral activation empha-sizes action as coming first, *before* thoughts and emotions, and because there is some risk that too much attention to thoughts and emotions when trying to initiate behaviors could stall action.

Practice #3: Go Small

In this exercise, I invite you to focus on a very small thing. It can be something that you find good, interesting, amusing, or neutral. Small is key here, because the goal of the exercise is not to change your entire life or mindset, but to narrow your focus to one small thing. Depression can feel overwhelming, as it swirls around our past hurt, current pain, and anticipation of future unhap-piness. Going small counteracts that storm. In mindfulness groups, we often hand out pennies, and encourage people to notice everything that they can about their penny. If the mind wanders, we gently notice that it has drifted and return our focus to the penny. In the groups, we noticed all sorts of new things about pennies, such the lower case "o" next to the upper case "F" on the tail side of the penny. Observing a small thing—in as much detail as possible—can shift depression because it changes our attention and promotes our mindfulness skill of being in this moment.

1. Choose a small object in your immediate environment.
2. Spend at least 5 minutes trying to observe all that you can about the object in as much detail as possible.
3. Use multiple senses: vision, touch, hearing (may be combined with touch if you tap the object), smell, and taste if appropriate to the object.
4. When your mind wanders, gently notice where it went and return

your focus back to the object without judging yourself for having had your attention wander.

5. After 5–10 minutes, check in with yourself about how you are feeling.

Another version of "go small" is to find some very small things that you like, to focus on their nuances in a mindful way, and to acknowledge that they, too, are in this world. Then, you can gradually make this list bigger. You might still feel down, but the depressive feelings can feel a bit more balanced. As a personal example, my list includes flourless chocolate cake, the aria "Deh vieni alla finestra" from Mozart's opera *Don Giovanni*, and Bethesda Fountain in Central Park. Reflecting upon even a few small pockets of fully positive experiences can provide a buffer when things feel overwhelmingly negative. This might feel a bit like Julie Andrews's overly saccharine approach in the Sound of Music ("I simply remember my favorite things, and then I don't feel so bad!"), and I do not mean to imply that it is simple or a cure-all. It is more like allowing the tiniest smidge of good feeling in, while recognizing and respecting that the depression is real. It is finding something tolerable in the broader context of feeling that things are intolerable—a buoy in the sea of depression.

The comic artist and blogger Allie Brosh (2013) described how a very small and seemingly mundane moment mysteriously shifted a prolonged depression:

> I was crying on the kitchen floor for no reason. As was common practice during bouts of floor-crying, I was staring straight ahead at nothing in particular and feeling sort of weird about myself. Then, through the film of tears and nothingness, I spotted a tiny, shriveled piece of corn under the refrigerator.
>
> I don't claim to know why this happened, but when I saw the piece of corn, something snapped. And then that thing twisted through a few permutations

of logic that I don't understand, and produced the most confusing bout of uncontrollable, debilitating laughter that I have ever experienced. (p. 150)

So, I invite you to try it. Look around the room or outside and go small, using all of your senses. "Going small" can feel counterintuitive because we have real, big problems that need attention. Going small can provide us some moments of relative ease, and relative ease is very welcoming in bearing depression and healing from it.

Practice #4: Mindfully Surfing Waves of Depression

The mindfulness teacher Jon Kabat-Zinn advised us that, "you can't stop the waves, but you can learn to surf" (1994, p. 30). This "surfing" involves observing the waves, so that we know more about what we are trying to handle, and practicing our approaches over and over so that we can begin to navigate the waves more skillfully.

Mindfully surfing depression involves exploring the following three questions:

1. What type of pain am I feeling right now?
2. How should I try to handle it?
3. How do I feel right now?

1. What type of pain am I feeling right now?

It is easy for depression to feel monolithic, but if we pay attention, we can notice subtle variations. I invite you take a moment and to tune in with your body right in this moment. Where in your body do you feel the depression? What are the physical sensations? You can take several moments just to observe and to be with those sensations. You might notice the way the air feels in your chest, a tightness or dryness around your eyes from having cried, the set of the muscles in your face, and any other physical accompaniments to depression. The benefit of focusing on physical sensations is that they tie us to our experiences in this precise moment, rather than to the broader levels of pain related to our past experiences, future worries, and thoughts. You can certainly broaden your inquiry of "What type of pain am I feeling right now?" to feelings (for example, "alone," "scared," or "heartbroken"). If you notice yourself on a train of thoughts or amidst memories, you can try to return to your feelings in this very moment (and returning to physical sensations is often an effective way to make that transition).

2. How should I try to handle it?

Here you have lots of choices. For instance, if you observe that you typically feel the worst in the early morning and late evening, and best in the mid-morning, you can plan ahead with the activities and comforts that seem to be most helpful for you. During moments that you feel your best, you can ride that energy towards recovery by engaging in behavioral activation, connecting with someone, or planning for how to get through the harder times. Noticing moments when things feel relatively easier can inspire us to use those pockets of time to accomplish small goals that in turn strengthen feelings of effectiveness.

When you encounter the most difficult moments, you might shift your focus towards caring for yourself and getting through those moments. You can benefit from having previously considered how you might comfort yourself or endure the pain until things feel somewhat more manageable. If it is a somewhat difficult time (not tremendously painful, but not easy), you have many options. You could try behavioral activation, or another mindfulness or self-compassion practice. You might also try to accomplish a task that is not your favorite. That way, you will have gotten through the moment, and you may also feel a small bit of satisfaction that you renewed your driver's license or paid your electric bill.

You also have the option of simply riding the wave—not trying to change or fix anything, but just observing the wave of depression as it comes and goes. There is no simple heuristic of what to do when, because each person and depression is different. Through practice, you can find the navigation style that works best for you. It is often helpful to have several options (e.g., take a walk; do the body scan exercise; accomplish one task), rather than just one coping strategy.

3. How do I feel right now?

After you have surfed the wave of depression by engaging in an activity, practicing a specific mindfulness skill, or by being mindfully present with the wave as it rises and falls, you can check back in with yourself. You can feel the sensations in your body and consider if there are any changes. You might feel different, and you might also sense other waves coming. No matter what the circumstance is, you can meet the waves with attention and care. You may consciously note that you are practicing riding waves: Each wave is an opportunity for practice and for taking care of yourself.

Practice #5: Noticing Triggers and Add-Ons

The movement of moods can be very mysterious. Mindfulness skills can illuminate some of their patterns. When we find that we have shifted from feeling more pleasant to less pleasant, or in any other direction, we can take a moment to ask ourselves about the thought or event (the "trigger") that contributed to the emotional shift. Sometimes these will feel quite obvious, such as receiving an upsetting e-mail or text message. At other times, we may need to reflect and to consider what perturbed us. This information might then inform the way that we surf this particular wave of feeling. Triggers for depression may emerge in the form of "add-ons"— the interpretations or appraisals that people ascribe to events. These add-ons feel like the truth: "The trauma happened or I feel this way because _____ [I am a terrible person/I am doomed/the world is out to get me]." Add-ons seem to carry great weight, and can keep us feeling down and depressed. Mindfulness practices can shed light on these add-ons, which can either be obvious or hidden. We all have add-ons, but we may not be aware of the ways that they maintain depression and other trauma-related problems.

Step 1: I invite you to explore your sensations right now, in this moment. You can set the invitation to investigate both the underlying feeling itself as well as the events today that contributed to it.

Step 2: Consider imagining the underlying physical and emotional feeling as a bit separate from the triggers or add-ons. Take a few minutes to be as present as you can with the underlying feelings of pain or hurt, and provide yourself with care and comfort about those feelings. Then, shift over to the triggers or add-ons. Try not to get lost in the train of thoughts themselves; rather, preserve your work in this exercise as a mindful witness, looking mindfully upon the triggers or add-ons. Try to provide yourself with comfort as you face those painful triggers or add-ons, as they have contributed to pain. Take a minute to reflect upon your bravery in being present in difficult realms—both with the pain itself as well as with the triggers and add-ons that may exacerbate it.

Step 3: Return to your sensations in this moment. Allow space for reflection about the process of attending to the different parts of your experience.

Practice #6: Oodles of Compassion

Depression is so very hard that we need all of the compassion we can get. The research evidence points to self-compassion being especially important in protecting us from depression. There is no risk of going overboard and being too kind to ourselves. Our kindness can take many forms. In her *Dialectical Behavior Therapy Skills Training* manual, Marsha Linehan (1993b) suggested that we can self-soothe using our five senses (for instance, mindfully drinking a cup of tea, taking a bubble bath, or watching a sporting event). I encourage you to incorporate small pleasures to comfort yourself. In addition to behaviors, we can treat our feelings with great compassion. When we take a compassionate stance towards our depression, we acknowledge the full extent of our suffering and our true hope that the suffering will be reduced. Rather than pretending the pain is not there, we meet it as bravely and openly as we can, and we try to offer our care.

Step 1: I invite you to check in with your physical and emotional sensations right now, in this moment.

Step 2: I invite you to notice the pain with a sense of kindness towards the pain, a spirit of care. You can stay with it, and offer it your company, your kind presence. You might notice any sensations or changes that accompany observing your pain kindly.

Step 3: You can visualize holding the pain in your hands with tenderness. You might consider ways to soothe this pain—by petting or patting it; by bringing it some imaginary food and drink; by giving the pain a hug. You can try to comfort the pain with words as well, as long as the words feel right for you. You might try something along the lines of, "I'm so sorry you are feeling this pain. I care about you. I am here to help. I can see how hard this is, and I want to take care of you and help you through this."

Suicidal Thoughts: Mindfulness Skills for Staying Alive

Suicidal thinking can emerge when people are depressed and feel in pain, hopeless, trapped, or as though life is meaningless. If the risk of suicide is imminent—that is, if you do not feel confident that you can keep yourself safe today—I encourage you to call an emergency number (such as 911) or to visit the nearest emergency room. If you are not at imminent risk of hurting or killing yourself but you are still struggling to handle suicidal thoughts, I encourage you to call a 24-hour crisis hotline and to make an appointment with a doctor or therapist to discuss your thoughts and to develop a sustainable plan to stay safe.

Suicidal thoughts can range from a vague sense of, "I wish I could just disappear," to specific ideas or plans. In the therapeutic setting, I work to build an understanding of the frequency and intensity of suicidal thinking. Do the thoughts come every day? How many times per day? How intense do they feel when they come? What are reasons for living, and what are reasons for dying? How can we work together to increase the reasons for living and change circumstances related to the reasons for dying? What are the "triggers" for the thoughts or impulses, and how can we work to change either the triggers themselves or what they seem to mean? Noticing these aspects of suicidal thinking can help illuminate the best way to manage them.

Suicidal thinking usually comes and goes, and varies in its intensity. You may find periods of relative calm or ease, and other instances of turmoil where things feel impossible. Observing this variability can provide some sense of relief and hope—it's not static, even if it feels that way. Even observing ambivalence about being alive can be helpful, because it provides an opportunity to acknowledge and engage with different parts of ourselves, including those parts that *do* want to take good care of ourselves and for things to improve. Many people report suicidal thinking but feel certain that they would never take action to harm or kill themselves. If this is the case, it is still helpful to observe suicidal thinking mindfully in case it becomes more serious.

In moments when things seem not quite as bleak, it can be helpful to carefully plan how to get through the bleaker times. Acts of self-harm or suicide are often impulsive, so the immediate goal is often to survive approximately 2 very difficult hours at a time. A safety plan for getting through the worst times usually involves removing dangerous objects from the home even before a crisis, distracting oneself using media or activities, reaching out to others for help, and calling 911 or a suicide hotline or going to the nearest emergency room if the other steps are insufficient. I encourage you to stay safe, even when it is very, very hard to do so.

In Their Own Words

For me, depression is being stuck wrestling with the past. At age 14, two men raped me and I sank into a deep depression. "I wish I had said no more!" was the thought that came back to me the most, and the one that I did everything in my power to avoid. I avoided it through blackout drinking, risky sex, and controlled eating. I was anywhere but in the here and now. I feared that if I told anyone, my words would crystalize the past and reify my feelings of shame and guilt.

After college, I started practicing mindfulness meditation. At first, all I could hear was my pounding heart. My mind raced: "Why did I let myself get raped? Why didn't I say no more?" Despite these thoughts, I started to feel safe and touch down into the present moment. I could choose when I started to practice, how to practice, and then when to finish. It was like a gentle self-guided exposure therapy. Over 10 years, meditation practice has granted me the access to the present. Through allowing my thoughts to be, I can tolerate them more. I feel safer within my thoughts, myself, and the world.

Depression Meets Poetry and Japanese Ceramics

The poet Rumi (1207–1273) wrote, "Don't turn your head. Keep looking at the bandaged place. That's where the light enters you" (1995, p. 142). Similarly, the poet Kabir (1440–1518) wrote, "Wherever you are is the entry point" (2002, p. 35). We often take it for granted that the desirable state is to be unbroken, with no flaws, cracks, or wounds. It is a deep shift to think of the ruptures in our lives with respect, or as vehicles for wisdom or beauty.

The Japanese ceramic tradition of *kintsugi*—"to patch with gold, [a] technique and artistic concept to repair ceramic using lacquer with gold or silver powder (*Flickwerk*, 2008, Glossary)" or *kintsukuroi*—"golden mend"—dates back to the sixteenth century. In the *kintsukuroi* tradition broken pottery, rather than being discarded, is repaired using silver or gold. The cracks in the pottery are not viewed as blemishes, but as signs of beauty, and as enhancing interest and meaning. This practice can be seen as "ennobling ceramics (Kopplin, 2008, Foreword)."

The origins of *kintsukuroi* date from the sixteenth century, and are linked to the tale of a Korean bowl prized by the ruler Toyotomi Hideyoshi (1537–1598). In the midst of a gathering, Hideyoshi's page dropped the bowl, and it broke into five pieces. The crowd was still, and all were fearful that Hideyoshi would become angry at the page. Then, another guest, Yusai, offered an improvised comic poem that skillfully referenced the former owner of the bowl, the style of the bowl, and a well-known verse in the *Tales of Ise*. Yusai's agile and complex humor made the guests laugh, and shifted Hideyoshi's reaction. The bowl was mended and revered for generations (sometimes becoming five pieces and then mended again). Bartlett (2008) wrote that,

> Mending gave the bowl new life, and in so doing forever immured a neophyte's awkward hands, a warrior's quick temper, a poet-scholar's brilliant mind in its sturdy body. Furthermore the bowl stood as talismanic proof that imagination and language had the power to make ill fortune good. Instead of the altered physical appearance of the bowl diminishing its appeal, a new sense of its vitality and resilience raised appreciation to even greater heights. (pp. 8–9)

We do not decide to be depressed or to have other posttraumatic symptoms. However, we do have options in determining how to handle them. When we approach depression with understanding, care, and honor, it becomes less painful. We can also learn valuable skills as we practice handling the thoughts and feelings of depression, such as patience, self-compassion, and nonjudgment. These skills can then ennoble our journey through depression, and promote resilience throughout our lives.

FINDING SOMETHING IN NOTHING: MINDFULNESS SKILLS FOR NUMBING

AFTER TRAUMA, many of us experience a dislike or distrust of feelings in general. We might wish that we were a robot, or like the character Spock in *Star Trek* (at least, his more prominent Vulcan side), unencumbered by the pain and messiness of human emotions. We may have learned to push our feelings away to cope with trauma, or to hide them so that we could appear strong or fit in with others' expectations. Feeling our feelings without helpful coping skills or support from others can certainly be overwhelming, or even unbearable. Numbing ourselves to our emotions can provide an escape, but it often prevents healing and diminishes our quality of life.

Trauma constricts emotional experiences by narrowing our focus to the current source of stress. It makes adaptive sense that we would allocate our cognitive and emotional energy in order to endure trauma or block feelings in general, even at the expense of ignoring other information. As a result, it can often feel that we lack the capacity to either feel a range of emotions or to handle them when they arise. We often absorb these tendencies into long-term beliefs about ourselves (e.g., "I'm really sensitive," or "I'm just not in touch with my feelings"). However, it is possible to change our emotional patterns, including the tendency to distance ourselves from our feelings or to numb them. To start, it is often helpful to determine the type of numbing that we experience, to consider how and why it began, and to examine its upsides and downsides.

Numbing can involve a range of physical, emotional, and cognitive experiences, and may include one or more of the following:[238]

- Having a diminished sense of being alive
- Feeling empty, dead, or shut down
- Being disinterested
- Feeling as though nothing matters
- Feeling paralyzed
- Being physically numb
- Experiencing "pins and needles" bodily sensations
- Feeling like a robot
- Having the sense of being stuck in a fog
- Having bodily sensations of feeling heavy or sluggish
- Having the sense that your mind is slowing down or going blank
- Struggling to pay attention
- Feeling unclear
- Losing track of time
- Being unaware of your own behaviors
- Having difficulties with memory
- Experiencing a disconnection between your own experience of emotion and that of other people
- Pretending to have feelings despite not really experiencing them
- Hearing from other people that you seem upset or mad but not knowing what they are referring to
- Feeling as though there is a wall between you and other people
- Having a diminished ability to feel care, love, affection, connection, and concern for others

We often become numb only to *positive* emotions following trauma. Trauma often unleashes a flood of negative emotions, but narrows our capacity to experience or express positive feelings.[239] PTSD involves substantial anxiety and fear, often accompanied by anger, irritability, and depression. From a survival perspective, it makes sense that we would become more attuned to potentially threatening cues, while disregarding neutral or pleasant feelings. We might have learned to associate having a feeling such as fear, concern, or surprise with a traumatic situation. We might also avoid experiencing positive emotions because we fear losing control.[240]

Emotions after trauma are often exhausting. With limited resources, we might find ourselves focusing only on the essential activities that are necessary to stay alive. Over time, hyperarousal—such as feeling nervous, jumpy, or "on guard"—can lead to numbing.[241] We may essentially wear ourselves out, such that numbing reflects the depletion of emotional reserves following persistent hyperarousal.[242] We might try to numb our feelings on purpose, or numbing might occur outside of our conscious intention or awareness. We can eventually reach the point where it seems that we stop feeling anything at all. Although some people report feeling numb to positive emotions only, others indicate feeling numb to anger or sadness as well.[243]

Emotional numbing may seem similar to avoidance and to depression. For instance, both numbing and avoidance indicate distancing from difficult thoughts and feelings. Numbing and depression both share a lack of interest and enjoyment in activities, and a diminished range of emotions. However, research indicates that numbing, depression and avoidance are distinct.[244]

Numbing differs from depression because it does not necessarily involve sadness or low mood.[245] Numbing may instead reflect a lack of any feelings, including sadness and depression.[246] Numbing differs from avoidance as well, although avoidance after trauma contributes to emotional numbing.[247] Nonetheless, numbing reflects a general distancing from feelings in particular, whereas avoidance usually involves efforts to limit a range of difficult thoughts, memories, or feelings, and to limit behaviors to avoid specific people, places, and situations.

Many of us develop a mental style that blocks our ability to notice and express emotions. *Alexithymia*, or literally, "a lack of words for feelings," is a term used for this tendency.[248] The term reflects a few types of challenges, including the difficulty some people experience when trying to identify, describe, or express their own feelings. Alexithymia is strongly related to trauma exposure and to PTSD, and particularly to hyperarousal and numbing symptoms.[249]

RESEARCH HIGHLIGHT What Happens in the Brain When We Become Numb to Feelings?

BOTH PTSD AND NUMBING in particular may reflect changes in the brain's patterns of regulating emotional arousal.[250] Numbing seems to reflect the brain's capacity to limit activity in its affective systems in order to reduce trauma-related distress.[251]

Studies that use functional magnetic resonance imaging (fMRI) to study brain activity have found that emotional numbing and alexithymia are linked with decreased activation in response to positive thoughts and images. For instance, one research experiment compared fMRI data from women with and without PTSD as they completed an emotional imagery task. Among the women with PTSD, emotional numbing symptoms corresponded with less positive emotion in response to positive imagery, along with decreased responses within the dorsomedial prefrontal cortex during imagery of positive and negative scenarios. This pattern could reflect impaired conscious and reflective emotional processing.[252]

Similarly, another research study[253] reported that individuals with PTSD rated happy facial expressions as less intense than trauma-exposed individuals without PTSD. Those with PTSD also demonstrated reduced activation in response to happy faces within brain regions thought to help us determine whether a signal is meaningful or threatening. The researchers suggested that this pattern of reduced activation could be associated with symptoms of emotional numbing. They also observed that their results were consistent with previously reported differences in fMRI data[254] between individuals with PTSD versus those without PTSD when engaging in a task that involved monetary gains and losses. The diminished activation was linked with self-reports of difficulty with motivation and social functioning, areas that may be challenging for people who experience numbing.

The scientific data regarding numbing indicate that it can involve our feelings about the past, as well as our emotions in the present. The researchers Mantani, Okamoto, Shirao, Okada, and Yamawaki (2005) conducted an fMRI study that contrasted individuals with high levels of alexithymia with those who indicated low degrees of alexithymia as they participated in a mental imagery task. Individuals with high levels of alexithymia demonstrated significantly less activation in brain regions related to perceiving, processing, or retrieving emotions or memories—results that might reflect an impaired ability to retrieve happy memories.

The studies above provide evidence that PTSD, and numbing specifically, are connected to how our brains respond to events. This research indicates that numbing occurs on a very deep level—one that may extend beyond the scope of immediate, conscious choice in how we respond to the world around us.

Upsides and Downsides of Numbing

When emotions are unpleasant or overwhelming, numbing can offer an alternative. Numbing may help us endure traumatic situations such as war, childhood abuse, and harassment, when we may have no other options. Focusing our attention *away* from emotions, rather than towards them, might allow us to get through difficult circumstances. In fact, distraction is a useful skill for tolerating emotional distress. For example, if I feel impatient and frustrated about waiting in a long line, but it is necessary for me to do so, it would probably help me more to engage in another task than to really get in touch with my feelings of impatience and frustration. However, it might also help me to be aware of my feelings at least a little bit, so that I do not do something destructive like shouting at another person.

Although numbing can provide a temporary respite from emotional pain, it comes with many drawbacks. It can lead to a general lack of awareness of our own feelings and those of others, with a range of negative consequences, such as not seeking needed care, negatively impacting our relationships, and impeding emotional changes. Numbing may worsen PTSD, or block recovery from trauma. Numbing is positively related to the severity of PTSD symptoms:[255] The more people report feeling numb, the more PTSD symptoms they report. Numbing is also related to chronic PTSD—that is, PTSD that lasts over a year.[256]

Numbing is often linked to substance use and addictions. For instance, we might use drugs to try to mitigate emotional pain after trauma, because using substances can numb negative feelings.[257] Using drugs to manage painful emotions is often reinforced by the temporary respite from pain that follows. Because many drugs are physically addictive, in addition to their potential to be emotionally reinforcing, habits and addictions can emerge. Numbing may be associated with these habits and addictions. For instance, emotional numbing is related to the amount of cigarettes that people smoke.[258]

Numbing can lead to the thought that "nothing matters." Numbing narrows our world, so that activities that might otherwise be interesting or fun lose their appeal. Perhaps not surprisingly, numbing is associated with depression and suicidal thinking. In fact, numbing may be the PTSD symptom most strongly associated with thoughts of suicide.[259] Numbing is also linked with deliberate self-harm.[260] Numbing can make self-harm worse: For instance, people who hurt themselves in order to feel something may become desensitized, so that they find themselves escalating the severity of self-harm to feel the same response. Numbing also seems to have a negative influence on our behavior towards other people, including increases in aggression.[261] If it is hard to feel anything, it makes sense that safety, well-being, and life itself might appear unimportant.

Numbing prevents us from engaging with other people, enjoying their company, or taking part in shared activities. Numbing our emotions interferes with family and intimate relationships, and decreases the amount of resources that we gain from interacting with other people.[262] Among couples, emotional numbing is also related to the likelihood of separation and divorce.[263]

On the bright side, becoming less numb can improve our well-being and relationships. Lower levels of numbing are associated with fewer symptoms of depression after trauma.[264] A reduction in emotional numbing appears to be related to positive outcomes in relationships.[265] For individuals with PTSD, decreases in numbing have been linked to improvements in family and social functioning.[266] Sharing our feelings with another person may help us to notice and express them. When we talk about our feelings with other people, we experience lower levels of emotional numbing.[267]

When emotions have been painful, it can be tempting to decide that it is not worth experiencing feelings at all. Although in certain situations, numbing can be an effective coping strategy, numbing also comes with serious costs. We can benefit from learning how to interact with our feelings, rather than resorting to a default style of numbing. It might be helpful to remember that we can experience emotions in ways that are not "all or nothing." As we learn new ways to notice and manage our feelings, we have more and more choices. Little by little, we can build the experience of allowing ourselves to experience feelings, and to observe the variety of consequences—both challenges and benefits—that ensue.

Numbing and Emotion Socialization

Our trauma exposure does not fully determine how we handle emotions; rather, our emotional styles are also shaped through years of input from our families, peers, media, and culture. We might become numb to certain emotions, or even to all emotions, depending on what our "emotion socialization" process has been. For instance, we may have learned that anger or crying is unacceptable, or that it is unseemly to express emotion in public. Many cultures look down on public displays of emotion, such as crying or smiling widely in public. Depending on the messages we have received about how to have and handle emotions, we might stop noticing how we feel, let alone expressing it. Over time, we can become numb—whether or not we have the compounded challenge of coping with trauma.

One aspect of emotion socialization has to do with gender. For instance, some women have been told to smile at men—even strangers—as though they have a duty to represent an outwardly happy persona, or to look pleasant as an object. They may also be socialized against expressing negative emotions, including anger, and they may therefore learn to repress anger.[268] Whereas women seem to be socialized to show emotions more than men, except for anger, men are often socialized not to display emotions at all, *except* for anger.[269] Perhaps for this reason, men generally have higher levels of alexithymia than do women.[270]

Gender-based emotion socialization may also influence responses to trauma. For instance, men report more anger after trauma than do women.[271]

It is also likely that this type of emotion socialization contributes to numbing after trauma, because men and women may have learned not to feel or express different types of emotions. Men who serve in the military might experience a double whammy, in which both broader and military cultures instruct them to repress emotions.[272]

Another important dimension of emotion socialization occurs in families. As children, we are keen observers of the ways that our parents or other caregivers handle emotions, and we absorb their explicit and implicit instructions about managing feelings. For instance, a child who never hears parents discuss their emotions may not be able to ascertain internal feeling states, or may be reluctant to disclose them. Having grown up with parents who were invalidating of emotions (including stating that a child is wrong in his or her statement about feelings, minimizing a child's feelings, or communicating that negative emotions are unacceptable) is related to an inhibited emotional style in adulthood.[273] The input about emotions that we receive from our parents appears to shape our emotional style beyond the influences of cultural background and gender.[274]

As we become more aware of our emotional styles, we have the potential to choose how we want to relate to our own emotions. Even if we have absorbed powerful messages from our families or broader cultural environments, we can begin to decide what we ourselves believe about how to relate to emotions. As we become more conscious and intentional about how we experience emotions, we can build the habits that seem to serve us best as we move forward.

What Good Are Emotions?

We use emotions constantly. Emotions contribute to how we understand the world around us, and influence how we interact with it. They also help us communicate information to other people—the words we choose, our body language, and our tone of voice are packed with emotional messages. In some situations, emotions can save time. We might wish to impart impending danger ("Watch out!") or exchange a meaningful glance. Emotions can help organize our experiences, motivate us to act, and surmount obstacles. Even difficult emotions, such as anger, can lead to positive changes. For example, anger can help us identify unfairness and spur our action to create a more humane world.

Emotions often signal us to pay attention. For instance, a feeling of sadness might alert us that we need additional care and support, or a strong feeling of discomfort on a date might indicate that it is not a good match. We sometimes feel a sudden burst of emotion that seems to come out of nowhere but that can indicate that there is something happening in our emotional lives—perhaps something mysterious or underneath the surface—that needs tending.

There are many myths about emotions, including the idea that they reflect weakness or stupidity, or that they are unnecessary.[275] The phrase "overly emotional" is often said in a disparaging way, as is the idea of being "unable to control" emotions. However, emotions are not wholly controllable. They can be cultivated, managed, and tended, but as long as we are human, total control over our emotions will remain elusive. Furthermore, being "underly" sensitive, such as mistreating others or ignoring our own needs, may be just as problematic as seeming "overly" sensitive.

After trauma and PTSD, emotional reactions can certainly become heightened, so that seemingly small events, such as hearing a loud noise or reading an upsetting story, can provoke a substantial response. However, trauma can also result in feeling numb or having blunted emotions. In both cases, mindful reflection about an emotional reaction, or a lack of it, can help us to appraise the situation wisely. For instance, discomfort on a date could indeed indicate that the match is not right; however, it could also reflect fear of getting into a relationship after one that was traumatic, or nervousness about wanting the date to go well.

Emotions help us make wise decisions. If we discount our emotions, we could suffer. For instance, I might save a lot of money if I shared a three-bedroom, one-bathroom house with ten other people. It even could seem, from a logical perspective, like a good idea to cut my rent by 90%. However, if I did not consider the aggravation I would feel about having to wait for the shower every day or the frustration I might feel about giving up my privacy, I would not make an effective decision. Trying to keep emotions out of decisions can result in poor decisions. Instead, we want to notice and use a range of available information when making decisions.

As we incorporate emotional information into our thinking and decision making, it is often helpful to balance it with other types of information as well. In his book *Blink: The Power of Thinking Without Thinking*, Malcolm Gladwell (2005) described instances in which "gut feelings" resulted in correct decisions, but also provided many examples—including stereotyping and prejudice—of when they resulted in poor decisions. After trauma, emotions can sometimes extend beyond the utility that they might provide. If after an interpersonal trauma, I feel fearful around other people and decide not to interact with other people at all, emotional remnants from the trauma may be overpowering my other goals and values. Practicing mindfulness towards our emotions can help us determine why an emotion is arising, and how much we should allow it to determine our decision making.

Mindfulness and Numbing

Practicing mindfulness can be daunting for those of us who numb our feelings. "I don't feel anything," is a common complaint from many individuals who begin to practice mindfulness, and from people used to numbing. If you do not feel much at all, that is just fine. There is no rush, and no prize for noticing many sensations versus a very few. You can start with noticing whatever arises, even if what arises is not being able to feel. For instance, if you are practicing the body scan (in Chapter 1) and you cannot feel your toes or your feet, you can notice the lack of sensation there. If you have emotional reactions to the challenge of noticing feelings, you can observe those reactions (for instance, frustration, annoyance, or confusion).

The research evidence shows that mindfulness seems to be particularly helpful for symptoms of avoidance and numbing.[276] Practicing mindfulness can counteract tendencies to ignore internal sensations and emotions. Simply setting an intention to notice even small variations in our experience might help us begin to shift from feeling nothing to feeling something. Other aspects of mindfulness, including curiosity, beginner's mind, patience, present-moment awareness, and nonjudging may also explain how mindfulness practice can bring about changes in numbing. For instance, the ability to observe experiences mindfully without judging them is associated with lower levels of numbing and of avoiding symptoms.[277]

It can be a bit scary to allow ourselves to feel feelings after a prolonged period of not feeling them. We might fear that allowing ourselves to experience any feelings at all will unleash a deluge of unmanageable feelings. However, it can feel empowering to choose the setting, process, and pace that seem most right for us. Whereas some people are caught off guard when trauma-related feelings arise after they stop numbing through alcohol, other drugs, or overwork, a deliberate and mindful approach to noticing feelings can help us maximize our comfort and reduce the likelihood of becoming overwhelmed. We can then become more aware of emotions gradually, and support ourselves in the process of connecting to our feelings in a way that matches our own comfort levels and preferences.

We can maximize our senses of comfort and safety as we work to decrease our numbing and begin to reconnect with our emotions. Many survivors of trauma find it helpful to build up their *distress tolerance skills,*[278] or the capacity to handle and endure challenging feelings. It can help to have a specific plan in place to use if emotions feel too difficult to sit with, such as calling a friend, practicing self-compassion, or self-soothing with the five senses.

It might also help to address numbing and the feelings that it masks within the context of counseling or psychotherapy. The presence of another person, especially one who is trained to handle trauma and its effects, may feel supportive and calming. That person can also help keep the level of emotional exposure manageable, check in about the level of comfort and difficulty in the moment, and help suggest specific distress tolerance practices to handle challenging feelings.

If we choose to open up to feel more, it might be a bit uncomfortable. That initial discomfort does not indicate that the unpleasant feelings will last forever, even if it seems that way. It might help to remember that any change can be challenging, and to also acknowledge if opening to sensations produces any awareness of pleasant or neutral sensations, along with more difficult feelings.

Mindfulness of physical sensations—the many sources of physical information about this moment that are contained within our own bodies—is a useful way to begin to address numbing. It can be more accessible to feel a breath than to feel a feeling, and often less scary. Mindfulness practice using the body also promotes the same perspective that is useful in noticing our feelings: one of awareness, patience, and nonjudgment. We can later return to mindfulness of bodily sensations in this moment if our attention to feelings becomes too intense.

In some cases, it might not be wise to begin to address numbing via bodily sensations. If the thought content within our fear, anxiety, or trauma is strongly related to our bodies (for instance, a physical illness or panic attacks that include anxiety about breathing), it might be wise to start with another mindfulness practice. In those cases, it might help to practice mindfulness in daily activities, or mindful walking as a starting point.

Mindfulness and self-compassion practices promote the acceptance of emotions, whereas trauma and numbing tend to limit our emotional experiences. Through cultivating our mindful attention to a fuller range of sensations, we can broaden our experience, so that our worlds become much larger than either the trauma or our attempts to escape trauma-related feelings. Practicing mindfulness also reduces the shame or fear that we might have about having difficult emotions. Mindfulness skills can provide a framework through which we can pause and attend to a "felt sense"—an implicit resonance among our thoughts, emotions, and sensations that is often beyond words or logic.[279]

Most moments are manageable on their own, one by one. Our suffering increases when we mentally project our present experience into the future. Every moment presents a new opportunity to deepen our presence right here, as we observe and feel this experience. These practices build the sense that "this is my only job: to notice the sensations in this moment, right now." They also present opportunities to observe self-judgments and beliefs that arise, and to note them gently before returning to present-moment sensations. By cultivating our relationship to this moment, our sense of being overwhelmed recedes, and we awaken new feelings and sensations.

Mindfulness Practices for Numbing

Practice #1: Mindfulness in Daily Activities

Most of us spend a substantial portion of our days on autopilot. We complete many tasks that are repetitive, that we know how to do, and that we have completed many times before. It is very easy to space out and let our minds wander when we are bathing, traveling, cooking, eating, or cleaning.

Our lack of consciousness means that we lose touch with the task that we are completing in the moment. In some real way, we do not feel the water or soap on our bodies, taste our food, feel our footsteps, or notice our movements. This zoning out may contribute to numbing; however, we can also practice zoning back in.

Getting more in touch with our physical sensations, including our five senses, during daily activities can be a manageable and approachable way to begin to feel after a period of numbness. It may seem less scary or overwhelming than trying to tune in to our emotions, because it is usually less highly charged.

We need to pick something and decide to do it, and then remember to do it. You might consider one of the following activities:

- Getting out of bed in the morning
- Brushing your teeth
- Bathing or showering
- Getting dressed
- Walking the dog
- Washing dishes
- Preparing a meal mindfully
- Eating a meal mindfully
- Engaging in mindful walking as part of your daily routine (e.g., walking to the bus stop)
- Cleaning

The key part is remembering to practice mindfulness during the daily task. It is often helpful to set a goal for a specific time and duration that we will practice mindfulness in the daily activity—for instance, the intention to pay mindful attention to washing the dishes after dinner every night for 1 week.

Once we decide on a task, we can set out to notice as much as we can, and to keep noticing. If we choose brushing teeth, we can notice it all: reaching to pick up the toothbrush, the feeling of holding it in our hand, the feel of the faucet as we turn it on, the act of squeezing the toothpaste and putting it onto the brush, the muscles involved in lifting the brush up to our teeth and to brushing, and the taste and touch of the toothpaste brush. The list could go on (rinsing the toothbrush), but you get the idea.

It may be especially challenging to try to focus on the sensations in this moment for actions that we usually complete with little if any conscious thought. We can expect to go back on autopilot many times. As we complete the exercise of mindfulness in daily activities, we can practice not judging ourselves for becoming distracted, and we can practice returning to our experience of that activity in the present moment.

What you notice does not have to be profound. The key here is to build up the muscles of noticing anything internal at all, including bodily movements, physical sensations, and emotions. Over time, our capacity to notice generalizes, and we become more practiced and comfortable accessing internal sensations, thoughts, and feelings.

Practice #2: The Curious Detective

Because it can be very hard to observe our own emotions and sensations after a period of numbing, it may be easier to start by noticing those of others around us. We may or may not be accurate in our assessments of others' emotional states, but we can observe the signs that are present. Signs of other people's feelings may emerge in their body language, facial expression, tone of voice, and the words that they use.

Psychologists such as Lorber and Garcia,[280] and Levant,[281] have helped individuals who have difficulty accessing their feelings by encouraging them to practice investigating other people's emotions. This process may assist us in labeling emotions with words, particularly when we are not used to doing so, or feel somehow as though we are not allowed to do so. As the skill of investigating others' emotions becomes stronger with practice, we can then turn this investigative ability towards our own feelings.

To practice being a Curious Detective, it can help to begin in a low-pressure situation, or one in which we have no other cognitive or emotional demands. That is, it may be easier to first practice the skill of noticing others' emotions on the bus, in a subway station, or at a store, rather than when we are engaged in a business meeting or a conversation. We can then commit to our "role" as the Curious Detective with some degree of focus, and return to that stance if we become distracted.

For this practice, we need to pick a spot where we can observe other people, such as the following:

- A park
- A bus, train, or transit station
- A store
- A shopping mall
- A street with a fair amount of passers-by

Once we find an appropriate spot, we can find a comfortable location, such as a seat or bench, or stay on our feet. Then, we can begin to observe. It is usually best not to stare in an obvious way at another person (that is, to look at someone for a prolonged period before looking away), but several short glances are usually unnoticeable (and acceptable if they were to be noticed). We can then be open to what we see.

We might see a smile, a frown, or a grimace. A person might yawn, or roll his or her eyes. We can overhear conversations that sound pleasant, neutral, or agitated. We may witness laughter, shouting, or humming. Once we notice something, we can then try to surmise how the person is feeling (amused? bored? dejected? delighted?). We might even detect a few pieces of information to string together. For instance, if you see a person bump into someone else when boarding a bus, and the person who was bumped sighs, frowns, and glares, you might gather that this person was upset and angry about having been bumped.

I invite you to try out the Curious Detective exercise for at least 5–10 minutes, and to return your attention to the task when your mind starts to wander. We can certainly be wrong in our assessments and interpretations of others' emotions, but we can still try to observe the facts that are available and to develop our best guess about how another person is feeling. For this exercise, being correct about another person's feelings is not as important as the simple act of noticing the emotional clues around us.

The Curious Detective exercise engages our curiosity and our ability to pay attention to the present moment. The "detective" mindset is one that is characterized by looking for clues, and by allowing patterns to emerge—but tries to refrain from limiting our assessment of the facts to fit our preconceived expectations. We may observe our own generalizations, judgments, or stereotypes as we engage in detecting others' emotions (such as, "everyone is the same," "people are all unhappy," or "there's nothing interesting to see"). If this occurs, we can note those thoughts gently before returning our attention to the specific evidence of emotions (or lack of emotions) that we observe before us.

After a week or two of practicing the Curious Detective when observing other people, we can begin to look for cues in ourselves. We might notice ourselves sighing, yelling, or yawning; what might these things mean? We can take our attention to the position of the muscles in our face. Does a tense forehead, tight jaw, or frown provide some indication about our emotional state? Even if we are not sure about how to interpret the clues, the Curious Detective exercise emphasizes gathering as much information as we can. As we notice more, we can broaden our awareness of emotional material—both others' emotional states and our own.

Practice #3: Finding Words for Emotions

Numbing often involves a disconnection between the parts of ourselves that experience feelings and the parts of ourselves that label, understand, and organize those feelings. As we address difficulties with numbing, finding the words for our feelings often presents one of the biggest stumbling blocks and challenges. The practice of matching words to feelings seems to help us alleviate some of our distress. A bundle of unnamed emotions can seem a lot more challenging than a few specific feelings. The psychologist Dan Siegel advocates a "name it to tame it" approach to feelings,[282] and references research[283] that indicates that the capacity to name a painful feeling actually does reduce our emotional distress.

Often, it is easier to recognize a term for an emotion that resonates with our experience, rather than trying to pick out the word from thin air. The list below can provide a starting point for noticing what emotions you might be feeling, either in the present moment or in the past. If it feels right for you, you can look over the list below, and consider which of the words relate to your experience.

As you read through the list, you might set an intention to read in a way that is slower than your usual pace. You might choose to read only a few words at a time before pausing. You can also set an intention to give yourself a moment to notice any physical or emotional reactions that you have to the words.

Words for Emotions				
Confused	Bewildered	Amused	Jaded	Aggravated
Animated	Serene	Affectionate	Annoyed	Resigned
Exuberant	Indignant	Worried	Dismayed	Wary
Forlorn	Abandoned	Beleaguered	Content	Heartbroken
Giddy	Befuddled	Concerned	Anguished	Enamored
Humiliated	Tender	Irked	Knotted Up	Flabbergasted
Relaxed	Grieving	Complacent	Disappointed	Bothered
Heartened	Suspicious	Resentful	Shocked	Disenchanted
Concerned	Impatient	Satisfied	Perplexed	Calm
Lonely	Disoriented	Exasperated	Peaceful	Ambivalent
Confident	Infuriated	Bitter	Energetic	Disillusioned
Elated	Relieved	Distraught	Hopeless	Remorseful
Frustrated	Delighted	Irritated	Uncomfortable	Ecstatic

Once you have found a word or two that reflects your experience, you can give yourself a moment with the word or words. You might notice a sensation of something settling or clicking into place; or, you might observe some sort of gap in between your mental understanding of your experience and an emotional "felt" sense. It can help to remember that you are in charge of determining whether and how to apply a word to your experience.

As a variation, some mindfulness practices advise people to try noticing if something feels *pleasant*, *neutral*, or *unpleasant*. Beginning with those categories may help as we begin to understand and organize our experiences. The simplicity of those categories can also help us if we feel overwhelmed with a range of emotions, or if we begin to ruminate on the complex story behind a sensation.

The words *pleasant, neutral,* or *unpleasant* can also help us remember to attend to all three categories, as we may fail to notice neutral or pleasant sensations. They may also help us to disentangle ourselves if we find ourselves overidentifying with an emotion—that is, feeling lost in the feeling or as though we *are* the feeling.

Practice #4: Exploring Numbing With Curiosity and Compassion

Once we decide that we want to make changes in how we experience feelings and emotions, the actual process of change can be a bit slow or frustrating. We might help ourselves by taking the pressure off: Instead of trying to feel, we can be curious about exploring what we do *not* notice or feel. Or, we might sense that there is some sort of feeling just out of reach. We can investigate how, when, where, and why we feel numb. For instance, we might notice when something seems to trigger a numb reaction in us, such as an unpleasant interpersonal exchange. A mindful perspective honors all these reactions as experiences—none inherently more worthy than another. Finally, we can offer ourselves compassion about the challenge of trying to feel things when we feel blocked.

Step 1: To explore numbing with curiosity and compassion, we first pick a practice such as mindful breathing, mindful walking, or the body scan. We can approach it with the intention to notice broadly—including the parts that seem inaccessible. For example, when practicing the body scan, we may observe that we can tune in to some of our body parts just fine, but that we cannot observe sensations in other parts of our body. We might take the opportunity to observe what we can about the distinction, such as where our ability to notice physical sensations starts and where it stops. I might be able to feel my ankle and foot, but not my toes.

Step 2: If we do notice a block, we can be curious about it. Where does it start, where does it end? What triggers it? What seems to promote or decrease our ability to access our own thoughts and feelings? A curious and interested stance can help us get through some of the judgments we might carry about an inability to have feelings or to notice them.

Step 3: As we notice our numbing, we might observe subtle variations. If everything just feels "blah" and "gray," we can even be curious about that. What sort of blah is it, and what shade of gray is it? Can we notice any moments of variation? Are there instances in which something sparks our interest for a moment, or annoys us?

Step 4: We can also offer ourselves compassion as we work with numbing. We might acknowledge that addressing numbing is challenging, and takes effort. We can provide ourselves with care and understanding about how our numbing developed, and the way that it functions in our lives. As we work to notice or shift our patterns of numbing, we can also encourage ourselves by giving ourselves credit for putting energy into the process.

In Their Own Words ———————————————————

> *I was in India (my hometown of Delhi) and I had a very serious first relationship for 3 years that started when I was about 17 years of age (currently 40+!). It felt so right but then things began to go wrong in the 2nd year. He became extremely possessive of me and jealous of my male friends and forbade me to meet any of them "if I loved him." Initially, I did this, but a few months into it, I realized I was losing good friends.*
>
> *I decided soon after to go back to those friendships, which made my partner so angry that he met up with me one night, slapped me on my face 4 times,*

and twisted my arm forcefully while I was pinned down and told me that next time "he would punch me if I met my male friends again". When I got home I told no one . . . just went to bed and sobbed my heart out. I never saw him again (despite his threats to kill himself, kill me, and so on). I was numb for many days and weeks. I felt a mix of guilt and anxiety. Eventually, I broke down and told my closest friend the truth. It felt so good, almost like a cleanse . . . he was incredibly supportive and told me that the best decision I made was to never go back to him.

I found ways to deal with the trauma. I focused on school, work, my future ahead and on my inner resilience and strength. I committed myself to doing many years of volunteer work at an Anti-Domestic Violence center and I think that was the true start and completion of my healing process—helping to empower victims of domestic violence to help themselves. Today, I am a confident professional woman, with a doctorate in sociology, a loving partner of 15 years, and a wonderful, intimate circle of family and friends.

Like many responses to trauma, numbing appears to develop for a logical set of reasons: to protect ourselves from painful information or emotions, to enhance our ability to focus and survive in threatening situations, and as a way of coping with an overload of difficult thoughts, memories, or feelings. However, numbing takes a negative toll on our well-being and relationships, and we may wish to shift our tendencies to numb our feelings. Because mindfulness practices and talking to other people about our feelings are associated with less numbing, they may help us reduce numbing. A curious and compassionate perspective towards not feeling can help us experience a fuller, more balanced, and more joyful life.

CULTIVATING PRESENCE: MINDFULNESS PRACTICES FOR DISSOCIATION

S ONIA SOTOMAYOR, the United States Supreme Court Justice, poignantly described her experience of dissociation on May 26, 2009, the day that her nomination was announced. "I felt like my spirit had left my body" (Owers & Kossler, 2015, p. 5), Sotomayor reflected.

> I was looking at myself from up there . . . I couldn't connect with my emotions and I knew, ultimately, that the reason for that was if I did, I wouldn't be able to do what I needed to do: to give a speech. I thought that feeling would end that day, but it lasted for about a year and a half. I watched myself doing things that I would have never thought possible. (p. 5)

Sotomayor's description portrays many aspects of dissociation: watching from above or having an "out of body" experience, disconnecting from emotions or even from ourselves in order to function, and maintaining these tendencies as a long-term way to manage stress. Her reflection highlights how dissociation can be adaptive during moments of stress. In addition to the experiences she describes, we may also notice ourselves "spacing out," feeling as though things are unreal or in a dream, having gaps in our awareness or memory, feeling "foggy," perceiving the world as odd, flat, or lifeless, or compartmentalizing our feelings and thoughts.

A common definition for dissociation is a separation among aspects of mental functioning that are usually integrated. Components of attention, identity, memory, and perception can become fragmented, and can make us confused, distressed, or unable to concentrate. These disruptions may reflect traumatic intrusions—unwanted thoughts, images, or memories—or difficulty accessing pieces of our thinking, memories, feelings, or identities.

Dissociation comes in many shapes and sizes. A classic example of everyday dissociation is "highway hypnosis," in which we find ourselves driving a car for many miles while our thoughts travel elsewhere. We can also lose track of ourselves or the outside world when we are engrossed in a book or a movie. Alcohol and other drugs can produce dissociation, as can fatigue, stress, and trauma. Mild episodes of *derealization*—the feeling that you or your surroundings are detached or not real—can be brought on by fatigue, stress, hypnosis, or alcohol or drug use. However, more severe instances of derealization can be distressing and cause problems. For instance, some people describe feeling as though they are in "the Twilight Zone" or "Alice in Wonderland."[284]

People describe dissociation in all sorts of ways: "I'll explode at my husband, and afterward I can't remember what I said," "I act differently with different people," "It's not feeling real or feeling that I'm just doing things automatically" (Steinberg & Schnall, 2001, pp. 4–5). One trauma survivor observed that, "it all still feels like a blurry sequence of dreams, it's a videotape with the sound turned off" (Barglow, 2014, p. 121). Everyone has moments of dissociation, and many of those moments do not cause problems. When dissociation is frequent and causes distress, it may require care and attention. Problematic types of dissociation can involve large gaps in memory, mental confusion, or a feeling of inner emptiness or lifelessness.[285]

What causes dissociation? The brain has multiple tracks that it uses to process factual and emotional information. When we become overwhelmed, these tracks can split off from each other, so that emotionally charged information becomes more isolated. As a result, we experience disconnections in awareness and memory.[286] Although dissociation can be challenging, it often functions as an attempt to preserve mental stability in the context of stress.

Dissociation is strongly associated with having experienced trauma.[287] Dissociation can be an adaptive response to trauma, because it can help us separate upsetting material from our awareness so that we can function. We might dissociate on purpose, as a coping strategy, or we might dissociate unintentionally. When it takes the shape of intrusions, dissociation may reflect efforts to integrate and process trauma-related material.[288]

Dissociation can cause many problems, because it impacts attention, concentration, and memory. When we dissociate, we might seem distracted and "out of it." For these reasons, it is easy to understand how people might mistake dissociation for attention deficit hyperactivity disorder (ADHD). Dissociation may impact our performance at work or in school, hinder our relationships, or increase our risk for trauma revictimization.[289] Many people experience short-lived episodes of dissociation, especially during moments of stress and trauma. However, when it persists, life can become "a joyless, 'empty dream'" (Steinberg & Schnall, 2001, p. 63).

The following experiences reflect different aspects of dissociation, sometimes called *depersonalization* (feeling cut off from yourself, your feelings, your thoughts, or your body), *derealization* (feelings of unreality or separation from the world around you), *identity confusion* (uncertainty, conflict or confusion about who you are), and *identity alteration* (observable changes in roles or identity):[290]

- Having a sense of being separate, disconnected, or detached from your body
- Looking at yourself as if you were an outsider or a stranger

- Having an "out of body" experience
- Feeling invisible
- Having the sense that you are watching yourself as if you were looking at a character in a movie
- Feeling that the world is a television show or movie,
- Feeling cut off from your emotions
- Feeling as though you are a robot, or that other people are robots
- Having feelings that are very compartmentalized
- Not recognizing your own face in the mirror
- Feeling as though your body or body parts are distorted or not real
- Listening to yourself as though someone else were speaking
- Doing something you would not normally do but feeling compelled to do it or unable to stop
- Feeling as though you are a "passenger" in your body, rather than the driver
- Having the perception that objects change their size, shape, or color
- Experiencing an internal struggle to figure out your identity
- Having facets of yourself that sharply contrast, such as enjoying certain foods or activities that you normally dislike
- Noticing handwriting that does not look like your usual writing
- Observing yourself acting like very different people
- Feeling like a stranger to yourself
- Having the sensation of being controlled
- Using different names
- Speaking in a different voice or manner
- Feeling as though you have different personalities
- Having the sensation of relinquishing control from yourself to another individual inside of you

- Finding objects in your possession that you do not remember receiving or purchasing
- Hearing from others that they interacted with you, but having no recollection of the conversation

Dissociative Disorders

Dissociative disorders are very complex. To get an accurate diagnosis for dissociative disorders, and to receive effective treatment, it is very important to consult a health provider who has undergone specific training in dissociative disorders. Because most therapists lack training in treating dissociative disorders, it is necessary to *ask* prospective health providers about their training and experience in assessing and treating these conditions. A dissociative "disorder" generally indicates a more serious or prolonged presentation of the types of dissociative experiences described above.

Depersonalization/derealization disorder involves episodes of feeling detached from yourself, your feelings, your thoughts, or parts of your body (depersonalization) or feelings of unreality or detachment from the world around you (derealization). The episodes persist and recur, and cause distress or dysfunction. Some people experience either depersonalization or derealization, while others experience both.

Amnesia is the experience of having gaps in memory, being unable to remember important personal information, or being unable to access specific events or periods of time. Amnesia refers to memory loss to a degree beyond common forgetfulness. It is often a trauma or important event that is forgotten, or a substantial period of time. There may also be "microamnesia," where people engaged in conversation forget what was said in the previous moment.

People may feel ashamed or embarrassed or try to hide instances of amnesia and other symptoms of dissociation.[291] Amnesia after trauma can take the form of either encoding or retrieval problems. That is, people who are impacted by numbing, derealization, and depersonalization may forget information because these experiences prevented information from being encoded in the brain so that it could be remembered. However, other types of dissociation, such as compartmentalizing feelings or aspects of identity, might interfere with the brain's ability to retrieve information.[292]

Dissociative amnesia refers to an inability to recall important personal information, or a loss of memory for your own identity, to an extent that is beyond normal forgetting. It might be confined to a specific event or period of time, to aspects of an experience, or generalized to your identity and life history. Dissociative amnesia is the most common of the dissociative disorders, and can last from a few days to a few years.[293] People are commonly unaware of their amnesia, but some people with dissociative amnesia know that they have memory loss. The memory loss is often reversible because the difficulty is in the retrieval process (that is, the trouble is with finding the memories, rather than with never encoding them in the first place). Dissociative amnesia may include *dissociative fugue*, which involves either sudden, unexpected travel or confused wandering, and is associated with amnesia for identity or other personal experiences.

Dissociative identity disorder (DID)—also known as multiple personality disorder—refers to having at least two distinct identities within yourself that can take charge of your thinking and behavior. With DID, life can seem very fragmented, because identities and experiences are separated into different pieces. The different personalities may have access to different information and coping styles. Some personalities may be aware of other personalities, but other personalities may lack this awareness. Because of these variations in awareness, some people with DID do not know that they have it. DID often involves derealization, depersonalization, identity confusion, and difficulty remembering information that is beyond ordinary forgetfulness.

Dissociative disorder not otherwise specified (DDNOS) is a diagnosis that reflects an early stage of one of the other diagnoses, or a presentation that is less serious than another diagnosis or does not meet all of the criteria. DDNOS is a common presentation of dissociative difficulties.

Common Misconceptions About Dissociation

Dissociative symptoms and disorders are often misunderstood. For instance, people may have the impression that the presence of dissociation indicates that a person has a very serious condition. However, dissociation is quite common in the general population, with approximately 25% of people reporting mild to severe levels of dissociation. Depictions of dissociative identity disorder in the media or public imagination are often overly dramatic. Dissociation, including DID, is often completely invisible. Many people who experience DID appear identical to the outside world from those without DID—that is, they can still function quite well and participate in activities of daily living.

Just as people often imagine flashbacks as being "all or nothing" breaks from reality, people might assume that dissociation is a wildly strange event. In reality, both flashbacks and dissociative experiences are often quite subtle. People may even have their minds partially in the present moment and partially elsewhere—or their experience of their own personal identity might be partially integrated and partially compartmentalized.

Finally, perhaps because DID has often been sensationalized in movies such as *Sybil* and *Fight Club*, there is sometimes a stigma associated with the diagnosis. Although it is common for people to believe that experiences of dissociative identity are strange or even "crazy," the science of dissociation indicates that DID and related experiences are quite logical, and that problems associated with dissociation are treatable.[294]

Mindfulness and Treatment for Dissociation

Because dissociation is often linked with stressful circumstances, the first step in healing is establishing safety and stability. The next steps often involve building skills that help us notice and tolerate emotions; control impulses; observe how, why, and when dissociation occurs; and improve skills involved in relating to other people.[295] When dissociative disorders are present, treatment providers often focus on cultivating safety, coping skills, as well as a connection to the patient, before discussing traumatic material itself. In fact, addressing trauma without a safe, trusting foundation can be destabilizing.[296]

Practicing mindfulness can change our experience of dissociation. For instance, we might notice if we try to escape mentally whenever something feels uncomfortable. If we pay attention, we can often discover signals that we are about to dissociate, including changes in vision, feeling bored or stressed, or physical discomfort. Changing our habits requires some awareness of those patterns and how they operate. As we develop insights into our dissociation, we may also shift our judgments about it. For instance, understanding how dissociation may have been helpful during trauma can help reduce negative thoughts or feelings about it.

In many ways, dissociation and mindfulness are opposites. When we dissociate, we leave our present-moment experience; when we practice mindfulness, we try to stay in the present moment. Because practicing mindfulness builds our capacity to stay in the present moment, implementing mindfulness practices may be an especially appropriate way to manage dissociation.[297]

Mindfulness offers a strong antidote to dissociation, because we can learn to become more present with thoughts, feelings, and sensations rather than detaching from them. We can also notice what it feels like to go away and to come back, and what our triggers are. As we practice observing these patterns, we can gain more awareness and control over the process.

In some cases, we may use mindfulness practices to separate ourselves from reality. Just as we might practice mindfully attending to certain aspects of the present moment in order to avoid awareness of painful feelings related to the past, some people describe using mindfulness to help them dissociate. It can be a voluntary process, in which individuals (often trauma survivors) try to zone out or self-hypnotize, and discover effective ways of doing so. They may even notice and implement this process in a mindful way, in which they are highly aware of transferring their focus out of the present moment.

Dissociation is often highly adaptive, but it becomes less so when it occurs outside of our conscious choice, as our only coping strategy, or in a way that disrupts our functioning in everyday life. We might choose to keep dissociation as one option for handling distress, while also building additional coping skills.

As we practice observing where our minds go, we become more skilled in shifting our attention so that it is most aligned with our goals. We build the element of conscious choice over our mental processes, and increase our options for managing our thoughts and feelings.

DISSOCIATION REFLECTS the brain's attempt to manage overwhelming emotional material. In fact, dissociation may involve an *overmodulation* of emotion in the brain.[298] Brain regions that help control emotions become overactive, and they impede emotions and emotional processing so that people feel cut off from their feelings or as though things are unreal. For instance, the brain's medial prefrontal cortex can decrease emotional processing in the brain's limbic regions,[299] resulting in a state of detachment or numbness. This brain activity contrasts with emotion *undermodulation* after trauma, in which symptoms such as intrusions and hyperarousal are undercontrolled by the brain's cortical regions.[300]

Over time, dissociation can produce changes in the brain, and it can impact recovery from trauma. Several research studies indicate neurological differences between individuals with high levels of dissociative tendencies and those with lower levels.[301] Because dissociation disrupts emotional processing of trauma-related material, dissociation can contribute to PTSD and maintain PTSD once it has developed.[302]

Several research studies demonstrate an inverse relationship between levels of mindfulness and levels of dissociation.[303] Practicing mindfulness can reduce dissociation,[304] perhaps because both mindfulness and dissociation reflect patterns of attention. Whereas dissociation restricts attention, mindfulness engages voluntary attention, and broadens the scope of our attention to a larger range of sensory input.[305]

Mindfulness Practices for Dissociation

Practice # 1: Grounding

Grounding is one of the most helpful practices for dissociation, because it enables us to engage our senses in this moment to keep our minds from floating away. You can use the grounding exercises presented in Chapter 3, "Anchor in the Present to Handle Pain From the Past," or you might find another form of grounding that works for you.

To practice grounding, we focus our attention towards one of the five senses. Touch is an especially powerful sensation: When we feel our minds drift into memories, we can literally hang on by grasping an object that exists in this moment, right now. Some people like to carry a stone or pebble in their pocket to ground themselves with touch, but you can also feel the fabric of a sofa or chair, or touch one hand with the other. It can help to use an object that is interesting to explore in a tactile way, such as a "stress ball," silly putty, or a toy or puzzle that is designed for fidgeting.

Once we have a sense and an object of focus picked out, we can begin the process of grounding ourselves. It is helpful to notice all that we can about the sensory information available. When practicing grounding with touch, we might observe an object's texture, its temperature, and the level of pressure of our touch (for instance, soft, firm, or in between). Expanding our awareness to the different properties of the touch can help keep our minds more tethered to our present-moment experience.

The next part involves returning our minds, over and over, to our object of focus. We do not need to aim for a "mind meld" in which our attention never leaves our chosen focus. Rather, we keep gathering our minds up and shifting our attention back. We might also observe split attention, in which our attention is partially focused on present-moment sensory information, but part of our attention is elsewhere. We can then shift the wandering attention back, so that *more* of our attention is focused on the sensation of touch (or other sensory experience) in this moment.

In addition to touch, you might explore senses of vision, smell, taste, and hearing. For instance, you can notice the colors of cars or leaves; boil spices in water and then breathe them in; listen carefully to a song; or taste food or beverages mindfully. You might notice that you can maintain your focus more easily on one sense than on another. For that reason, you might choose a more accessible grounding practice as your "go to" way of handling dissociation, and another for when you want to give yourself a bit more of a challenge.

Practice #2: Mindfulness in Observing Dissociative Triggers and Tendencies

Dissociation commonly occurs outside of our conscious awareness. In fact, the "automatic" nature of dissociation is part of its adaptive function, as dissociation can help keep threatening information tucked away from our conscious minds. However, this feature makes working with dissociation extremely challenging. How can we shift mental processes that are hidden from our conscious minds?

We can begin by approaching dissociation from a perspective of curiosity and care. This stance alone reflects a shift from the tendency to ignore and push away difficult material. It may feel a bit subtle, but approaching mental material, instead of avoiding it, can fuel many changes in our thoughts and feelings.

When we begin to observe dissociation, we might have only bits and pieces to work with. We can try to accept that condition as normal, and use whatever information we have. For instance, we might notice that a slight visual haze precedes dissociation, or that it happens when we are feeling stressed or bored.

It is common for reminders of our trauma to trigger dissociation, or to be triggered by any sort of pain or discomfort. There may also be specific sensory experiences that trigger us, such as the smell of a particular soap or a specific style of music.

In addition to noticing triggers for dissociation, we can notice the process itself. Do our minds wander away gradually, or are we suddenly elsewhere? Do we tend to gravitate to the same mental landscapes (such as the details of a romantic relationship or imagining how tomorrow will go), or do our minds go somewhere new each time? How do we notice our own dissociation? How does noticing the dissociation change it?

Sometimes other people can help us notice dissociation. We might feel glad to have a friend or counselor point out to us when we have mentally departed, as long as it feels kind rather than critical. If there are people in your life with whom you want to share your experience of handling dissociation, you might consider asking them what they notice about the process.

Because dissociation often functions to keep traumatic information from conscious awareness, dissociation often decreases when people bring more conscious awareness to the trauma. Acknowledging trauma may reduce the brain's attempts to push it away through dissociation. Depending on our available resources and comfort level, we can communicate about trauma with friends, therapists, and support groups, or we can write about it in a journal. However, experts who work with individuals who have experienced trauma and dissociation advocate focusing first on stabilization and safety, before addressing trauma experiences directly.

Noticing dissociative triggers and tendencies becomes easier over time. Our awareness might arise gradually, or we might have an "Aha!" moment where we recognize a common trigger. As we become more skilled in noticing when our minds are wandering, we have more choices about whether and how to return to the present moment.

Practice #3: Exploring the Magic Moment

The "magic moment" (Salzberg, 2011, p. 49) reflects the point in our awareness when we realize our minds have wandered away from the present moment. It is "magic" because it is the moment of insight and power. Instead of using the recognition that our minds have drifted as an occasion to berate ourselves, we can instead regard the magic moment as a precious gift. The magic moment gives us an opportunity to learn about our mental patterns, to shift our attention to whatever we choose, or to try a new response that departs from our old patterns. It is a moment of empowerment and agency.

As we practice mindfulness, the goal is not to retain tense, unwavering, constricted attention on our object of focus, such that we regard deviations of attention as failures. Rather, it is to notice when our mind wanders, and to then bring it back to our chosen focus, again and again and again, with as little judgment as possible. The repetition of this process—the way that we handle the magic moment—builds our "muscle" of mindfulness, and can be considered "the essential art of meditation practice" (Salzberg, 2011, p. 49).

To explore the magic moment, we can begin by beginning any mindfulness exercise, including mindful breathing (in Chapter 1), the body scan (in Chapter 1), or grounding (in Chapters 5 and 11). Soon enough, our mind will depart from the experience, and our noticing its departure is the magic moment. Most of us will have many magic moment opportunities in any session of mindfulness practice.

Once we notice our dissociation, we have the opportunity to return to the present moment. As we gain more and more awareness about this process, we can use that awareness to notice what it is like to return. Is it comforting to return, or distressing? Does the return happen suddenly, or gradually? Are there any physical sensations that accompany the return of our attention to the present moment? How do we relate to ourselves when we observe that our minds have wandered—in a friendly way, or with self-judgment?

As we build awareness for the ebb and flow of dissociation, we might notice that our experience of dissociation changes. After all, we usually begin to dissociate automatically, whereas the process of noticing the movements of our minds cultivates our voluntary attention skills. We may be able to observe changes in our dissociation over time.

Attending to the magic moment also provides an opportunity to work with dissociation in a compassionate way. Just as the magic moment provides an opportunity to shift our attention, it also offers the possibility of choosing a different way of relating to ourselves. If we choose to relate to ourselves compassionately, we might say to ourselves something like, "It's totally understandable that you zoned out the moment that you got uncomfortable. That was such an important and useful habit to have, given all that you have been through." Or, we may need to comfort ourselves, such as, "That must have been so scary to have lost your focus right in the middle of chopping the carrots. I'm so sorry you had to experience that."

Besides the benefits to our well-being that compassion confers, self-compassion during the magic moment also reinforces our developing attentional skills. It is absolutely fine to exaggerate, and to respond to the magic moment with an over-the-top, "Hooray! You noticed that you were gone, and now you've managed to gather up your attention again and point it where you want. Wonderful! I'm so glad you came back." In acknowledging the magic moment with vigor, we send ourselves a powerful message that we can be effective and successful in working with our attention. Working with the magic moment in a curious and compassionate way can help grow our attentional control and our confidence in the process.

Practice #4: Mindfulness in Tolerating Discomfort

We all experience at least small discomforts in our daily lives. We might feel aggravated at having to wait in a long line, or feel upset after leaving a glove on the bus. We may feel sad after reading news about a tragedy, angry after an argument with a sibling, or scared about an upcoming dental procedure. Or perhaps our feet hurt.

Dissociation is certainly one option in all of these situations, because if we avoid being mentally present, we can escape the discomfort (at least temporarily). However, dissociation becomes problematic if it is our only option, and if it causes us other problems.

To practice mindfulness in tolerating discomfort, we try to observe uncomfortable feelings in the moment, and to resist the urge to escape mentally. When choosing a practice opportunity, it is helpful to pick a moment of discomfort at about level 2 to level 4 on a scale of 0–10, where 0 indicates no discomfort, and 10 reflects the most discomfort possible. For this practice, the ideal level of discomfort will be noticeable and contain distinctive features, but will be somewhat tolerable. As our ability to remain present grows, we can then try to stay present with more difficult material.

It may feel counterintuitive to stay with discomfort instead of dissociating. As you begin, you might encourage yourself a bit in a self-compassionate way (for example, "OK, here goes. It can be hard to try new ways to handle discomfort, but it might also feel kind of brave."). Then, try to stick with your thoughts and feelings in the moment, and to notice whatever is there. A hollow feeling in your chest, regret, shallow breaths, fear, the words that someone has just spoken, a pattern on the carpet that seems to be making you dizzy—anything is appropriate for observation.

If you feel the urge to distract yourself or to dissociate in another way, you might do your best to notice the urge without yielding to it. You might experiment with gently noticing the tug to dissociate, and then redirecting your attention to your thoughts and feelings in this moment. It is absolutely fine if you need to repeat this process over and over, or if you need to return from having departed the present moment.

When practicing Mindfulness in Tolerating Discomfort, it can be useful to incorporate an expansive perspective (see the practice There's More in This Moment in Chapter 3). That is, we can try to make our experience of this moment larger than our discomfort alone by noticing its less obvious components. If our feet hurt, we might notice the specific kind of pain we feel, but also the temperature and position of our feet, or the sensation of our socks. We hope to become open to the fullness of this moment, rather than tethered to only one aspect or caught up in the impulse to escape.

After practicing Mindfulness in Tolerating Discomfort, you might close with offering yourself some appreciation and self-compassion for having practiced the exercise. It might help to remind yourself of the logical reasons that dissociative patterns developed, or of your goals for gaining more control over your attention. If the exercise was challenging, you can acknowledge that experience. You might also reflect about an aspect that went well, or something about it that you found surprising (e.g., "I didn't think I would be able to just stand there and feel my annoyance about waiting in line, but it wasn't as hard as I thought it would be. It was especially strange that as I approached my feeling of anger with curiosity, the anger itself seemed to diminish.").

Practice #5: Choose to Stay Present

We often dissociate without any conscious choice. Suddenly, our minds are just gone—off somewhere else. Although distraction can be a valuable tool in managing distress, we get into problems when it happens constantly and automatically. Our goal in bringing mindfulness to dissociation is to enhance our ability to *choose* whether to stay mentally present or to encourage our minds to go elsewhere. There are many situations where we want to pay attention or even need to pay attention—for instance, when the pharmacist explains how to take a new medication, when a friend asks us for advice, or when we are taking an exam.

In this exercise, we can practice staying present on purpose. The word "stay" is not meant to imply absolute fixed, unwavering attention, as it is quite normal for our minds to go here and there for a few seconds even while focusing. Rather, "staying present" means that our overarching experience is one of consistent attention, one that seems to flow with only momentary mental departures. When we notice our minds have gone elsewhere, we gently bring our focus back to the task at hand. Staying present is therefore a bit relative, as we can each strive to increase our mental presence in this moment. To start, we might set an intention of being more mentally here than mentally elsewhere.

It can help to pick a specific situation in which we want to try staying present. For instance, if you find that you often multitask when having phone conversations with friends, you might try to stay focused on the conversation alone, without doing anything else. You can also choose a mindfulness exercise (such as Mindful Breathing, the Body Scan, or Mindful Walking), as all mindfulness practices cultivate staying present in this moment.

When we notice that we have departed from the present moment, we can use our five senses to help ourselves return. I often consider this an intermediate step when trying to reengage attention towards a complex task in in the present moment. For instance, you can imagine a college student who is distraught about the end of a recent relationship, and is having a hard time paying attention in class. If the student tries to bring his brain straight from the intricate details and feelings of the breakup right to a complex sociology theory, he might be unsuccessful. If he instead first focuses on bringing his mind back to the room he is in, by noticing the desks, the clock, the chairs, and the professor's shirt, it may be a bit easier. Returning physically to our surroundings can be a helpful transitional step.

In Their Own Words

I was scuba diving near Koh Phi Phi, Thailand during the 2004 Tsunami. I gripped the hand of my dive buddy and tried to surface. I didn't know that the breaking waves overhead came from a 9.1 earthquake. I spent two weeks in Bangkok getting a new passport, glasses, and treatment for decompression sickness. When I went back to Southern Thailand to help, I started to feel almost normal again. But when I returned to the States two weeks later, airplanes and icy roads scared me. I slept on the floor of my father's room. I stopped leaving the house. I slept all of the time.

Two years later, my body that had reacted to help me during the disaster was still responding with hypersensitivity, anxiety, and dissociation. In the car, I coached myself to feel my feet on the floor, my thighs and back on the seat, my hands on the steering wheel.

It's been ten years since the tsunami. I still practice coming back to my body through mindfulness, breathing, meditation, yoga, touch, and body scans. It's easier to change the sensations in my body through breath than it is to change a memory. These exercises calm my body and help me to accept what's happening with less judgment. When I remember to use exercises to feel myself embodied, my mind starts to believe that I am safe.

Working with our mental habits can be daunting. It may help to remember that the goal is not to quash dissociation completely, but to become more aware of its role in our lives and to expand our range of coping skills. Rather than taking an "all or nothing" approach to dissociation, we can work on observing it and increasing our options. Along the way, we can celebrate many victories: noticing where our minds went, returning them to the present moment, and practicing self-compassion towards ourselves in the process. If the process is frustrating, we can acknowledge that difficulty, and we can even use the frustration as an opportunity to stay present with those feelings and to offer ourselves some care. Over time, attending to our experiences in this moment with curiosity and tenderness can help us feel stronger, more flexible, and more present.

chapter 12

PARTICIPATE AND CONNECT: MINDFULNESS PRACTICES FOR RELATIONSHIPS

TRAUMA PRESENTS MANY obstacles to connecting with other people. Because handling trauma takes energy, we may have fewer resources with which to relate to others. Trauma often leads to depression, with its urge to isolate ourselves or withdraw from social interactions, and its sense of worthlessness or being "damaged goods." After trauma, we may be wary of going places where trauma could occur. Being in any uncontrollable environment—a grocery store, a party, a movie theater—can feel quite alarming, as we might be hypervigilant to all possible sources of danger.

After interpersonal trauma, we may feel wary of being retraumatized if we interact with other people, we may struggle to trust people, and we may remain generally uncomfortable in social settings. We might also avoid other people because we anticipate negative responses from them—such as pity, judgment, sadness, an insensitive curiosity, a lack of understanding, or any treatment that suggests we are different or "other." Alternatively, we might refrain from getting close to people because we fear hurting them in some way, either by being too needy or burdensome, or because of our own anger, sadness, distrust, or instability.

Trauma can also generate a sense of separation from other people and from the flow of the world around us. Public attention might seem riveted to an election, a sporting event, or celebrity gossip—issues that can feel worlds away from our own hardships. A sense of invisibility and loneliness can increase our suffering after trauma. As the saying goes, "we compare our insides to other people's outsides." We can develop the false impression that everyone else around us is coping well with life, whereas we are all alone in our pain.

The emotional styles that we develop after trauma—often as a way to handle overwhelming feelings—can impact our relationships substantially. For instance, fear of emotion may impede supportive social interactions among individuals with PTSD.[306] Fear of emotions, emotional avoidance, and "emotional numbing" are each associated with less satisfaction in and engagement in family relationships.[307]

Another roadblock to discussing our feelings with others involves the sense that it is better not to complain, or the idea that, "other people have it worse." I hear this sentiment often in clinical settings. I usually respond with a physical health example: "Some people need medical attention because they have lost a leg. Does that mean that you should not get treatment for a broken ankle?" For some reason, a physical health example convinces most people that psychological challenges can be worthy of care. However, others continue to feel unworthy of any sort of attention (perhaps as an emotional remnant from past trauma), or are convinced that it is more virtuous to keep one's problems to oneself. We may feel the need to uphold an identity of being stoic and self-sufficient, or we might have learned that others are unreliable.

We often keep our trauma-related struggles hidden, or do not ask for support, because we are afraid of others' responses to our disclosures. We may be concerned about the possibility of burdening others, or worry that a person's response to our trauma might make us feel even worse. If one person reacts to our trauma in a negative way, we can become reluctant to share with anyone else. Many people are uncomfortable hearing about trauma. Unfortunately, this even includes some therapists and health providers, who may respond by changing the subject or by encouraging patients to focus on the "here and now." However, there are many others (therapists, friends, partners, colleagues, and family members) who *can* stay present and provide support without feeling that trauma-related information is burdensome. In fact, many people derive positive meaning from helping others. Sharing our feelings can also help build intimacy and strengthen relationships.

All of these obstacles can be seen as understandable outcomes of trauma. For instance, it is logical that we would want to conserve our energy, numb our feelings, and avoid potential sources of stress after trauma. These tendencies also reflect basic human learning processes, through which we learn from past experiences and project that information onto new circumstances. However, our posttraumatic thinking often involves beliefs, rather than facts. For example, we might believe that "other people will always hurt me," or "I have nothing to offer," and these beliefs can hold us back from developing relationships. When we continue to avoid social interactions, our beliefs about other people—and about our own social capacities—become calcified. We never have the opportunity to expand or change our beliefs through new interactions.

It can feel easier and more comfortable to simply avoid social interactions altogether. As with other forms of avoidance, we might notice an immediate sense of relief at the thought of staying in again, rather than going out. We feel more in control of our environment, less vulnerable to danger, and calmer. Being alone can feel much more predictable and familiar. While it is true that some environments do present high levels of danger, such as war zones or neighborhoods with substantial levels of community violence, we often overestimate the amount of danger in our current situation based on our past trauma experiences.

There are many downsides to isolation. Social support staves off depression and PTSD, whereas isolation perpetuates those conditions. Our physical health also improves when we connect with other people. Isolating ourselves narrows our life and our perspectives, and keeps us right where we are, with no possibility of positive change. We miss out on the satisfaction of helping another person, the delight of sharing a humorous moment, and the warmth of feeling as though we are part of a community. Engaging with other people can also be a welcome distraction from our own pain. We often feel less alone with our problems when we connect with others who have been through trauma. And if we socialize, we have the opportunity to form new beliefs about other people and about our own potential.

Cultivating Empowerment

After trauma, we can work to build a sense of empowerment. Trauma happens to us without our control or consent. It can feel liberating to establish our own patterns and boundaries, as long as they continue to feel like choices, rather than barriers. We get to decide what thoughts, feelings, and experiences we want to share with other people. Depending on the circumstances, we can also choose whom to see, where to go, and what to do.

We can mindfully attend to our feelings around other people. For instance, if we choose to tell someone about our trauma experiences, that person's response usually affects our feelings. Supportive responses promote trauma recovery, but unsupportive responses, such as blaming the victim, worsen PTSD and other mental health difficulties. We might feel misunderstood or invalidated by a friend who encourages us to "look on the bright side" when we are feeling miserable. However, looking for opportunities where it is safe to share our feelings can be beneficial; for instance, it can reduce emotional numbing.[308]

It can be tempting to regard others in our lives with an all-or-nothing perspective, and to dismiss them quickly if they let us down. Sometimes taking a break or ending a relationship *is* the wisest course of action (for instance, distancing oneself from a perpetrator of abuse, or from friends with alcohol and other drug problems when in recovery from addictions). However, in other circumstances we might mindfully decide how to engage in a particular relationship. Within each relationship, we can ask ourselves how often we want to be in contact with that person, and what kind of contact feels right for us. There may be people in our lives with whom we enjoy watching movies or attending sporting events, but to whom we would prefer not to disclose trauma.

We can decide how much information we want to share, and how, and when. For instance, a person who has been mugged may have friends and family members ask for the story of what happened. It might feel comforting or empowering to tell the story, and to receive support. Or, it might feel quite upsetting to repeat the details over and over again. In that case, it is certainly possible to say something like, "I appreciate your interest and concern, but I'm finding that retelling the story isn't right for me just now." Similarly, if a therapist or other health provider asks about trauma, we can choose to disclose the details, or to say, "I'd rather not discuss that at this time. Perhaps I will feel differently after we've gotten to know each other better. I would prefer to focus on (relaxation techniques; emotion regulation skills; anger management) first."

We can also *ask* for the specific type of support that we want. This idea can seem radical at first. After interpersonal trauma, we may have learned to be submissive, accommodating, or agreeable. We might also have developed the belief that others are incapable or uninterested in helping us. It might feel strange or uncomfortable to ask for the support that we want, and it requires some degree of mindful awareness to identify what would feel best to us. However, it gets easier and easier with practice. We can say something like, "What feels best to me right now is to have friends just listen, without offering suggestions." Or, "What I need most right now is a ride to my doctor's appointment." Although we ultimately cannot control others' responses to us, we stand a much better chance of getting the type of support we need if we ask for it.

Another benefit of clarifying the type of support we want is that it strengthens relationships. Those close to us might not know what to do or say after trauma. It helps them to know what kind of support is right for us, and makes them feel more effective when they provide it. Asking for a specific form of support can also prevent resentment (for instance, feeling upset that a friend did not respond to our feelings in the way that we had hoped) and defensiveness (such as feeling mad that our partner criticized us when we were just trying to be helpful). It can also help us to feel more interpersonally effective, as the process of asking for what we want strengthens our own communication skills and sense of agency.

We might choose not to share much about our trauma or our feelings with most people, and in many circumstances, that approach may feel best for us, and produce few adverse consequences. However, concealing important information about how we are doing from those closest to us can harm relationships and impede our recovery from trauma. Research shows that "emotional hiding" from friends, family, and spouses or partners is linked to higher levels of PTSD.[309]

When building or rebuilding our sense of empowerment with others after trauma, it may help to remember that *empowerment* is not the same as *comfort*. Whenever we decide to share our feelings with someone, we take a risk, and it is often uncomfortable. We may not receive the response that we hoped for, and it can hurt. However, that does not mean that we should not have tried. We can give ourselves credit for having taken the risk, for tolerating the discomfort, and for trying to connect with another person. Reinforcing our own efforts, rather than the results, can make it more likely that we will try again with someone else. Through our attempts, we can identify supportive people in our lives and build our own sense of interpersonal effectiveness.

RESEARCH HIGHLIGHT How Does Social Support Reduce PTSD?

OUR LEVELS OF perceived social support and interpersonal connections are strongly related to PTSD.[310] Others' supportive responses help us recover from trauma, whereas unsupportive responses worsen PTSD and related problems.[311]

Other people in our lives can help us interpret and understand the trauma in a healthy way. If we do not receive support from other people after trauma, we might blame ourselves, view the world as dangerous, and other people as untrustworthy—appraisals that are linked with PTSD.[312] For instance, a research study of 170 survivors of intimate partner violence and 208 survivors of motor vehicle accidents examined individuals' posttraumatic appraisals about themselves (e.g., that the abuse was their fault), the world (e.g., that the world is a dangerous place), and their levels of social support (e.g., being able to talk about difficulties with friends). The researchers found that social support, posttraumatic thoughts, and PTSD were strongly interrelated, and that support from family and friends was associated with fewer problematic posttraumatic thoughts.[313]

Another way that social support can help us recover from trauma is that it often involves social activities. After trauma, people often become more withdrawn, isolated, and lonely, and may reduce the amount of activities in which they take part. Increasing activities, including social activities, can reduce levels of PTSD and depression.[314]

Mindfulness skills can assist us to understand and improve a range of experiences that demand relating to other people—including friendships, family relationships, romantic and intimate partnerships, work relationships, caregiving, and participating in community—and can improve our levels of social support.[315] Each interpersonal context may elicit unique vulnerabilities stemming from past trauma, and can also provide new opportunities for making mindful changes to our current patterns.

Friendships

Friendships can be wonderful, frustrating, destructive, uplifting, or neutral, and sometimes the same friendship seems to be several of these at once. When we consider our friendships, it can help to cultivate a broad and balanced perspective, in which we view an instance of a friend's behavior as but one small part of a larger picture. We also need to recognize that friends bring their own prior hardships and feelings into every interaction, so that their responses to us always have as much to do with them as they have to do with us.

Trauma might hold us back from forming new friendships, or it may throw a wrench into friendships that we thought were solid. However, it can also be a catalyst for deepening friendships—for instance, if a friend responds to our trauma in an understanding and caring way. Because all relationships contain a certain amount of mystery—especially as each human develops in unpredictable ways—we can try our best to be flexible in how we view our friendships. As friendships present us with ups and downs, we can benefit from paying mindful attention to our own feelings and hopes as we interact with our friends.

A mindful perspective after trauma can help us navigate through the challenges of friendships, because it can bring insight into our own reactions and interpretations. For instance, if a friend seems to drop out of contact for a period of time, I might automatically (but perhaps not accurately) assume that the person does not like me or want to be friends anymore. A mindful view could allow me to recognize my interpretation as an "add-on," a thought that I am adding to an ambiguous situation. While it is possible that the person no longer desires to be my friend, there might be other explanations for the behavior.

As we become more mindful of our own mental and emotional patterns, we can consider ways that our previously established ideas about relationships might be impacting the dynamics in our current relationships. *Relational schemas* are mental frameworks or "blueprints" that we develop from our earliest significant relationships (for instance, with our parents or other caregivers). Depending upon the nature of those early relationships, we might expect other people in our lives to neglect, abandon, insult, or mistreat us—expectations that we often bring and project onto new relationships. Or, we might have positive expectations about relationships, and assume that other people will be kind and helpful. Whatever the nature of these relational schemas, we can bring awareness to these expectations, and change our ideas about what a relationship could or should look like, as well as how we want to function within the relationship.

Our interpersonal expectations impact our feelings and coping styles, and influence whether or not we will seek support from other people.[316] Once we become aware of our relational schemas, we can shift our beliefs and behaviors from "automatic pilot" to "manual." As present-moment situations arise, we can begin to ask ourselves to what extent our thoughts and feelings reflect past experiences. We can also try new ways of relating—including ways that depart from our past relationship blueprints.

We can also become aware of our *conditioned emotional responses*[317]—our learned emotional reactions to interpersonal conflict or distress, such as avoidance, anger, and fear. For instance, if a friend seems agitated about something, and I have learned in the past that agitation can be dangerous, I might avoid the person. In other instances, conditioned emotional responses arise from physical characteristics of a person who harmed us, so that we react fearfully or angrily to other people with similar attributes, such as hair color, physical build, or gender. Because conditioned emotional responses reflect basic human learning processes—and because learning is more salient when coupled with threat—it takes a bit of time and energy to unlearn them.

Friendships present us with many opportunities to notice our feelings, thoughts, and behaviors, and to make new changes. We may feel emotionally triggered by an event or nonevent in a friendship (e.g., a friend asks too many favors; does not show up; or does not provide the support that we hoped for). Often, after trauma, people feel as though they do not deserve to have boundaries with friends, or relationships that feel mutual. As a result, we may experience unhealthy relationships with friends, in which we experience unmet needs or a loss of integrity. The psychologist and trauma expert Laura Brown explained that healthy friendships "nourish decency" (2015, p. 56); that is, they help us to interact and function in ways that are compatible with our own integrity.

When we experience difficult emotions related to a friendship, we can observe our own feelings and reflect upon the situation. We can be compassionate and understanding towards ourselves, and we can ask to what extent our feelings reflect add-ons, or the mental patterns we have developed from past relationships. We may even choose to relate in a new way, such as asking for the specific kind of support that would feel helpful, or by discussing conflict gently instead of avoiding it. With time, the new skills that we practice become more and more natural, so that our default ways of relating align with our goals and values, rather than reflecting a continuation of past relationships.

Family

The author Leo Tolstoy began his famous novel *Anna Karenina*, published in installments from 1873-1877, with the pronouncement that "All happy families are alike; each unhappy family is unhappy in its own way" (1873/2002, p. 1). Tolstoy's assertion holds up to scientific investigation in many respects. Even though healthy families may differ in their configurations, cultures, and personalities, they share several common ingredients: warmth; attunement, positive communication, and care for each person's needs; appreciation of family members' company; physical and emotional safety; and space for members to learn, grow, and develop as individuals within the family context and beyond.[318]

When families are healthy, they provide us with a deep sense of support, connection, and care. Individuals with healthy families feel as though they can depend on family members during crises. Healthy families nurture a sense of hope, and of self-encouragement. After growing up in a healthy family, a person often leaves with a positive sense of self, a feeling of being loveable, and mental models of relationships that include feelings of safety, empowerment, mutual caring, and joy.

Unfortunately, many families do not provide the conditions that nurture emotional health and well-being. People who grow up in *invalidating environments*[319] that ignore, minimize, punish, or deride children's emotional experiences are more likely to face mental health challenges in adulthood. Other adverse environments include emotional, physical, or sexual abuse; neglect; parental alcohol and drug abuse; family illness, the loss of a parent or parents, and poverty. Some parents put pressure on their children to be perfect, or to fit their own preferences and ideals; other parents are aloof and uninvolved, and require that children take care of their own emotional needs. There are, in short, many ways that things can go wrong.

Many people are surprised to learn the extent to which childhood experiences contribute to mental and physical health in adulthood—on levels that include thinking, emotions, the brain, and the body. The research literature, including prospective studies, has established a very strong connection between childhood abuse (and other adverse childhood experiences) and adult physical and mental health difficulties.[320] People absolutely can and do recover from negative childhood experiences. Sharing these data is not meant to suggest that recovery is hopeless, but to underscore how incredibly hard it can be to feel good after a difficult childhood, and to validate the courage and effort often involved in recovery. After childhood trauma, creating a healthy life with healthy relationships may necessitate a great deal of attention and care

Trauma in adulthood can also disrupt family functioning. Responses to trauma such as PTSD and depression can result in withdrawing from family members, or being unable to fulfill a caregiving role effectively. PTSD symptoms are linked with less positive family engagement among trauma survivors.[321] For instance, partners of Veterans with higher levels of PTSD severity reported wishes that those individuals would engage in more emotional intimacy, physical intimacy, shared activities, and participation in financial decision-making and other family responsibilities.[322] Coping with trauma by withdrawing from family support impedes healing from trauma.[323] When family members do not understand a person's trauma responses, they might respond by blaming the traumatized person or themselves for the changes that they observe. In those instances, it is often helpful for families to learn about trauma and its effects together (for instance, in counseling, or through self-educating), and to think about how to manage trauma-related symptoms as a team.

Because trauma can impact how people function as parents, it is often helpful for parents who have endured trauma to obtain support from health professionals or others. In general, the mental health of parents is linked to improved outcomes in children. Conversely, parents who experienced negative treatment from their own parents may strive to do the opposite, and may in fact go too far—such as always saying "yes" to a child if their own needs were denied, or ignoring their own needs if their own parents were overly focused on themselves. Mindful awareness of these topics, intentional self-education regarding parenting philosophies, and support from health professionals can all help trauma survivors to parent healthfully.

Whether trauma occurred in childhood or in adulthood, strong family relationships help individuals recover from trauma. However, if family itself is the source of trauma, it can help to build a "family of choice" in which a person chooses the individuals (often, nonblood relatives) with whom to associate in a familial way. Brown (2015) explains how families of choice may be especially meaningful for individuals whose families have misunderstood or rejected them for being lesbian, gay, bisexual, transgender, questioning, or for expressing a nontraditional, nonbinary sexual or gender identity. After family trauma, it can feel hard to make your own way in a culture that often propagates a "one size fits all" vision of families in its media and advertising; but it is certainly possible to create your own traditions within a family of choice, such as a "Friendsgiving" holiday party, vacations, game nights, and celebrations.

Whether or not we have experienced healthy family dynamics, recovery from trauma often involves learning to be our own "good parent." Just as we would want to take good care of a child we love whose well-being is our responsibility, we can learn to be as effective and helpful as possible in caring for our own emotional needs. Building mindful awareness for how we are feeling, and for what helps—and actually devoting the time and energy to "parent" ourselves—can yield lifelong benefits. It is through such efforts, linked with a nurturing mindset, that we can grow, learn, and heal.

Romantic and Intimate Relationships

Our past experiences may have taught us that relationships necessarily hurt, or left us feeling as though we deserve to be mistreated. In her book *Not the Price of Admission: Healthy Relationships After Childhood Trauma*, Laura Brown (2015) described some of the ways that love and pain can become deeply interconnected in our minds after trauma, and provides steps for healing. Brown noted that many of us come to learn that attachment to other humans comes at a steep price—such as the price of losing our own identity, feeling bad about ourselves, or consistently ignoring our own needs to please others. She explained that these costs differ from the challenges of healthy relationships, which may involve conflict, anger, or distress, but within a framework that feels respectful, balanced, and safe.

We commonly seek out relationships that feel familiar, even if their dynamics are abusive or otherwise unhealthy. It can feel strangely comforting to find partners with known challenges, such as high levels of anxiety, struggles with addiction, or rigid ideas of gender roles. Brown (2015) explained that people who have experienced abuse might even feel more comfortable with some form of continued abuse occurring, rather than "waiting for the other shoe to drop." Conversely, we might seek out the opposite experience. For instance, if we experienced neglect in our family of origin, we might feel drawn to a highly controlling or even abusive relationship that at least seems to fulfill our need for attention.

Sometimes, in order to maintain relationships, we try to banish troubling information from awareness. For instance, if the same person on whom we must depend, such as a caregiver, is hurting us, those pieces of information may be hard to process because they are incompatible; we might consciously or unconsciously choose to ignore the problematic information so that we can continue to survive, to elicit care, or live within an unavoidable situation.[324] We may even develop cognitive and emotional styles that allow us to attend selectively to some information within relationships, while ignoring others. Over time, we may adapt to traumatic relationships by developing "betrayal blindness," in which we learn to deactivate our "cheater detectors."[325]

As we broaden our attention regarding our own thoughts and feelings, we can use the "beginner's mind" perspective to pay attention to a fuller range of experiences, rather than maintaining our usual narrow focus on selective information (such as hypervigilance to a partner's moods). We can learn to develop trust in our own experience and impression of a situation. We can ask ourselves about our own thoughts, feelings, needs, and desires, and consider how they might fit or depart from those of our partners.

Our mental attention is essential to ending dangerous relationships. Brown (2015) emphasized that it is crucial to notice if we are involved with someone who cannot accept the word "no," or if there is any sense of coercion or control in a relationship. No one deserves to experience violence and abuse. It is vital to prioritize your life and your safety over such a relationship, and to go to a place where the person does not have access to you or any children involved. As Brown (2015) emphasized: In situations where a person threatens to kill you, kill children, or issues suicide threats, such threats mean that someone is likely to die. If this is the case for you, *stop reading right now* and do not wait another minute; get to safety immediately.

Mindfulness can benefit our relationships by helping us to avoid either repeating the same problems from our past or creating new problems. As we approach our relationships, we can work to become more mindful about each relationship dynamic, and how it represents either a repetition or a departure from our past relationships. We can also consciously allow ourselves room to have some new experiences, even if they are a bit uncomfortable at first (for example, the new sensation of feeling cared for but not controlled). When a partner or partners within a relationship have been impacted by trauma, it can help to discuss trauma-related challenges together with an emphasis on caring for both individuals' experiences as well as the ways that they impact the relationship.

In every relationship, some things inevitably go wrong—including misunderstandings, hurt feelings, and conflicting needs. However, we can develop the ability to address problems and tolerate their discomfort, while trusting that a relationship is strong and healthy. If we attend to our own and others' experiences mindfully and respectfully, we can even use challenges as opportunities to learn about ourselves and our partners, and to strengthen our relationships.

Work

When work goes well, we can feel interested and satisfied in our work, and as though we are taking part in a meaningful endeavor. We may also feel connected to other people through our work, and respected in our roles. However, trauma can impact our work in many ways. It takes mental resources to cope with trauma and to recover. Because trauma responses such as depression and PTSD can reduce our concentration, interest in things, ability to sleep, and physical health, it may be hard to work effectively. Furthermore, the workplace may actually be the location in which the trauma occurred. Or, our work environment might include being exposed to the trauma of others. Trauma can also take a toll on our relationships with other people at work.

Paid work is not the only kind of work with value. Whether it is paid or not, we can enhance our well-being through work that engages and inspires us, and through work that reflects our own values and provides us with a sense of meaning. Our work might be painting, writing, cleaning, handling bills, caring for children or others, being politically active, or advancing social justice—either paid or unpaid. The process of looking for a job itself is also work, and often includes researching possibilities, completing cover letters or job applications, and networking. Similarly, the time and energy we might put into recovery from physical and mental illness (either our own or others') may be accurately described as work in that it usually involves a great deal of energy, focus, advocacy, and logistical details, such as arranging appointments and managing health insurance.

When we work for other people, companies, or institutions, we depend on our bosses and our institutions in ways that mirror how children depend on their parents. Our dependence includes our physical sustenance—our livelihoods—as conferred through a paycheck. In the United States, the context of our work also constricts our options regarding health insurance, family leave, and work flexibility. The workplace environment can impact our physical health through exposure to toxic chemicals, other physically unsafe conditions, or through stress.[326]

We are often emotionally dependent on our jobs, as well as physically dependent. Many of us spend a large proportion of our waking hours at work. The emotional dynamics among bosses, co-workers, and employees affect us. If our boss seems like a friendly individual, an aloof graduate advisor, or an insensitive taskmaster, we often absorb the way in which our boss treats us and take it personally. To some extent, we depend, physically and emotionally, upon our boss's approval and support. If a worker is disrespected, harassed, or abused, or reports a problem in the workplace, the company or institution may respond in a way that helps the situation. However, if the response contains indifference or retaliation, it can compound the negative experience substantially.[327]

Just as we bring our relational schemas into our friendships and romantic relationships, those schemas impact our experiences and work satisfaction as well.[328] For instance, a survivor of family abuse might be unusually attuned to a boss's moods; perhaps for good reason in the current work context, but perhaps as a lingering adaptation to childhood trauma. In this situation it can be helpful to validate our feelings, both as they relate to the present and to the past. It is normal to feel upset about a difficult situation at work—especially one that involves mistreatment by those who have higher levels of power. It can also help to remember that as adults, we have increased options and resources: We can try to seek other employment, problem-solve the situation with trusted cowork-ers, or report the issue. We can also support ourselves mentally, by attending to our own well-being beyond the scope of our jobs.

As we become stronger during the process of recovering from trauma, we can take our strength into the workplace. We can assert the ways in which we hope to grow and develop in our careers, and we can discern which people at work might be good confidants and those with whom we want to be more guarded. We can decide how much information we want to share, and to pro-tect our own privacy. For instance, you might decide to say "I have a health appointment on Wednesday afternoon," rather than disclosing that you have a psychotherapy appointment, if that is more comfortable. Noticing our rela-tional schemas, including the impulse to defer to another person's wishes, can also help us make positive changes. We can consciously choose to treat our own workplace experiences with care, respect, and attention—even in circum-stances when others around us do not—and to take action to better our expe-riences when we can.

Mindfulness skills may be helpful for a variety of challenges related to work, including attention, concentration, and problems with workplace relationships. We often have unreasonable expectations about what kind of job we "should" have or how much we "should" have accomplished in a day. Because mindfulness can help reduce negative judgments, it may be a useful way to handle negative thoughts about ourselves related to work. Mindfulness can also help decrease workplace stress,[329] and appears to be negatively related to burnout.[330]

Caregiving

Many individuals provide substantial care to others: children, spouses or part-ners, parents or other relatives, or to those for whom we work in the health, teaching, or service professions. Providing care can feel extremely rewarding.

For instance, we may see someone else's well-being flourish, and be gratified to know that we played a role in improving that person's experience. We can feel satisfaction in providing company, care, or support to another person during a difficult time. The experience of tuning in to another person's needs is valuable on its own, as a moment of presence and connection.

Even as it nourishes us, caregiving can also deplete our resources when we are not able to attend to our own needs sufficiently. Caregiving roles can be both physically and emotionally exhausting. For instance, parents of young children are often caring for others all day and all night, without any break; health professionals may be handling the needs of multiple patients in dire straits; and teachers may be expected to be case managers for children facing trauma, poverty, and disabilities, on top of their educational roles. Putting our own needs on the back burner—especially when we push them out of awareness—can become a habit. For instance, we might neglect our own physical needs, such as by delaying going to the bathroom, refraining from rest, or feeling unable to make time to eat. Or, we may fail to notice the signs—such as feeling exhausted or apathetic—that indicate that we need a break. In short, we can burn out.

Self-care is the antidote to burnout, and it requires mindful attention. We need to take a few moments to check in with ourselves about how we are doing, and to address our own unmet needs to the extent possible. Ideally, we might benefit from taking a day or a week off; however, if we only have a few minutes, we can still use them to care for ourselves. We can breathe, practice self-compassion, give ourselves a hug, and recognize that caregiving is hard and that we are not alone, even if it feels like it. Even within moments of caregiving, we can still attend to our own needs. For instance, if a child or a patient shouts at us, we can observe and care for that person's feelings while also acknowledging (sometimes silently) our own.

Mindfulness-based programs have been shown to improve well-being among several types of caregivers, including mothers of children with disabilities,[331] those caring for dying individuals,[332] and caregivers for family members with chronic conditions.[333] Mindfulness also improves mental health among teachers[334] and nurses.[335] The general benefits of mindfulness practice, such as stress reduction, may explain how it is helpful to these populations. However, mindfulness practice also requires tuning in to our own experiences. This may assist those of us in caregiving roles to remember to balance our own needs with those of others.

Participate and Connect

Trauma can leave us with the impression—and the actual experience—of being alone. This isolation can perpetuate difficult trauma-related feelings, as it prevents us from having new experiences of other people or things as good or interesting, or of the world as a safe or enjoyable place. Recovery often involves "getting out there"—engaging with other people, groups, and communities.

The evidence shows that participating in activities, clubs, and groups enhances our sense of connection with other people, as well as our view of our own personal strengths.[336] The content of the activity may be less important than the act of doing something with other people. Various types of group activities have demonstrated meaningful reductions in PTSD and depression among participants, including horticulture,[337] group drumming,[338] and archaeology.[339] Involvement with several different kinds of groups and activities seems especially beneficial. In fact, research indicates that the diversity of our social engagement is even more protective against PTSD than our perceived levels of social support.[340]

Participating in activities in the company of others can benefit us in multiple ways at the same time. For instance, walking groups often promote physical health, reduce depression, and facilitate social connections.[341] Taking part in a drumming group corresponded to improved attention, along with decreased levels of PTSD.[342] When we engage in activities with other people, the process might help shift our attention away from our own difficulties and onto other, potentially enjoyable, facets of life. Either the activities, the people with whom we pursue them, or both may provide us with new experiences that improve our feelings.

The exercises in this chapter provide some starting points for enhancing our engagement with the people around us. Even actions that require a small amount of effort, such as simply interacting pleasantly with the person serving us in a store, may improve our sense of community and our well-being. As we become more practiced and accustomed to engaging with other people, we can explore more complex activities and organizations that appeal to us; and remember that participating—just showing up—can improve our well-being.

Mindfulness, Relationships, and Community

Our interactions with other people present a great potential for feelings of support, connection, and joy. Our mindfulness skills can help us "sync up" with other people as we become more attuned to our own thoughts and feelings, as well as the ways that we relate to others. We can also practice providing ourselves with awareness and care for the times when encounters with other people are frustrating. Such instances present an opportunity to practice self-compassion and skills for tolerating distress.

The research evidence confirms that the practice of mindfulness, self-compassion, and kindness boosts our well-being and enhances our connectedness to other people. These practices may also help us tolerate interpersonal interactions that we find stressful. For instance, people with depression who engaged in 8 weeks of mindfulness practice reported decreased emotional reactivity to social stress.[343]

Even a few minutes of loving-kindness meditation increases feelings of connection to other people.[344] Loving-kindness meditation can also reduce levels of prejudice and bias towards stigmatized populations, such as homeless people.[345] Furthermore, self-compassion can increase our likelihood of helping others,[346] and helping others benefits both the person helping and the recipient.[347]

There are several reasons that our helping behavior can improve our own well-being. Midlarsky (1991) identified five reasons that this could occur: (a) increased social integration, (b) distraction from our own difficulties, (c) a greater sense of meaningfulness, (d) enhanced perception of ourselves as competent and effective, and (e) an improved mood from being more active. In addition, Midlarsky and Kahana (1994) demonstrated an association between adult altruism and enhanced morale, self-esteem, positive feelings, and well-being.

The present moment is where we can find the most connection to other people. Chapter 3 explored how trauma disrupts our sense of time and of being in the world, and creates its own temporal structures and rhythms. Because trauma can disrupt our experience of time, when we become stuck in our own difficult thoughts and memories we can feel generally disoriented and alienated. As the writer Alan Lightman observed in his book *Einstein's Dreams*, "Each person who gets stuck in time gets stuck alone" (1994, p. 49). Connecting with other people may buoy us into a more shared experience of time. When we attend to meeting others in the present moment, we synchronize with them, which can help us feel more anchored in this moment, in this world.

Mindfulness is a key element in interrupting my trauma reactions. Sometimes when I am triggered, I recognize that I am becoming stressed and activated inside. Through the practice of mindfulness, I've learned to neutralize many of my trauma reactions. I've learned to be mindful when my muscles tense, my breath shortens or stops, and my heart pounds as adrenaline pumps through me. I can feel I am on the verge of yelling—something that was done to me plenty of times—something my tense nervous system says will feel so much better after I do. But my awareness of this tense part is what helps me keep my lips pressed together and start to breathe again, so I can reply calmly. Mindfulness helps me reply in a way that is in line with my best self.

Mindfulness Practices to Participate and Connect

Practice #1: Notice Others' Positive Contributions to This Moment

We can feel astoundingly lonely. After trauma, there are understandable reasons why we may feel separate and cut off from other people. However, we often perpetuate these feelings of alienation in our minds and behaviors. We get into the habit of thinking about ourselves in an isolated way, and our physical isolation can reinforce this view.

An alternative to "isolation thinking" is to practice recognizing just how many people have made positive contributions to this very moment—our being right in this spot, right here, right now. For instance, if you are drinking tea, you might reflect that other people most likely planted the tea seeds, tended the leaves, picked the leaves, packaged the leaves, transported them to you, and made your cup. You might try pausing to picture an actual person completing each of these activities. It is one thing to acknowledge these unknown individuals in an abstract way, but it may feel different to reflect upon them as real, living people, with thoughts, feelings, strengths, and vulnerabilities. Considering our connections to others can help us feel less isolated.

To begin this mindfulness practice, it can help to first cultivate a mindful state. You might begin with some mindful breathing or with a body scan, with the goal of settling in to this moment with an intention of being curious and nonjudgmental. An attitude of curiosity can help us open up to connections that we might not have noticed before.

Next, we can ask ourselves the question: Who are all the people who have contributed to my being here today, right here, right now? Perhaps there was a bus driver who helped you get to this spot; people who made your clothes; or someone who made food that nourished you today.

As we continue to reflect, we can recognize a broad range of others' contributions. For instance, the meditation teacher Sharon Salzberg, from whom I learned this exercise, often shares that she thinks of the individuals on the committee who provided her with the college scholarship that enabled her to study in India, to begin meditating, and to become a meditation teacher. We might consider teachers and other helpers in our lives, or acquaintances who introduced us to a meaningful person or idea.

We may find that as we open to the different people who have impacted our being here, we have mixed feelings. Perhaps the same teacher who helped you learn to read was cruel in another way. Or, remembering the bus driver reminds you of a belligerent passenger who rode with you the following week. The exercise of acknowledging others' contributions is not meant to deny trauma or to suggest that all human actions are harmonious. However, many of us feel overly focused on the "bad stuff" already, and noticing some of the more positive contributions can help us feel better about the way we are connected to other people in the world. If we do observe ourselves feeling upset when a painful memory is triggered, we can notice it gently before returning our attention to the helpful contributions from others that have influenced our being in this moment.

Practice #2: Directing Loving-kindness to Other Beings Around Us

We often judge others around us. We might mentally register our own opinions of their clothing or speech, or speculate about how their lives are going. After trauma, we might judge people in another way—by assessing whether or not they seem dangerous. These mental processes are usually habitual, rather than the result of a consciously chosen mental style.

When we quickly label people, we can make them objects in our mind. When we view others as scenery, or even as supporting actors in our own story, we may proceed from a worldview that suggests that we alone experience deep feelings. We perpetuate our sense of disconnection. As mentioned earlier, even a few minutes of loving-kindness meditation increases feelings of connection to other people.[348]

Part of the reason that loving-kindness meditation resonates with many people is that it acknowledges that all beings wish to be safe, happy, healthy, and to live with ease. After we have become comfortable with loving-kindness practice, we can try applying it to others around us. That is, we focus our attention on another person, and silently wish, "May you be safe. May you be happy. May you be healthy. May you live with ease," or alternative phrases or good wishes.

To practice directing loving-kindness towards others around us in this moment, it can help to have an environment such as a bus, park, or café—anywhere where we are likely to encounter many other people. We might want to first engage our loving-kindness in a way that feels comfortable or familiar. For instance, if you have been practicing loving-kindness towards yourself, you might start with a few minutes of self-directed phrases (e.g., "May I be peaceful and calm"). Once you feel somewhat rooted in loving-kindness, you can mentally choose an individual person (or animal) and mentally direct the loving-kindness phrases towards them. Next, you can choose another individual, and send that person your loving-kindness wishes; then another; and then another. We can silently offer the phrases to each person in our surroundings.

After we practice loving-kindness towards others around us, we can take a few moments to just be. We can observe how we feel, and be curious about what happens. We might feel nothing, or we might not feel much until we practice the exercise a few times. We might continue to notice judgments about others, even as we send them our good wishes. Many people report that practicing loving-kindness towards others does not necessarily change their feelings towards them, but that it impacts their own emotions. With time, this practice can ease the delusion of separateness, as it acknowledges that all beings seek happiness.

Practice #3: Generosity

This practice involves giving to others. In giving, we gain a feeling of connection to another person, and our sense of isolation recedes. We also notice that our actions matter. They can make a difference to another person's experience, and to our own. Our giving can also counteract trauma-related feelings. After trauma, we might feel powerless, ineffective, or ashamed. Being generous to others (in ways that do not compromise our own needs) can help us feel empowered and effective, and to know ourselves as good.

Helping others seems to help us. Across cultures, financial generosity is related to emotional well-being.[349] After trauma, higher levels of altruism are associated with lower levels of PTSD.[350] Our helping behaviors seem to activate brain regions and chemical processes that protect us against stress.[351] It may be that when we choose to do something active and positive, our feelings gravitate towards our actions.

Gifts can be small: a smile, a compliment, or the tremendous gift of our full attention. Depending on our physical capabilities, we might hold the door open for someone, or pick something up that has fallen. Other gifts can certainly involve charitable donations of money or time. If a friend is going through a difficult time, we can offer that person our company, or our logistical support in arranging meals, transportation, or errands. Sharing our own thoughts and experiences with other people can also be generous, because it can help people gain information and feel less alone.

After trauma, our cognitive and emotional resources can feel depleted. It might be difficult to consider being generous towards other people if we are barely able to take care of our own needs. As we begin to feel stronger, we can experiment with offering other people moments of attention and care. It may be easier to tune in to generosity by starting with some little things.

First, we can set the intention to be generous in the world; then, we can pick a specific opportunity to practice. For instance, the meditation teacher Alison Laichter describes her practice in sending e-mail: she takes a moment to ask herself if she can make it just a little bit kinder, and she finds that she always can. We can then check in with ourselves before, during, and after this practice.

Examples of generosity:

- Offer a compliment to someone
- Greet a stranger (such as a grocery store clerk) with kindness
- Send a text or e-mail to a friend
- Mail a card to someone

- Express gratitude or appreciation to another person
- Listen to someone
- Initiate a conversation
- Accept an invitation graciously
- Express interest in someone else's work or thoughts
- Share your own experience with another person or online

Kindly engaging with other people typically improves our own feelings. Our interactions with people who drive the bus, help us purchase food or other items, or assist us with errands can begin to feel less lonely and transactional when we offer even a few moments of our kind attention. In addition, kindness seems to be a key ingredient in sustaining healthy relationships.[352] Cultivating generosity can also change our beliefs about ourselves, as we learn that even our small actions can improve others' experiences.

Practice #4: Ask for Help

Asking for help strengthens our connections to others. However, there are many reasons why we may fear asking for help—for example, wanting to be independent, feeling scared to need another person, or having the sense that we should not need help or that we are already a burden to others. Trauma can leave us feeling especially reluctant to interact with other people or to ask for help, as we may have learned not to trust others. However, the benefits from asking for help are substantial. When we receive support, it strengthens our relationships, as well as our own sense that we can make requests effectively. In addition, people often like helping, and get a boost in their own mood from helping another person effectively. A request for help is actually generous in the sense that it provides this opportunity to the person who can help.

When asking for help, it is most effective to be specific. For instance, we give the other person more information if we ask, "Can you please come with me to the pharmacy?" than if we say more generally, "I'd really like your support right now." We can also express our gratitude specifically: "Hanging out last night and watching that movie with you, without any pressure to talk, was just what I needed. Thank you!" or "Thank you so much for listening; I really needed to express my feelings about what happened."

Because asking for help might feel overwhelming, we can decide whether to make big requests or small requests. You can ask for clarification during a health appointment. You can ask for directions. You can ask for an opinion. Or, you can ask someone for a specific kind of support. Asking for help gets easier with practice. We may feel uncomfortable asking, but we need to do it in order to get more comfortable. If asking for help is difficult, we can mindfully practice tolerating distress, or soothing ourselves with the five senses.

To begin, we need to set a conscious intention to ask for help sometimes. We need to recognize that as humans, we all need help, and that it is all right to ask for it. Next, we can choose a particular request, and a specific person to whom we will make our request. As we make the request, we can try to ask in a kind way that acknowledges the efforts that would be involved in fulfilling the request, and we can thank that person afterwards for the time and help provided.

We might try one of the following to develop our capacity to ask for help. Even if these practices seem unnecessary in terms of the specific request that we articulate, we can think of them as practices to build our "asking for help" capacity.

- Call a customer service number to ask a question or to request information

- Make a special request at a restaurant (e.g., "May I have the sauce on the side?")
- Contact a friend or friends to ask for their company
- Ask someone's opinion or advice
- Call a radio station and ask to hear a specific song

Before, during, and after the request, we can mindfully notice our sensations and thoughts. It can also help to give ourselves credit for trying something difficult.

Practice #5: Participate

In this practice, we build the skill of "showing up." We may feel that there are many things we want to do—such as attend an exercise class, check out a neighborhood organization, hear a lecture, or investigate a martial arts studio—but there is often a reason not to follow through that seems compelling. I might think, "I don't have the right gear for that class," or "I'm way too busy this week," or "I feel too stressed right now to go out and meet new people."

The considerations that prevent our participation may be understandable and valid; however, the benefits of participating are robust (see "Research Highlight: How Does Social Support Reduce PTSD?" earlier in this chapter). For this reason, it is often wise to plan to participate, despite our reasons not to. If we think too long about participating, we can get lost in our thoughts, our energy can go towards managing our thoughts, and we might lose the impetus to act. To prevent this from happening, you might plan to participate first and think later. Just go.

Participation is a form of *behavioral activation*, an "outside-in" approach to mental health that is highly effective. To participate, it works best to have a specific plan about what you are going to do ("attend a small concert at 2:00 PM on Saturday," or "show up for pickup basketball on Monday at 7:00 PM"), and then put your energy into the physical steps required to complete the activity—getting dressed, leaving the house, and attending the event. It may help to concentrate on getting your feet to step out of your home and into the event, rather than to wrestle with your mind and emotions about whether to go.

Just go. Then, give yourself credit for going. For this exercise—building the skill of participating—it does not matter how your chosen activity went. Just the fact that you attended an event in the company of other people can be sufficient, and you can practice appreciating yourself for that achievement. If you find yourself engaging in judgments and evaluations about how you participated (e.g., "I was so awkward"), you can practice mindfully returning to the thought, "I went, and that's enough for now. I did it."

Any moments of discomfort before, during, or after the event can be opportunities to acknowledge our feelings with self-compassion, and to redirect our attention to participating. We may need to practice participating many times to begin to feel comfortable, and that is perfectly fine. The act of participating helps us to engage instead of withdraw, to be active instead of stagnant, and to build new interests and connections.

Practice #6: Loving-Kindness Comes Full Circle

As described by Sharon Salzberg (1995) in *Lovingkindness*, this powerful practice reflects the classical Buddhist progression of loving-kindness meditation, and it can unfold slowly over weeks, months, or years. The practice involves setting an intention towards an expansive sense of goodwill.

To practice, we silently repeat to ourselves a few phrases that convey good wishes, and we keep repeating them, over and over, for several minutes. Phrases that are commonly used are:

- May I be safe
- May I be happy
- May I be healthy
- May I live with ease

We can also consider a range of alternative phrases, such as:

- May I be calm
- May I be peaceful
- May my actions be skillful and kind

In the classical progression of loving-kindness practice, we first direct the phrases towards ourselves. After some period of time in which those good wishes have taken root, we next direct them towards a teacher or "benefactor" for whom we feel respect and gratitude. In the next step, we direct loving-kindness towards a dear friend. After practicing these categories over the course of some time and establishing a sense of comfort in generating good wishes towards these people, we can direct loving-kindness towards someone about whom we feel neutral. This person might be an acquaintance, or someone about whom we have no strong feelings or opinion. In the next step, we direct loving-kindness towards an individual with whom we have experienced conflict (we start by focusing on someone with whom we have experienced relatively minor conflict, rather than someone who was involved in our experience of trauma). In the final step, we direct loving-kindness towards all beings.

As we progress through directing loving-kindness to different beings, the form of the phrases changes. When we direct them towards another person, the phrases commonly take the form of, "May you be safe; may you be happy; may you be healthy; may you live with ease." When we direct them to all beings, we can repeat, "May all beings be safe; may all beings be happy; may all beings be healthy; may all beings live with ease."

These phrases reflect several classical Buddhist teachings. For instance, the Buddha's teaching on loving-kindness encourages people to "develop an unlimited heart of friendliness" (Lokamitra, 2004, p. 52), a perspective that includes friendliness towards ourselves. As the Buddha exhorts (McDonald, 2010),

In gladness and in safety,
May all beings be at ease.
Whatever living beings there may be;
Whether they are weak or strong, omitting none. (p. xi)

Or, as the physician and mindfulness teacher David Kearney (personal communication, July 28, 2015) advises the individuals who participate in his loving-kindness groups, "You don't have to like everyone. You just have to love them."

Loving-kindness practice typically takes some time. The effects may or may not be immediately observable. Research reports do indicate that people report benefits after a few weeks of practice;[353] however, many individuals consider loving-kindness to be a practice, like mindfulness, that continues to evolve over a lifetime.

Connecting with others is a key ingredient in recovering from trauma. Mindfulness provides a vehicle to recondition and transform the ways that we interact (or avoid interacting) with others. As we make the brave effort to connect despite understandable fears, we can regard moments of awkwardness, uncertainty, and trepidation as opportunities for self-compassion. With practice, we can develop confidence interacting with others as well as the comfort that feeling connected can provide.

Interacting with other people after trauma can feel uncomfortable. It is indeed a risk to try to trust people, or to share with them. After trauma, it is common for a range of relationships (friendships, romantic relationships, work relationships) to feel confusing and scary.[354] However, there is risk in both directions. If we try to connect, we risk feeling misunderstood, rejected, or hurt; however, if we do not try we risk becoming more isolated, depressed, and anxious, and we risk missing the benefits of connecting with others. We need to find some way to allow the risk to be present. Being gentle and kind to ourselves may help us to take such risks.

Part of the way we can tolerate the risk of connecting with others is to open up to having a mixed experience—to view the interaction as a learning opportunity in which we do not expect perfection. We might feel awkward or nervous, or worry that we have said the wrong thing. Although such concerns can feel dangerous after trauma, or even trigger memories of interpersonal interactions that did in fact involve danger, being awkward or nervous on their own cannot hurt us. Human interactions contain millions of imperfections, and it is quite common to feel awkward or nervous in reaching out to other people. However, we can use our mindfulness and self-compassion practices to support ourselves in a kind and gentle way as we experiment with connecting with others. Our efforts can then lead us toward feeling increasingly engaged and positively intertwined with the world around us.

BEYOND TRAUMA AND PTSD:
POSTTRAUMATIC GROWTH AND RESILIENCE

TRAUMA SHAKES US up and causes suffering. The healing process is often complex, and takes us places we may not have been before. As we heal, we may establish new strengths within ourselves. Because life will continue to present us with challenges, we can then draw on those strengths to handle a full range of experiences, and to enhance our overall well-being.

Our experiences after trauma are often not what we expect. Many of us anticipate that healing from trauma might parallel healing from a treatable physical injury: After some period of time, our function returns to normal, and we feel pretty much the same as we did before. However, healing from psychological trauma can involve complex mental processes that lead us in new directions. After traumatic experiences, we may be different than before in ways that endure. Although some of those differences can cause suffering, they can also be vehicles towards new growth, opportunities, and wisdom.

Perhaps we never noticed certain types of feelings prior to the trauma, and the process of tending to them opened up new levels of awareness. We may have learned a skill with which we can soothe ourselves that we did not have before—one that we can use for a range of challenging situations beyond those that involve trauma. Or, we might start to notice our patterns. Perhaps we can catch stress or anger when they are just starting to simmer, before they boil over and become destructive towards ourselves or others.

Our history, literature, and popular culture are rich with stories of individuals—trauma survivors such as Nelson Mandela, Viktor Frankl, and Garchen Triptrul Rinpoche, along with stories ranging from superheroes to Odysseus in Homer's *The Odyssey*— who somehow manage not only to endure trauma, but to use it as a catalyst for personal development and meaningful contributions to the world. The posttraumatic growth researchers Lawrence Calhoun and Richard Tedeschi cited an African proverb asserting that "smooth seas do not make skillful sailors" (2013, p. 6). The science is also clear that people can and do transform trauma into personal growth and resilience.

When we practice mindfulness skills, we often have the opportunity to observe that how we handle what happens is at least as important as what happens, if not more so. The process of cultivating mindfulness and self-compassion towards ourselves demonstrates that we do have a degree of choice in our mental approach to whatever life brings. Although they do not confer complete control, mindfulness skills give us more options regarding the ways that we notice our experiences (both internal and external) and the ways that we can respond.

After trauma, many of us find a new normal, and it might even be an appealing normal. We can consider where we want to mentally "hang out" or reside, and consider effective ways to maintain that mental home for ourselves. This idea is depicted in Buddhist mindfulness traditions through discussions of the four "abodes," or "sublime attitudes" called *brahmāviharas*, and explanations of how to cultivate them through mindfulness and compassion practice. Each of the four abodes is viewed as having a "far enemy" or opposite state that represents an obvious detractor from that attitude. Each state is also considered to have a "near enemy," or a state that is similar enough to the abode that we can become confused by it, that can even masquerade as the positive state, and that is potentially problematic. The four abodes are as follows (Brahma Vihara Foundation, n.d.):

1. Loving-kindness (*metta* in Pāli, the original language of Buddhist texts) is a feeling of care and affection towards ourselves and others. It involves the wish that all beings, excepting none, be happy. It is a loving state without any sense of attachment or control, and a state that is inclusive of all beings, rather than a state that differentiates between different categories of beings or promotes separation or exclusion. Its far enemy is ill will towards someone (including negative self-judgment), and its near enemy is selfish affection.

2. Compassion (*karuna* in Pāli) refers to the movement in our hearts in response to suffering, and our wish that the suffering be removed. Compassion's motivation to alleviate suffering reflects all aspects of suffering—personal, political, social, physical, and mental. Compassion includes feelings of empathy and understanding, and the ability to acknowledge another being's position. This abode emphasizes caring for and about all beings. Its far enemy is cruelty, while its near enemy has been described as pity (which contains a sense of aversion), or anger, fear, or grief on another person's behalf—emotions that can overwhelm us and distract us from compassion.

3. Sympathetic joy or empathetic joy (*mudita* in Pāli) describes joy and rejoicing in others' positive outcomes, including their accomplishments, success, virtues, and prosperity. It includes being nondemeaning towards other people, and it is an antidote for comparisons, jealousy and competitiveness. It is the ability to be happy when we notice that other people are happy, so much so that their joy becomes ours, and we welcome their decrease in suffering and increase in hap-

piness.[355] Salzberg notes that impediments to *mudita* are judgment, comparing, discriminating, demeaning, envy, avarice, and boredom. Qualities that support it are gratitude, compassion, loving-kindness, and rapture. Its far enemy is jealousy and resentment, and its near enemy is exultation—becoming so excited about others' prosperity that our state of mind becomes agitated, overly excited, manic, or grasping towards joy.

4. Equanimity (*upekkhā* in Pāli) refers to balance. The concept of equanimity can be a challenging one. It reflects a sense of stability, serenity, peace, calmness and balance that rounds out the other abodes. However, equanimity does not convey indifference, imply that things should never bother us, or suggest that we should not feel things. It is a clear-minded, tranquil, "middle way" state of mind—not being overpowered by stress, tension, delusions, mental dullness, or agitation—but also a state without clinging, attachment, detachment, or indifference. Sharon Salzberg (1995) teaches that this attitude towards our experiences is like an adult parent of grown children. Equanimity includes feelings of warmth and love, but it also encompasses an acceptance of things as they are. A sense of equanimity helps us to accept and handle what the Buddha taught were the "eight worldly vicissitudes" that we all encounter throughout our lives: gain and loss, good-repute and ill-repute, praise and blame, pleasure and pain. Equanimity enables us to respond to challenges with flexibility, rather than applying our ingrained rules and understandings. Equanimity can strengthen our faith, confidence, honesty and sincerity, and help resolve vacillation or feeling unsettled. The far enemy of equanimity is clinging, attachment, or craving, whereas the near enemy is isolation, superiority, indifference, or "a cold distance from a heartfelt sense of life," that scorns the human process.

Buddhist traditions view the divine abodes as boundless, infinite, and limitless. These traditions offer specific approaches to cultivating these divine abodes (for a helpful introduction, see *Lovingkindness* by Sharon Salzberg, 1995). The abodes are not meant to be exclusive mental states, but rather complementary qualities that strengthen each other. For instance, Salzberg refers to equanimity as a "secret ingredient" that makes loving-kindness and compassion more effective and resilient. She explains that when we are suffering, we often seek help from someone who can offer *both* care and perspective. That element of balance makes support more effective than if we were to receive a deep understanding and kindness alone that somehow confirmed that we *should* despair, without any hope or greater perspective.

Western psychology also provides some information about how to handle life's difficulties. Researchers have studied *posttraumatic growth*—defined as the ability to learn or grow after trauma—and *resilience*—or the capacity to encounter stressors while remaining relatively unshaken. Much of the research to date examines the factors that contribute to posttraumatic growth and resilience; research regarding how to cultivate these experiences is just beginning.

At times, discussions of posttraumatic growth and resilience can have a pathologizing tone. Well-meaning people may even suggest that these concepts reflect attitudes that can be readily adopted ("You need to pull yourself up by your bootstraps" or "look on the bright side"). In reality, these processes are quite complex, and reflect a constellation of factors, many of which may reside outside our control. Posttraumatic growth and resilience can take time to build, and they do not necessarily reflect the phenomenon of being unshaken by trauma. In fact, being shaken up—and then going through the recovery process—can be the catalyst that yields growth and resilience.

Posttraumatic Growth

The term *posttraumatic growth* refers to the beneficial changes that many people report after trauma, and acknowledges the many ways in which trauma survivors can grow. Trauma can help people build skills and capacities that bolster their ability to cope with subsequent challenging events.[356]

Descriptions of posttraumatic growth often incorporate Piaget's (1952) learning models of assimilation and accommodation.[357] Piaget viewed learning as comprising both assimilation and accommodation. Accommodation requires adjusting our mental landscapes, and it can be a difficult process. In fact, we seem to have a bias towards assimilation—because it is easier to fit information into the mental maps that we already have. Despite the relative ease of assimilation as compared with accommodation, trauma often demands accommodation, and pushes us to stretch the boundaries of our known experiences and coping skills in order to adapt. The process of accommodating our understanding of the world to a new, posttraumatic reality can take considerable mental effort. Although it is often difficult, this effort can pay off. The adjustments we make to handle trauma can generate a range of benefits. As we work to heal from trauma, we also build new skills for handling stressful circumstances. We can boost our *proactive coping*—our efforts in our thinking and behavior that we direct towards strengthening our basic emotional resources.[358]

The book *Upside: The New Science of Posttraumatic Growth* (Rendon, 2015) notes that at least half of trauma survivors say that they have experienced positive changes since the trauma. The book also illustrates the meaning-making and new skills demonstrated by a number of survivors of trauma, including Clementina Chery, a mother who lost a son to a stray bullet and later founded an institute to assist families who had lost a member to gun violence, and New

York's Empire Dragon Boat Team, a competitive rowing team of breast cancer survivors. Rendon also discusses Luther Delp, who became disabled after a terrible accident and after a period of depression became a volunteer, advocate, and public speaker addressing the needs of individuals with disabilities. Delp contrasted his life before and after the accident by saying, "I had a good life then, but I have a great life now" (Rendon, 2015, p. 9).

Richard Tedeschi and Lawrence Calhoun (2004) described the following five aspects of posttraumatic growth: (a) new possibilities or opportunities; (b) an augmented sense of closeness or connection to others, including to other people who have experienced trauma; (c) an increased appreciation for one's own strength in coping with difficulties; (d) greater appreciation for life in general; and (e) shifts or deepening in one's religious, spiritual, or belief systems. Although one might assume that these categories reflect some type of positive attitude that would run contrary to trauma-related distress, posttraumatic growth seems to be highly intertwined with posttraumatic stress symptoms after trauma. Instead of occurring in opposition to trauma responses such as PTSD, posttraumatic growth appears to take shape alongside distress or even because of it. Posttraumatic growth appears to reflect the idea that a journey *through* trauma and its effects—rather than steering around it— is necessary to yield meaningful transformation.

Tedeschi and Calhoun observe that not everyone reports posttraumatic growth, and assert that the concept of posttraumatic growth is not meant to imply that trauma is a good experience or necessarily beneficial. Instead, the concept is useful in describing the types of positive changes that many individuals experience after trauma. The concept of posttraumatic growth can also be seen as a way to reframe our experience of trauma and instill hope that we can recover with new strength and opportunities.

RESEARCH HIGHLIGHT What Are Some of the Factors That Promote Posttraumatic Growth?

SEVERAL INTERNAL and external factors have emerged as meaningful predictors of a person's likelihood to experience posttraumatic growth after trauma. For instance, a longitudinal study of 653 women diagnosed with breast cancer indicated that a longer time since diagnosis, higher levels of education, and increases in social support, spirituality, and active coping strategies each contributed to posttraumatic growth.[359] Other studies have identified openness to experience, positive affect, effective emotion regulation, perceptions of self-efficacy, and lower levels of stress as factors associated with posttraumatic growth.[360]

Increased PTSD symptoms are associated with posttraumatic growth in many samples, including survivors of earthquakes.[361] This evidence provides support for the theory that PTSD symptoms may reflect cognitive efforts to process trauma.[362] Whereas events that do not impact us very much may spark few possibilities for personal growth, traumas that challenge our core beliefs or central aspects of our identity may lead to ongoing mental processing.[363] Rumination may even help us work through the trauma. However, it appears that *deliberate rumination* is more strongly associated with positive outcomes than *automatic rumination*.[364] Traumas may provoke growth when they require us to make room for the event within our perspectives about ourselves and the world.[365]

Many studies demonstrate a connection between social support and posttraumatic growth.[366] For example, trauma survivors' sense of their partners' responsiveness following stressful events has been linked to posttraumatic growth.[367] In another study,[368] adults who were abused in childhood were asked to identify the factors and "turning points" that helped them move on. Participants identified five factors, the first three of which involved social support: (a) genuine acceptance, (b) feeling loved and nurtured, (c) having a sense of belonging and connection, (d) feelings of liberation and freedom, and (e) feelings of accomplishment and mastery.

Practicing mindfulness may also facilitate posttraumatic growth. One research study[369] included 50 women with breast and gynecologic cancer who took part in eight weekly 2-hour mindfulness sessions. The researchers reported that increased levels of mindfulness were significantly linked with decreased distress, and with higher levels of quality of life and posttraumatic growth. This study adds to other research[370] demonstrating that engaging in constructive mental practices after trauma can promote posttraumatic growth.

In Their Own Words

For me the most powerful benefit of mindfulness is choice. My mindfulness practice allows me to choose new responses in the face of triggering circumstances that would otherwise be fraught with the drama of unconscious responses. For example, as the middle child in a family with 9 other siblings, I have been prone to intense experiences of abandonment in many different types of situations. One time I was going to go on a date with my partner. I left work early for this special evening. I arrived home, changed into a lovely, black cocktail dress, and was waiting with anticipation for him to arrive home. After 30 minutes of waiting I began to feel irritated. I then tried to call and text him and couldn't get any response. I then began to feel very anxious. My heart beat began to race. My mind was filled with worries and thoughts about his safety, about whether or not he was still coming, about why he wasn't responding. I wanted to lash out in anger, and in the next moment I want to break down in fear. What I chose to do was sit on my couch and bring conscious awareness to my feelings. I brought compassion to the little girl inside that was afraid; I offered her reassurance. I began to take slow, deep breaths. I closed my eyes and meditated for quite some time. He ended up arriving nearly 2 hours late, and where I would have typically been emotionally drained and likely very upset, I was able to accept his beautiful flowers and the explanation about traffic, the flower shop, his phone, etc . . . In short, I was able to have a wonderful evening instead of having it ruined by not having the tools to manage my personal triggers.

Resilience

As with the word *trauma*, there are many meanings associated with the word *resilience*. Sources list the origins of the word *resilience* as the Latin *resiliens* meaning "leaping back" or "rebounding."[371]. *Resilience* can be defined as "positive adaptation, or the ability to maintain or regain mental health, despite experiencing adversity" (Hermann et al., 2011, p. 259). With its emphasis on "the ability to maintain or regain mental health," this definition provides a helpful framework that reflects both coping with past trauma and building new capacities to handle future challenges. It indicates that we may be able to encounter trauma without having it derail us, and also reflects our ability to reestablish our well-being if trauma does knock us down.

In the mental health field, *resilience* has been used to refer to a personality trait, such as hardiness, optimism or determination; to reflect a process of responding constructively to stress; or to describe our bodies' physiological reactions to challenges. In developmental psychology literature, it can refer to children who thrive despite deleterious home environments. The word *resilient* has also been used to describe individuals who encounter trauma but who do not experience PTSD.[372] Some definitions emphasize the role that social support plays in resilience, and include the roles of families, cultures, and communities to mitigate stress and trauma.[373] Another area of resilience work focuses on the genetic markers that influence responses to trauma.[374] Finally, the resilience field addresses interactions among the personal, genetic, and environmental factors that influence trauma responses.[375]

These definitions and associations illuminate the complexity of resilience, and reveal the variety of factors that influence how we handle trauma and its aftermath. Resilience becomes even more complex when we consider that people, contexts, and cultures prioritize different aspects of resilience, and that individuals can demonstrate levels of resilience that vary across domains.[376] For instance, mothers who are survivors of childhood sexual abuse may demonstrate considerable resilience in their ability to be effective parents while still struggling with their own depression.[377]

Resilience is a topic that lends itself to misunderstandings regarding its supposed ease as a chosen mindset or character trait. If we could each just "zap" our way to better mental health by snapping our fingers, we would all do so. The idea that we can become more resilient merely by deciding to seems relatively pervasive, at least in American culture. The assumption can even be dangerous, as it can lead to our blaming ourselves and others during times of pain, thereby increasing suffering. In fact, there is a healthy balance between believing that we can control everything and believing that we can control nothing. Both of these perspectives can cause problems; we must acknowledge that we exist in a "middle ground" of controllability.

Our brains have a substantial capacity for resilience, and they can be engaged to redirect functioning towards better health.[378] There are several factors that we can implement to enhance our brains' resilience to stressors. McEwen cites evidence that regular physical activity,[379] mindfulness-based stress reduction,[380] and social support and integration[381] each exert positive influences on the brain.

Resilience is strongly linked to mindfulness and self-compassion.[382] Self-compassion also seems to involve resilience in that it may have a protective function, beyond that of mindfulness, against symptoms of depression and post-traumatic stress.[383] Overall, the evidence shows that we can actively increase our resilience,[384] and that mindfulness and self-compassion practice can contribute to this goal.

Mindfulness practices seem to boost our responses to stressors. For instance, Johnson and colleagues (2014) described a study of two groups of marines, 147 of whom were randomly chosen to receive mindfulness training and 134 of whom were randomized not to receive the training. The mindfulness training was associated with significant improvements in physical recovery (as measured by heart rate, blood oxygen, and plasma neuropeptide Y concentration) and brain activity after a stressful combat training session. Mindfulness may also be linked to resilience among individuals with high-stress jobs, such as firefighters,[385] and mindfulness training can reduce burnout among those working in high-stress environments.[386] Neuroimaging research also suggests that mindfulness training may help our brain to process stressful situations more effectively.[387]

The factors that influence the development of resilience mirror those that promote mental health in general.[388] The American Psychological Association (2016) advises the following ways of coping with stressful events:

- Make connections with others, maintain healthy ties to loved ones and communities, accept help from others, and provide it to others when possible
- Avoid seeing crises as insurmountable
- Accept that change is a part of life, and focus on ways that you can be effective

- Move towards goals that are realistic and that you can pursue regularly
- Take action rather than avoiding or detaching from problems
- Seek out opportunities for self-discovery, growth, and new strengths
- Cultivate a positive view of yourself that includes trust and confidence in your instincts and ability to handle challenges
- Keep things in perspective by pursuing a broad, long-term outlook
- Nurture hope and optimism
- Practice self-care in the form of attending to your own needs, feelings, physical health and exercises, enjoyable activities, spiritual practices, and meditation

Mindfulness and self-compassion practices can help in each of these areas. By building awareness, self-encouragement, and self-confidence through developing a wide range of skills, we can increase our resilience. For instance, mindful awareness of small physical changes, such as variations between breaths when practicing mindful breathing, or exploring sensations within the body during body scans, can increase our awareness and acceptance of change in general, and help us to expand our perspective beyond the particular challenge of each moment. Handling obstacles that arise in mindfulness practice—such as frustration, discomfort, or boredom—can build our skills for handling other challenges. Self-compassion practices such as loving-kindness can promote a more positive view of ourselves, along with the knowledge that we deserve support and care from others and that we are capable of providing care as well. Successes with mindfulness practice—from remembering to do it at all to noticing positive changes—can also help us to cultivate optimism and hope.

Maintaining Trauma Recovery and Resilience

If mindfulness, compassion, or self-compassion skills have helped you manage trauma or life in general more effectively, it may be wise to continue your practice as you move forward. You may find that your practice shifts over months or years—that you put it down and then pick it up, or discover that different practices are more helpful in different stages of trauma recovery and in life. In general, any type of behavioral change or skill that confers positive effects—including physical exercise, mindfulness practice, socializing, or being kind to yourself—works best when we keep it up.

Whether or not trauma occupies the foreground or the background of our lives, everyday life is often hard, and we can anticipate that both external and internal challenges will continue to arise. In his remarkable book *The Trauma of Everyday Life*, Epstein (2013) asserted that we deal with traumas daily. Even if we have experienced some degree of recovery from trauma, everyday life provides plenty of traumas. We have only to read a newspaper to find it, or notice the challenging dynamics that can emerge within ourselves in relation to others.

We can be sure that various forms of trauma will continue to appear, both large and small—either reminders of past trauma or brand new stressors. It is an inextricable part of human experience. We often encounter racism, sexism, economic concerns, misunderstandings, crowded buses, or health worries. It is unrealistic to expect to feel great all the time, but it is realistic to become more confident about our able to get through difficult times. By cultivating our attention to a range of experiences, we can come to feel more and more as though the painful aspects of life can be balanced by finding moments of connection, contentment, peace—and even bliss or joy.

A range of stressors can impact our mindfulness practice. Changes in our living situation, workplace, physical or mental health, childrearing or other care-giving responsibilities—as well as changes in our broader social, political, and economic circumstances—can each create new demands on our time, energy, and attention. It can feel frustrating to have external circumstances impinge on our mindfulness routines; however, we can also grow from the opportunity to be flexible as we integrate mindfulness practices into different situations. We can bring our curiosity to the ways that outside circumstances influence us, and attempt to refrain from judging ourselves when this occurs.

We may need to shift something about our practice during times of transition or hardship. When life becomes overwhelming, the simple act of *getting through the day* without destructive acts towards ourselves or others is of paramount importance. It is a bonus to have any mindful moments during such times, or to refrain from criticizing ourselves. One way to shift mindfulness practices when life becomes especially challenging is to incorporate them into our daily activities (see Practice #1, Mindfulness in Daily Activities, in Chapter 10), or to practice self-compassion for ways that challenges impact us (see Chapter 4). Just as a range of mindfulness skills may help us with specific post-traumatic difficulties, different practices may be most useful for different life circumstances.

In addition to external difficulties, we can expect to encounter internal challenges (termed "hindrances" in Buddhist tradition) that may impact mindfulness practice. The Insight Meditation Center (n.d.) in Redwood City, California advises that,

> We absolutely will encounter hindrances. The main instruction is to turn them into your focus of mindfulness. It does not matter whether a hindrance arises, but it does matter how you handle it. You can make a friendly relationship, rather than an adversarial one with the hindrances.

Categories of hindrances include (a) sensual desire or greed; (b) ill will or aversion; (c) sloth and torpor; (d) restlessness, anxiety, or worry; and (e) doubt.

The Insight Meditation Center (n.d.) suggests addressing hindrances through the "RAIN" formula, in which we

- **Recognize** the hindrance
- **Accept** its presence
- **Investigate** it curiously (how does it emerge physically, emotionally, energetically, cognitively, or motivationally—for example, are there urges to act, push it away, or cling?)
- **Nonidentification,** in which we remember that the hindrance is a passing challenge that does not reflect who we are

Although often the RAIN framework is sufficient to address a hindrance, there are also remedies or counterbalances to the hindrances, such as reflecting on the harmful consequences of unhealthful desires; narrowing your focus or practicing loving-kindness as a remedy against ill will; cultivating mindfulness practices that generate both tranquility and alertness to ward off feeling mentally dull; concentrating, sitting still, or smiling to address restlessness; or reflecting on unresolved questions and consulting with others to handle doubt.

Balance Acceptance and Change

It is something of a paradox that we may benefit from changing some aspects of our lives or the world around us, while simultaneously learning to tolerate life exactly as it is. The psychologist Marsha Linehan (1993b) described cultivating this balance as a key foundation for improving and maintaining mental health. Many of us may experience an imbalance between acceptance and change—

that is, either feeling overly certain that we cannot change and that things will remain exactly as they are, or placing demands on ourselves to make big or fast changes in ways that are unkind or unreasonable. It can help to mindfully inquire whether our tendencies toward acceptance or toward change might themselves reflect elements of our past trauma or self-judgment, and provide ourselves with compassion and understanding if either is the case.

To add to the paradox, cultivating acceptance—our awareness of how things are right now, along with some degree of tolerance for things and ourselves exactly as they are—is itself a meaningful change for most of us, and one that can boost our mental health. When we are suffering from trauma or self-criticism, we can experience a desire to change everything, and to feel a sense of urgency and striving. Some of that urgency may propel positive changes, but too much can lead to frustration and disappointment. Balancing acceptance and change can help us appreciate the benefit from even one new mindfulness skill, or one new idea or perspective. Holding on to this idea of balance can also help us through periods of challenges with mindfulness practice, or encounter a new obstacle to the development that we seek.

In Their Own Words ──────────────────────

Every time I ride the subway during rush hour, I transform into a mindfulness ninja. I remind myself to breathe out deeply. The simple act of mindful breathing helps to release some of the stress and tension that can accumulate when elbows, armpits and briefcases are touching me.

Immediately upon releasing an exhalation, I feel my body unwind a bit. I consciously (and silently) breathe in the word "space" and breathe out the word "stress". I continue to discreetly apply this mantra or slogan as best as I can until I reach my destination. Simultaneously, I bring my attention to both of my feet making contact with the subway floor (or the seat if I am fortunate enough to be sitting). I intentionally ground down into the parts of my body that are in contact with the floor (chair), and invite myself to stand (or sit) taller with each inhalation. I visualize the front of my spine getting longer with each breath in ("space"), and tension melting down my back as I breath out ("stress").

My mindfulness practice guides me more peacefully through busy City life, and I am forever grateful for this practice. It is exactly that— an ongoing practice— and as one of my teachers once said, "What we practice, we strengthen". I will continue to be a stealth mindfulness ninja—especially during rush hour.

We can practice mindfulness and self-compassion anytime and anywhere. As we practice, we realize that we can learn new ways to manage and improve our mental states. We also benefit from providing ourselves with care, companionship, and encouragement as we encounter the ups and downs of life. There is no one right way to practice mindfulness, to heal from trauma, or to cultivate resilience, but we can each determine for ourselves which practices we find most helpful.

As we practice, we can discover new inner landscapes, or ways of perceiving ourselves and the world. Although the mindfulness skills included in this book are grounded in research evidence, their practice necessarily entails some degree of personal adaptation, creativity, and even mystery. We might practice for a variety of reasons—for instance, in order to maintain benefits of calmness or confidence that we may have cultivated, or to continue to grow in our ability to handle challenges with more choice, comfort, and ease. We have good reason to think that mindfulness skills will help us, but we might also wind up being surprised where our practice takes us. We may find ourselves developing new perspectives, insights, emotions, daily rhythms, friendships, spiritual sensibilities, goals, or values. As we incorporate new mindfulness and self-compassion skills into our lives, we are likely to emerge still ourselves, yet also transformed through our own efforts and care. Like the artists who craft precious Japanese *kintsukuroi* bowls out of broken pieces of pottery, by working lovingly and creatively with trauma we can transfigure our own brokenness into new manifestations of strength, recovery, and resilience.

Adenauer, H., Catani, C., Gola, H., Keil, J., Ruf, M., Schauer, M., & Neuner, F. (2011). Narrative exposure therapy for PTSD increases top-down processing of aversive stimuli—evidence from a randomized controlled treatment trial. *BMC Neuroscience, 12*, 127.

Affleck, G., & Tennen, H. (1996). Construing benefits from adversity: Adaptational significance and dispositional underpinning. *Journal of Personality, 64*, 899–922.

Aikens, K. A., Astin, J., Pelletier, K. R., Levanovich, K., Baase, C. M., Park, Y. Y., & Bodnar, C. M. (2014). Mindfulness goes to work: Impact of an online workplace intervention. *Journal of Occupational and Environmental Medicine, 56*(7), 721–731.

Aknin, L. B., Barrington-Leigh, C. P., Dunn, E. W., Helliwell, J. F., Burns, J., Biswas-Diener, R., . . . Norton, M. I. (2013). Prosocial spending and well-being: Cross-cultural evidence for a psychological universal. *Journal of Personality and Social Psychology, 104*(4), 635–52.

Allwood, M. A., Bell, D. J., & Horan, J. (2011). Posttrauma numbing of fear, detachment, and arousal predict delinquent behaviors in early adolescence. *Journal of Clinical Child and Adolescent Psychology, 40*(5), 659–667.

Amaro. (2010). Don't push – Just use the weight of your own body [Audio podcast]. Talk recorded June 20, 2010 at Spirit Rock Meditation Center. Retrieved from http://dharmaseed.org/

American Psychological Association. (2016). The road to resilience. Retrieved April 1, 2016 from http://www.apa.org/helpcenter/road-resilience.aspx

Anders, S. L., Frazier, P. A., & Frankfurt S. B. (2011). Variations in Criterion A and

PTSD rates in a community sample of women. *Journal of Anxiety Disorders, 25*(2), 176–184.

Ando, M., Morita, T., Akechi, T., Ito, S., Tanaka, M., Ifuku, Y., & Nakayama, T. (2009). The efficacy of mindfulness-based meditation therapy on anxiety, depression, and spirituality in Japanese patients with cancer. *Journal of Palliative Medicine, 12*(12), 1091–1094.

Andrews, B., Brewin, C. R., Rose, S., & Kirk, M. (2000). Predicting PTSD symptoms in victims of violent crime: The role of shame, anger and childhood abuse. *Journal of Abnormal Psychology, 109*, 69–73.

Arch, J. J., Brown, K. W., Dean, D. J., Landy, L. N., Brown, K. D., & Laudenslager, M. L. (2014). Self-compassion training modulates alpha-amylase, heart rate variability, and subjective responses to social evaluative threat in women. *Psychoneuroendocrinology, 42*, 49–58.

Asmundson, G. J., Stapleton, J. A., & Taylor, S. (2004). Are avoidance and numbing distinct PTSD symptom clusters? *Journal of Traumatic Stress, 17*(6), 467–475.

Atlas, J. A., & Ingram, D. M. (1998). Betrayal trauma in adolescent inpatients. *Psychological Reports, 83*, 914.

Avery, M., & McDevitt-Murphy, M. (2014). Impact of combat and social support on PTSD and alcohol consumption in OEF/OIF veterans. *Military Behavioral Health, 2*(2), 217–223.

Babyak, M., Blumenthal, J. A., Herman, S., Khatri, P., Doraiswamy, M., Moore, K., . . . Krishnan, K. R. (2000). Exercise treatment for major depression: Maintenance of therapeutic benefit at 10 months. *Psychosomatic Medicine, 62*, 633–638.

Badura, A. S. (2003). Theoretical and empirical exploration of the similarities between emotional numbing in posttraumatic stress disorder and alexithymia. *Journal of Anxiety Disorders, 17*(3), 349–360.

Baer, R. A., Smith, G. T., & Allen, K. B. (2004). Assessment of mindfulness by self-report: The Kentucky Inventory of Mindfulness Skills. *Assessment, 11*, 91–206.

Banks, K., Newman, E., & Saleem, J. (2015). An overview of the research on mindfulness-based interventions for treating symptoms of posttraumatic stress disorder: A systematic review. *Journal of Clinical Psychology, 71*(10), 935–963. doi:10.1002/jclp.22200

Barglow, P. (2014). Numbing after rape, and depth of therapy. *American Journal of Psychotherapy, 68*, 117–139.

Barnes, J. (2011). *The sense of an ending*. New York, NY: Alfred A. Knopf.

Bartlett, C. (2008). A tearoom view of mended ceramics. In *Flickwerk: The aesthetics of mended Japanese ceramics*. Münster, Germany: Museum für Lackkunst.

Batten, S. V., Follette, V. M., & Aban, I. B. (2001). Experimental avoidance and high-risk sexual behavior in survivors of child sexual abuse. *Journal of Child Sexual Abuse, 10*(2), 101–120.

Bazarko, D., Cate, R. A., Azocar, F., & Kreitzer, M. J. (2013). The impact of an innovative mindfulness-based stress reduction program on the health and well-being of nurses employed in a corporate setting. *Journal of Workplace Behavioral Health, 28*(2), 107–133.

Beiser, M., & Hyman, I. (1997). Refugees' time perspective and mental health. *American Journal of Psychiatry, 154*, 996-1002.

Beng, T. S., Ahmad, F., Loong, L. C., Chin, L. E., Zainal, N. Z., Guan, N. C., . . . Meng, C. B. (2015). Distress reduction for palliative care patients and families with 5-minute mindful breathing. *The American Journal of Hospice and Palliative Medicine, 33*(6), 555–560.

Berliner, L., & Elliott, D. M. (1996). Sexual abuse of children. In J. Briere, L. Berliner, J. A. Bulkley, C. Jenny, & T. Reid (Eds.), *The American Professional Society on the Abuse of Children handbook on child maltreatment* (pp. 4–20). Thousand Oaks, CA: Sage Publications.

Berry, L. M., May, J., Andrade, J., & Kavanagh, D. (2010). Emotional and behavioral reaction to intrusive thoughts. *Assessment, 17*(1), 126–317.

Black, D. S., Milam, J., & Sussman, S. (2009). Sitting-meditation interventions among youth: A review of treatment efficacy. *Pediatrics, 124*(3), doi:10.1542/peds.2008-3434

Blom M., & Oberink, R. (2012). The validity of the DSM-IV PTSD criteria in children and adolescents: a review. *Clinical Child Psychology and Psychiatry, 17*(4), 571-601.

Bockers, E., Roepke, S., Michael, L., Renneberg, B., & Knaevelsrud, C. (2014). Risk recognition, attachment anxiety, self-efficacy, and state dissociation predict revictimization. *PLoS One, 9*(9). doi:10.1371/journal.pone.0108206

Boden, M. T., Bernstein, A., Walser, R. D., Bui, L., Alvarez, J., & Bonn-Miller, M. O. (2012). Changes in facets of mindfulness and posttraumatic stress disorder treatment outcome. *Psychiatry Research, 200*(2–3), 609–613. doi:10.1016/j.psychres.2012.07.011

Bonanno, G. A. (2004). Loss, trauma, and human resilience: Have we underestimated the human capacity to thrive after extremely aversive events? *American Psychologist, 59*(1), 20–28.

Bonnan-White, J., Hetzel-Riggin, M. D., Diamond-Welch, B. K., & Tollini, C. (2015). "You blame me, therefore I blame me": The importance of first disclosure partner responses on trauma-related cognitions and distress. *Journal of Interpersonal Violence.* doi:10.1177/0886260515615141

Boorstein, S. (1997). *It's easier than you think: The Buddhist way to happiness.* New York, NY: HarperCollins.

Boscarino, J. A. (2004). Posttraumatic stress disorder and physical illness: Results from clinical and epidemiologic studies. *Annals of the New York Academy of Sciences, 1032,* 141–153.

Bourne, E. J. (1995). *The anxiety and phobia workbook* (2nd ed.). Oakland, CA: New Harbinger Publications.

Brach, T. (2015). Healing traumatic fear: The wings of mindfulness and love. In V. M. Follette, J. Briere, D. Rozelle, J. W. Hopper, & D. I. Rome (Eds.), *Mindfulness-oriented interventions for trauma* (pp. 31–42). New York, NY: The Guilford Press.

Brach, T. (2015). "Morning Q and response—working with trauma." Presentation on April 20, 2015, at Insight Meditation Community of Washington DC. Retrieved June 16, 2016, from the Dharma Seed website: http://dharmaseed.org/talks/?search=working+with+trauma#

Brahma Vihara Foundation. (n.d.). Upekkha. Retrieved [insert date] from http://www.brahmaviharas.org/upekkha.htm

Brand, B. L., Myrick, A. C., Loewenstein, R. J., Classen, C. C., Lanius, R. A., McNary, S. W., . . . Putnam, F. W. (2012). A survey of practices and recommended treatment interventions among expert therapists treating patients with dissociative identity disorder and dissociative disorder not otherwise specified. *Psychological Trauma: Theory, Research, Practice, & Policy, 4,* 490–500.

Bratman, G., Hamilton, J. P., Hahn, K., Daily, G., & Gross, J. (2015). Nature experience reduces rumination and subgenual prefrontal cortex activation. *Proceedings of the Natural Academy of Sciences, 112*(28), 8567–8572.

Brefczynski-Lewis, J. A., Lutz, A., Schaefer, H. S., Levinson, D. B., & Davidson, R. J. (2007). Neural correlates of attentional expertise in longterm meditation practitioners. *Proceedings of the National Academy of Sciences of the United States of America, 104*(27), 11483–11488.

Breines J. G., & Chen, S. (2012). Self-compassion increases self-improvement motivation. *Personality & Social Psychology Bulletin, 38*(9), 1133–1143.

Breines, J. G., McInnis, C. M., Kuras, Y. I., Thoma, M. V., Gianferante, D., Hanlin, L., . . . Rohleder, N. (2015). Self-compassionate young adults show lower salivary alpha-amylase responses to repeated psychosocial stress. *Self and Identity, 14*(4), 390–402.

Breslau, N., & Davis, G. C. (1992). Posttraumatic stress disorder in an urban population of young adults: Risk factors for chronicity. *American Journal of Psychiatry, 149*(5), 671–675.

Brewin, C. R., Andrews, B., & Valentine, J. D. (2000). Meta-analysis of risk factors for posttraumatic stress disorder in trauma-exposed adults. *Journal of Consulting and Clinical Psychology, 68*(5), 748–766.

Briere, J. (1992). *Child abuse trauma: Theory and treatment of the lasting effects.* Newbury Park, CA: Sage Publications.

Briere, J. (2002). Treating adult survivors of severe childhood abuse and neglect: Further development of an integrative model. In J. E. B. Myers, L. Berliner, J. Briere, C. T. Hendrix, T. Reid, & C. Jenny (Eds.), *The APSAC handbook on child maltreatment* (2nd ed.). Newbury Park, CA: Sage Publications.

Briere, J. (2015). Pain and suffering: A synthesis of Buddhist and western approaches to trauma. In V. M. Follette, J. Briere, D. Rozelle, J. W. Hopper, & D. I. Rome (Eds.), *Mindfulness-oriented interventions for trauma* (pp. 11–30). New York, NY: The Guilford Press.

Brion, J. M., Leary, M. R., & Drabkin, A. S. (2014). Self-compassion and reactions to serious illness: The case of HIV. *Journal of Health Psychology, 19*(2), 218–229.

Britton, W. B., Shahar, B., Szepsenwol, O., & Jacobs, W. J. (2012). Mindfulness-based cognitive therapy improves emotional reactivity to social stress: Results from a randomized controlled trial. *Behavior Therapy, 43*(2), 365–380.

Brockman, C., Snyder, J., Gewirtz, A., Gird, S. R., Quattlebaum, J., Schmidt, N., . . . DeGarmo, D. (2015). Relationship of service members' deployment trauma, PTSD symptoms, and experiential avoidance to postdeployment family reengagement. *Journal of Family Psychology, 30*(1), 52–62.

Brosh, A. (2013). *Hyperbole and a half: Unfortunate situations, flawed coping mechanisms, mayhem, and other things that happened.* New York, NY: Simon & Schuster.

Brown, L. S. (2015). *Not the price of admission: Healthy relationships after childhood trauma.* Author.

Brown, R. J. (2006). Different types of "dissociation" have different psychological mechanisms. *Journal of Trauma and Dissociation Trauma, 7*(4), 7–28.

Brown, R. P., Gerbarg, P. L., & Muench, F. (2013). Breathing practices for treatment of psychiatric and stress-related medical conditions. *Psychiatric Clinics of North America, 36,* 121–140.

Brown, S. L., & Brown, R. M. (2015). Connecting prosocial behavior to improved physical health: Contributions from the neurobiology of parenting. *Neuroscience and Biobehavioral Reviews, 55,* 1–17.

Buddharakkhita, A. (1995). Metta: The philosophy and practice of universal love. Retrieved July 21, 2015 from http://www.accesstoinsight.org/lib/authors/budd harakkhita/wheel365.html

Calhoun, L. G., & Tedeschi, R. G. (2013). *Posttraumatic growth in clinical practice.* New York, NY: Routledge.

Campbell, S. B., & Renshaw, K. D. (2013). PTSD symptoms, disclosure, and relationship distress: Explorations of mediation and associations over time. *Journal of Anxiety Disorders, 27*(5), 494–502.

Canevello, A., Michels, V., & Hilaire, N. (2015). Supporting close others' growth after trauma: The role of responsiveness in romantic partners' mutual posttraumatic growth. *Psychological Trauma: Theory, Research, Practice, and Policy.* doi:10 .1037/tra0000084.supp

Carlson, L., Ursuliak, Z., Goodey, E., Angen, M., & Speca, M. (2001). The effects of a mindfulness meditation-based stress reduction program on mood and symptoms of stress in cancer outpatients: 6-month follow-up. *Supportive Care in Cancer,* 112–123.

Carlson, M. C., Erickson, K. I., Kramer, A. F., Voss, M. W., Bolea, N., Mielke, M., . . . Fried, L. P. (2009). Evidence for neurocognitive plasticity in at-risk older adults: The experience corps program. *The Journals of Gerontology: Series A, Biological Sciences and Medical Sciences, 64,* 1275–1282.

Carmody, J., & Baer, R. A. (2008). Relationships between mindfulness practice and levels of mindfulness, medical and psychological symptoms and well-being in a mindfulness-based stress reduction program. *Journal of Behavioral Medicine, 31*(1), 23–33.

Chawla, N., & Ostafin, B. (2007). Experiential avoidance as a functional dimensional approach to psychopathology: An empirical review. *Journal of Clinical Psychology, 63*(9), 871–890.

Chekhov, A. P. (2000). *Selected stories of Anton Chekhov.* (R. Pevear & L. Volokhonsky, Trans.). New York, NY: Modern Library.

Chemtob, C., Roitblat, H. L., Hamada, R. S., Carlson, J. G., & Twentyman, C. G. (1988). A cognitive action theory of posttraumatic stress disorder. *Journal of Anxiety Disorders, 2,* 253–275.

Chiesa, A., Anselmi, R., & Serretti, A. (2014). Psychological mechanisms of mindfulness-based interventions: What do we know? *Holistic Nursing Practice, 28*(2), 124–148.

Chu, J. A., Dill, D. L., & Murphy, D. E. (2000). Depressive symptoms and sleep disturbance in adults with histories of childhood abuse. *Journal of Trauma & Dissociation, 1,* 87–97.

Cicchetti D. (2010). Resilience under conditions of extreme stress: A multilevel perspective. *World Psychiatry, 9,* 145–154.

Cloitre, M., Stovall-McClough, K. C., Nooner, K., Zorbas, P., Cherry, S., Jackson, C. L., . . . Petkova, E. (2010). Treatment for PTSD related to childhood abuse: A randomized controlled trial. *American Journal of Psychiatry, 167*(8), 915–924.

Codrington, R. (2010). A family therapist's look into interpersonal neurobiology and the adolescent brain: An interview with Dr. Daniel Siegel. *Australian and New Zealand Journal of Family Therapy, 31*(3), 285–299.

Cohen-Katz, J., Wiley, S. D., Capuano, T., Baker, D. M., Kimmel, S., & Shapiro, S. (2005). The effects of mindfulness-based stress reduction on nurse stress and burnout, Part II: A quantitative and qualitative study. *Holistic Nursing Practice, 19*(1), 26–35.

Colcombe, S. J., Kramer, A. F., Erickson, K. I., Scalf, P., McAuley, E., Cohen, N. J., . . . Elavsky, S. (2004). Cardiovascular fitness, cortical plasticity, and aging. *Proceedings of the Natural Academy of Sciences of the United States of America, 101,* 3316–3321.

Contractor, A. A., Armour, C., Wang, X., Forbes, D., & Elhai, J. D. (2015). The mediating role of anger in the relationship between PTSD symptoms and impulsivity. *Psychological Trauma: Theory, Research, Practice, & Policy, 7,* 138–145.

Copeland, W. E., Keeler, G., Angold, A., & Costello, E. J. (2007). Traumatic events and posttraumatic stress in childhood. *Archives of General Psychiatry, 64*(5), 577–584.

Cortina, L. M., & Magley, V. J. (2003). Raising voice, risking retaliation: Events following interpersonal mistreatment in the workplace. *Journal of Occupational Health Psychology, 8*(4), 247–265.

Cottle, T. J. (1969). The location of experience: A manifest time orientation. *Acta Psychologia, 28,* 129–149.

Cottle, T. J. (1976). *Perceiving time: A psychological investigation of men and women.* New York, NY: John Wiley & Sons.

Coupland, D. (1995). *Microserfs.* New York, NY: HarperCollins.

Cox, B. J., MacPherson, P. S., Enns, M. W., & McWilliams, L. A. (2004). Neuroticism and self-criticism associated with posttraumatic stress disorder in a nationally representative sample. *Behaviour Research and Therapy, 42*(1), 105–114.

Cremeans-Smith, J. K., Greene, K., & Delahanty, D. L. (2015). Trauma history as a resilience factor for patients recovering from total knee replacement surgery. *Psychology & Health, 30*(9), 1005–1016.

Crick, F., & Mitchison, G. (1983). The function of dream sleep. *Nature, 304,* 111–114.

Cromer, L. D., & Smyth, J. M. (2010). Making meaning of trauma: Trauma exposure doesn't tell the whole story. *Journal of Contemporary Psychotherapy, 40*(2), 65–72.

Dalai Lama, & Cutler, H. C. (1998). *The art of happiness: A handbook for living.* New York, NY: Penguin.

Dalai Lama. (2003). *The compassionate life.* Somerville, MA: Wisdom Publications.

Dalai Lama. (n.d.). Dalai Lama quotes. Retrieved June 20, 2016 from http://thinkexist.com/quotation/compassion_is_not_religious_business-it_is_human/145362.html

Danhauer, S. C., Case, L. D., Tedeschi, R., Russell, G., Vishnevsky, T., Triplett, K., . . . Avis, N. E. (2013). Predictors of posttraumatic growth in women with breast cancer. *Psychooncology, 22*(12), 2676–2683.

Dawson Rose, C., Webel, A., Sullivan, K. M., Cuca, Y. P., Wantland, D., Johnson, M. O., . . . Holzemer, W. L. (2014). Self-compassion and risk behavior among people living with HIV/AIDS. *Research in Nursing & Health, 37*(2), 98–106.

de Bruin, E. I., Topper, M., Muskens, J. G., Bögels, S. M., & Kamphuis, J. H. (2012). Psychometric properties of the Five Facets Mindfulness Questionnaire (FFMQ) in a meditating and a non-meditating sample. *Assessment, 19*(2), 187–197.

Declercq, F., Vanheule, S., Deheegher, J. (2010). Alexithymia and posttraumatic stress: Subscales and symptom clusters. *Journal of Clinical Psychology, 66*(10), 1076–1089.

DeFrain, J. D., & Asay, S. M. (Eds.) (2007). *Strong families around the world: Strengths-based research and perspectives.* Binghamton, NY: Haworth Press.

DePrince, A. P., Chu, A.T., & Pineda, A. S. (2011). Links between specific posttrauma appraisals and three forms of trauma-related distress. *Psychological Trauma: Theory, Research, Practice, and Policy, 3*(4), 430–441.

DePrince, A. P., Zurbriggen, E. L., Chu, A. T., & Smart, L. (2010). Development of the Trauma Appraisal Questionnaire. *Journal of Aggression, Maltreatment, & Trauma, 19*, 275–299.

Detweiler, M. B., Self, J. A., Lane, S., Spencer, L., Lutgens, B., Kim, D. Y., . . . Lehmann, L. P. (2015). Horticultural therapy: A pilot study on modulating cortisol levels and indices of substance craving, posttraumatic stress disorder, depression, and quality of life in veterans. *Alternative Therapies in Health and Medicine, 21*(4), 36–41.

Dewey, D., Schuldberg, D., & Madathil, R. (2014). Do peritraumatic emotions differentially predict PTSD symptom clusters? Initial evidence for emotion specificity. *Psychological Reports, 115*(1), 1–12.

Di Benedetto, M., & Swadling, M. (2014). Burnout in Australian psychologists: Correlations with work-setting, mindfulness and self-care behaviours. *Psychology, Health, & Medicine, 19*(6), 705–715.

Dillon, L. M., Nowak, N., Weisfeld, G. E., Weisfeld, C. C., Shattuck, K. S., Imamoglu, O. E., . . . Shen, J. (2015). Sources of marital conflict in five cultures. *Evolutionary Psychology, 13*(1), 1–15.

Dorahy, M. J., & van der Hart, O. (2015). DSM-5's posttraumatic stress disorder with dissociative symptoms: Challenges and future directions. *Journal of Trauma & Dissociation, 16*(1), 7–28.

Dorahy, M. J., Corry, M., Shannon, M., Macsherry, A., Hamilton, G., McRobert, G., . . . Hanna, D. (2009). Complex PTSD, interpersonal trauma and relational consequences: Findings from a treatment-receiving Northern Irish sample. *Journal of Affective Disorders, 112*(1–3), 71–80.

Dorahy, M. J., Corry, M., Shannon, M., Webb, K., McDermott, B., Ryan, M., & Dyer, K. F. (2012). Complex trauma and intimate relationships: The impact of shame, guilt and dissociation. *Journal of Affective Disorders, 147*(1–3), 72–79.

Drescher, K., Foy, D., Kelly, C., Leshner, A., Schutz, A., & Litz, B. T. (2011). An exploration of the viability and usefulness of the construct of moral injury in war veterans. *Traumatology, 17*(1), 8–13.

Duax, J. M., Bohnert, K. M., Rauch, S. A., & Defever, A. M. (2014). Posttraumatic stress disorder symptoms, levels of social support, and emotional hiding in returning veterans. *Journal of Rehabilitation Research and Development, 51*(4), 571–578.

Dunkley, D. M., Sanislow, C. A., Grilo, C. M., & McGlashan, T. H. (2009). Self-criticism versus neuroticism in predicting depression and psychosocial impairment for 4 years in a clinical sample. *Comprehensive Psychiatry, 50*(4), 335-346.

Dunmore, E., Clark, D. M., & Ehlers, A. (1999). Cognitive factors involved in the onset and maintenance of posttraumatic stress disorder (PTSD) after physical or sexual assault. *Behaviour Research and Therapy, 37*(9), 809–829.

Dunn, R., Callahan, J. L., & Swift, J. K. (2013). Mindfulness as a transtheoretical clinical process. *Psychotherapy, 50*(3), 312–315.

Dutton, M.A., Bermudez, D., Matas, A., Majid, H., & Myers, N. L. (2013). Mindfulness-based stress reduction for low-income, predominantly African American women with PTSD and a history of intimate partner violence. *Cognitive and Behavioral Practice, 20,* 23–32.

Dykens, E. M., Fisher, M. H., Taylor, J. L., Lambert, W., & Miodrag, N. (2014). Reducing distress in mothers of children with autism and other disabilities: A randomized trial. *Pediatrics, 134*(2). doi:10.1542/peds.2013-3164d

Eagleman, D. M. (2008). Human time perception and its illusions. *Current Opinion in Neurobiology. 18*(2), 131–6.

Eftekhari, A., Stines, L. R., & Zoellner, L. A. (2006). Do you need to talk about it? Prolonged exposure for the treatment of chronic PTSD. *The Behavior Analyst Today, 7*(1), 70–83.

Ehlers, A. (2010). Understanding and treating unwanted trauma memories in posttraumatic stress disorder. *Zeitschrift fur Psychologie, 218*(2), 141–145.

Ehlers, A., & Clark, D. M. (2000). A cognitive model of posttraumatic stress disorder. *Behaviour Research and Therapy, 38*, 319–345.

Ehret, A. M., Joormann J., & Berking, M. (2014). Examining risk and resilience factors for depression: The role of self-criticism and self-compassion. *Cognition and Emotion, 29*(8):1496–1504.

Eichhorn, S., Brähler, E., Franz, M., Friedrich, M., & Glaesmer, H. (2014). Traumatic experiences, alexithymia, and posttraumatic symptomatology: A cross-sectional population-based study in Germany. *European Journal of Psychotraumatology, 5*(0). doi:10.3402/ejpt.v5.23870

El Khoury-Malhame, M., Lanteaume, L., Beetz, E. M., Roques, J., Reynaud, E., Samuelian, J. C., . . . Khalfa, S. (2011). Attentional bias in post-traumatic stress disorder diminishes after symptom amelioration. *Behaviour Research and Therapy, 49*(11), 796–801.

Elman, I., Lowen, S., Frederick, B. B., Chi, W., Becerra, L., & Pitman, R. K. (2009). Functional neuroimaging of reward circuitry responsivity to monetary gains and losses in posttraumatic stress disorder. *Biological Psychiatry 66*(12), 1083–1090.

Epstein, M. (2013). *The trauma of everyday life.* New York, NY: Penguin Books.

Erogul, M., Singer, G., McIntyre, T., & Stefanov, D. G. (2014). Abridged mindfulness intervention to support wellness in first-year medical students. *Teaching and Learning in Medicine, 6*(4), 350–356.

Farb, N. A. S., Anderson, A. K., & Segal, Z. V. (2012). The mindful brain and emotion regulation in mood disorders. *Canadian Journal of Psychiatry, 57*(2), 70-77.

Farley, M., Golding, J. M., & Minkoff, J. R. (2002). Is a history of trauma associated with a reduced likelihood of cervical cancer screening? *The Journal of Family Practice, 51*(10), 827–831.

Farley, M., Minkoff, J. R., & Barkan, H. (2001). Breast cancer screening and trauma history. *Women & Health, 34*(2), 15–27.

Farnsworth, J. K., & Sewell, K. W. (2011). Fear of emotion as a moderator between PTSD and firefighter social interactions. *Journal of Traumatic Stress, 24*(4), 444–450.

Fava, G. A., & Tomba, R. (2009). Increasing psychological well-being and resilience by psychotherapeutic methods. *Journal of Personality, 77*(6), 1903–1934.

Feeny, N. C., Zoellner, L. A., Fitzgibbons, L. A., & Foa, E. B. (2000). Exploring the roles of emotional numbing, depression, and dissociation in PTSD. *Journal of Traumatic Stress, 13*(3), 489–498.

Feldman, C., & Kuyken, W. (2011). Compassion in the landscape of suffering. *Contemporary Buddhism, 12*(1), 143–155.

Feldman, R. R. (2007). Parent-infant synchrony and the construction of shared timing; physiological precursors, developmental outcomes, and risk conditions. *Journal of Child Psychology and Psychiatry, 48*(3-4), 329–354.

Felitti, V. J., Anda, R. F., Nordenberg, D., Williamson, D. F., Spitz, A. M., Edwards, V., . . . Marks, J. S. (1998). Relationship of childhood abuse and household dysfunction to many of the leading causes of death in adults. *American Journal of Preventive Medicine, 14*(4), 245–258.

Felmingham, K. L., Falconer, E. M., Williams, L., Kemp, A. H., Allen, A., Peduto, A., & Bryant, R. A. (2014). Reduced amygdala and ventral striatal activity to happy faces in PTSD is associated with emotional numbing. *PLoS One, 9*(9):e103653.

Ferreira, C., Matos, M., Duarte, C., & Pinto-Gouveia, J. (2014). Shame memories and eating psychopathology: The buffering effect of self-compassion. *European Eating Disorders Review, 22*(6), 487–494.

Feuer, C. A., Nishith, P., & Resick, P. (2005). Prediction of numbing and effortful avoidance in female rape survivors with chronic PTSD. *Journal of Traumatic Stress, 18*(2):165–170.

Fidler, T., Dawson, K. A., & Gallant, R. (1992). Empirical evidence for assumptions underlying time orientation in undergraduates. *Perceptual and Motor Skills, 74*(3c), 1171–1180.

Flack, W. F., Jr, Milanak, M. E., & Kimble, M. O. (2005). Emotional numbing in relation to stressful civilian experiences among college students. *Journal of Traumatic Stress, 18*(5), 569–573.

Flickwerk: The aesthetics of mended Japanese ceramics. (2008). [Glossary] Münster, Germany: Museum für Lackkunst.

Foa, E. B., & Kozak, M. J. (1986). Emotional processing of fear: Exposure to corrective information. *Psychological Bulletin, 99,* 20–35.

Foa, E. B., & Riggs, D. S. (1995). Posttraumatic stress disorder following assault: Theoretical considerations and empirical findings. *Current Directions in Psychological Science, 4,* 61–65.

Foa, E. B., & Rothbaum, B. O. (1998). *Treating the trauma of rape: Cognitive-behavioral therapy for PTSD.* New York, NY: Guilford.

Foa, E. B., Ehlers, A., Clark, D. M., Tolin, D. F., & Orsillo, S. M. (1999). The Posttraumatic Cognitions Inventory (PTCI): Development and validation. *Psychological Assessment, 11,* 303–314.

Foa, E. B., Riggs, D., & Gershuny, B. (1995). Arousal, numbing, and intrusion: Symptom structure of PTSD following assault. *American Journal of Psychiatry, 152,* 116–120.

Forbes, D., Phelps, A. J., McHugh, A. F., Debenham, P., Hopwood, M., & Creamer, M. (2003). Imagery rehearsal in the treatment of posttraumatic nightmares in Australian veterans with chronic combat-related PTSD: 12-month follow-up data. *Journal of Traumatic Stress, 16,* 509–513.

Foynes, M. M. & Freyd, J. J. (2011). The impact of skills training on responses to the disclosure of mistreatment. *Psychology of Violence, 1,* 66–77.

Freed, S., & D'Andrea, W. (2015). Autonomic arousal and emotion in victims of interpersonal violence: Shame proneness but not anxiety predicts vagal tone. *Journal of Trauma and Dissociation, 16*(4), 367–383.

Frewen, P. A., & Lanius, R. A. (2006). Toward a psychobiology of posttraumatic self-dysregulation: Reexperiencing, hyperarousal, dissociation, and emotional numbing. *Annals of the New York Academy of Sciences, 1071,* 110–124.

Frewen, P. A., Dozois, D. J., Neufeld, R. W., Lane, R. D., Densmore, M., Stevens, T. K., & Lanius, R. A. (2012). Emotional numbing in posttraumatic stress disorder: A functional magnetic resonance imaging study. *Journal of Clinical Psychiatry, 73*(4), 431–436.

Frey, R. J. (2001). Dissociative disorders. In *The Gale Encyclopedia of Medicine,* 2nd Edition (5 Vol.) (pp. 1085-1088). Farmington Hills, MI: Gale Group.

Freyd, J. J.& Birrell, P. J. (2013). *Blind to betrayal.* Hoboken, NJ: John Wiley & Sons.

Freyd, J. J., Klest, B., & Allard, C. B. (2005). Betrayal trauma: Relationship to physical health, psychological distress, and a written disclosure intervention. *Journal of Trauma and Dissociation, 6*(3), 83–104.

Freyd, J. J. (1996). *Betrayal trauma: The logic of forgetting childhood abuse.* Cambridge, MA: Harvard University Press.

Fried, L. P., Carlson, M. C., Freedman, M., Frick, K. D., Glass, T. A., Hill, J., . . . Zeger, S. (2004). A social model for health promotion for an aging population: Initial evidence on the experience corps model. *Journal of Urban Health, 81,* 64–78.

Furini, C., Myskiw, J., & Izquierdo, I. (2014). The learning of fear extinction. *Neuroscience and Biobehavioral Reviews, 47,* 670–683.

Galla, B. M., O'Reilly, G. A., Kitil, M. J., Smalley, S. L., Black, D. S. (2014). Community-based mindfulness program for disease prevention and health promotion: Targeting stress reduction. *American Journal of Health Promotion, 30*(1), 36–41.

Galovski, T. E., Mott, J., Young-Xu, Y., & Resick, P. A. (2011). Gender differences in the clinical presentation of PTSD and its concomitants in survivors of interpersonal assault. *Journal of Interpersonal Violence, 26*(4), 789–806.

Garber, M. (2004). Compassion. In P. Gilbert, & L. Berlant (Eds.), *Compassion: The culture and politics of an emotion* (pp. 15–28). New York, NY: Routledge.

Garland, E. L., Fredrickson, B., Kring, A. M., Johnson, D. P., Meyer, P. S., & Penn, D. L. (2010). Upward spirals of positive emotions counter downward spirals of negativity: Insights from the broaden-and-build theory and affective neuroscience on the treatment of emotion dysfunctions and deficits in psychopathology. *Clinical Psychology Review, 30,* 849–864.

Gecht, J., Kessel, R., Forkmann, T., Gauggel, S., Drueke, B., Sherer, A., & Mainz, V. (2014). A mediation model of mindfulness and decentering: Sequential psychological constructs or one and the same? *BMC Psychology, 2*(1), 18.

Germer, C. K., & Neff, K. D. (2013). Self-compassion in clinical practice. *Journal of Clinical Psychology, 69*(8), 856–867.

Gibb, B. E., Chelminski, I., & Zimmerman, M. (2007). Childhood emotional, physical, and sexual abuse, and diagnoses of depressive and anxiety disorders in adult psychiatric outpatients. *Depression and Anxiety, 24*(4), 256–263.

Giesbrecht, T., Smeets, T., Merckelbach, H., & Jelicic, M. (2007). Depersonalization experiences in undergraduates are related to heightened stress cortisol responses. *The Journal of Nervous and Mental Disease, 195*(4), 282–287.

Gilbert, P. (2009). *The compassionate mind: A new approach to life's challenges.* London: Constable & Robinson.

Gilbert, P. (2010). *Compassion focused therapy: Distinctive features.* London: Routledge.

Gilbert, P., & Proctor, S. (2006). Compassionate mind training for people with high shame and self-criticism: Overview and pilot study of a group therapy approach. *Clinical Psychology & Psychotherapy, 13*(6), 353–379.

Gilbert, P., McEwan, K., Matos, M., & Rivis, A. (2011). Fears of compassion: Development of three self-report measures. *Psychology and Psychotherapy, 84*(3), 239–255.

Ginzburg, K., Butler, L. D., Giese-Davis, J., Cavanaugh, C. E., Neri, E., Koopman, C., . . . Spiegel, D. (2009). Shame, guilt, and posttraumatic stress disorder in adult survivors of childhood sexual abuse at risk for human immunodeficiency virus: Outcomes of a randomized clinical trial of group psychotherapy treatment. *The Journal of Nervous and Mental Disease, 197*(7), 536–542.

Gladwell, M. (2005). *Blink: The power of thinking without thinking.* New York, NY: Little Brown.

Glover, H. (1992). Emotional numbing: A possible endorphin-mediated phenomenon associated with posttraumatic stress disorders and other allied psychopathologic states. *Journal of Traumatic Stress, 5,* 643–675.

Glover, H., Ohlde, C., Silver, S., Packard, P., Goodnick, P., & Hamlin, C. L. (1994). The Numbing Scale: psychometric properties, a preliminary report. *Anxiety, 1*(2), 70-79.

Goldsmith, R. E., Gerhart, J. I., Chesney, S. A., Burns, J. W., Kleinman, B., & Hood, M. M. (2014). Mindfulness-based stress reduction for posttraumatic stress symptoms: Building acceptance and decreasing shame. *Journal of Evidence-Based Complementary and Alternative Medicine, 19,* 227–234.

Goldstein, J. (2015, April 12). You can't fail at meditation. Interview by D. Harris. Retrieved May 25, 2016 from Lion's Roar website: http://www.lionsroar.com/cant-fail-meditation/

Goodman, J. H., Guarino, A., Chenausky, K., Klein, L., Prager, J., Petersen, R., . . . Freeman, M. (2014). CALM Pregnancy: Results of a pilot study of mindfulness-based cognitive therapy for perinatal anxiety. *Archives of Women's Mental Health, 17*(5), 373–387.

Grasso, D. J., Cohen, L. H., Moser, J. S., Hajcak, G., Foa, E. B., & Simons R. F. (2012). Seeing the silver lining: Potential benefits of trauma exposure in college students. *Anxiety, Stress & Coping, 25*(2), 117–136.

Greenglass, E. (2002). Proactive coping. In E. Frydenberg (Ed.), *Beyond coping: Meeting goals, visions and challenges* (pp. 37–62). Oxford, UK: Oxford University Press.

Grepmair, L., Mitterlehner, F., Loew, T., & Nickel, M. (2007). Promotion of mindfulness in psychotherapists in training: Preliminary study. *European Psychiatry, 22*(8), 485–489.

Grindler Katonah, D. (2015). Focusing-oriented psychotherapy: A contemplative approach to healing trauma. In V. Follette, J. Briere, D. Rozelle, J. W. Hopper, & D. I. Rome (Eds.). *Mindfulness-oriented interventions for trauma – Integrating contemplative practices* (pp.157–170). New York, NY: Guilford Press.

Guerra, V. S, & Calhoun, P. S. (2011). Examining the relation between posttraumatic stress disorder and suicidal ideation in an OEF/OIF veteran sample. *Journal of Anxiety Disorders, 25*(1), 12–18.

Haase, L., Thom, N. J., Shukla, A., Davenport, P. W., Simmons, A. N., Stanley, E. A., . . . Johnson, D. C. (2014). Mindfulness-based training attenuates insula response to an aversive interoceptive challenge. *Social Cognitive and Affective Neuroscience, 11*(1), 182–190.

Hagenaars, M. A., & van Minnen A. (2010). Posttraumatic growth in exposure therapy for PTSD. *Journal of Traumatic Stress, 23*(4), 504–508.

Hall, C. W., Row, K. A., Wuench, K. L., & Godley, K. R. (2013). The role of self-compassion in physical and psychological well-being. *Journal of Psychology, 147,* 311–323.

Hamilton, J. L., Connolly, S. L., Liu, R. T., Stange, J. P., Abramson, L. Y., & Alloy, L. B. (2015). It gets better: Future orientation buffers the development of hopelessness and depressive symptoms following emotional victimization during early adolescence. *Journal of Abnormal Child Psychology, 43*(3), 465–474.

Hansen, A. M., Hogh, A., Persson, R., Karlson, B., Garde, A. H., & Ørbaek, P. (2006). Bullying at work, health outcomes, and physiological stress response. *Journal of Psychosomatic Research, 60*(1), 63–72.

Hanson, R. (2009). *Buddha's brain: The practical neuroscience of happiness, love, and wisdom.* Oakland, CA: New Harbinger.

Hanson, R. (2013). *Hardwiring happiness: The new brain science of contentment, calm, and confidence.* New York, NY: Crown Publishing.

Hanson, S., & Jones, A. (2015). Is there evidence that walking groups have health benefits? A systematic review and meta-analysis. *British Journal of Health Medicine, 49*(11), 710–715.

Hariri, A. R., Bookheimer, S. Y., & Mazziotta, J. C. (2000). Modulating emotional responses: Effects of a neocortical network on the limbic system. *Neuroreport, 11*(1), 43–48.

Hartmann, E. (1998). Nightmare after trauma as paradigm for all dreams: A new approach to the nature and functions of dreaming. *Psychiatry, 61*(3), 223–238.

Hassija, C. M., Jakupcak, M., & Gray, M. J. (2012.) Numbing and dysphoria symptoms of posttraumatic stress disorder among Iraq and Afghanistan war veterans: A review of findings and implications for treatment. *Behavior Modification, 36*(6), 834–856.

Hayes, J. P., Vanelzakker, M. B., & Shin, L. M. (2012). Emotion and cognition interactions in PTSD: A review of neurocognitive and neuroimaging studies. *Frontiers in Integrative Neuroscience, 6*, 89.

Hayes, S. C., Wilson, K. G., Gifford, E. V., Follette, V. M., & Strosahl, K. (1996). Experiential avoidance and behavioral disorders: A functional dimensional approach to diagnosis and treatment. *Journal of Consulting and Clinical Psychology, 64*, 1152–1168.

Held, P., & Owens, G. P. (2015). Effects of self-compassion workbook training on trauma-related guilt in a sample of homeless veterans: A pilot study. *Journal of Clinical Psychology, 71*(6), 513–526.

Hemmingsson, E., Johansson, K., & Reynisdottir, S. (2014). Effects of childhood abuse on adult obesity: A systematic review and meta-analysis. *Obesity Reviews, 15*(11), 882–893.

Herrman, H., Stewart, D. E., Diaz-Granados, N., Berger, E. L., Jackson, B., & Yuen, T. (2011). What is resilience? *Canadian Journal of Psychiatry, 56*(5), 258–265.

Hiraoka, R., Meyer, E. C., Kimbrel, N. A., DeBeer, B. B., Gulliver, S. B., & Morissette, S. B. (2015). Self-compassion as a prospective predictor of PTSD symptom severity among trauma-exposed U.S. Iraq and Afghanistan war veterans. *Journal of Traumatic Stress, 28*(2), 127–133.

Ho, P., Tsao, J. C., Bloch, L., & Zeltzer, L. K. (2011). The impact of group drumming on social-emotional behavior in low-income children. *Evidence-Based Complementary and Alternative Medicine, 2011*, 1–14. doi:10.1093/ecam/neq072

Hofmann, S. G., Heering, S., Sawyer, A. T., & Asnaani, A. (2009). How to handle anxiety: The effects of reappraisal, acceptance, and suppression strategies on anxious arousal. *Behaviour Research and Therapy, 47*, 389–394.

Hofmann, S. G., Grossman, P., & Hinton, D. E. (2011). Loving-kindness and compassion meditation: Potential for psychological interventions. *Clinical Psychology Review, 31*(7), 1126–1132.

Hölzel, B. K., Carmody, J., Vangel, M., Congleton, C., Yerramsetti, S. M., Gard, T., & Lazar, S. W. (2011). Mindfulness practice leads to increases in regional brain gray matter density. *Psychiatry Research, 191*, 36–43.

Hölzel, B. K., Hoge, E. A., Greve, D. N., Gard, T., Creswell, J. D., Brown, K. W., . . . Lazar, S. W. (2013). Neural mechanisms of symptom improvements in generalized anxiety disorder following mindfulness training. *NeuroImage: Clinical, 2*, 448–458.

Hopper, E., & Emerson, D. (2011). *Overcoming trauma through yoga: Reclaiming your body.* Berkeley, CA: North Atlantic Books.

Horstmanshof, L., & Zimitat, C. (2007). Future time orientation predicts academic engagement among first-year university students. *The British Journal of Educational Psychology, 77*(3), 703–718.

Horwitz, A. V., Widom, C. S., McLaughlin, J., & White, H. R. (2001). The impact of childhood abuse and neglect on adult mental health: A prospective study. *Journal of Health and Social Behavior, 42*, 184–201.

Hou, R. J., Wong, S. Y., Yip, B. H., Hung, A. T., Lo, H. H., Chan, P. H., . . . Ma, S. H. (2014). The effects of mindfulness-based stress reduction program on the mental health of family caregivers: A randomized controlled trial. *Psychotherapy and Psychosomatics, 83*(1), 45–53.

Hundt, N. E., Mott, J. M., Miles, S. R., Arney, J., Cully, J. A., & Stanley, M. A. (2015). Veterans' perspectives on initiating evidence-based psychotherapy for posttraumatic stress disorder. *Psychological Trauma: Theory, Research, Practice, and Policy,7*(6), 539–546.

Hutcherson, C. A., Seppala, E. M., & Gross, J. J. (2008). Loving-kindness meditation increases social connectedness. *Emotion, 8*(5), 720–724.

Hyland, M. E., Alkhalaf, A. M., & Whalley, B. (2013). Beating and insulting children as a risk for adult cancer, cardiac disease and asthma. *Journal of Behavioral Medicine, 36*(6), 632–40.

Insight Meditation Center. (n.d.). The five hindrances. Retrieved April 1, 2016 from http://insightmeditationcenter.org/articles/FiveHindrances.pdf

Isa, M. R., Moy, F. M., Abdul Razack, A. H., Zainuddin, Z. M., & Zainal, N. Z.

(2013). Impact of applied progressive deep muscle relaxation training on the level of depression, anxiety and stress among prostate cancer patients: A quasi-experimental study. *Asian Pacific Journal of Cancer Prevention, 14,* 2237–2242.

Isaac, V., Stewart, R., Artero, S., Ancelin, M. L., & Ritchie, K. (2009). Social activity and improvement in depressive symptoms in older people: A prospective community cohort study. *The American Journal of Geriatric Psychiatry, 17*(8), 688–696.

Jack, D. C. (1991). *Silencing the self: women and depression.* Cambridge, MA: Harvard University Press.

Jakupcak, M., Tull, M. W., McDermott, M. J., Kaysen, D., Hunt, S., & Simpson, T. (2010a). PTSD symptom clusters in relationship to alcohol misuse among Iraq and Afghanistan war veterans seeking post-deployment VA health care. *Addictive Behaviors, 35,* 840–843.

Jakupcak, M., Wagner, A., Paulson, A., Varra, A., & McFall, M. (2010b). Behavioral activation as a primary care-based treatment for PTSD and depression among returning veterans. *Journal of Traumatic Stress, 23*(4), 491–495.

Jallo, N., Bourguignon, C., Taylor, A. G., Ruiz, J., & Goehler, L. (2009). The biobehavioral effects of relaxation guided imagery on maternal stress. *Advances in Mind-Body Medicine, 24,* 12–22.

Janoff-Bulman, R. (1989). Assumptive worlds and the stress of traumatic events: Applications of the schema construct. *Social Cognition, 7,* 113–136.

Janoff-Bulman, R. (1992). *Shattered assumptions: Towards a new psychology of trauma.* New York, NY: Free Press.

Jaquier, V., Hellmuth, J. C., & Sullivan, T. P. (2013). Posttraumatic stress and depression symptoms as correlates of deliberate self-harm among community women experiencing intimate partner violence. *Psychiatry Research, 206*(1), 37–42.

Játiva, R., & Cerezo, M. A. (2014). The mediating role of self-compassion in the relationship between victimization and psychological maladjustment in a sample of adolescents. *Child Abuse & Neglect, 38*(7), 1180–1190.

Jerath, R., Edry, J. W., Barnes, V. A., & Jerath, V. (2006). Physiology of long pranayamic breathing: Neuralrespiratory elements may provide a mechanism that explains how slow deep breathing shifts the autonomic nervous system. *Medical Hypotheses, 67,* 566–571.

Jobson, L., & O'Kearney, R. T. (2009). Impact of cultural differences in self on cognitive appraisals in posttraumatic stress disorder. *Behavioural and Cognitive Psychotherapy, 37*(3), 249–266.

Johnson, D. C., Thom, N. J., Stanley, E. A., Haase, L., Simmons, A. N., Shih, P. A., . . . Paulus, M. P. (2014). Modifying resilience mechanisms in at-risk individuals: A controlled study of mindfulness training in marines preparing for deployment. *American Journal of Psychiatry, 171,* 844–853.

Johnson, D. M., Palmieri, P. A., Jackson, A. P., & Hobfoll, S. E. (2007). Emotional numbing weakens abused inner-city women's resiliency resources. *Journal of Traumatic Stress, 20*(2), 197–206.

Joseph, S. (2011). *What doesn't kill us: The new psychology of posttraumatic growth.* New York: Basic Books.

Kabat-Zinn, J. (1994). *Wherever you go, there you are: Mindfulness meditation in everyday life.* New York, NY: Hyperion.

Kabir. (2002). *The bijak of Kabir* (L. Hess & S. Singh, Trans.). New York, NY: Oxford University Press.

Kang, Y., Gray, J. R., & Dovidio, J. F. (2014). The nondiscriminating heart: Lovingkindness meditation training decreases implicit intergroup bias. *Journal of Experimental Psychology, 143*(3), 1306–1313.

Kashdan, T. B., & Kane, J. Q. (2011). Posttraumatic distress and the presence of posttraumatic growth and meaning in life: Experiential avoidance as a moderator. *Personality and Individual Differences, 50*(1), 84–89.

Kassavou, A., Turner, A., Hamborg, T., & French, D. P. (2014). Predicting maintenance of attendance at walking groups: Testing constructs from three leading maintenance theories. *Health Psychology, 33*(7), 752–756.

Katerelos, M., Hawley, L. L., Antony, M. M., & McCabe, R. E. (2008). The exposure hierarchy as a measure of progress and efficacy in the treatment of social anxiety disorder. *Behavior Modification, 32*(4), 504–518.

Kearney, D. J., Malte C. A., McManus, C., Martinez, M. E., Felleman, B., Simpson, T. L. (2013). Loving-kindness meditation for posttraumatic stress disorder: A pilot study. *Journal of Traumatic Stress, 26*(4), 426–434.

Kearney, D. J., McDermott, K., Malte, C., Martinez, M., & Simpson, T. L. (2010). Association of participation in a mindfulness program with measures of PTSD, depression and quality of life in a veteran sample. *Journal of Clinical Psychology, 68*, 101–116.

Kearney, D. J., McDermott, K., Malte, C., Martinez, M., & Simpson, T. L. (2013). Effects of participation in a mindfulness program for veterans with posttraumatic stress disorder: A randomized controlled pilot study. *Journal of Clinical Psychology, 69*(1), 14–27.

Kelly, A. C., Zuroff, D. C., & Shapira, L. B. (2009). Soothing oneself and resisting self-attacks: The treatment of two intrapersonal deficits in depression vulnerability. *Cognitive Therapy and Research, 33*(3), 301–313.

Kemper, K. J., Mo, X., & Khayat, R. (2015). Are mindfulness and self-compassion associated with sleep and resilience in health professionals? *Journal of Alternative and Complementary Medicine, 21*(8), 496–503.

Kendall-Tackett, K. (2002). The health effects of childhood abuse: Four pathways by which abuse can influence health. *Child Abuse & Neglect, 26*(6–7), 715–729.

Kenny, L. M., Bryant, R. A., Silove, D., Creamer, M., O'Donnell, M., & McFarlane, A. C. (2009). Distant memories: A prospective study of vantage point of trauma memories. *Psychological Science, 20*(9), 1049–1052.

Kerig, P. K., Bennett, D. C., Chaplo, S. D., Modrowski, C. A., & McGee, A. B. (2016). Numbing of positive, negative, and general emotions: Associations with trauma exposure, posttraumatic stress, and depressive symptoms among justice-involved youth. *Journal of Traumatic Stress, 29*(2), 111–119.

Kern, R. P., Libkuman, T. M., Otani, H., & Holmes, K. (2005). Emotional stimuli, divided attention, and memory. *Emotion, 5*(4) 408–417.

Kim, S. H., Schneider, S. M., Bevans, M., Kravitz, L., Mermier, C., Qualis, C., & Burge, M. R. (2013). PTSD symptom reduction with mindfulness-based stretching and deep breathing exercise: Randomized controlled clinical trial of efficacy. *Journal of Clinical Endocrinology & Metabolism, 98*(7), 2984–2992.

Kimbrough, E., Magyari, T., Langenberg, P., Chesney, M., Berman, B. (2010). Mindfulness intervention for child abuse survivors. *Journal of Clinical Psychology, 66*, 17–33.

King, A. P., Erickson, T. M., Giardino, N. D., Favorite, T., Rauch, S. A., Robinson, E., . . . Liberzon, I. (2013). A pilot study of group mindfulness-based cognitive therapy

(MBCT) for combat veterans with posttraumatic stress disorder (PTSD). *Depression and Anxiety, 30*(7), 638–645.

Kishon-Barash, R., Midlarsky, E., & Johnson, D. R. (1999). Altruism and the Vietnam War veteran: The relationship of helping to symptomatology. *Journal of Traumatic Stress, 12*(4), 655–662.

Kluft, R. P. (1993a). Clinical approaches to the integration of personalities. In R. P. Kluft & C. G. Fine (Eds.), *Clinical perspectives on multiple personality disorder* (pp. 101–133). Washington, DC: American Psychiatric Press.

Kögler, M., Brandstätter, M., Borasio, G. D., Fensterer, V., Küchenhoff, H., & Fegg, M. J. (2015). Mindfulness in informal caregivers of palliative patients. *Palliative & Supportive Care, 13*(1), 11–18.

Kopplin, M. (2008). [Foreword]. In *Flickwerk: The aesthetics of mended Japanese ceramics.* Münster, Germany: Museum für Lackkunst.

Körner, A., Coroiu, A., Copeland, L., Gomez-Garibello, C., Albani, C., Zenger, M., & Brähler, E. (2015). The role of self-compassion in buffering symptoms of depression in the general population. PLoS One. 10(10):e0136598. doi:10.1371/journal.pone.0136598.

Kornfield, J. (1994). *Buddha's little instruction book.* New York, NY: Bantam Books.

Krakow, B. (2004). Imagery rehearsal therapy for chronic posttraumatic nightmares: A mind's eye view. In R.I. Rosner, W.J. Lyddon, & A. Freeman (Eds.), *Cognitive therapy and dreams* (pp. 89–109). New York, NY: Springer Publishing Company.

Krakow, B., Hollifield, M., Johnston, L., Koss, M., Schrader, R., Warner, T. D., . . . Prince, H. (2001). Imagery rehearsal therapy for chronic nightmares in sexual assault survivors with posttraumatic stress disorder: A randomized controlled trial. *JAMA, 286*(5), 537-545.

Krause, E. D., Mendelson, T., & Lynch, T. R. (2003). Childhood emotional invalidation and adult psychological distress: The mediating role of emotional inhibition. *Child Abuse & Neglect, 27*(2), 199–213.

Krieger, T., Altenstein, D., Baettig, I., Doerig, N., & Holtforth, M. G. (2013). Self-compassion in depression: Associations with depressive symptoms, rumination, and avoidance in depressed outpatients. *Behavior Therapy, 44*(3), 501–513.

Krusche, A., Cyhlarova, E., King, S., & Williams, J. M. G. (2013). Mindfulness online: A preliminary evaluation of the feasibility of a web-based mindfulness course for stress, anxiety, and depression. *BMJ Open*, *3*(11). doi:10.1136/bmjopen-2013-003498

Kubany, E. S. (2000). Application of cognitive therapy for trauma-related guilt (CT-TRG) with a Vietnam veteran troubled by multiple sources of guilt. *Cognitive and Behavioral Practice*, *3*, 213–244.

Kubany, E. S., & Watson, S. B. (2003). Guilt: Elaboration of a multidimensional model. *The Psychological Record*, *53*, 51–90.

Kubany, E. S., Abueg, F. R., Owens, J. A., Brennan, J. M., Kaplan, A. S., & Watson, S. B. (1995). Initial examination of a multidimensional model of trauma-related guilt: Applications to combat veterans and battered women. *Journal of Psychopathology and Behavioral Assessment*, *17*, 353–376.

Kuyken, W., & Moulds, M. L. (2009). Remembering as an observer: How is autobiographical memory retrieval vantage perspective linked to depression? *Memory*, *17*(6), 624–634.

LaMotte, A. D., Taft, C. T., Reardon, A. F., & Miller, M. W. (2015). Veterans' PTSD symptoms and their partners' desired changes in key relationship domains. *Psychological Trauma – Theory, Research, Practice, and Policy*, *7*(5), 479–484.

Lancaster, S. L., Kloep, M., Rodriguez, B. F., & Weston, R. (2013). Event centrality, posttraumatic cognitions, and the experience of posttraumatic growth. *Journal of Aggression, Maltreatment & Trauma*, *22*, 1–15. doi:10.1080/10926771.2013.775983

Landes, S. J., Garovoy, N. D., & Burkman, K. M. (2013). Treating complex trauma among veterans: Three stage-based treatment models. *Journal of Clinical Psychology*, *69*(5), 523–533.

Lang, P. J., Davis, M., & Öhman, A. (2000). Fear and anxiety: Animal models and human cognitive psychophysiology. *Journal of Affective Disorders*, *61*(3), 137–159.

Lanius, R. A. (2015). Trauma-related dissociation and altered states of consciousness: A call for clinical, treatment, and neuroscience research. *European Journal of Psychotraumatology*, *6*, 10.

Lanius, R. A., Frewen, P. A., Vermetten, E., & Yehuda, R. (2010). Fear conditioning and early life vulnerabilities: Two distinct pathways of emotional dysregulation and brain dysfunction in PTSD. *European Journal of Psychotraumatology*, *1*(0). *doi:10.3402/ejpt.v1i0.5467*

Lanius, R. A., Vermetten, E., Loewenstein, R. J., Brand, B., Schmahl, C., Bremner, J. D., & Spiegel, D. (2010). Emotion modulation in PTSD: Clinical and neurobiological evidence for a dissociative subtype. *American Journal of Psychiatry, 167,* 640–647.

Lawrence, V. A., & Lee, D. (2014). An exploration of people's experiences of compassion-focused therapy for trauma, using interpretative phenomenological analysis. *Clinical Psychology & Psychotherapy, 21*(6), 495–507.

Le, H. N., Berenbaum, H., & Raghavan, C. (2002). Culture and alexithymia: mean levels, correlates, and the role of parental socialization of emotions. *Emotion, 2*(4), 341–360.

Leonard, D., Brann, S., Tiller, J. (2005). Dissociative disorders: Pathways to diagnosis, clinician attitudes and their impact. *The Australian and New Zealand Journal of Psychiatry, 39*(10), 940–946.

Leskela, J., Dieperink, M., & Thuras, P. (2002). Shame and posttraumatic stress disorder. *Journal of Traumatic Stress, 15*(3), 223–226.

Levant, R. F. (1998). Desperately seeking language: Understanding, assessing, and treating normative male alexithymia. In W. Pollack & R. Levant (Eds.), *New psychotherapy for men* (pp. 35–56). New York: Wiley.

Levant, R. F., Hall, R. J., Williams, C., & Hasan, N. T. (2009). Gender differences in alexithymia: A meta-analysis. *Psychology of Men & Masculinity, 10,* 190–203.

Levant, R. F., Halter, M. J., Hayden, E. W., & Williams, C. M. (2009). The efficacy of alexithymia reduction treatment: A pilot study. *The Journal of Men's Studies, 17,* 75–84.

Levine, P. (2000). Call it music. *Poetry,* Sept. 2000, 311–313.

Lewis, H. B. (1971). *Shame and guilt in neurosis.* New York, NY: International Universities Press.

Lewis, M. (1995). *Shame: The exposed self.* New York, NY: The Free Press.

Lieberman, M. D., Eisenberger, N. I., Crockett, M. J., Tom, S. M., Pfeifer, J. H., & Way, B. M. (2007). Putting feelings into words: Affect labeling disrupts amygdala activity in response to affective stimuli. *Psychological Science, 18*(5), 421–428.

Lightman, A. (1994). *Einstein's dreams.* New York, NY: Warner Books.

Linden, D. E. (2008). Brain imaging and psychotherapy: Methodological considerations and practical implications. *European Archives of Psychiatry and Clinical Neurosciences, 258*(55), 71–75.

Lindsay, E. K., & Creswell, J. D. (2014). Helping the self help others: Self-affirmation increases self-compassion and pro-social behaviors. *Frontiers in Psychology, 5*, 421.

Lindstrom, C. M., Cann, A., Calhoun, L. G., & Tedeschi, R. G. (2013). The relationship of core belief challenge, rumination, disclosure, and sociocultural elements to posttraumatic growth. *Psychological Trauma: Theory, Research, Practice, and Policy, 5*, 50–55. doi:10.1037/a0022030

Linehan, M. M. (1993a). *Cognitive behavioral treatment of borderline personality disorder.* New York, NY: Guilford Press.

Linehan, M. M. (1993b). *Skills training manual for treating borderline personality disorder.* New York, NY: Guilford Press.

Lipka, J., Hoffman, M., Miltner, W. H., & Straube, T. (2013). Effects of cognitive-behavioral therapy on brain responses to subliminal and supraliminal threat and their functional significance in specific phobia. *Biological Psychiatry, 76*(11), 869–877.

Liss, M., & Erchull, M. J. (2015). Not hating what you see: Self-compassion may protect against negative mental health variables connected to self-objectification in college women. *Body Image, 14*, 5–12.

Litz, B. T., Schlenger, W. E., Weathers, F. W., Caddell, J. M., Fairbank, J. A., & LaVange, L. M. (1997). Predictors of emotional numbing in posttraumatic stress disorder. *Journal of Traumatic Stress, 10*(4), 607–618.

Litz, B. T., Stein, N., Delaney, E., Lebowitz, L., Nash, W. P., Silva, C., & Maguen, S. (2009). Moral injury and moral repair in war veterans: A preliminary model and intervention strategy. *Clinical Psychology Review, 29*(8), 695–706.

Llewellyn, N., Dolcos, S., Iordan, A. D., Rudolph, K. D., & Dolcos, F. (2013). Reappraisal and suppression mediate the contribution of regulatory focus to anxiety in healthy adults. *Emotion, 13*, 610–615.

Lokamitra. (2004). Opening our hearts to the world. In D. Nagabodhi (Ed.), *Metta: The practice of loving kindness.* Cambridge, UK: Windhorse Publications.

Lommen, M. J., Engelhard, I. M., Sijbrandij, M., van den Hout, M. A., & Hermans, D. (2014). Pre-trauma individual differences in extinction learning predict posttraumatic stress. *Behaviour Research and Therapy, 51*(2), 63–67.

Longe, O., Maratos, F. A., Gilbert, P., Evans, G., Volker, F., Rockliff, H., & Rippon, G. (2010). Having a word with yourself: Neural correlates of self-criticism and self-reassurance. *Neuroimage, 49*(2), 1849–1856.

Lorber, W., & Garcia, H. A. (2010). Not supposed to feel this: Traditional masculinity in psychotherapy with male veterans returning from Afghanistan and Iraq. *Psychotherapy, 47*(3), 296–305.

Lucenko, B.A., Gold, S.N., & Cott, M.A. (2000). Relationship to perpetrator and post-traumatic symptomology among sexual abuse survivors. *Journal of Family Violence, 15*, 169–179.

Lynch, J., & Mack, L. (n.d.). PTSD recovery program treatment manual. Retrieved June 21, 2016 from http://www.miren.d.cc.va.gov/docs/visn6/PTSD_Recovery_Group_Client_Manual.pdf

MacBeth, A., & Gumley, A. (2012). Exploring compassion: A meta-analysis of the association between self-compassion and psychopathology. *Clinical Psychology Review, 32*(6), 545–552.

Maldonado, J. R., Butler, L. D., & Spiegel, D. (2002). Treatments for dissociative disorders. In P. E. Nathan & J.M. Gorman (Eds.). *A guide to treatments that work*, 2nd ed. (pp. 463–496). New York, NY: Oxford University Press.

Malinowksi, P. (2013). Neural mechanisms of attentional control in mindfulness meditation. *Frontiers in Neuroscience, 7*: 8.

Malta, L. S., Wyka, K. E., Giosan, C., Jayasinghe, N., & Difede, J. (2009). Numbing symptoms as predictors of unremitting posttraumatic stress disorder. *Journal of Anxiety Disorders, 23*(2), 223–229.

Mantani, T., Okamoto, Y., Shirao, N., Okada, G., & Yamawaki, S. (2005). Reduced activation of posterior cingulate cortex during imagery in subjects with high degrees of alexithymia: A functional magnetic resonance imaging study. *Biological Psychiatry, 57*(9), 982–990.

Manzoni, G.M., Pagnini, F., Castelnuovo, G., & Molinari, E. (2008). Relaxation training for anxiety: A ten-years systematic review with meta-analysis. *BMC Psychiatry, 8*, 41.

Marchand, W. R. (2013). Mindfulness meditation practices as adjunctive treatments for psychiatric disorders. *Psychiatric Clinics of North America, 36*(1), 141–152.

Martin, C. G., Cromer, L. D., DePrince, A. P., & Freyd, J. J. (2013). The role of cumulative trauma, betrayal, and appraisals in understanding trauma symptomatology. *Psychological Trauma: Theory, Research, Practice, & Policy, 52*(2),110–118.

Martin, L. E., Stenmark, C. K., Thiel, C. E., Antes, A. L., Mumford, M. D., Connelly, S., & Devenport, L. D. (2011). The influence of temporal orientation and affective frame on use of ethical decision-making strategies. *Ethics & Behavior, 21*(2), 127–146.

Masten, C. L., Guyer, A. E., Hodgdon, H. B., McClure, E. B., Charney, D. S., Ernst, M., . . . Monk, C. S. (2008). Recognition of facial emotions among maltreated children with high rates of posttraumatic stress disorder. *Child abuse and neglect, 32*(1), 139–153.

Mathew, K. L., Whitford, H. S., Kenny, M. A., Denson, L. A. (2010). The long-term effects of mindfulness-based cognitive therapy as a relapse prevention treatment for majordepressive disorder. *Behavioural and Cognitive Psychotherapy, 38*(5), 561–576.

Mathew, A. R., Cook, J. W., Japuntich, S. J., & Leventhal, A. M. (2015). Post-traumatic stress disorder symptoms, underlying affective vulnerabilities, and smoking for affect regulation. *The American Journal of Addictions, 24*(1), 39–46.

Mayo, K. R. (2009). Support from neurobiology for spiritual techniques for anxiety: A brief review. *Journal of Health Care Chaplaincy, 16*, 53–57.

McCranie, E. W., & Hyer, L. A. (1995). Self-critical depressive experience in posttraumatic stress disorder. *Psychological Reports, 77*(3 Pt 1), 880–882.

McDonald, K. (2010). *Awakening the kind heart: How to meditate on compassion.* Somerville, MA: Wisdom Publications.

McDonough, M. H., Sabiston, C. M., & Wrosch, C. (2014). Predicting changes in posttraumatic growth and subjective well-being among breast cancer survivors: The role of social support and stress. *Psychooncology, 23*(1), 114–120.

McEwen, B. S. (2016). In pursuit of resilience: Stress, epigenetics, and brain plasticity. *Annals of the New York Academy of Sciences*, doi:10.1111/nyas.13020

McFarlane, A. C., & van der Kolk, B. (1996). Trauma and its challenge to society. In B. A. van der Kolk, A. C. McFarlane, & L. Weisaeth (Eds.), *Traumatic stress: The effects of overwhelming experience on mind, body, and society* (pp. 417–440). New York, NY: The Guilford Press.

McFarlane, A. C., Weber, D. L., & Clark, C. R. (1993). Abnormal stimulus processing in posttraumatic stress disorder. *Biological Psychiatry, 34*(5), 311-320.

McGee, R., Williams, S., Howden-Chapman, P., Martin, J., & Kawachi, I. (2006). Participation in clubs and groups from childhood to adolescence and its effects on attachment and self-esteem. *Journal of Adolescence, 29*(1), 1–17.

McLaughlin, K. A., & Nolen-Hoeksema, S. (2011). Rumination as a transdiagnostic factor in depression and anxiety. *Behaviour Research & Therapy, 49*(3), 186–193.

McLean, C. P., Yeh, R., Rosenfield, D., & Foa, E. B. (2015). Changes in negative cognitions mediate PTSD symptom reductions during client-centered therapy and prolonged exposure for adolescents. *Behaviour Research and Therapy, 68*, 64–69.

McNamer, S. (2010). *Affective meditation and the invention of medieval compassion.* Philadelphia, PA: University of Pennsylvania Press.

Meiklejohn, J., Phillips, C., Freedman, L., Griffin, M. L., Biegel, G. M., Roach, A., . . . Saltzman, A. (2012). Integrating mindfulness training into K–12 education: Fostering the resilience of teachers and students. *Mindfulness, 3*, 291–307.

Mellman, T. A., & Hipolito, M. M. (2006). Sleep disturbances in the aftermath of trauma and posttraumatic stress disorder. *CNS Spectrums, 11*(8), 611–615.

Meyer, E. C., Zimering, R., Daly, E., Knight, J., Kamholz, B. W., & Gulliver, S. B. (2012). Predictors of posttraumatic stress disorder and other psychological symptoms in trauma-exposed firefighters. *Psychological Services, 9*(1), 1–15.

Michl, L. C., McLaughlin, K. A., Shepherd, K., & Nolen-Hoeksema, S. (2013). Rumination as a mechanism linking stressful life events to symptoms of depression and anxiety: Longitudinal evidence in early adolescents and adults. *Journal of Abnormal Psychology, 122*(2), 339–352.

Michopoulos, V., Powers, A., Moore, C., Villarreal, S., Ressler, K. J., & Bradley B. (2015). The mediating role of emotion dysregulation and depression on the relationship between childhood trauma exposure and emotional eating. *Appetite, 91*, 129–136.

Midlarsky, E. (1991). Helping as coping. *Prosocial Behavior: Review of Personality and Social Psychology, 12*, 238–264.

Midlarsky, E., & Kahana, E. (1994). *Altruism in later life.* Thousand Oaks, CA: Sage.

Miller, J. J., Fletcher, K., & Kabat-Zinn, J. (1995). Three-year follow-up and clinical implications of a mindfulness meditation-based stress reduction intervention in the treatment of anxiety disorders. *General Hospital Psychiatry, 17*, 192–200.

Miyahira, S. D., Folen, R. A., Hoffman, H. G., Garcia-Palacios, A., Spira, J. L., & Kawasaki, M. (2012). The effectiveness of VR exposure therapy for PTSD in returning warfighters. *Studies in Health Technology and Informatics, 181*, 128–132.

Monson, C. M., Macdonald, A., Vorstenbosch, V., Shnaider, P., Goldstein, E. S., Ferrier-Auerbach, A. G., & Mocciola, K. E. (2012). Changes in social adjustment with cognitive processing therapy: effects of treatment and association with PTSD symptom change. *Journal of Traumatic Stress, 25*(5), 519-526.

Monti, D. A., Kash, K. M., Kunkel, E. J., Brainard, G., Wintering, N., Moss, . . . Newberg, A. B. (2012). Changes in cerebral blood flow and anxiety associated with an 8-week mindfulness programme in women with breast cancer. *Stress and Health, 28*, 397–407.

Moore, A., Gruber, T., Derose, J., & Malinowski, P. (2012). Regular, brief mindfulness meditation practice improves electrophysiological markers of attentional control. *Frontiers in Human Neuroscience, 6*, 1–15.

Moore, T. (1992). *Care of the soul: A guide for cultivating depth and sacredness in everyday life.* New York, NY: HarperCollins.

Moore, T. (2004). *Dark nights of the soul: A guide to finding your way through life's ordeals.* New York, NY: Gotham Books.

Mosewich, A. D., Crocker, P. R. E., Kowalski, K. C., & Delongis, A. (2013). Applying self-compassion in sport: An intervention with women athletes. *Journal of Sport & Exercise Psychology, 35*(5), 514–524.

Müller, M., Vandeleur, C., Rodgers, S., Rössler, W., Castelao, E., Preisig, M., & Ajdacic-Gross, V. (2015). Posttraumatic stress avoidance symptoms as mediators in the development of alcohol use disorders after exposure to childhood sexual abuse in a Swiss community sample. *Child Abuse & Neglect, 46*, 8–15.

Myrick, A. C., Chasson, G. S., Lanius, R. A., Leventhal, B., & Brand, B. L. (2015). Treatment of complex dissociative disorders: A comparison of interventions reported by community therapists versus those recommended by experts. *Journal of Trauma and Dissociation, 16*(1), 51–67.

Nappi, C. M., Drummond, S. P., Thorp, S. R., & McQuaid, J. R. (2010). Effectiveness of imagery rehearsal therapy for the treatment of combat-related nightmares in veterans. *Behavior Therapy, 41*(2), 237-244.

Naveh-Benjamin, M., Guez, J., & Sorek, S. (2007). The effects of divided attention on encoding processes in memory: Mapping the locus of interference. *Canadian Journal of Experimental Psychology, 61*(1), 1–12.

Neff, K. (2011). *Self-compassion: Stop beating yourself up and leave insecurity behind.* New York, NY: HarperCollins.

Neff, K. D., & Germer, C.K. (2013). A pilot study and randomized controlled trial of the mindful self-compassion program. *Journal of Clinical Psychology, 69*(1), 28–44.

Neff, K. D., & McGehee, P. (2010). Self-compassion and psychological resilience among adolescents and young adults. *Self and Identity, 9*(3), 225–240.

Nhât Hạnh, T. (1998). *The heart of the buddha's teaching: Transforming suffering into peace, joy, and liberation.* New York, NY: Harmony Books.

Nickerson, A., Barnes, J. B., Creamer, M., Forbes, D., McFarlane, A. C., O'Donnell, M., . . . Bryant, R. A. (2014). The temporal relationship between posttraumatic stress disorder and problem alcohol use following traumatic injury. *Journal of Abnormal Psychology, 123*(4), 821–834.

Nimenko, W., & Simpson, R. G. (2014). Rear Operations Group medicine: A pilot study of psychological decompression in a Rear Operations Group during Operation HERRICK 14. *Journal of the Royal Army Medical Corps, 160*(4), 295–297.

Nishith, P., Resick, P. A., & Griffin, M. G. (2002). Pattern of change in prolonged exposure and cognitive-processing therapy for female rape victims with posttraumatic stress disorder. *Journal of Consulting and Clinical Psychology, 70*(4), 880–886.

Nolen-Hoeksema, S. (1991). Responses to depression and their effects on the duration of depressive episodes. *Journal of Abnormal Psychology, 100*(4), 569-582.

Nolen-Hoeksema, S., Wisco, B. E., & Lyubomirsky, S. (2008). Rethinking rumination. *Perspectives on Psychological Science, 3*(5), 400–424.

Noll, J. G., Horowitz, L. A., Bonanno, G. A., Trickett, P. K., & Putnam, F. W. (2003). Revictimization and self-harm in females who experienced childhood sexual abuse: Results from a prospective study. *Journal of Interpersonal Violence, 18*(12), 1452–1471.

Norman, S. B., Means-Christensen, A. J., Craske, M. G., Sherbourne, C. D., Roy-Byrne, P. P., & Stein, M. B. (2006). Associations between psychological trauma and physical illness in primary care. *Journal of Traumatic Stress, 19*(4), 461–470.

Norman, S. B., Wilkins, K. C., Myers, U. S., & Allard, C. B. (2014). Trauma informed guilt reduction therapy with combat veterans. *Cognitive and Behavioral Practice, 21*(1), 78–88.

North, C. S. (2001). The course of post-traumatic stress disorder after the Oklahoma City bombing. *Military Medicine, 166*(12 Suppl), 51–52.

Novaco, R. W., & Chemtob, C. M. (1998). Anger and trauma: Conceptualization, assessment and treatment. In: V. M. Follette, J. I. Ruzek, & F. R. Abueg (Eds.), *Cognitive-behavioral Therapies for Trauma* (pp. 162–190). New York, NY: Guilford Press.

Noyes, R., & Kletti, R. (1977). Depersonalization in response to life-threatening danger. *Comprehensive Psychiatry, 18*, 375–384.

Nunnink, S. E., Goldwaser, G., Afari, N., Nievergelt, C. M., & Baker, D. G. (2010). The role of emotional numbing in sexual functioning among veterans of the Iraq and Afghanistan wars. *Military Medicine, 175*(6), 424–428.

O'Bryan, E. M., McLeish, A. C., Kraemer, K. M., & Fleming, J. B. (2015). Emotion regulation difficulties and posttraumatic stress disorder symptom cluster severity among trauma-exposed college students. *Psychological Trauma: Theory, Research, Practice, and Policy, 7*(2), 131–137.

Orth, U., & Wieland, E. (2006). Anger, hostility and posttraumatic stress disorder in trauma-exposed adults: A meta-analysis. *Journal of Consulting and Clinical Psychology, 74*, 698–706.

Owers, C., & Kossler, C. (2015, September 3). Sotomayor shares Supreme Court insight, advice. *The Observer*, Retrieved July 2, 2016 from http://ndsmcobserver.com/2015/09/sotomayor-shares-supreme-court-insight-advice/

Ozer, E., Best, S., Lipsey, T., & Weiss, D. (2003). Predictors of posttraumatic stress disorder and symptoms in adults: A meta-analysis. *Psychological Bulletin, 129*(1), 52–73.

Palmieri, P. A., Marshall, G. N., & Schell, T. L. (2007). Confirmatory factor analysis of posttraumatic stress symptoms in Cambodian refugees. *Journal of Traumatic Stress, 20*(2):207–16.

Paquette, V., Lévesque, J., Mensour, B., Leroux, J. M., Beaudoin, G., Bourgouin, P., & Beauregard, M. (2003). "Change the mind and you change the brain": Effects of cognitive-behavioral therapy on the neural correlates of spider phobia. *Neuroimage, 18*, 401–409.

Paramananda. (2006). *Change your mind: A practical guide to Buddhist meditation.* Birmingham, UK: Windhorse Publications.

Patsiopoulos, A. T., & Buchanan, M. J. (2011). The practice of self-compassion in counseling: A narrative inquiry. *Professional Psychology: Research and Practice, 42*(4), 301–307.

Pavlov, I. P. (1927). *Conditioned reflexes.* London: Routledge and Kegan Paul.

Pawlow, L. A., & Jones, G. E. (2002). The impact of abbreviated progressive muscle relaxation on salivary cortisol. *Biological Psychology, 60,* 1–16.

Pence, P. G., Katz, L. S., Huffman, C., & Cojucar, G. (2014). Delivering Integrative Restoration-Yoga Nidra Meditation (iRest®) to women with sexual trauma at a veteran's medical center: A pilot study. *International Journal of Yoga Therapy, 24,* 53–62.

Peretti-Watel, P., L'Haridon, O., & Seror, V. (2013). Time preferences, socioeconomic status and smokers' behaviour, attitudes and risk awareness. *European Journal of Public Health, 23*(5), 783–788.

Peri, T., Ben-Shakhar, G., Orr, S. P., & Shalev, A. Y. (2000). Psychophysiologic assessment of aversive conditioning in posttraumatic stress disorder. *Biological Psychiatry, 47*(6), 512–519.

Perona-Garcelán, S., García-Montes, J. M., Rodríguez-Testal, J. F., López-Jiménez, A. M., Ruiz-Veguilla, M., Ductor-Recuerda, M. J., . . . Pérez-Álvarez, M. (2014). Relationship between childhood trauma, mindfulness, and dissociation in subjects with and without hallucination proneness. *Journal of Trauma and Dissociation, 15*(1), 35–51.

Piaget, J. (1952). *The origins of intelligence in children.* New York, NY: International Universities press.

Pickett, S. M., & Kurby, C. A. (2010). The impact of experiential avoidance on the inference of characters' emotions: Evidence for an emotional processing bias. *Cognitive Therapy and Research, 34*(6), 493–500.

Pidgeon, A. M., Ford, L., & Klassen, F. (2014). Evaluating the effectiveness of enhancing resilience in human service professionals using a retreat-based Mindfulness with Metta Training Program: A randomised control trial. *Psychology, Health, & Medicine, 19*(3), 355–364.

Pierce, T., & Lydon, J. (1998). Priming relational schemas: Effects of contextually activated and chronically accessible interpersonal expectations on responses to a stressful event. *Journal of Personality and Social Psychology, 75*(6), 1441–1448.

Pietrzak, R. H., Johnson, D. C., Goldstein, M. B., Malley, J. C., & Southwick, S. M. (2009). Psychosocial buffers of traumatic stress, depressive symptoms, and psychosocial difficulties in veterans of Operations Enduring Freedom and Iraqi Freedom: The role of resilience, unit support, and postdeployment social support. *Depression and Anxiety, 26*(8), 745–751.

Pinto-Gouveia, J., Duarte, C., Matos, M., & Fráguas, S. (2014). The protective role of self-compassion in relation to psychopathology symptoms and quality of life in chronic and in cancer patients. *Clinical Psychology & Psychotherapy, 21*(4), 311–323.

Platt, J., Keyes, K. M., & Koenen, K. C. (2014). Size of the social network versus quality of social support: Which is more protective against PTSD? *Social Psychiatry and Psychiatric Epidemiology, 49*(8), 1279–1286.

Plumb, J. C., Orsillo, S. M., & Luterek, J. A. (2004). A preliminary test of the role of experiential avoidance in post-event functioning. *Journal of Behavior Therapy, 35*, 245–257.

Poerio, G. L., Totterdell, P., & Miles, E. (2013). *Consciousness and Cognition, 22*, 1412–1421.

Price, C. J., Wells, E. A., Donovan, D. M., & Rue, T. (2012). Mindful awareness in body-oriented therapy as an adjunct to women's substance use disorder treatment: A pilot feasibility study. *Journal of Substance Abuse Treatment, 43*(1), 94–107.

Price, J. L., MacDonald, H. Z., Adair, K. C., Koerner, N., & Monson, C. M. (2014). Changing beliefs about trauma: A qualitative study of cognitive processing therapy. *Behavioural and Cognitive Psychotherapy*, 1–12.

Putnam, E. W. (1985). Dissociation as an extreme response to trauma. In R. P. Kluft (Ed.), *Childhood antecedents of multiple personality* (pp. 66–97). Washington, DC: American Psychiatric Press.

Quidé, Y., Witteveen, A. B., El-Hage, W., Veltman, D. J., & Olff, M. (2012). Differences between effects of psychological versus pharmacological treatments on functional and morphological brain alterations in anxiety disorders and major depressive disorder: A systematic review. *Neuroscience and Biobehavioral Reviews, 36*, 626–644.

Raes, F., Dewulf, D., Van Heeringen, C., Williams, J. M. (2009). Mindfulness and reduced cognitive reactivity to sad mood: Evidence from a correlational study and a non-randomized waiting list controlled study. *Behaviour Research and Therapy*. *47*(7), 623–627.

Ramaswamy, V. (2009). Gender and transcendence in early India. In B. Chattopadhyaya (Ed.), *A social history of early India*. New Dehli, India: Center for Studies in Civilizations.

Ramirez, S. M., Glover, H., Ohlde, C., Mercer, R., Goodnick, P., Hamlin, C., & Perez-Rivera, M. I. (2001). Relationship of numbing to alexithymia, apathy, and depression. *Psychological reports*, *88*(1), 189–200.

Rasid, Z. M., & Parish, T. S. (1998). The effects of two types of relaxation training on students' levels of anxiety. *Adolescence*, *33*, 99–101.

Ray, S. L., & Vanstone, M. (2009). The impact of PTSD on veterans' family relationships: An interpretative phenomenological inquiry. *International Journal of Nursing Studies*, *46*(6), 838–47.

Reich, C. M., Jones, J. M., Woodward, M. J., Blackwell, N., Lindsey, L. D., & Beck, J. G. (2015). Does self-blame moderate psychological adjustment following intimate partner violence? *Journal of Interpersonal Violence*, *30*(9), 1493–1510.

Rendon, J. (2015). *Upside: The new science of posttraumatic growth*. New York: Touchstone.

Resick, P. A., Galovski, T. E., Uhlmansiek, M. O., Scher, C. D., Glum, G. A., & Young-Xu, Y. (2008). A randomized clinical trial to dismantle components of cognitive processing therapy for posttraumatic stress disorder in female victims of interpersonal violence. *Journal of Consulting and Clinical Psychology*, *76*, 243–258.

Resilience. (n.d.). In Online Etymology Dictionary. Retrieved June 28, 2016 from http://www.etymonline.com/index.php?term=resilience

Resilient. (n.d.). In Oxford Dictionary (American English). Retrieved June 28, 2016 from http://www.oxforddictionaries.com/us/definition/american_english/resilient

Reynolds, M., & Wells, A. (1999). The Thought Control Questionnaire--psychometric properties in a clinical sample, and relationships with PTSD and depression. *Psychological Medicine*, *29*(5), 1089-1099.

Rieffe, C., & De Rooij, M. (2012). The longitudinal relationship between emotion awareness and internalising symptoms during late childhood. *European Child & Adolescent Psychiatry*, *21*(6), 349–356.

Riggs, D. S., Byrne, C. A., Weathers, F. W., & Litz, B. T. (1998). The quality of the intimate relationships of male Vietnam veterans: Problems associated with post-traumatic stress disorder. *Journal of Traumatic Stress, 11*(1), 87–101.

Rizzo, A. A., Parsons, T. D., Kenny, P., & Buckwalter, J. G. (2012). Using virtual reality for clinical assessment and intervention. In L. L'Abate & D. Palmer (Eds.), *Handbook of technology in psychology, psychiatry, and neurology: Theory, research, and practice* (pp. 277–318). Hauppauge, NY: Nova Science Publishers.

Roberts-Wolfe, D., Sacchet, M. D., Hastings, E., Roth, H., & Britton W. (2012). Mindfulness training alters emotional memory recall compared to active controls: Support for an emotional information processing model of mindfulness. *Frontiers in Human Neuroscience, 6,* 15.

Roffman, J. L., Marci, C. D., Glick, D. M., Dougherty, D. D., & Rauch, S. L. (2005). Neuroimaging and the functional neuroanatomy of psychotherapy. *Psychological Medicine, 35,* 1385–1398.

Rosenbaum, S., Sherrington, C., Tiedemann, A. (2015). Exercise augmentation compared with usual care for post-traumatic stress disorder: A randomized controlled trial. *Acta Psychiatrica Scandinavica, 131*(5), 350–359.

Rosenthal, M. Z., Cheavens, J. S., Lynch, T. R., & Follette, V. (2006). Thought suppression mediates the relationship between negative mood and PTSD in sexually assaulted women. *Journal of Traumatic Stress, 19*(5), 741–745.

Rothbaum B. O., & Davis M. (2003). Applying learning principles to the treatment of post-trauma reactions. Annals of the New York Academy of Sciences, 1008, 112–121.

Rumi, Jalal al-Din. (1995). The essential Rumi. (C. Barks & J. Moyne, Trans.). San Francisco: HarperCollins.

Ruscio, A. M., Weathers, F. W., King, L. A., & King, D. W. (2002). Male war-zone veterans' perceived relationships with their children: The importance of emotional numbing. *Journal of Traumatic Stress, 15*(5), 351–357.

Sachs-Ericsson, N., Verona, E., Joiner, T., & Preacher, K. J. (2006). Parental verbal abuse and the mediating role of self-criticism in adult internalizing disorders. *Journal of Affective Disorders, 93*(1–3), 71–78.

Safran, J., & Segal, Z. (1990). *Interpersonal process in cognitive therapy.* New York, NY: Basic Books.

Sailer, U., Rosenberg, P., Nima, A. A., Gamble, A., Gärling, T., Archer, T., & Garcia,

D. (2014). A happier and less sinister past, a more hedonistic and less fatalistic present and a more structured future: Time perspective and well-being. *PeerJ, 2*. doi:10.7717/peerj.303

Salzberg, S. (1995). *Lovingkindess: The revolutionary art of happiness.* Boston, MA: Shambhala.

Salzberg, S. (1999). *Lovingkindness: The revolutionary art of happiness.* Boston: Shambhala Publications, Inc.

Salzberg, S. (2010). *Equanimity and Faith.* [Audio podcast]. Talk recorded January 13, 2010 at the Insight Meditation Center. Retrieved from http://insightmeditationcenter.org

Salzberg, S. (2011). *Real happiness: The power of meditation.* New York, NY: Workman Publishing Company.

Salzberg, S. (2012). Practicing equanimity with Sharon Salzberg [Audio podcast]. New York, NY: The Interdependence Project. Retrieved from http://theidproject.org/media/Buddhism

Salzberg, S. (2015). You can't fail at meditation. Interview by D. Harris. Retrieved May 25, 2016 from Lion's Roar website: http://www.lionsroar.com/cant-fail-meditation/

Samper, R. E., Taft, C. T., King, D. W., & King, L. A. (2004). Posttraumatic stress disorder symptoms and parenting satisfaction among a national sample of male Vietnam veterans. *Journal of Traumatic Stress, 17*(4), 311–315.

Sarapas, C., Cai, G., Bierer, L. M., Golier, J. A., Galea, S., Ising, . . . Yehuda, R. (2011). Genetic markers for PTSD risk and resilience among survivors of the World Trade Center attacks. *Disease Markers, 30*(2–3), 101–110.

Sauer, S., & Baer, R. A. (2010). Mindfulness and decentering as mechanisms of change in mindfulness- and acceptance-based interventions. In R. A. Baer (Ed.), *Assessing mindfulness and acceptance processes in clients: Illuminating the theory and practice of change* (pp. 25–50). New Harbinger.

Sbarra, D. A., Smith, H. L., & Mehl, M. R. (2012). When leaving your ex, love yourself: Observational ratings of self-compassion predict the course of emotional recovery following marital separation. *Psychological Science, 23*(3), 261–269.

Schachter, C. L., Stalker, C. A., & Teram, E. (1999). Toward sensitive practice: Issues for physical therapists working with survivors of childhood sexual abuse. *Physical Therapy, 79*(3), 248–261.

Shnaider, P., Vorstenbosch, V., Macdonald, A., Wells, S. Y., Monson, C. M., & Resick,

P. A. (2014). Associations between functioning and PTSD symptom clusters in a dismantling trial of cognitive processing therapy in female interpersonal violence survivors. *Journal of Traumatic Stress, 27,* 526–534.

Schoenefeld, S. J., & Webb, J. B. (2013). Self-compassion and intuitive eating in college women: Examining the contributions of distress tolerance and body image acceptance and action. *Eating Behaviors, 14*(4), 493–496.

Schuettler, D., & Boals, A. (2011). The path to posttraumatic growth versus posttraumatic stress disorder: Contributions of event centrality and coping. *Journal of Loss and Trauma: International Perspectives on Stress & Coping, 16*(2), 180-194.

Schumm, J. A., Dickstein, B. D., Walter, K. H., Owens, G. P., & Chard, K. M. (2015). Changes in posttraumatic cognitions predict changes in posttraumatic stress disorder symptoms during cognitive processing therapy. *Journal of Consulting and Clinical Psychology, 83*(6), 1161–1166.

Shapiro, D. H., Jr. (1992). Adverse effects of meditation: A preliminary investigation of long-term meditators. *International Journal of Psychosomatics, 39,* 62–67.

Shapiro, S. L., Carlson, L. E., Astin, J. A., & Freedman, B. (2006). Mechanisms of mindfulness. *Journal of Clinical Psychology, 62,* 373–386.

Sharkin, B. S. (1993). Anger and gender: Theory, research, and implications. *Journal of Counseling and Development, 71*(4), 386–389.

Sierra, M., & Berrios, G. E. (1998). Depersonalization: Neurobiological perspectives. *Biological Psychiatry, 44,* 898–908.

Sifneos, P. E. (1973). The prevalence of "alexithymic" characteristics in psychosomatic patients. *Psychotherapy and Psychosomatics, 22,* 255–262.

Silverman, A. B., Reinherz, H. Z., & Giaconia, R. M. (1996). The long-term sequelae of child and adolescent abuse: A longitudinal community study. *Child Abuse & Neglect, 20*(8), 709–723.

Sippel, L. M., & Marshall, A. D. (2013). Posttraumatic stress disorder and fear of emotions: The role of attentional control. *Journal of Traumatic Stress, 26*(3), 397–400.

Sirois, F. M., Kitner, R., & Hirsch, J. K. (2015). Self-compassion, affect, and health-promoting behaviors. *Health Psychology, 34*(6), 661–669.

Smeets, E., Neff, K. D., Alberts, H., & Peters, M. (2014). Meeting suffering with kindness: Effects of a brief self-compassion intervention for female college students. *Journal of Clinical Psychology, 70*(9), 794–807.

Smith, A. K., Conneely, K. N., Kilaru, V., Mercer, K. B., Weiss, T. E., Bradley, B., . . .

Ressler, K. J. (2011). Differential immune system DNA methylation and cytokine regulation in post-traumatic stress disorder. *American Journal of Medical Genetics, Part B: Neuropsychiatric Genetics,156B*, 700–708.

Smith, B. W., Ortiz, J. A., Steffen, L. E., Tooley, E. M., Wiggins, K. T., Yeater, E. A., . . . Bernard, M. L. (2011). Mindfulness is associated with fewer PTSD symptoms, depressive symptoms, physical symptoms, and alcohol problems in urban firefighters. *Journal of Consulting and Clinical Psychology, 79*(5), 613–617.

Smith, C. P., & Freyd, J. J. (2014). Institutional betrayal. *American Psychologist, 69*, 575–587.

Smyth, J. M., Heron, K. E., Wonderlich, S. A., Crosby, R. D., & Thompson, K. M. (2008). The influence of reported trauma and adverse events on eating disturbance in young adults. *The International Journal of Eating Disorders, 41*(3), 195–202.

Snell, F. I., & Padin-Rivera, E. (1997). Group treatment for older veterans with post-traumatic stress disorder. *Journal of Psychosocial Nursing and Mental Health Services, 35*(2), 10-16.

Soler, J., Cebolla, A., Feliu-Soler, A., Demarzo, M. M. P., Pascual, J. C., Baños, R., & García-Campayo, J. (2014). Relationship between meditative practice and self-reported mindfulness: The MINDSENS Composite Index. *PLoS ONE 9*(1). doi:10.1371/journal.pone.0086622

Spiegel, D., & Cardeña, E. (1991). Disintegrated experience: The dissociative disorders revisited. *Journal of Abnormal Psychology, 100*(3), 366–78.

Springs, F. E., & Friedrich, W. N. (1992). Health risk behaviors and medical sequelae of childhood sexual abuse. *Mayo Clinic Proceedings, 67*(6), 527–532.

Srinivas, T., DePrince, A. P., & Chu, A. T. (2015). Links between posttrauma appraisals and trauma-related distress in adolescent females from the child welfare system. *Child Abuse & Neglect, 47*, 14–23.

St. John, D. (2014). The braid of time. Workshop presented at Hugo House: A Place for Writers on May 4, 2014, in Seattle, WA.

Stafford, L., Foley, E., Judd, F., Gibson, P., Kiropoulos, L., & Couper, J. (2013). Mindfulness-based cognitive group therapy for women with breast and gynecologic cancer: A pilot study to determine effectiveness and feasibility. *Supportive Care in Cancer, 21*(11), 3009–3019.

Stankovic, L. (2011). Transforming trauma: A qualitative feasibility study of integrative restoration (iRest) yoga Nidra on combat-related post-traumatic stress disorder. *International Journal of Yoga Therapy, 21,* 23–37.

Staugaard, S. R., Johannessen, K. B., Thomsen, Y. D., Bertelsen, M., & Berntsen, D. (2015). Centrality of positive and negative deployment memories predicts post-traumatic growth in Danish veterans. *Journal of Clinical Psychology, 71*(4), 362–377.

Steil, R., & Ehlers, A. (2000). Dysfunctional meaning of posttraumatic intrusions in chronic PTSD. *Behaviour Research and Therapy, 38*(6), 537–58.

Stein, D. J., Ives-Deliperi, V., & Thomas, K. G. (2008). Psychobiology of mindfulness. *CNS Spectrum, 13*(9), 752–756.

Steinberg, M., & Schnall, M. (2001). The stranger in the mirror: Dissociation—the hidden epidemic. New York, NY: HarperCollins.

Steinberg, M. (1995). *Handbook for the assessment of dissociation: A clinical guide.* Washington, D.C.: American Psychiatric Press.

Steinberg, M., Cicchetti, D., Buchanan, J., Hall, P., & Rounsaville, B. (1993). Clinical assessment of dissociative symptoms and disorders: The Structured Clinical Interview for DSM-IV Dissociative Disorders (SCID-D). *Dissociation: Progress in the Dissociative Disorders, 61*(1), 108–120.

Stevenson, V. E., & Chemtob, C. M. (2000). Premature treatment termination by angry patients with combat related post-traumatic stress disorder. *Military Medicine, 165,* 422–424.

Substance Abuse and Mental Health Services Administration. (n.d.). Trauma definition. Retrieved August 12, 2014, from http://www.samhsa.gov/traumajustice/traumadefinition/definition.aspx

Sullivan, T. P., & Holt, L. J. (2008). PTSD symptom clusters are differentially related to substance use among community women exposed to intimate partner violence. *Journal of Traumatic Stress, 21*(2), 173–178.

Taku, K., Calhoun, L. G., Cann, A., & Tedeschi, R. G. (2008). The role of rumination in the coexistence of distress and posttraumatic growth among bereaved Japanese university students. *Death Studies, 32,* 428–444. doi:10.1080/07481180801974745

Tanaka, M., Wekerle, C., Schmuck, M. L., Paglia-Boak, A., & MAP Research Team. (2011). The linkages among childhood maltreatment, adolescent mental health, and self-compassion in child welfare adolescents. *Child Abuse & Neglect, 35*(10), 887–898.

Taylor, V. A., Daneault, V., Grant, J., Scavone, G., Breton, E., Roffe-Vidal, S., . . . Beauregard, M. (2013). Impact of meditation training on the default mode network during a restful state. *Social Cognitive and Affective Neuroscience, 8*(1), 4-14.

Tedeschi, R. G., & Calhoun, L. G. (2004). Posttraumatic growth: Conceptual foundations and empirical evidence. *Psychological Inquiry, 15*(1), 1–18.

Teicher, M. H., & Samson, J. A. (2013). Childhood maltreatment and psychopathology: A case for ecophenotypic variants as clinically and neurobiologically distinct subtypes. *American Journal of Psychiatry, 170*(10), 1114–1133.

Terry, M. L., Leary, M. R., Mehta, S., & Henderson, K. (2013). Self-compassionate reactions to health threats. *Personality & Social Psychology Bulletin, 39*(7), 911–926.

Thomaes, K., Dorrepaal, E., Draijer, N., Jansma, E. P., Veltman, D. J., & van Balkom, A. J. (2014). Can pharmacological and psychological treatment change brain structure and function in PTSD? A systematic review. *Journal of Psychiatric Research, 50*, 1–15.

Thompson, B. L., & Waltz, J. (2010). Mindfulness and experiential avoidance as predictors of posttraumatic stress disorder avoidance symptom severity. *Journal of Anxiety Disorders, 24*(4), 409–415.

Thompson, R. W., Arnkoff, D. B., & Glass, C. R. (2011). Conceptualizing mindfulness and acceptance as components of psychological resilience to trauma. *Trauma, Violence, & Abuse. 12*(4), 220–235.

Tolstoy, L. (2002). *Anna Karenina.* (R. Pevear & L. Volokhonsky, Trans.). London: Penguin Classics. (Original work published 1873–1877).

Towler, A. J., & Stuhlmacher, A. F. (2013). Attachment styles, relationship satisfaction, and well-being in working women. *The Journal of Social Psychology, 153*(3), 279–298.

Troy, A. S., Wilhelm, F. H., Shallcross, A. J., & Mauss, I. B. (2010). Seeing the silver lining: Cognitive reappraisal ability moderates the relationship between stress and depressive symptoms. *Emotion, 10*, 783–795.

Trungpa, C. (1984). *Shambhala: The Sacred Path of the Warrior.* Boulder, CO: Shambhala Publications.

Tull, M. T., Jakupcak, M., McFadden, M. E., & Roemer, L. (2007). The role of negative affect intensity and the fear of emotions in posttraumatic stress symptom severity among victims of childhood interpersonal violence. *Journal of Nervous and Mental Disease, 195*(7), 580–587.

Tylka, T. L., Russell, H. L., & Neal, A. A. (2015). Self-compassion as a moderator of thinness-related pressures' associations with thin-ideal internalization and disordered eating. *Eating Behaviors, 17,* 23–26.

Ullman, S. E., Filipas, H. H., Townsend, S. M, & Starzynski, L. L. (2007). Psychosocial correlates of PTSD symptom severity in sexual assault survivors. *Journal of Traumatic Stress, 20*(5), 821–831.

Ungar, M. (2013). Resilience, trauma, context, and culture. *Trauma, Violence, & Abuse, 14*(3), 255–266.

Ursano, R. J., & Fullerton, C. S. (1999). Posttraumatic stress disorder: Cerebellar regulation of psychological, interpersonal, and biological responses to trauma? *Psychiatry, 62*(4), 325-328.

Ussher, M., Spatz, A., Copland, C., Nicolaou, A, Cargill, A., Amini-Tabrizi, N., & McCracken, L. M. (2014). Immediate effects of a brief mindfulness-based body scan on patients with chronic pain. *Behavioral Medicine, 37*(1), 127–134.

Van Dam, N. T., Sheppard, S. C., Forsyth, J. P., & Earleywine, M. (2011). Self-compassion is a better predictor than mindfulness of symptom severity and quality of life in mixed anxiety and depression. *Journal of Anxiety Disorders, 25*(1), 123–130.

Vøllestad, J., Sivertsen, B., & Nielsen, G. H. (2011). Mindfulness-based stress reduction for patients with anxiety disorders: Evaluation in a randomized controlled trial. *Behaviour Research and Therapy, 49,* 281–288.

Vujanovic, A. A., Youngwirth, N. E., Johnson, K. A., & Zvolensky, M. J. (2009). Mindfulness-based acceptance and posttraumatic stress symptoms among trauma-exposed adults without axis I psychopathology. *Journal of Anxiety Disorders, 23*(2), 297–303. doi:10.1016/j.janxdis.2008.08.005

Wagner, B., Knaevelsrud, C., & Maercker, A. (2007). Post-traumatic growth and optimism as outcomes of an internet-based intervention for complicated grief. *Cognitive Behaviour Therapy, 36,* 156–161.

Wahbeh, H., Lu, M., & Oken, B. (2011). Mindful awareness and non-judging in relation to posttraumatic stress disorder symptoms. *Mindfulness, 2*(4), 219–227.

Walach, H., Buchheld, N., Buttenmüller, V., Kleinknecht, N., & Schmidt, S. (2006). Measuring mindfulness: The Freiburg Mindfulness Inventory (FMI). *Personality and Individual Differences, 40,* 1543–1555.

Watson-Johnson, L. C., Townsend, J. S., Basile, K. C., & Richardson, L. C. (2012).

Cancer screening and history of sexual violence victimization among U.S. adults. *Journal of Womens Health, 21*(1), 17–25.

Way, B. M., Creswell, J. D., Eisenberger, N. I., & Lieberman, M. D. (2010). Dispositional mindfulness and depressive symptomatology: Correlations with limbic and self-referential neural activity during rest. *Emotion, 10*(1), 12–24. doi:10.1037/a0018312

Webster, J. D., & Ma, X. (2013). A balanced time perspective in adulthood: Well-being and developmental effects. *Canadian Journal on Aging, 22*, 1–10.

Webster, J. D., Bohlmeijer, E. T., & Westerhof, G. J. (2014). Time to flourish: The relationship of temporal perspective to well-being and wisdom across adulthood. *Aging & Mental Health, 18*(8), 1046–1056.

Weems, C. F., Saltzman, K. M., Reiss, A. L., & Carrion, V. G. (2003). A prospective test of the association between hyperarousal and emotional numbing in youth with a history of traumatic stress. *Journal of Clinical Child and Adolescent Psychology, 32*(1), 166–171.

Weinstein, N., & Ryan, R. M. (2010). When helping helps: Autonomous motivation for prosocial behavior and its influence on well-being for the helper and recipient. *Journal of Personality and Social Psychology, 98*(2), 222–244.

Wessa, M., & Flor, H. (2007). Failure of extinction of fear responses in posttraumatic stress disorder: Evidence from second-order conditioning. *The American Journal of Psychiatry, 164*(11), 1684–1692.

White, D. L., Savas, L. S., Daci, K., Elserag, R., Graham, D. P., Fitzgerald, S. J., . . . El-Serag, H. B. (2010). Trauma history and risk of the irritable bowel syndrome in women veterans. *Alimentary Pharmacology & Therapeutics, 32*(4), 551–561.

Whitebird, R. R., Kreitzer, M., Crain, A. L., Lewis, B. A., Hanson, L. R., & Enstad, C. J. (2013). Mindfulness-based stress reduction for family caregivers: a randomized controlled trial. *The Gerontologist, 53*(4), 676–686.

Wing Lun, L. M. (2008). A cognitive model of peritraumatic dissociation. *Psychology and psychotherapy, 81*(Pt 3), 297–307.

Wittman, M. (2009). The inner experience of time. *Philosophical Transactions of the Royal Society of London B, 364*(1525), 1955–1967.

Woodward, C., & Joseph, S. (2003). Positive change processes and post-traumatic growth in people who have experienced childhood abuse: Understanding vehicles of change. *Psychology and Psychotherapy: Theory, Research and Practice, 76*(3), 267–283.

Woodward, M. J., Eddinger, J., Henschel, A. V., Dodson, T. S., Tran, H. N., & Beck, J. G. (2015). Social support, posttraumatic cognitions, and PTSD: The influence of family, friends, and a close other in an interpersonal and non-interpersonal trauma group. *Journal of Anxiety Disorders, 35*, 60–67.

Woodward, S. H., Kuo, J. R., Schaer, M., Kaloupek, D. G., & Eliez, S. (2013). Early adversity and combat exposure interact to influence anterior cingulate cortex volume in combat veterans. *Neuroimage: Clinical, 2*, 670–674.

Woud, M. L., Holmes, E. A., Postma, P., Dalgleish, T., & Mackintosh, B. (2012). Ameliorating intrusive memories of distressing experiences using computerized reappraisal training. *Emotion, 12*(4), 778–784.

Wright, M. O., Fopma-Loy, J., & Fischer, S. (2005). Multidimensional assessment of resilience in mothers who are child sexual abuse survivors. *Child Abuse & Neglect, 29*(10), 1173-1193.

Xu, J., & Liao, Q. (2011). Prevalence and predictors of posttraumatic growth among adult survivors one year following 2008 Sichuan earthquake. *Journal of Affective Disorders, 133*(1–2), 274–280.

Yoshimura, S., Okamoto, Y., Yoshino, A., Kobayakawa, M., Machino, A., & Yamawaki, S. (2014). Neural basis of anticipatory anxiety reappraisals. *PLoS ONE 9*(7), e102836. doi:10.1371/journal.pone.0102836

Yü, Chün-fang. (2001). *Kuan-yin: The Chinese transformation of Avalokiteśvara.* New York, NY: Columbia University Press.

Yu, Y., Peng, L., Tang, T., Chen, L., Li, M., & Wang, T. (2014). Effects of emotion regulation and general self-efficacy on posttraumatic growth in Chinese cancer survivors: Assessing the mediating effect of positive affect. *Psychooncology, 23*(4), 473–478.

Zajac, K., Ralston, M. E., & Smith, D. W. (2015). Maternal support following childhood sexual abuse: Associations with children's adjustment post-disclosure and at 9-month follow-up. *Child Abuse & Neglect, 44*, 66–75.

Zantvoord, J. B., Diehle, J., & Lindauer, R. J. (2013). Using neurobiological measures to predict and assess treatment outcome of psychotherapy in posttraumatic stress disorder: Systematic review. *Psychotherapy and Psychosomatics, 82*, 142–51.

Zeidan, F., Martucci, K. T., Kraft, R. A., McHaffie, J. G., & Coghill, R. C. (2014). Neural correlates of mindfulness meditation-related anxiety relief. *Social Cognitive and Affective Neuroscience, 9,* 751–759.

Zeller, M., Yuval, K., Nitzan-Assayag, Y., & Bernstein A. (2015). Self-compassion in recovery following potentially traumatic stress: Longitudinal study of at-risk youth. *Journal of Abnormal Child Psychology, 43*(4), 645–653.

Zeng, X., Chiu, C. P., Wang, R., Oei, T. P., & Leung, F. Y. (2015). The effect of loving-kindness meditation on positive emotions: A meta-analytic review. Frontiers in Psychology, 6. doi:10.3389/fpsyg.2015.01693

Zerubavel, N., & Messman-Moore, T. L. (2015). Staying present: Incorporating mindfulness into therapy for dissociation. *Mindfulness, 6,* 303–314.

Zimbardo, P. G., & Boyd, J. N. (1999). Putting time in perspective: A valid, reliable individual-difference metric. *Journal of Personality and Social Psychology, 77*(6), 1271–1288. doi:10.1037/0022-3514.77.6.1271

end notes

1   Briere, 2002

2   Brefczynski-Lewis, Lutz, Schaefer, Levinson, & Davidson, 2007; Dutton, Bermudez, Matas, Majid, & Myers, 2013; Kearney, McDermott, Malte, Martinez, & Simpson, 2010; Kearney, McDermott, Malte, Martinez, & Simpson, 2013; Kim et al., 2013; Kimbrough, Magyari, Langenberg, Chesney, & Berman, 2010; Pence, Katz, Huffman, & Cojucar, 2014; Stankovic, 2011

3   Goldsmith et al., 2014; Pence et al., 2014

4   King et al., 2013

5   Wahbeh, Lu, & Oken, 2011

6   e.g., Thompson, Arnkoff, & Glass, 2011; Boden, Bernstein, Walser, Bui, Alvarez, & Bonn-Miller, 2012

7   Soler, Cebolla, Feliu-Soler, Demarzo, Pascual, Baños, & García-Campayo, 2014

8   Hanson, 2013

9   Shapiro, Carlson, Astin, & Freedman, 2006

10 Salzberg, 1999

11 Feldman & Kuyken, 2011; Gilbert, 2009

12 Breines & Chen, 2012; Hall, Row, Wuench, & Godley, 2013; Kelly, Zuroff, & Shapira, 2009

13 Arch, Brown, Dean, Landy, Brown, & Laudenslager, 2014

14 Longe, Maratos, Gilbert, Evans, Volker, Rockliff, & Rippon, , 2010

15 Brach, 2015b

16 Marchand, 2013

17   Shapiro, 1992

18   Grepmair, Mitterlehner, Loew, & Nickel, 2007; Kang, Gray, & Dovidio, 2014; Lindsay & Creswell, 2014

19   Substance Abuse and Mental Health Services Administration, n.d.

20   Brewin et al., 2000; Felitti et al., 1998

21   Atlas & Ingram, 1998; Copeland, Keeler, Angold, & Costello, 2007; Freyd, Klest, & Allard, 2005; Lucenko, Gold, & Cott, 2000

22   Zajac, Ralston, & Smith, 2015

23   Avery & McDevitt-Murphy, 2014; Meyer et al., 2012; Pietrzak, Johnson, Goldstein, Malley, & Southwick, 2009

24   see Smith & Freyd, 2014

25   Le, Berenbaum, & Raghavan, 2002

26   see Linehan, 1993a

27   Teicher & Samson, 2013

28   Martin, Cromer, DePrince, & Freyd, 2013

29   see Ehlers & Clark, 2000

30   Janoff-Bulman, 1989

31   Lanius, Frewen, Vermetten, & Yehuda, 2010

32   Masten et al., 2008

33   Hayes, VanElzakker, & Shin, 2012

34   Lanius, Frewen, Vermetten, & Yehuda, 2010; Teicher & Samson, 2013; Woodward, Kuo, Schaer, Kaloupek, & Eliez, 2013

35   Chemtob, Roitblat, Hamada, Carlson, & Twentyman, 1988

36   Malinowski, 2013

37   Taylor, 2013

38   Farb, Anderson, & Segal, 2012

39   Sachs-Ericsson, Verona, Joiner, & Preacher, 2006

40   Michopoulos, Powers, Moore, Villarreal, Ressler, & Bradley, 2015

41   Hemmingsson, Johansson, & Reynisdottir, 2014; Smyth et al., 2008

42   Boscarino, 2004; Felitti et al., 1998; Hyland, Alkhalaf, & Whalley, 2013; Mellman & Hipolito, 2006; Norman et al., 2006; White et al., 2010

43   Foynes & Freyd, 2011

44   Briere, 2002

45 Cremeans-Smith, Greene, & Delahanty, 2015

46 Beiser & Hyman, 1997; Freyd, 1996

47 Hanson, 2009

48 Lanius, 2015

49 Fidler, Dawson, & Gallant, 1992

50 Eagleman, 2008

51 Noyes & Kletti, 1977; Ursano et al., 1999

52 Zimbardo & Boyd, 1999

53 Cottle, 1969; Cottle, 1976

54 Wittman, 2009

55 Horstmanshof & Zimitat, 2007; Martin et al., 2011; Peretti-Watel, L'Haridon, & Seror, 2013

56 Hamilton et al., 2015

57 Poerio, Totterdell, & Miles, 2013

58 Sailer et al., 2014

59 Beiser & Hyman, 1997

60 Webster & Ma, 2013; Webster, Bohlmeijer, Westerhof, 2014

61 Roberts-Wolfe, Sacchet, Hastings, Roth, & Britton, 2012

62 Naveh-Benjamin, Guez, & Sorek, 2007

63 Kern, Libkuman, Otani, & Holmes, 2005

64 Cloitre et al., 2010; Landes, Garovoy, & Burkman, 2013

65 Kearney, Malte, McManus, Martinez, Felleman, & Simpson, 2013; Kearney, McDermott, Malte, Martinez, & Simpson, 2010; Kearney, McDermott, Malte, Martinez, & Simpson, 2013

66 Although in some contexts, the word *ruminate* means to simply go over *any* subject in the mind repeatedly, or to engage in contemplation, its use throughout this book connotes its common use within the fields of mental health and cognitive science to indicate replaying *negative* thoughts and memories over and over.

67 Nolen-Hoeksema, 1991

68 McLaughlin, & Nolen-Hoeksema, 2011

69 Michl, McLaughlin, Shepherd, & Nolen-Hoeksema, 2013

70 Nolen-Hoeksema, Wisco, & Lyubomirsky, 2008

71 Black, Milam, & Sussman, 2009

72   Carmody & Baer, 2008

73   Moore, Gruber, Derose, & Malinowski, 2012

74   Bratman, Hamilton, Hahn, Daily, & Gross, 2015

75   Carmody & Baer, 2008

76   Gilbert, 2009; Feldman & Kuyken, 2011

77   Paramananda, 2006

78   Kenny et al., 2009; Kuyken & Moulds, 2009

79   Rosenbaum, Sherrington, & Tiedemann, 2015

80   Gilbert & Proctor, 2006

81   Dunn, Callahan, & Swift, 2013; Grepmair, Mitterlehner, Loew, & Nickel, 2007; Patsiopoulos & Buchanan, 2011

82   Garber, 2004; McNamer, 2010; Ramaswamy, 2009

83   Dunkley, Sanislow, Grilo, & McGlashan, 2009

84   Breines & Chen, 2012; Hall, Row, Wuench, & Godley, 2013; MacBeth & Gumley, 2012

85   Ehret, Joormann, & Berking, 2014

86   Longe et al., 2010

87   Breines et al., 2014; Breines et al., 2015

88   Dawson Rose et al., 2014

89   Liss & Erchull, 2015; Tylka, Russell, & Neal, 2015

90   Ferreira, Matos, Duarte, & Pinto-Gouveia, 2014

91   Brion, Leary, & Drabkin, 2014; Pinto-Gouveia, Duarte, Matos, & Fráguas, 2014

92   Neff & McGehee, 2010; Tanaka et al., 2011

93   Játiva & Cerezo, 2014

94   Sbarra, Smith, & Mehl, 2012

95   Zeller, Yuval, Nitzan-Assayag, & Bernstein, 2015

96   Hiraoka et al., 2015

97   Schoenefeld & Webb, 2013

98   Hall, Row, Wuensch, & Godley, 2013

99   Mosewich, Crocker, Kowalski, & Delongis, 2013

100   Arch et al., 2014; Galla, O'Reilly, Kitil, Smalley, & Black, 2014

101   Pidgeon., Ford, & Klassen, 2014; Smeets, Neff, Alberts, & Peters, 2014

102   Held & Owens, 2015; Kearney et al., 2013

103   Krieger, Altenstein, Baettig, Doerig, Holtforth, 2013

104   Hofmann, Grossman, Hinton, 2011

105   Breines & Chen, 2012

106   Gilbert, 2010

107   Gilbert, McEwan, Matos, & Rivis, 2011

108   Salzberg, 2011

109   Germer & Neff, 2013; Neff, 2011; Brach, 2015a

110   McFarlane, Weber, & Clark, 1993

111   Ehlers, 2010

112   Berry, May, Andrade, & Kavanagh, 2010

113   Berry, May, Andrade, & Kavanagh, 2010

114   Steil & Ehlers, 2000

115   Hartmann, 1998

116   Crick & Mitchison, 1983

117   Nappi, Drummond, Thorp, & McQuaid, 2010; Krakow et al., 2001

118   Forbes, Phelps, McHugh, Debenham, Hopwood, & Creamer, 2003

119   "Change the Channel" is a technique that I learned while training to provide PTSD symptom management classes for veterans at the Portland Veterans Affairs Medical Center, under the supervision of Drs. Amy Wagner and Lynn Van Male.

120   Lang et al., 2000

121   Chemtob et al., 1988

122   Hayes, VanElzakker, & Shin, 2012

123   Teicher & Samson, 2009

124   Paquette et al., 2003; Roffman, Marci, Glick, Dougherty, Rauch, 2005

125   Lipka, Hoffman, Miltner, & Straube, 2013

126   Monti et al., 2012

127   Adenauer et al., 2011; Quidé, Witteveen, El-Hage, Veltman, & Olff, 2012

128   Thomaes et al., 2014; Zantvoord, Diele, & Lindauer, 2013

129   Adenauer et al., 2011; Linden, 2008; Quidé, Witteveen, El-Hage, Veltman, & Olff, 2012

130   Mayo, 2009

131   Zeidan et al., 2014

132 Carlson, Ursuliak, Goodey, Angen, & Speca, 2001; Krusche, Cyhlarova, King, & Williams, 2013

133 "Circle Breathing" is a technique that I learned while training to provide PTSD symptom management classes for veterans at the Portland Veterans Affairs Medical Center, under the supervision of Drs. Amy Wagner and Lynn Van Male.

134 Salzberg, 2011

135 Goodman et al., 2014; Monti et al., 2012; Rasid & Parish, 1998; Vøllestad, Silvertsen, & Nielsen, 2011

136 Manzoni, Pagnini, Castelnuovo, & Molinari, 2008

137 Miller, Fletcher, & Kabat-Zinn, 1995

138 Jerath et al., 2006

139 Jerath et al., 2006

140 Brown, Gerbarg, & Muench, 2013

141 Isa et al., 2013; Rasid & Parish, 1998

142 Pawlow & Jones, 2002

143 Hoffman et al., 2009; Llewellyn, Dolcos, Iordan, Rudolph, & Dolcos 2013; Yoshimura et al., 2014

144 Roffman, Marci, Glick, Dougherty, Rauch, 2005

145 Thomaes et al., 2014; Yoshimura et al., 2014

146 Troy, Wilhelm, Shallcross, & Mauss, 2010

147 Snell & Padin-Rivera, 1997

148 Jallo, Bourguignon, Taylor, Ruiz, & Goehler, 2009

149 Safran & Segal, 1990

150 Sauer & Baer, 2010

151 Gecht et al., 2014

152 Arch et al., 2014; Garland et al., 2010; Hoffman et al., 2009

153 Arch et al., 2014

154 Goodman et al., 2014

155 Garland et al., 2010

156 Salzberg, 1995

157 O'Bryan, McLeish, Kraemer, & Fleming, 2015; Plumb, Orsillo, & Luterek, 2004

158 Hayes, Wilson, Gifford, Follette, & Stroshahl, 1996

159 Hayes et al., 1996

160 Goldsmith et al., 2014

161 Sullivan & Holt, 2008

162 Asmundson, Stapleton, & Taylor, 2004

163 Farley, Golding, & Minkoff, 2002; Farley, Minkoff, & Barkan, 2001; Springs & Friedrich, 1992; Watson-Johnson, Townsend, Basile, & Richardson, 2012

164 Schachter, Stalker, & Teram, 1999

165 Steil & Ehlers, 2000

166 Hundt et al., 2015

167 Hayes et al., 1996

168 Chawla & Ostafin, 2007; North, 2001; Ullman, Filipas, Townsend, & Starzynski, 2007

169 Rosenthal, Cheavens, Lynch, & Follette, 2006

170 Pickett & Kurby, 2010

171 El Khoury-Malhame et al., 2011

172 Müller et al., 2015; Nickerson et al., 2014

173 Batten, Follette, & Aban, 2001

174 Flack, Milanak, & Kimble, 2005

175 Rieffe & De Rooij, 2012

176 Peri, Ben-Shakhar, Orr, & Shalev, 2000; Rothbaum & Davis, 2003

177 Lommen, Engelhard, Sijbrandij, van den Hout, & Hermans, 2014

178 Thompson & Waltz, 2010

179 Asmundson, Stapleton, & Taylor, 2004; Eftekhari, Stines, & Zoellner, 2006; Hagenaars & van Minnen, 2010

180 Furini, Myskiw, & Izquierdo, 2014

181 Banks et al., 2015; Chiesa, Anselmi, & Serretti, 2014; Stein, Ives-Deliperi, & Thomas, 2008

182 Kashdan & Kane, 2011

183 Wessa & Flor, 2007

184 Foa & Rothbaum, 1998

185 Foa & Kozak, 1986

186 Miyahira et al., 2012; Rizzo, Parsons, Kenny, & Buckwalter, 2012

187 Eftekhari, Stines, & Zoellner, 2006

188 Resick et al, 2008

189 Nishith, Resick, & Griffin, 2002

190 Briere, 2002

191 Hopper & Emerson, 2011

192 adapted from Katerelos, Hawley, Antony, & McCabe, 2008

193 Lynch & Mack, n.d.

194 Grindler Katonah, 2015

195 Tull, Jakupcak, McFadden, & Roemer, 2007

196 Sippel & Marshall, 2013

197 Schumm, Dickstein, Walter, Owens, & Chard, 2015

198 McLean, Yeh, Rosenfield, & Foa, 2015

199 Dunmore, Clark, & Ehlers, 1999

200 Andrews, Brewin, Rose, & Kirk, 2000; Cromer & Smyth, 2010; DePrince, Chu, & Pineda, 2011

201 Ginzburg et al., 2009; Price, MacDonald, Adair, Koerner, & Monson, 2014; Woud, Holmes, Postma, Dalgleish, & Mackintosh, 2012

202 Freed & D'Andrea, 2015; Leskela, Dieperink, & Thuras, 2002

203 e.g., Lewis, 1971

204 Litz et al., 2009

205 Lewis, 1995

206 Ginzburg et al., 2009

207 Reich et al., 2015

208 Cox, MacPherson, Enns, & McWilliams, 2004; McCranie & Hyer, 1995

209 Dunkley, Sanislow, Grilo, & McGlashan, 2009

210 Sachs-Ericsson, Verona, Joiner, & Preacher, 2006

211 Freyd, 1996

212 Martin, Cromer, DePrince, & Freyd, 2013

213 DePrince, Zurbriggen, Chu, & Smart, 2010

214 Janoff-Bulman, 1989; 1992

215 Andrews et al., 2000; Dewey, Schuldberg, & Madathi, 2014; Orth & Wieland, 2006

216 Contractor, Armour, Wang, Forbes, & Elhai, 2015

217 Stevenson & Chemtob, 2000

218 Novaco & Chembtob, 1998

219 Kubany et al., 1995; Kubany, 2000; Kubany & Watson, 2003

220 Norman, Wilkins, Myers, & Allard, 2014

221 Drescher et al., 2011; Litz et al., 2009

222 Jobson & O'Kearney, 2009; Srinivas, DePrince, & Chu, 2015

223 Goldsmith et al., 2014

224 Lieberman et al., 2007

225 Teicher & Samson, 2013

226 see Briere, 1992, and Freyd, 1996

227 Ando et al., 2009; Mathew, Whitford, Kenny, & Denson, 2010

228 Mathew, Whitford, Kenny, & Denson, 2010

229 Raes, Dewulf, Van Heeringen, & Williams, 2009

230 Way, Creswell, Eisenberger, & Lieberman, 2010

231 Ehret, Joormann, & Berking, 2014; Körner et al., 2015

232 Ehret, Joormann, & Berking, 2014

233 Krieger, Altenstein, Baettig, Doerig, & Holtforth, 2013

234 Pinto-Gouveia, Duarte, Matos, Fráguas, 2014

235 Van Dam, Sheppard, Forsyth, & Earleywine, 2011

236 Zeller, Yuval, Nitzan-Assayag, Bernstein, 2015

237 Jakupcak, Wagner, Paulson, Varra, & McFall, 2010b

238 Glover, Ohlde, Silver, Packard, Goodnick, & Hamlin, 1994

239 Hassija, Jakupcak, & Gray, 2012

240 Kashdan & Kane, 2011

241 Feuer, Nishith, & Resick, 2005; Weems, Saltzman, Reiss, & Carrion, 2003

242 Litz et al., 1997

243 Allwood, Bell, & Horan, 2011

244 Asmundson, Stapleton, & Taylor, 2004; Blom & Oberink, 2012; Palmieri, Marshall, & Schell, 2007; Ramirez et al., 2001

245 Ramirez et al., 2001

246 Glover, 1992

247 Flack, Milanak, & Kimble, 2005

248 Sifneos, 1973

249 Badura, 2003; Declercq, Vanheule, & Deheegher, 2010; Eichhorn, Brähler, Franz, Friedrich, & Glaesmer, 2014

250 Frewen & Lanius, 2006

251   Foa, Riggs, & Gershuny, 1995

252   Frewen et al., 2012

253   Felmingham et al., 2014

254   Elman et al., 2009

255   Feeny, Zoellner, Fitzgibbons, & Foa, 2000

256   Breslau & Davis, 1992; Malta et al., 2009

257   Jakupcak et al., 2010a

258   Mathew, Cook, Japuntich, & Leventhal, 2015

259   Guerra & Calhoun, 2011

260   Jaquier, Hellmuth, & Sullivan, 2013

261   Allwood, Bell, & Horan, 2011

262   Johnson, Palmieri, Jackson, & Hobfoll, 2007; Nunnink, Goldwaser, Afari, Nievergelt, & Baker, 2010; Ruscio, Weathers, King, & King, 2002; Ray & Vanstone, 2009; Samper, Taft, King, & King, 2004

263   Riggs, Byrne, Weathers, & Litz, 1998

264   Kerig et al., 2016

265   Schnaider et al., 2014

266   Monson et al., 2012

267   Campbell & Renshaw, 2013

268   Jack, 1991

269   Sharkin, 1993

270   Levant, Hall, Williams, & Hasan, 2009

271   Galovski, Mott, Young-Xu, & Resick, 2011

272   Lorber & Garcia, 2010

273   Krause, Mendelson, & Lynch, 2003

274   Le, Berenbaum, & Raghavan, 2000

275   Linehan, 1993b

276   Kimbrough, Magyari, Langenberg, Chesney, & Berman, 2010

277   Wahbeh, Lu, & Oken, 2011

278   Linehan, 1993b

279   Grindler Katonah, 2015

280   Lorber & Garcia, 2010

281   Levant, 1998; Levant, Halter, Hayden, & Williams, 2009

282   Codrington, 2010

283   Hariri et al., 2000

284   Steinberg, 1995; Steinberg & Schnall, 2001

285   Steinberg & Schnall, 2001

286   Steinberg & Schnall, 2001

287   Putnam, 1985

288   Dorahy & van der Hart, 2015

289   Bockers, Roepke, Michael, Renneberg, & Knaevelsrud, 2014; Dorahy et al., 2012; Noll, Horowitz, Bonanno, Trickett, & Putnam, 2003

290   Steinberg & Schnall, 2001

291   Leonard, Brann, & Tiller, 2005

292   Brown, 2006

293   American Psychiatric Association, 2000; Frey, 2001; Maldonado et al., 2002; Spiegel & Cardeña, 1991; Steinberg et al., 1993

294   Steinberg & Schnall, 2001

295   Brand et al., 2012; Myrick, Chasson, Lanius, Leventhal, & Brand, 2015

296   Kluft, 1993a

297   Zerubavel & Messman-Moore, 2015

298   Lanius et al., 2010

299   Sierra & Berrios, 1998

300   Lanius et al., 2010

301   Giesbrecht, Smeets, Merckelbach, & Jelicic, 2007

302   Foa & Riggs, 1995

303   Baer, Smith, & Allen, 2004; de Bruin, Topper, Muskens, Bögels, & Kamphuis, 2012; Perona-Garcelán et al., 2014; Walach, Buchheld, Buttenmüller, Kleinknecht, & Schmidt, 2006

304   Price, Wells, Donovan, & Rue, 2012

305   Wing Lun, 2008

306   Farnsworth & Sewell, 2011

307   Brockman et al., 2015; Campbell & Renshaw, 2013; Ruscio, Weathers, King, & King, 2002; Samper, Taft, King, & King, 2004

308   Campbell & Renshaw, 2013

309   Duax, Bohnert, Rauch, & Defever, 2014

310 Brewin, Andrews, & Valentine, 2001; Dorahy et al., 2009; Grasso et al., 2012; McFarlane & van der Kolk; 1996; Ozer, Best, Lipsey, & Weiss, 2003

311 Berliner & Elliott, 1996; Bonnan-White, Hetzel-Riggin, Diamond-Welch, & Tollini, 2015

312 Foa et al., 1999

313 Woodward et al., 2015

314 Isaac, Stewart, Artero, Ancelin, & Ritchie, 2009; Jakupcak, Wagner, Paulson, Varra, & McFall, 2010b

315 Whitebird, Kreitzer, Crain, Lewis, Hanson, & Enstad, 2013

316 Pierce & Lydon, 1998

317 Briere, 2002

318 DeFrain & Asay, 2007; Feldman, 2007

319 see Linehan, 1993b

320 e.g., Felitti et al., 1998; Horwitz, Widom, McLaughlin, & White, 2001; Kendall-Tackett, 2002; Silverman, Reinherz, & Giaconia, 1996

321 Brockman et al., 2015

322 LaMotte, Taft, Reardon, & Miller, 2015

323 Ray & Vanstone, 2009

324 Freyd, 1996

325 Freyd & Birrell, 2013

326 Hansen et al., 2006

327 Cortina & Magley, 2003

328 Towler & Stuhlmacher, 2013

329 Aikens et al., 2014

330 Di Benedetto & Swadling, 2014

331 Dykens, Fisher, Taylor, Lambert, & Miodrag, 2014

332 Kögler et al., 2015

333 Hou et al., 2014

334 Meiklejohn et al., 2012

335 Bazarko, Cate, Azocar, Kreitzer, 2013

336 McGee, Williams, Howden-Chapman, Martin, & Kawachi, 2006

337 Detweiler et al., 2015

338 Ho, Tsao, Bloch, & Zeltzer, 2011

339 Nimenko & Simpson, 2014

340 Platt, Keyes, & Koenen, 2014

341 Hanson & Jones, 2015; Kassavou, Turner, Hamborg, French, 2014

342 Ho et al., 2011

343 Britton, Shahar, Szepsenwol, & Jacobs, 2012

344 Hutcherson, Seppala, & Gross, 2008

345 Kang, Gray, & Dovidio, 2014

346 Lindsay & Creswell, 2014

347 Weinstein & Ryan, 2010

348 Hutcherson, Seppala, & Gross, 2008

349 Aknin et al., 2013

350 Kishon-Barash, Midlarsky, & Johnson, 1999

351 Brown & Brown, 2015

352 Dillon et al., 2015

353 Zeng, Chiu, Wang, Oei, & Leung, 2015

354 Brown, 2015

355 Salzberg, 1995

356 Cremeans-Smith, Greene, & Delahanty, 2015

357 e.g., Joseph, 2011

358 Greenglass, 2002

359 Danhauer et al., 2013

360 McDonough, Sabiston, & Wrosch, 2014; Staugaard, Johannessen, Thomsen, Bertelsen, & Berntsen, 2015; Yu et al., 2014

361 Xu & Liao, 2011

362 Ehlers & Clark, 2000

363 Schuettler & Boals, 2011; Lindstrom, Cann, Calhoun, & Tedeschi, 2013

364 Affleck & Tennen, 1996; Taku, Calhoun, Cann, & Tedeschi, 2008

365 Lancaster, Kloep, Rodriguez, & Weston, 2013

366 McDonough, Sabiston, & Wrosch, 2014; Staugaard, Johannessen, Thomsen, Bertelsen, & Berntsen, 2015

367 Canevello, Michels, & Hilaire, 2015

368 Woodward & Joseph, 2003

369 Stafford et al., 2013

370   Wagner, Knaevelsrud, & Maercker, 2007

371   Resilient, n.d.; Resilience, n.d.

372   e.g., Bonanno, 2004

373   Cicchetti, 2010

374   e.g., Sarapas et al., 2011

375   Herrman et al., 2011

376   Herrman et al., 2011; Ungar, 2013

377   Wright, Fopma-Loy, & Fischer, 2005

378   McEwen, 2016

379   Babyak et al, 2000; Colcombe, et al., 2004

380   Hölzel et al., 2011; Hölzel et al., 2013

381   Carlson et al., 2009; Fried et al., 2004

382   Erogul, Singer, McIntyre, Stefanov, 2014; Kemper, Mo, & Khayat, 2015

383   Zeller, Yuval, Nitzan-Assayag, & Bernstein, 2015

384   Fava, & Tomba, 2009

385   Smith et al., 2011

386   Cohen-Katz, Wiley, Capuano, Baker, Kimmel, & Shapiro, 2005

387   Haase et al., 2014

388   Herrman et al., 2011

Note: Italicized page locators refer to figures; tables are noted with *t*.

anxiety (*continued*)
   personal reflection on, 204
   posttraumatic, brain and, 137–39
   reappraising, 134–35
   as response to trauma, 45
   rumination and, 71
   self-criticism and, 19, 54, 96
   walking alongside of, 152–54
appraisals
   changing, trauma recovery and, 192–93
   common, 193–203
   intrusions and, 118–19
   negative, 210–11
   of trauma, 189
Ask for Help practice, 309–11
assault survivors, appraisal changes and, 192
assimilation, posttraumatic growth and, 321
attachment styles, 57
attention, mindfulness and, 7
attentional bias, 52
attentional control, increasing, 4
attention deficit hyperactivity disorder (ADHD), 264
automatic judgments, problems with, 9–10
automatic reactions, reducing, 4
automatic rumination, 323
avoidance, 4, 6, 57
   experiential, 161, 165
   forms of, 160

   intrusions and, 116, 122
   judging self about, 162
   learning and unlearning, 166–69
   mindfulness practices for, 173–87, 250
   noting, 174–76
   numbing *vs.*, 241, 242
   problematic *vs.* unproblematic, 162–64
   problems associated with, 165–66
   reducing through exposure, 166, 171–73
   relief and, 159–60
   safety behaviors and, 184–85
   self-compassion for, 176–78
   self-perpetuating nature of, 164
   what helps with, 169–71
awareness, 26. *see also* mindfulness; present moment

balance, mindfulness and, 2, 22–23
balanced perspective, cultivating, 5
Barnes, J., 67
Bartlett, C., 238
beginner's mind, 8–9, 296
behavioral activation
   mindful, 226–28
   mindfulness and, 223–25, 231
   participation and, 311–12
Beng, T. S., 78
betrayal, 193, 196–98
betrayal blindness, 295
betrayal trauma, 196–97
Birrell, P., 42

mindfulness exercises for, 225–35

mindfulness for changing behaviors contributing to, 223–25

mindfulness practices and decrease in, 220–21

"moonlight" of, 222–23

nightmares, insomnia, and, 120

numbing vs, 241

"observer" standpoint towards trauma and, 91

personal reflection on, 236–37

poetry, Japanese ceramics, and, 237–38

reduced, self-compassion, mindfulness, and, 221–22

as response to trauma, 44–45, 216–17, 282

rumination and, 71

self-criticism and, 19, 54, 96

symptoms of, 216, 217–18

understanding after trauma, 218–20

work and, 297

derealization, 263, 264

DESNOS. *see* disorders of extreme stress not otherwise specified (DESNOS)

"detective" mindset, 256

Dialectical Behavior Therapy Skills Training (Linehan), 234

DID. *see* dissociative identity disorder (DID)

Dill, D. L., 120

Directing Loving-kindness to Other Beings Around Us practice, 306–7

discomfort, tolerating, 277–78

disorders of extreme stress not otherwise specified (DESNOs), 49

dissociation, 32, 67, 160

adaptations to trauma and, 271

avoidance and, 161

causes of, 263–64

common misconceptions about, 268–69

defining, 52, 263

description of, 262

different aspects of, 264–66

everyday examples of, 263

grounding and, 123

mindfulness practices for, 269–70, 272–80

personal reflection on, 280–81

trauma and, 52–53

"witness" aspect of self-compassion *vs.*, 91

dissociative amnesia, 267

dissociative disorders, 266–68

diagnosis of, 266

forms of, 266–68

dissociative disorders not otherwise specified (DDNOS), 268

dissociative fugue, 267

dissociative identity disorder (DID), 53, 267–68

distractions, 33, 163, 244

distress level, rating, 32

distress tolerance skills, 251

drug abuse, trauma and, 54–55

Noting practice, 204–6

Not the Price of Admission: Healthy Relationships After Childhood Trauma (Brown), 294

numbing, 161, 162
    avoidance *vs.*, 241, 242
    brain and, 242–43
    depression *vs.*, 241
    emotion socialization and, 246–47
    mindfulness and, 249–52
    mindfulness practices for, 252–60
    physical, emotional, and cognitive experiences of, 240
    upsides and downsides of, 243–46
    see also emotions; feelings

obesity, trauma and, 55
objects, grounding with, 124
Observe Layers of Meaning practice, 206–8
Okada, G., 243
Okamoto, Y., 243
Oodles of Compassion practice, 234–35
operant conditioning, 168
"out of body" experience, 262, 265
overidentification, 13–14, 206

pain
    approaching, mindfulness and, xvii
    compassion and recognition of, 17
panic attacks, 112, 139, 140
parasympathetic nervous system, deep breathing and, 150

parents, trauma and functioning of, 293
Parker, C., 68
Participate practice, 311–12
participation
    mindfulness practices for, 304–15
    in social activities, 301–2
patience, mindfulness and, 11–12
Pavlov, I., 167, 168
paying attention, making positive changes and, xii
physical abuse, 43
physical health problems, trauma and, 55–56
physical location, for mindfulness practice, 31
physical sensations, mindfulness of, 251. *see also* body sensations
Piaget, J., 321
PMR. *see* progressive muscle relaxation (PMR)
poetry, depression and, 237–38
positive changes
    mindfulness, self-compassion, and, xvi
    paying attention and, xii
positive emotions, numbing of, after trauma, 241
positive word recall, mindfulness practice and, 70
posttraumatic growth, 213
    defined, 320
    descriptions of, 321
    dimensions of, 62